The Modernization of British Government

The Modernization of British Government

Edited by
William Thornhill
Department of Political Theory and Institutions,
The University of Sheffield

Rowman and Littlefield
Totowa, New Jersey

First published in the United States 1975
by ROWMAN AND LITTLEFIELD, Totowa, N.J.

© Pitman Publishing Ltd 1975

ISBN 0–87471–759–0

Printed in Great Britain

Contents

Foreword

By the Rt. Hon. Lord Armstrong of Sanderstead, G.C.B., M.V.O.

In 1938 when I entered the Civil Service, the Cabinet had 22 members. Of these no fewer than eight were concerned with foreign affairs and defence; in addition to the Foreign Secretary there was the Secretary of State for Dominion Affairs, the Secretary of State for India and Burma, and the Secretary of State for the Colonies: in addition to the three Service Ministers there was the Minister for Co-ordination of Defence. Today, in a Cabinet of 21 members there are only two Ministers responsible for these matters, the Foreign Secretary and Secretary of State for Defence. On domestic affairs there are no fewer than 15 members of the Cabinet. These facts, striking though they are, do not by themselves bring out the full extent of the changes that have occurred. All today's domestic Departments are materially different in the make-up of their functions, from their pre-war counterparts. Even the three whose names have not changed have had changes in function. The Treasury is no longer in charge of the management of the Civil Service, the Home Office has lost its responsibility for Northern Ireland and for children's work, while the Lord Chancellor's Department has acquired a much increased responsibility for the administration of the courts. Moreover, simply to take snapshots of the position in 1938 and now loses sight of all the Departments which were created during the period and have since disappeared—the Ministry of Town and Country Planning, the various Departments concerned with Aviation, the Ministry of Materials and the Department of Economic Affairs.

There can therefore be no gainsaying but that the last 25 years or so have seen very many changes in the machinery of the government and the distribution of functions between Ministers and Government Departments. Even though to the outsider a Government Department may look peculiarly solid and unyielding, to those who work inside it often appears strangely fragile and subject to sudden and even inexplicable change. It is therefore of particular interest to look back over the period and try to trace some of the forces, both those of external circumstances and those represented by the ideas of successive Prime Ministers and Governments, which have led to the various changes and so to the shape which the Central Government takes today.

In parallel with all this there have been a comparable series of changes in our other public institutions. In many of these I have myself been personally involved. I remember well the arguments in the early days of the first post-war Labour government about the right form of organization for a nationalized industry—should it be a government department like the Post Office, or should it be a public corporation like the BBC? That argument was resolved in favour of

I*

the public corporation and many years later the Post Office itself followed suit, ceasing to become a government department; but the relationship between the central government and these new bodies is still subject to controversy and no settled principles seem yet to have emerged. I have taken part also in a whole series of discussions leading to changes in Parliamentary procedure and institutions—about the streamlining of the rules governing subordinate legislation, about the introduction of new select committees and the abolition of old rules, and the modernizing of the form of the Estimates. I remember too years which seemed to consist almost entirely of a series of constitutional conferences preceding the setting up of new independent states in the place of former colonies and the gradual transformation of the Commonwealth into the multi-racial grouping it is today.

All of these changes and many more need to be chronicled both so that we can all look back with some historical perspective on what we have lived through the better to understand why the various institutions have the shape they have today. For these reasons I welcome very much the appearance of this book. I welcome too the decision of the editor to get the book written by experts and as far as possible by those who actually took part in the changes described.

It is no detraction from the value of the book to remark that by the time it is published it will probably be out of date at least in some details. The speed of change which has been so marked in recent years is, in my opinion, unlikely to slacken for a good while yet. Nevertheless, if a proper historical perspective is to be attained then a point must be set for the chronicling of change and a decent interval must be allowed to pass before the attempt is made again. I hope that those who find themselves engaged in the further development of our institutions over the next 25 years will benefit from the historical lessons contained in this book.

Preface

The changes which have taken place during the last 25 years in the organization and working of the institutions of British Government are so many and complex that a lengthy treatise would be required if all of them were to be recorded in chronological order and their effects were to be assessed and evaluated. Even if the publication of such a treatise was feasible, it would overwhelm all but the most meticulous of students concerned with the minutiae of administrative development. The aim of this volume is to give an account of the development of governmental institutions over this period, and to assess their significance, in a manner which serves the purposes of the non-specialist student and also which provides the general reader with a concise and intelligible review. It is hoped that overseas readers will also find that the book provides them with a clear and overall picture of the manner in which British Government has evolved in the fast-moving years since the resumption of ordinary life after World War II.

My first thanks are due to my contributors. All of them have given their full co-operation, both by working within the brief specifications laid down for the various chapters in order to ensure some cohesiveness for the volume as a whole, and by producing their manuscript within the time allowed. Without exception, they have all been extremely busy with their normal work, and I am all the more grateful for their promptitude knowing what pressures they have been working against.

My thanks are also due to the editorial staff at Pitman Publishing for their ready and unstinted help and advice, from the initial planning of the volume to its publication. It is also necessary to record the help given to my contributors and to me by our many friends in the public services; they must inevitably remain anonymous.

My friend, Elizabeth Dawson, has shared with me all of the editorial work; she has prepared the final typescript and has assisted with all the final stages before publication. Her unfailing and efficient help, and her enthusiastic interest in seeing the book to its eventual publication, leave me with a debt of admiration and gratitude which I can scarcely hope ever to repay.

To my wife, who has forgone countless hours of my company in the interests of editorial harmony, my gratitude is immeasurable.

The University of Sheffield   W. Thornhill
May, 1974.

The Modernization of British Government

Introduction: W. Thornhill, M.Sc. (Econ.)

This collection of essays is concerned with the developments which have taken place in British Government in the quarter of a century or so since 'normal' life was resumed after World War II. The term 'normal' perhaps needs some qualification since there were many aspects of life which did not return to their pre-war state, and these contributed to the need to change British Government to fit the new conditions. We are not, however, concerned with the immediate post-war years in which readjustment from a war economy and austerity were the dominant features. The author of each essay is concerned with the developments which have taken place in his area of British Government in response to peace time changes in society.

The period covered varies in the different essays; but the aim has been to accommodate all of them to a period of approximately 25 years from about 1948–50. In this period there have been significant changes in all the aspects of Government which are dealt with. These developments collectively have modernized our system of government, but they have not been pursued as part of a pre-determined programme of modernization. There has been interaction between developments in some of the areas, but for the most part different influences have been at work in the various sectors. For this reason, each author begins his contribution on the foundations which are most appropriate for his subject. Most of the contributions have been completed early in 1974, and this has determined the final point of some of the essays. The Dissolution of Parliament and the General Election of 1974 occurred at an appropriate moment to enable the immediate consequences to be taken into account in the chapters on the Cabinet and the Machinery of Government. The same cannot be done in the chapters dealing with Northern Ireland and with Britain's membership of the European Economic Communities, for it will take time for the consequences of the election to work out in these two areas.

The essays provide a retrospective examination of the events which have re-shaped much of our system of government. The aim is two-fold: to provide a concise account of the significant developments in each sector, and to make an assessment of their value. Six of the contributors have been, and some of them remain, participants in the processes which they describe and evaluate. The other five are academics with close research and other connections with their subjects. The aim of all has been to provide information and a critical assessment

1

of the manner in which British Government has been changed to meet the circumstances of the third quarter of the twentieth century.

The turmoil created by the two major European wars in which Britain has been involved, the continual extension of the franchise, the spread of education, and the improvement of communications and the mobility of the individual, have been the waves which have lashed the rocks of British Government. This metaphor has some justification, since there are aspects of our governmental institutions which have been in existence for centuries and which have withstood the onslaught of events in much the same manner that the rocks around our coasts have remained firm through the centuries. Indeed, the system of government which carried the country through the 1939–45 war was last remodelled over a century ago, and not only has it had to cope with movements within British society but it has also had to deal with events taking place overseas, particularly in those countries which a century ago comprised that unique Victorian institution known as the British Empire.

The changes which have taken place in the various sectors of British Government cannot all be put down to a common cause, even though their attainment occurred within a single generation and with a common backcloth of social, economic and political movements. Within this period there have been enormous developments in technology, exemplified by man's arrival on the Moon. Not only has technological development affected the services of government—atomic energy, motorways, nuclear armaments—but it has also invaded the processes of government, especially by the use of the computer. Socially, it has been the age of permissiveness, and though the mini-skirt will probably go down in history as the ensign of this era, there is no doubt that people have in general become more sceptical of government and have been less overawed by the pomp and majesty of the affairs of state. The consequence has been that governmental institutions have found it more difficult to carry people with them solely by the exercise of authority, and processes of explanation and consultation have become an essential part of the conduct of public business. In the economic sphere, continual inflation has been the constant adversary of post-war Governments. Management of the economy, in order to gain both a larger cake and a better distribution of it, has finally been accepted, in practice, if not altogether in principle, as a function of all Governments; but the means for achieving it are still embryonic. In sum, the last generation has witnessed vast changes and developments, and so many of the things which are now almost commonplace were unknown to the great majority of people a quarter of a century ago. Government has been carried on despite all these upheavals; the chapters which follow describe how changes have been made in the different aspects of Government to accommodate it to these great developments in society as a whole.

The parliamentary and local government changes which are described here can best be seen as a further instalment of processes which were started in the reform era of the nineteenth century. Indeed, it has been said that the local government re-organization which became effective on 1st April 1974 was achieving nothing more than the re-organization which was originally proposed in 1888, but which was so effectively thwarted by the amendments made during the enactment of the legislation. Even this is an overstatement, however, since the 1888 proposals were rather more radical in intent than the new system which has been established. In Parliament, many of the recent developments have been concerned with improving the system of control associated with the Exchequer and Audit Act of 1866. In both spheres, the nineteenth century settlements have endured with only minimal changes as the years have passed. It remains to be seen whether the increased tempo of change during the last 25 years has been effective in remodelling these two institutions to enable them to cope with modern needs.

The Cabinet and the machinery of government share a common aspect since they both reflect the ministerial structure. In this sense, they have a common pattern of development; for example, the growth of the large departments has meant that most, if not all, ministerial heads of departments are now members of the Cabinet, whereas only about half of them were 25 years ago. But whilst discussion of Cabinet problems tends to be in terms of the personnel who compose it and their interrelationships, problems of machinery of government are usually discussed in the rather more abstruse terminology of management and organizational theory. It is also necessary to remember that, in spite of their common meeting point, these two areas of governmental activity enjoy vastly differing publicity. There are many official documents, such as the 1970 White Paper *The Reorganization of Central Government* (Cmnd. 4506) which explained changes in the machinery of government, and regular publications such as the annual *Civil Service Year Book* (formerly the *British Imperial Calendar and Civil Service List*) and the more frequent *Her Majesty's Ministers and Senior Staff in Public Departments* which provide a clear, open and authoritative guide to the Central Government machinery and to the location and spheres of interest of public officials. Not so, however, with the Cabinet; its only official publicity is the list of Cabinet Ministers included in the publications just mentioned. As Dr Jones points out in his chapter, the working of the Cabinet is officially shrouded in secrecy and, apart from the occasional publication of memoirs by former members (which are not always reliable on facts and frequently throw a partisan gloss on the assessment of events and personalities), the 30-year embargo on the publication of Cabinet minutes and other official papers makes life difficult for the student of contemporary Cabinet government. Small wonder, therefore, that the assessment of the status of the Prime Minister in relation to his colleagues, as well as accounts of the working of the Cabinet, can provoke such different opinions as those which have been expressed by former Cabinet Ministers such as the late Mr Richard Crossman and Mr Gordon Walker.

The effects of external events on British Government are described in the chapters which deal with the grant of self-government to the former colonial territories and with the problems of Northern Ireland. In both cases, the British Government had difficulties in keeping up with the speed of developments, and in both spheres the benefit of hindsight suggests that different action would have been taken at an earlier stage if the full evolution of events could have been foreseen. In the case of relations with Europe, Britain's main problem seems to have been how to get into the European Economic Communities, and again with the benefit of hindsight successive British Governments might well have acted differently had the course of events been clear. Whilst most of the colonial problems have now been solved, except for the future development of Commonwealth institutions, Britain's relations with both Northern Ireland and with the E.E.C. remain clouded by uncertainty, of which the results of the 1974 General Election are only one element.

No discussion of the institutions of government would be adequate without some consideration of the public service personnel. In both the Civil Service and the local government service there have been important developments which stem from two distinct causes. On the one hand, the developments in the structure and functions of government at both national and local levels, and the accompanying developments in the techniques of administration and management, have led to changes in the number of public servants, in their qualifications and training, and in the manner of their deployment. On the other hand, the post-war generation have shown less veneration than their fathers and grandfathers (the public services were predominantly masculine before 1939) for public employment. This changed attitude combined with improved employment opportunities in the private sphere and improved educational opportunities to diminish the supply of entrants to the two services. The chapters devoted to them deal with the very important changes which have taken place in each service to accommodate the changed conditions. In spite of the differences which existed before 1939 in the structure of the two services, they have faced similar problems, of which recruitment, training and the development of effective personnel management are the most significant. The emphasis on modern management techniques in both central and local government has done much to bring the two services closer to each other than at any previous time in the last 150 years.

The lower regard shown by the post-war generation towards the public services has been paralleled by a similar attitude towards the decisions and actions of public bodies and public officials. There has been a growing desire in the post-war period to challenge official actions over a wide area. The courts' long-standing role of providing redress to aggrieved citizens who could prove some breach of the law was augmented by a vast array of administrative tribunals in the early post-war period in order to deal with grievances arising from the extension of the social services and official regulation in various spheres of activity, such as agriculture and health services. Administrative tribunals were, of course, a relatively old device but public unease with this form of justice was not placated by the pre-war Donoughmore Committee on Ministers' Powers. The *cause célèbre* of the post-war era was not, however, a matter which concerned this sort of adjudication: the Crichel Down affair brought to public notice the possibility of public officials acting unfairly, for which there was no apparent remedy except the ultimate one of political remonstrance. Increasingly, in the 1950s and 1960s, there were attempts to raise public concern at issues of this kind, and in the event our period has been one in which a wider front has been created for the redress of grievances.

The nationalization of major industries after the war brought a new institution into extensive use in British Government, the public corporation. Care must be taken to distinguish between public enterprise and the institutional form in which it is managed. The extension of public enterprise, which has a long history in Great Britain, had other justifications than the so-called socialist tenets of the post-war Labour Government which carried through the nationalization programme between 1946 and 1950. But the public corporation device which was used for this purpose was largely an essay in idealism. The best one can say after 25 years' experience is that the ideal set out by John Reith half a century ago is still a long way from attainment. It seems that public enterprise, like 'Topsy' and the rest of the British Constitution, has 'just grown' and will eventually become an undistinguishable part of the system of government.

In conclusion, we wish to emphasize that this collection of essays is concerned with the institutions of British Government. No attempt has been made to deal with the wider framework of political activity and political processes. To have done so would have produced a volume too large and unwieldy, but more importantly the political aspects of British life since 1945 have already received considerable attention from psephologists and political sociologists. For much the same reasons, the volume does not deal with the major issues which Governments have faced in the period since the end of the war: industrial relations, the management of the economy, the development of social policy, and the encouragement of innovation and technological progress. All of these are important aspects of British life; their exclusion from this volume is a practical matter, not a denial of their significance. But we really need no excuse for devoting a volume entirely to British governmental institutions; they exist, and some have done so for almost a thousand years. During that time issues have waxed and waned; political causes have been fought for and established and in turn have given way to others; but the institutions have remained. It is through the institutions of government that issues are settled and causes are assuaged. It is right that we should take time to examine our institutions after a generation of extensive and undreamt of changes.

Developments in the Parliamentary System   2

M. T. Ryle

A tourist who first viewed the Palace of Westminster from across the river in 1950 and who came again today would see little change. The incredible detail of Pugin's Victorian Gothic craftsmanship may appear anachronistic and confusing but still does not detract from the simple classical lines of Barry's great building —and no modern extensions, modifications or contractions have been allowed to mar the façade. But if the visitor were to be invited inside or, poor man, were to try to find his way round the maze of temporary huts, extra floors and new corridors that have nearly filled all usable space within the Palace—or, worse, if he were to find employment there and be required to try to use the old Victorian halls (designed as a cross between a cathedral and a gentlemen's club) for the purposes of a modern Parliament—he would quickly become aware of the extent of improvisation that has occurred in recent years to keep the place working. Outside appearances and overall purpose may not have changed in the last 25 years: many of the less publicly observed details have.

It is the same with the practices and procedures of the House. It would be tedious in this chapter to catalogue and classify every change in the workings of Parliament since 1950. The various experiments and false starts that are inherent in any institutional evolution are of less interest in respect of Parliament than the overall extent and nature of that change. Nor are detailed statistical analyses particularly helpful to the understanding. This chapter therefore mainly comprises a series of 'before and after' pictures, as recorded by one whose working life has happily spanned the years concerned, with only as much discussion of intervening years as is necessary to make the evolution intelligible.

One last word of explanation. As both the power (such as it is) and the public interest lies in the House of Commons, this chapter, except for one short section, is exclusively concerned with developments in that House. But the increasing willingness of the Lords to accept change in many fields should not be overlooked.

CHANGE AND REFORM

Much has been written describing or urging Parliamentary reform (the word 'change' may be preferable—one man's reform is another man's phobia—but I have used the terms almost interchangeably), but it is worthwhile looking at how

7

this has been brought about, and at the changes in the process of change itself.

The changes that have taken place in the House of Commons in the last 25 years have been partly forced on the House, for example by the increased volume and complexity of Government business which the House has to consider, have been partly in response to a more critical and less rigid attitude of people in general towards inherent institutions and customs, and have partly resulted from increased Parliamentary activity by Members. These factors are, of course, interrelated, but together mean that there is more business to be done and more Members want to take part in doing it.

Some quantifications of the growing volume of Parliamentary business are given below.[1] But the central factor conditioning the procedures of the House of Commons is the number of Members wishing to take part in the transaction of that business in the limited time available; and an increasing proportion of the Members[2] are increasingly active. For example, in Session 1951–52, 155 Members (excluding Ministers and Opposition front-bench spokesmen) spoke five or more times in the House (excluding debate on the committee and report stages of bills, debate on statutory instruments and the daily half-hour adjournment debates); in 1971–72, the corresponding figure was 249.[3] Impressionistically, there are more young (or even not so young) energetic 'eager beavers' today; there are fewer strong silent men.

These impressions were endorsed by the Report of the Review Body on Top Salaries under Lord Boyle published in 1971. Statistics showed that 'there has been a distinct growth over the last 20 years or so in the number of Members drawn from professional backgrounds', constituency pressures had become more demanding, and it was clear to them that 'a growing number of Members are not content simply to . . . leave the business of Government entirely to the front benches . . . they wish and feel that they ought to participate more fully in the process of policy-making and in influencing what the Government actually does. They ask more questions, they make greater demands for information, and they are more active on standing and select committees'.[4]

Whatever the statistics and impressions, it is clear that many of the changes in the House's procedure and practices since 1950 have been a direct consequence of this increasing desire on the part of Members to participate actively and the decreasing number of Members who are content to sit, listen and vote.

As a result of these pressures, Parliamentary reforms have been advanced for two overriding purposes. First there are new procedures and practices intended to protect the majority against obstruction by the minority—to secure the passage of Government business. And, second there are reforms intended to help the House exercise its scrutiny of Government more effectively. The maintenance of the balance between these two purposes is the art of the Parliamentary systems. The Government, in the end, must get approval for their bills, money, taxes etc., but Parliament (both the official Opposition and back-benches collectively) must have full opportunity to criticize the Government proposals—to require explanations and justifications both before and after the passage of the necessary legislation. This has been the theme of much of the thinking on Parliamentary reform, particularly in the 1960s,[5] and was clearly expressed by Mr Crossman when he was Leader of the House in 1966.[6]

The sources and process of reform also vary. Some changes have obviously been made on the direct initiative of the Government of the day; occasionally the official Opposition may propose a change (although because of the alternation of the parties in power, the interests and attitudes of the two front-benches are frequently surprisingly similar); but much of the initiative for change, especially in the latter half of the period with which this book is concerned, has come from back-benchers themselves. This has been partly facilitated by, and partly reflected in, the appointment of a sessional Procedure Committee.

Before the war, and until 1963, Select Committees on Procedure had been appointed from time to time when either the Government wanted to introduce some changes (as in 1945–46) or when it seemed desirable to have a review to satisfy back-bench criticisms. The last such Committee reported in 1959. The Orders of Reference of such committees were usually broad, empowering them to look generally at the procedures in the public business of the House. In 1962, however, a new type of Procedure Committee was appointed to which specific matters were from time to time referred. In 1964 this was further extended and a Committee was once again set up with broad powers. This Committee wished to carry out a broad review of the House's work and to report on many different problems,[7] and from that time onwards the Committee have been re-appointed each session and have been free to conduct their enquiries as they chose. Some have resulted in major and fairly comprehensive reports, e.g. those on the Scrutiny of Public Expenditure and Administration[8] (which led to the appointment of the Expenditure Committee) and on the Process of Legislation.[9] Many other Reports have been on detailed procedural problems which had been informally referred to them, often by the Speaker, as a result of matters raised in the House.

In general, therefore, these two decades have seen (particularly since the return of a Labour majority in 1964) not only increased Parliamentary activity by back-benchers, but also increased—and more systematic—participation by back-benchers, of all parties, in the evolution of the House's procedures and practices.

USE OF PARLIAMENTARY TIME

The House normally sits on Mondays to Fridays, and in the period with which we are concerned there has been little change in the number of days per session (ignoring abnormally short or long sessions caused by spring or summer General Elections). In 1951–52, for example, the House sat on 157 days; in 1971–72 it sat on 180 days. The recesses at Christmas, Easter, Whitsun and in the summer have remained inviolate, although their length has occasionally been curtailed to match the exigencies of the political situation. Nor have the average lengths of sittings varied markedly. For those involved, certain sessions are scarred on the memory; 1950–51, for example, when the House was frequently required to sit late into the night—or all through it—debating prayers against statutory instruments, and 1951–52 when the famous 'midnight hags' (Messrs Bing, Hale and Paget) ensured full consideration of the Isle of Man Customs Bill and other measures. But despite steps taken to restrict such opportunities for late debate, the volume of Government business has continued to ensure that the 'Ten o'clock rule' (when the House should theoretically, under Standing Orders, finish its work with a short debate on the adjournment) has frequently had to be suspended. The average length of sitting (including Fridays when the House normally only sits for $5\frac{1}{2}$ hours) in 1951–52, was 8 hours 48 minutes; in 1971–72 it was 9 hours 17 minutes.

The continuance of relatively late sittings (the average hour of rising on Mondays to Thursdays in 1971–72 was about midnight), disguises the real efforts that have been made to reduce the number of occasions when the House sits long into the night; but for these steps the average hour of rising would have become later and later as the volume of Government business has increased. This has partly been avoided by informal arrangements through 'the usual channels'; although formal guillotines on bills are still fairly rare (there were only three in the 1970–74 Parliament) the Whips will nowadays often agree a voluntary timetable on a bill, so that, for example, on the report stage the Opposition will not debate each amendment unduly long provided the Government agrees to move the adjournment at a reasonable hour. Bills are rarely obstructed today on report.

Other limitations of time, however, have been secured by Standing Orders. In regard to statutory instruments, affirmative resolutions are nowadays not normally debated for more than $1\frac{1}{2}$ hours and negative 'prayers' may not continue after 11.30 p.m. Debate on money resolutions is now limited to 45 minutes and they are frequently not debated at all. Debate on guillotine motions is limited to 2 hours. And the practice of imposing *ad hoc* time limits for specified debates is increasing. In general, there is a tendency, favoured by both front-benches, to pre-package debate in accordance with an agreed timetable, with divisions, for example, at pre-arranged times. This is clearly helpful for the Government's business managers, for the Whips and, indeed, for many back-benchers; it may handicap the expression of opinion by independent-minded Members, rebels or minority groups.

Mr Crossman attempted to end late sittings when he was Leader of the House in 1966. An order was passed to permit morning sittings for certain business and a number of such sittings were held, but they proved unpopular with many Members, particularly the Opposition of the day, and without general co-operation they were doomed to fail.

Within the time available (or used by) the House, there has been little change since 1950 in the distribution of that time between Government, Opposition and private Members, nor in the use of time for particular types of business. The only significant changes have been an increased number of 'emergency' debates under S.O. No. 9 (see p. 18), which are taken in Government time, but usually initiated by Opposition members, and a slight increase in the number of occasions on which private Members' motions and bills have precedence. In the 1950s there were 20 Fridays set aside for such business (10 for motions and 10 for bills); in 1959 four more half-days for motions were added. Under the Labour Government the bill opportunities were increased for a short while, with only four Fridays for motions and 16 for bills, and four half other days for motions; since 1970 there have been eight Fridays for motions and 12 for bills, and four other half days for motions.

LEGISLATION

The striking feature of the legislative process, from the point of view of this book, is how *little* it has changed in the last 25 years. The structure of presentation and first reading, second reading, committee, report stage, third reading, and transmission to the Lords (for Commons bills) has remained unchanged for centuries. And, at a time when, in other fields, Members have successfully developed new techniques for informing themselves and scrutinizing Government proposals by taking evidence in select committees, the normal process of considering bills remains that of public debate. The Select Committee on Procedure in their Report of 1971 on the Process of Legislation recommended a return to an earlier practice (it fell into disuse between the wars) and one which is employed in many other Parliaments, namely the committal of certain bills, especially those which are not politically controversial, to select committees who would hear evidence on the bill; parts of other, more controversial, bills could be so committed.[10] But so far this advice has not been followed by the Government.

The major change in Government legislation is simply stated—a marked growth in volume. The statute book for 1952 was one volume of 1437 pages; that for 1972 was three volumes of 2565 pages. The volume of delegated legislation has similarly doubled over these years. The reasons for this increase are partly political—modern governments of both major parties are more ready to legislate than used to be thought proper by conservative opinion—but partly, it would seem, the result of a natural momentum in government. Once government has moved into certain fields of public life, such as housing and town and country planning, further legislation, simply to keep the law up to date and relevant to contemporary problems, becomes necessary from time to time, whatever the political beliefs of the party in power.

Handling this increased work load has involved certain procedural changes. There has been no significant change in respect of second readings on the floor of the House (although, perhaps, a more tolerant view is now taken by the Chair of the scope of debate than formerly), but there has been an important innovation in the setting up of a Second Reading Committee, comprising Members appointed specially for each bill, to which less controversial bills (often those received from the Lords) may be sent for their second reading debate; when reported by the Committee there may be no further debate on the floor of the House. Some half dozen bills have been considered in this way in each of recent sessions. The Members concerned can still all speak on the bill, but the time of the House is saved.

Major bills, such as the Industrial Relations Bill of 1970–71 and the European Communities Bill of 1971–72 are still committed to a Committee of the whole House, and there has been no noteworthy change here, but standing committees have been further developed. In particular the number of committees has increased, and the number of sittings. In 1951–52 twenty-six bills were committed to four standing committees, which sat for a total of 66 sittings. In 1971–72 the corresponding figures were 44 bills, ten committees and 399 sittings.

This growth of committee work has only been made possible by a reduction in the size of committees. Whereas in the early 1950s committees of 45 were fairly standard, nowadays most committees on bills have 16 or 20 Members. This also means that far fewer Members are required to attend simply to keep the quorum and vote; a much higher proportion of the Members of standing committees now take part in the debates, which must make membership of these committees more attractive.

There have been no major changes in the nature of the report stage, although there is an increasing tendency for the official Opposition to prepare a planned attack on certain selected points rather than following up numerous detailed points arising from the committee proceedings. Standing Orders now provide for the report stage of bills that were originally considered by a Second Reading Committee to be referred to a standing committee, but as such bills are rarely controversial and as uncontroversial bills rarely have many amendments tabled to them on report, this standing order is almost a dead-letter; it has only been operated once.[11]

The Standing Orders of the House also suggest a major change in respect of third readings in that since 1967 they have required that the question on third reading shall be put forthwith, without debate, unless six members have tabled a motion to the contrary. In practice, on Government bills of any substance, such a motion is now nearly always tabled, and thus little time has been saved in the House by the adoption of this procedure.

As far as private Members' bills are concerned, few procedural changes have been made, but the demand for the limited opportunities available has steadily mounted. Some 400 Members now enter the ballot for bills each year and nearly every one of the twice-weekly occasions for moving for leave to bring in a bill under the '10-minute rule' is now reserved at the first opportunity, which was not so in the 1950s.

Despite the limited time available, however, a number of measures brought in by back-benchers reach the statute book—an average of some 20 a session in recent years. Many of these are bills of agreed value, which the Government has helped prepare; others have been more controversial proposals—such as amendments to the law of defamation, abolition of capital punishment, divorce reform, homosexual law reform and changes in the law regarding abortion. Most of these could only pass with Government assistance, and a significant change in the course of the years since 1951 was the willingness of the Labour Government to give time (if needed) for the report stages of private Members' bills which they and a majority of the House favoured, which must be contrasted with the view of the Conservative Governments that all private Members' bills should compete on equal terms within the time allotted for this purpose.

A recurring concern of Members throughout this period has been how to examine the continually growing mass of delegated legislation. First a 'scrutiny' committee was set up (the Select Committee on Statutory Instruments) with a quasi-legal function of seeing that Statutory Instruments had been properly made and of drawing the attention of the House to any novel features in an instrument. This Committee has clearly been successful in establishing a good code of practice in the drafting of instruments, and the declining number of instruments they have reported on adversely is a measure of their success. But the Committee was not concerned with the merits of instruments; that was left to the House. Time for debate on affirmative resolutions has, of course, to be provided by the Government, but finding time to debate 'prayers' (for instruments subject to the negative procedure) has proved increasingly difficult (partly because of the rule that debate cannot go beyond 11.30 p.m.). As a result even many 'prayers' desired by the official Opposition have remained undebated and the chances of a back-bencher moving a prayer (as Sir Herbert Williams used to in 1950) have become almost nought.

A solution was recommended by a joint select committee in 1972[12] and has operated since 1973. They recommended two separate sorts of committee. First, a joint committee of Commons and Lords to continue the quasi-legal scrutiny, and second the use of standing committees to debate the merits of both affirmative and negative instruments referred to them, in place of debate on the floor of the House. So far most of the instruments considered have been subject to the affirmative procedure, and this has clearly saved the House several hours of later sittings, but the extent to which the new committees have increased the opportunities for debate on instruments subject to the negative procedure is not yet proved.

To sum up in respect of legislation, the growing volume of bills and instruments to be looked at, coupled with an apparently increasing concern on the part of Members with matters of detail, has led to a great extension of the standing committee system but otherwise to few changes of practice in the last 25 years. Whether the desire of Members for more information, and frustration with the limited process of debate,[13] will persuade them further towards using the techniques of select committees in the next 25 years is as yet uncertain. The principal problem remains one of securing that all the legislation desired by the Government can be given all the scrutiny desired by the House, and yet be ensured its passage within the confines of a single session.

SCRUTINY OF EXPENDITURE AND TAXATION

In no area is Parliamentary practice further separated from theory than that of control of expenditure. In theory the House of Commons exercises strict control over voted money, appropriating the total amounts, in some detail, to the various services; in practice the House rubber-stamps the Estimates presented to the House by the Government. In return for this automatic endorsement the House has secured two opportunities—first, the ability on a number of specified occasions to debate topics that the Government might not themselves choose to have discussed, and, second, the establishment of other machinery for the examination of the details of Government administration and expenditure and for making advisory comment on them. The story of the development of Parliamentary scrutiny of expenditure since 1950 has been largely one of increasing recognition of this reality—a recognition reflected in the procedures and practices of the House.

There are now 29 Supply days each Session, on which occasions the subject of debate is chosen by the Opposition. But whereas business of Supply used to be largely confined to consideration of Estimates set down at the request of the Opposition as pegs on which to hang a general debate—and from time to time independently-minded Members such as Lord Hinchingbrooke and Mr Ellis Smith would insist on debating the actual Estimates or such esoteric matters as the virement between the service votes (often to the embarrassment of Government and Opposition alike)—such business may now consist of almost any kind of debate, except consideration of legislation; in particular many Supply debates are now substantive motions on matters of policy. As far as specific scrutiny of expenditure proposals is concerned, this is now largely left to the Expenditure Committee (apart from one broad debate a year on the Public Expenditure White Paper with its five-year forward look). And even in the Committee it is now recognized that the Estimates are largely a statement of the annual bills presented to meet the costs of spending decisions already taken or expenditures already committed (e.g. goods and services previously ordered). For the development of this Committee and others see pp. 20–24.

In regard to taxation, however, the House exercises much more direct scrutiny. The Government's tax proposals are set out first in the Budget statement and resolutions and then in the annual Finance Bill, and the lengthy examination of this bill in committee and on report gives ample opportunity for every detail of the changes proposed—and also many proposals for reducing continuing taxes—to be debated. With three exceptions, practice has changed little since 1950. Although Finance Bills tend to be longer and longer as the skills of the Treasury and Inland Revenue are used to devise further forms of taxation, and as the wits of the Parliamentary draftsmen are pitted against those tax experts who specialize in finding the loopholes in tax legislation, the ancient ritual of Budget day is largely unchanged. There is still the occasional top hat, the battered dispatch-box is still produced, the Chancellor still sips that mysterious fluid in the flask as he turns to 'my fiscal proposals for this financial year', and Members draw in their breath, a packed Chamber falls silent, and the TV reporters in the gallery scurry to and fro. Budget day is still a big day in Parliament.

The first new development has been the practice of committing most of the Finance Bill to a standing committee. The growth in complexity of these bills, coupled with desire to save some of the time devoted to lengthy committee stages in a Committee of the whole House, led first to an experiment (which did not prove acceptable to the Opposition) of sending the whole of the bill upstairs. Since 1969, however, it has been the practice, with the agreement of both sides, to have debates on the clauses involving major political decisions—the rates of income tax or VAT for example—on the floor of the House, but to commit the remainder of the bill to a standing committee. This appears to have worked well.

The second development has been a deliberate policy of permitting the House to consider the operation of proposed new tax policies before their final incorporation in legislation. Although the Government have not been willing to permit the appointment of a regular select committee on taxation (like that on Expenditure), as in effect recommended by the Procedure Committee,[14] they have taken two steps designed to enable Members to play a more active part in the formulation of tax policy. First, the Chancellor, instead of introducing totally new tax systems with little prior discussion in Parliament, has taken the opportunity in recent Budgets to give forewarning of future tax changes to be implemented in a later year, and has coupled this with the publication of 'green papers' as the basis for public discussion; this was done in respect of corporation tax, value-added tax and the tax credit system. Furthermore, in respect of the first and last of these, select committees were appointed to consider the Government's draft proposals and to make recommendations.[15] The Chancellor, in finalizing his proposals for corporation tax in his 1972 Budget, paid tribute to the helpful report of the select committee, whose recommendations he proposed to accept.[16] In this way Members have contributed to tax thinking at the formative stage.

Thirdly, although it is clear that the substance of Parliamentary control of expenditure and taxation has changed little in the last 25 years (at least on the floor of the House) there has been a major simplification of the procedural framework of this control. In accordance with the ancient practices of the House increases in both expenditure and taxation must be initiated by a Minister on behalf of the Crown, but the rule, dating from 1667, that such proposals must first be proposed in a committee has been abolished. As a result the former Committees of Ways and Means and Supply and committees on money resolutions for bills are no longer appointed. This has simplified procedures on the Budget and on days when the House votes Supply under the guillotine (the procedures for which have also been 'streamlined').

To some observers the relatively minor character of the developments in the House's scrutiny of expenditure, particularly over the last 25 years, has been disappointing. In a period when the techniques of Government for planning and controlling the growth of public expenditure have been improved (particularly following the report of the Plowden Committee in 1961)[17] some people hoped that there would be matching improvements in the practices of the House of Commons in scrutinizing and criticizing that process.[18] But, as evidenced for example in the poor attendance at, and limited public interest in, the annual debates on the Public Expenditure White Papers,[19] the response to that challenge by the House itself has been limited. More has been done in select committees (see p. 22), but in debate Members clearly prefer to confine themselves to general debates on specific aspects of current policy, rather than attempting to control the longer term growth of expenditure as a whole. Perhaps this is inevitable. As Gladstone said, expenditure is but the reflection of policy decisions, and politicians naturally are more concerned with straight political issues than with the complex arts of expenditure management. Nevertheless it remains a weakness of Parliament that the central political decisions of the Cabinet regarding the overall allocation of public expenditure are not more fully probed by the House of Commons.

DEBATES — THE MOOD OF THE HOUSE, PERSONALITIES AND BIG OCCASIONS

Most academic studies of Parliament concentrate on the more readily describable procedures and practices of the House, and on examining the evolution of the machinery for legislative scrutiny, the select committee system, etc.—as, indeed, does this chapter. But the House as seen by the newspapers and television, and indeed by most Members of Parliament, is much more the public forum for political debate, the stage upon which the major political actors of the state play their parts, rather than simply an institution for the passage of bills, or approval of the Estimates. The question must be asked, therefore, as it is of senior Members when they come to the end of their service in the House, how the House itself has changed over the last 25 years.

The answers must be impressionistic. In the absence of filmed record or even of attendance registers (which are never kept in the Commons), one cannot prove whether debates are better or worse attended than they used to be; and without the aid of decibel-meters one cannot be sure that the House is noisier (or more restrained) than it used to be. But some general impressions are widely held (and largely confirmed by this writer's memory).

As far as attendance is concerned—except, of course, on the really major occasion such as Budget day or the opening and closing hours of a big, controversial, debate—it is widely thought that debates are not as well attended as they were in the early 1950s. One can speculate on the reasons—the increasingly technical nature of many political issues, the fact that many debates are of limited or only local interest, the increasing specialization of Members on matters in which they are expert, the growth of other forms of Parliamentary activity outside the Chamber, increased correspondence from and visits by constituents, or simply (it has been said) that the debates are duller—but the fact that fewer Members are willing simply to sit and listen without seeking to take part in the debate is generally apparent. Whether this matters is another question; many Members would argue that they are contributing little to the effectiveness of Parliament, to the furtherance of their party or even to the advancement of their own political careers by simply filling up the green benches.

The behaviour of the House is even harder to measure with confidence. Of course there are excited and noisy occasions—highlighted by the press—when men and women who genuinely feel strongly about some issue confront each other across the floor of a crowded chamber in which all the passions of the moment have been focused, and only a House of calculating robots or saints (who would not be representative of any electorate) would be otherwise. But there are many more hours of sober and often sensible debate. Both are important features of Parliamentary democracy. But the relative frequency of these different moods (and of all the other moods of the Commons—the humorous occasions, the sentimental moments, the bitter anger, the cheaper forms of political fighting, and the occasions of deep and generous sympathy) cannot be spelt out. It varies enormously according to the issues of the day and the personalities of the period. In the course of these years such diverse personalities as Winston Churchill and Harold Wilson have, when speaking from the dispatch-box, been listened to with rapt attention and on other occasions so heavily interrupted that they could not be heard (Churchill's technique for dealing with such behaviour is, incidentally, worth recalling; he would look studiously over his spectacles at his notes, drop his voice as low as possible, and continue his speech in a barely audible monotone; and the House would then fall silent as there is no point in interrupting a speaker if you cannot hear what he is saying!).

In general, no major change in the behaviour of the House is apparent over the last 25 years. Speakers, from Mr Speaker Clifton Brown to Mr Speaker Lloyd have generally succeeded in mastering the House and only on four occasions since 1950 has the House had to be suspended or adjourned because of grave disorder.

Much of the flavour of Parliament depends on the personalities of its Members. It is sometimes said that we lack today the giants of the past, but one suspects that the men of our youth always loom larger than those who are contemporary. Certainly in the 1950s there were two Parliamentarians who were outstanding by the tests of any age—Churchill and Aneurin Bevan; both were men who, whether speaking as leaders of their party from the front bench or as isolated rebels, could exercise an imaginative power that required their listeners to see an old problem in a new way, and both, of course, had a magnificent command of language. But the House has always been rich in personalities if not in giants, and Parliaments which have contained, apart from major ministerial figures, such varied characters as Bob Boothby, Leslie Hale, Emrys Hughes and Dame Irene Ward, such independent intellects as those of Sir John

Foster and Richard Crossman, or such outstandingly effective debaters as Enoch Powell and Michael Foot, are not poor. And who today can be sure that some young giant is not beginning to flex his political muscles. Again it would be rashly dogmatic to insist on any falling of the Parliamentary standards.

As far as the themes of major Parliamentary debate are concerned, however, there have been significant changes since 1950. Neither foreign affairs nor defence bulk as large on the political scene as they used to do, nor do they command attendances in the House as hitherto. In terms of big debates, their place has been taken by economic affairs and industrial relations (it used to be the consensus view that while there was an industrial dispute as little as possible should be said about it in the House, and when it was settled no one wished to say anything more, but all that has changed). Social questions and housing have also loomed larger. And, in recent years, the problems of Northern Ireland have reminded the House that certain sores in the British body politic seem never finally healed.

Procedurally, however, the opportunities for major debates have, with one exception, remained largely unchanged: the debate on the Address, the Budget, Supply day debates on topics chosen by the Opposition, debates in Government time on White Papers etc. and occasional motions of censure. The only significant extension has been that which followed the modification, in 1967, of Standing Order No. 9 which permits debate on a matter of urgency to take priority over the previously announced business. Until 1967, on average less than one application a Session for such a debate was granted; since 1967 it has averaged four a session. One other change, of importance to the Members concerned, should also be noted; there has been an increase in the opportunities for debating purely Scottish and Welsh matters in the relevant Grand Committees.

PARLIAMENTARY QUESTIONS

Whatever the interest in full debates may have been, the interest in Question hour has continued unabated. This is the one occasion when back-benchers from both sides have a reasonable chance to raise matters that concern them. Questions are therefore popular and, as a result of increasing responsibilities of Ministers and greater general participation of Members, the demand for a share of Question time has steadily risen.[20] This is only partly revealed by the statistics because, as described below, various restrictions have been imposed deliberately to squeeze demand, but nevertheless in 1951–52, some 14,000 Questions (for both oral and written answer) were tabled; in 1971–72 the corresponding figure was 30,000. And, to illustrate the frustration flowing from this demand, of 15,107 Questions tabled for oral answer in 1971, only 4,907 were actually answered orally.[21]

The increasing desire of Members to ask oral Questions led, over the years, to a situation whereby, to make sure of being reached for oral answer, a Member had to hand in his Question a long time in advance. This led to Question hour being increasingly pre-empted by certain regular questioners asking Questions which tended to be stale; it became harder and harder for any Member to obtain an oral answer to a Question of immediate concern.

In response to this, following several inquiries by select committees, the rules regulating the tabling of Questions have been radically altered. In 1950, any Member could table any number of Questions for oral answer for any day of the Session (provided he gave at least 48 hours notice), and on any one day he could have on the Order Paper not more than three oral questions to any Minister. Today Questions are rationed so that no more than eight Questions may be tabled for oral answer by any one Member in any period of ten sitting days (i.e. two weeks), and questions may not be tabled for more than ten sitting days ahead; furthermore, a Member may not now table more than two Questions for oral answer on any one day, and only one Question may be tabled by him to any Minister on that day. These rules were introduced experimentally in Session 1972–73, but have now been approved by the House. It is too early to judge their longer-term effect on Question hour, but it is clear that the earlier mischief of the Order Paper being blocked up with stale Questions, many of which could not be asked orally, has been eliminated. Whether the rationing of Questions has handicapped the most persistent Questioners and so, perhaps, weakened the House in this respect in its scrutiny of the executive remains to be seen.

Increasing desire to ask Questions combined with the difficulty in getting an oral answer has led to a huge increase in the number of Questions (whether originally tabled for oral reply or not) which receive written answers. In 1951–52 the daily average number of Questions put down for written answer was 17; in 1971–72 it was 100. Indeed the Question for written answer has now become the most valuable instrument in the political surgeons dissecting kit when he is searching for detailed information relating to some aspect of government.

The rules that determine the admissibility of Questions are derived in the main from decisions given over a long period by successive Speakers in relation to individual Questions.[22] Anxiety has been expressed from time to time about the restrictive effect of these accumulated precedents, and the matter was reviewed by the Select Committee in 1971–72.[23] As a result, some of the restrictions have been lifted (particularly in respect of certain matters on which previous Ministers had refused to answer) and the Speaker has been relieved of the inhibitions placed on him by the rulings of his predecessors. This has gone some way to reduce the number of Questions that are ruled out of order and to moderate the frustration of Members seeking to ask them. (It was Lord Boothby who said, on asking his first Question in the House of Lords, that this was the first time he had been able to ask a Question in his own words rather than in those permitted by Erskine May.)

Whatever the rules regarding the tabling and admissibility of Questions, and while it may be true, as Sir Norman Chester has said, that 'as a Parliamentary device the starred (i.e. oral) Question is but a shadow of its former self', it is also true (to quote the same authority) that 'as a spectacle Question time has retained a significant place in the House'.[24] It is still the market place where every Minister has to sell his wares, and where he is liable to be called to account for every matter for which he is responsible—be it Mrs Smith's pension or the health of the national economy. And it remains the most testing forum for Ministers and for their interrogators.

This is particularly true of Questions to the Prime Minister (now taken for at least 15 minutes and often considerably longer on every Tuesday and Thursday on which the House sits, which is an extension of the opportunities to question the Prime Minister that were available in the early 1950s). The chance to ask these Questions is much sought after; many a brave young knight on the Opposition side is happy to risk breaking a lance in combat with the enemy general; older hands like to spar or tease (those who heard them will long remember—for pure enjoyment if nothing else—the exchanges between Mr Emrys Hughes and Mr Churchill in the 1951–55 Parliament); and the Leader of the Opposition and his fellow front-benchers are always on the look out for the chance to land a knock-out blow. The confrontation of the party champions is part of the tradition of the House, and is largely exhibited today in their exchanges at Question time.

Here, of course, the pattern and style is always changing, according to the personalities involved, but whatever the content of the actual Questions (the Select Committee deplored a 'tendency to trivialize Prime Minister's Question time'[25]) the political importance of this Parliamentary proceeding is growing. Recent Prime Ministers and Leaders of the Opposition have been widely judged by their performance on such occasions—much more so, it would seem, than 20 years ago; their successes and failures are reported and commented on, and only the absence of direct televising of the House averts the final public presentation of the Parliamentary 'big fight'.

In general, to quote Sir Norman Chester once more, 'In recent years Question time has become more party political than ever before'.[26] Although this may well help the public airing of political issues and stimulate wider debate, and while it retains for the floor of the House the public critique of persons and policies, it nevertheless weakens the information gathering processes. And without information most criticism is handicapped. So Members wishing to inform themselves will not, nowadays, put Questions for oral answer; they will turn to other sources and procedures.

SELECT COMMITTEES

It is probable that the anxiety of some Members, particularly of a number of those who entered the House in the 1960s, for alternative sources of information to that provided by Questions, contributed to the pressure from the backbenches for the appointment of more select committees. This pressure was heeded by the front-benches, and the biggest single change in the procedures and practices of the House, over the period with which this work is concerned, has been the revival and growth of the select committee system.

Select committees had flourished in the 19th century—when (in the first half at least) they made a major contribution towards social reform—but their number and importance had slowly withered so that their role reached its nadir in the 1930s. The work of the National Expenditure Committee during the last war gave this form of investigating committee a new impetus. After the war the revived Estimates Committee was certainly much more active and effective than its pre-war counterpart, but in 1950 it was still a relatively restricted body playing a useful—but essentially minor—role. Twenty-five years later, much has changed: more committees have been appointed, their powers are greater, the techniques of enquiry have been developed, they have made more contact with a wider public, and their reports are fuller and based on more extensive evidence.

Let us take these points separately. The number of committees has increased. In 1950, apart from such 'domestic' administrative and procedural committees as the old 'Kitchen Committee', the Committee of Selection and the Statutory Instruments Committee, the only regularly appointed select committees looking at Government administration or public matters were the Public Accounts Committee and the Select Committee on Estimates (with five working sub-committees). In 1973–74 the corresponding list included the Public Accounts Committee, the Expenditure Committee (with six sub-committees), the National-ized Industries Committee (with two sub-committees), the Select Committee on the Parliamentary Commissioner for Administration, the Science and Technology Committee (with three working sub-committees), the Race Relations and Immigration Committee and the Overseas Development Committee; other specialist committees appointed for a few Sessions in recent years have included committees on Education, Agriculture and Scottish Affairs.

Furthermore the number and length of committee sittings have increased. This has involved a major increase in the time devoted by Members to this work. In 1951–52 a total of 198 Members were appointed to select committees which held a total of 278 sittings; in 1971–72 the corresponding figures were 250 and 628.

Equally striking have been the changes in the approach of committees to their enquiries and in the techniques of enquiry. This has been stimulated by the broader orders of reference given to committees today; the sort of explicit prohibition on the examination of policy questions by which the Estimates Committee were bound has not inhibited the work of the Expenditure Committee or the recent specialist committees. And so, for example, whereas the Estimates Sub-committee that looked at the subject of Rearmament in 1950, 1951 and 1952 were largely concerned with such matters as manpower problems, prices and delivery dates for equipment, storage and other problems of ad-ministering the defence policies of the day, the Defence and External Affairs Sub-committee of the Expenditure Committee could, in 1973, report on defence policy itself in respect of British nuclear weapon systems. Even the Public

Accounts Committee—the most ancient and respected of the committees concerned—have extended the scope of their work, for whereas they used only to report briefly on every matter which they thought merited it, in recent years they have also reported in greater depth on certain matters of major concern, e.g. certain Ferranti contracts, Concorde and the exploitation of North Sea mineral resources.

The exercise of such wider powers has required a broadening of the field of evidence. Following practices first explored by the first of the specialist committees—the Select Committee on Nationalized Industries—committees today are no longer content to rely on official witnesses from the Civil Service or local government. Many more witnesses from outside are now heard—from industry, from trade unions and other staff associations (an Estimates Sub-committee which reported on H.M. Dockyards in 1951, for example, received neither oral nor written evidence from any trade union), from universities and from other experts. Certain committees, particularly the Education and Science Committee of 1967–70 and the Race Relations and Immigration Committee have not been content to rely on evidence from nominated spokesmen of various interests or bodies, but have sought out 'grass roots' evidence in schools, youth clubs, factories and colleges; evidence has even been heard from a group of West Indian youths in a café in Notting Hill. This could be a significant development, echoing, as it does, the practice of earlier 19th century committees when investigating such matters as the slave trade.

Nor is Government evidence given solely by civil servants. Since 1967 committees looking at the policies of Government departments have expected also to examine the Minister himself at some stage; this was never done by the Estimates Committee.

Concern with policy and the hearing of Ministers has led many (but not all) committees to hearing evidence in public. At first this was regarded with some scepticism by some Members and others who feared it would detract from the serious and largely non-partisan spirit of committee inquiry. Others, especially a few journalists, forecast enhanced prestige for the committees in terms of greater public interest in their work and benefit for the public in terms of education about current policy issues. Perhaps both the fears and the hopes were exaggerated. Public hearings appear to have had little influence on the conduct of evidence sessions. On the other hand the committees' hearings have not generally attracted large audiences or much press attention. Overall, however, the hearing of evidence in public appears to have been well worth while and is generally approved by the Members of the Committees that have permitted it.

Committees have also opened up in another way, although in this case the development was pioneered by some of the Estimates Sub-committees in the 1950s. Many committees are no longer content to call witnesses to appear before them at Westminster, but travel widely, both in this country and overseas, to visit relevant establishments, to meet people concerned locally with the subject of their enquiry, or (particularly overseas) to learn from other places with relevant parallel experience. For example, Members of the Race Relations and Immigration Committee and of the Overseas Aid Committee have visited Bangladesh, India and Pakistan for periods of two or three weeks to take evidence that was essential for their enquiries, and other committees have held valuable hearings or made visits in the U.S.A. This was not done 25 years ago. The greater depth and complexity of select committees' enquiries and a massive increase in the volume of written evidence have led Members to ask for expert assistance in briefing themselves for hearings and preparing their reports. The briefs prepared by the Clerks to the committees have, since 1967, been supplemented by the use of specialist advisers, many of them from universities, who work for a part-time fee for a committee on an *ad hoc* basis (i.e. new advisers would be sought for each enquiry), to elucidate complex questions or to supply information that is not readily available. The Expenditure, Nationalized Industries and Science and Technology Committees have made much use of their powers to appoint such specialist advisers—in particular professional economists. It is not surprising that out of this growing committee activity—charged with the enthusiasm, concern or impatience of a certain number of active Members—has emerged an impressive volume of reports and evidence on many subjects. Whether their conclusions are any wiser is a matter for others to judge, but certainly the reports of most select committees today are more fully argued and more comprehensive than they were 25 years ago. Some are substantial volumes of detailed argument (although mercifully shorter than the reports of many Royal Commissions); others are punchy and to the point. Many of them enjoy a good press coverage on publication—more so than in the earlier years.

This section has emphasized the extent of change since 1950. However, it would be misleading not to conclude with a note of warning on the limited significance of this change. The strength of the select committee system throughout this period has been the non-partisan nature of the committees' work. Members of all parties have so worked together and have had such respect for the facts and evidence before them, that they have usually produced unanimous reports—often strongly critical of the Government or of a particular department—or, if they have divided, such divisions have seldom been on party lines. This all-party agreement certainly lends weight to their conclusions. It has, however, only been achieved at a price, namely that the work of select committees remains peripheral to the main political argument and national issues. Therefore they have not attracted many of the front rank politicians to their membership and so they minimize their own political significance.

Thus the select committees of the House of Commons have not evolved—as some had hoped and more had feared—in the pattern of the committees of the U.S. Congress or even on the continental model. They do not, for example, yet consider Government legislation and they have no power to sanction or veto Government spending, taxing or other decisions. Select committees remain purely advisory. Through their reports they can enrich debate in the House and outside; the members of committees can bring to debate a fund of information, experience and understanding that they could not find elsewhere; and the committees give Members a chance to involve themselves in subjects that interest them in a way that debates in the Chamber cannot do. But select committees have not replaced debate. They are more extensive and more effective—but no more than that—than they were 25 years ago.

FACILITIES FOR MEMBERS

No description of the changes in the House of Commons over the last 25 years would be complete without some references to the major reforms that have been achieved regarding the salaries, accommodation and conditions of service of Members, including, in particular, the provision of research facilities.[27] Members today do not regard themselves as living in paradise. But Members who remember life in the Palace of Westminster in 1950 must now consider those years as spent in purgatory.

Take first, salaries, pensions and other remuneration. Following several enquiries, culminating in the Boyle Report of 1971,[28] fairly substantial increases have been made in Members' salaries (from £750 p.a. in 1950 to £4500 at the time of writing), a subsistence allowance of up to £750 p.a. is now paid to Members who have to live away from home, pensions have been provided and improved, various necessary expenses are now covered, including postage and travel expenses and Members now have a secretarial allowance of £1000. Finally, pay now continues during the period of a General Election and help—in the form of a terminal grant—is given to Members who then lose their seats.

Apart from salaries, services provided at the House itself have also been improved. Much of this has been achieved by the Services Committee which was first set up in 1965 to keep a continuing watch on the accommodation, administrative, catering and Library services provided for Members and to advise the Speaker and other responsible officers of the House.

Although, as the Boyle Report said in 1971, 'many Members are sharing cramped quarters with each other, and most have to work at a considerable distance from their secretaries',[29] and although Members have worse accommodation than those in many other countries, the situation has greatly improved since 1950. At that time the only private space the ordinary back-bencher had for his sole use (as opposed to use of a table in the Library) was a small cupboard in which he could keep his papers; all his work at the House, including reading, writing, meeting constituents etc., had to be done in corridors, the Library or other public rooms. In 1974 103 back-bench Members had rooms for themselves, and 382 Members shared with one or more other Members.[30] Furthermore there are now many more rooms outside the Palace for Members and conference rooms which can be used for meeting delegations etc., and more accommodation has been provided for Members' secretaries. The use of duplicating machines has also been a boon to many. Lastly, amid much controversy and some heart-searching, a great underground car park is being built.

Apart from his own, personal or party, research facilities, Members have the benefit of the services provided by the Library. In addition to the use of a fine, well-stocked Library, a research and information service provides rapid answers to inquiries from Members. This service, which started in 1946 with two graduate librarians, has now been expanded; today there are over 60 Library staff, including 22 graduates, 12 of whom are concerned full time with research and information services (including statisticians and a scientist). Considerable help with Questions, amendments, preparation of bills and select committee work—as well as procedural advice—is also given by the Department of the Clerk of the House.

Finally, for investigation of constituents' complaints about the administration within Government departments, Members now have the benefit of the work of the Parliamentary Commissioner for Administration (the 'Ombudsman'). Primarily regarded as providing a service for the public at large, he also provides valuable relief for Members; for example, 571 cases were referred to him in 1973. This, alone, is a remarkable change since 1950.

The most important *non*-change over the last 25 years, as far as facilities are concerned, has been the failure to start—or even to agree on—a new Parliamentary building. There has, throughout this period, been much talk about this—*The Economist* even suggested that Parliament should be re-built on Marston Moor in Yorkshire—and currently a major extension building is planned, but at the time of writing not an ounce of concrete has been poured. If this book is revised in 25 years time, will this paragraph need to be re-written?

THE HOUSE OF LORDS

Without a doubt the most significant feature of the last 25 years in regard to the House of Lords was a non-event—the failure of the Commons to agree to the Parliament (No. 2) Bill in Session 1968–69. This was a major attempt by the Government of the day, broadly supported by the official Opposition front-bench, to 'make the Lords respectable' by amending both their composition and their powers. It failed because, for very different reasons, it was not acceptable to a number of active and influential back-benchers on both sides of the House. Thus, at the end of our period, the powers of the Upper House are as they were at the beginning, after the passage of the Parliament Act 1949.

The composition of the Lords has, of course, changed. To a primarily hereditary body there have been added life peers and peeresses totalling 199 as at December 1973, and from that body have been lost some dozen former peers who have disclaimed their peerages under the Peerage Act 1963. And this change has clearly had a marked effect on the style and approach of the House of Lords so that, in some ways, it has become a much more lively institution than 25 years ago. This has been reflected in the willingness of the Lords to accept change, particularly social change, for example in respect of private Members' legislation on such matters as divorce reform, reform of the law relating to homosexuality, abolition of capital punishment and amendment of the law relating to abortions. Indeed on some of these matters the Lords have taken the initiative.

The Lords have also continued to play an active role in regard to Government legislation, and many bills benefit from the additional scrutiny to which the Lords subject them. To further this process, the Lords now sometimes employ a form of committee similar to the Commons' Standing Committees. In regard to other matters the Lords have also shown themselves willing to make more use of select committees. New Members who have served in the Commons, such as Lord Brockway, have sought to invigorate the Lords Question Time. And in general the Lords have been ready to reform their procedures and practices to suit changed conditions.

The most important constructive achievement, however, during this period, has been the practical and realistic acceptance by the Lords—and especially, of course, by the Conservative peers—of their subordinate role within Parliament. The testing time came during the period of the Labour Government of 1964–70 when the Lords (with a Conservative majority) made it clear that they did not wish a show-down with the Commons or the Government. They sought to amend many bills, but they did not push their opposition to any to the point where they could be accused of frustrating the will of the Commons or the people; they have not thrown out any Government bill on second or third reading; and the Parliament Act 1949 has never been invoked.

In general, therefore, the Lords and Commons have reached a good mutual, but unwritten, understanding. But whether those who prefer constitutional tidiness will permit the continuance of what many regard as a constitutional anachronism remains to be seen.

CONCLUSIONS

History does not break up naturally into neat segments like a bar of chocolate, although historians may, in retrospect, seek to distinguish eras and patterns. There is no magic about a particular span of 25 years in the life of Parliament. Procedures, practices, attitudes and style are constantly changing in response to outside influences and to each other; while practice is being consolidated in one area, elsewhere the ice is breaking and reform is the fashion. And so, at the time of writing, as one Parliament comes to an end and another is about to begin, this chapter cannot end with a set of definite conclusions—or at least not ones that will remain true for long. Even now fresh questions are posed—in particular, are we to see a growth of minor parties which will seek to play an independent, active part and so, perhaps, cause (as did the Irish party in the last century) new pressures for change; and are we to experience an extended period of minority governments?

Another area of uncertainty is how the U.K. Parliament will adjust itself to life within the European Community. Already much thought has been given to this and select committees of both Houses have reported on the subject.[31] Many Members are clearly anxious to be informed about and to have opportunity to comment on proposals and decisions of the European Commission and Council of Ministers that affect British interests and their constituents. Such information is now available in the Library, copies of Community documents can be obtained by Members and Ministers make periodic statements to the House, especially after meetings of the Council. The Select Committees have also proposed further machinery, in particular, the establishment of a select committee for the scrutiny of Community legislation. At the time of writing, however, it is not certain what machinery will be established or how it will work.

Looking back over the last 25 years, a few general observations may be relevant. Many of the procedural and practical changes in this time are a recognition of the changing role of Parliament. Less and less can Parliament claim to govern or even—in the direct sense of the word—control the Government; rather, in a two party system, the Government through its control of the majority party controls Parliament. But more and more the House is becoming alive to its role as the forum for constant and public scrutiny of Government. This is partly reflected in the attitude of Members. They appear less concerned today than they were in the 1950s with the traditional privileges and customs of the House; they are less sensitive, perhaps, to public criticism (few questions of contempt or privilege of this type are now raised); they are more concerned with their opportunities, particularly from the back-benches on either side, to play an active part on behalf of their constituents or as the critics of Ministers; and they are more concerned with the effective representation and operation of their parties in the House and its committees. Members, generally, are much more active, and are anxious to be consulted at as early a stage as possible so as to play their part in the evolution of policies—both of the Government and of the Opposition. The development of 'green papers' and consultative documents has been a valuable move forward in this respect.

At the end of this period, however, there is one matter on which many Members and a number of academic observers have begun to express some concern. If Parliament is to be an effective forum for the public critique of Government, there should be a two way dialogue through the medium of Parliament, with the Government (and the Opposition) speaking to the people and the people speaking to the Government; Parliament, as Lloyd George said, should be the 'sounding board of the nation'. But many people fear that this medium of communication is blocked and that Parliament is being by-passed, particularly by television. Do Ministers pay sufficient heed to the opinions of Parliament as reflecting those of the people? Do the debates in Parliament—and the reports of select committees, for example—have any influence on public opinion? Anxiety on both scores may well be justified.

Directly relevant to the relationship between Parliament and the public is the question of televising Parliament itself. The last 25 years have seen the emergence of television as one of the most powerfully influential factors in people's lives and yet Parliament as an institution has, on several occasions, deliberately refused to allow its proceedings to be televised. This is certainly one of the most notable non-changes of this period. It remains highly controversial (across party lines) and will surely be raised again.

Indeed most of the matters with which this chapter is concerned will be raised again, for Parliament is an evolving institution. The façade may not change, but the internal workings do. Over the last 25 years the opportunities for Members of Parliament to perform the various tasks for which they were elected have been modified and improved. But those opportunities still exist today, and the effectiveness of Parliament depends on their being taken.

NOTES AND REFERENCES

1 See pp. 11, 12, 18 and 21.

2 There were 630 Members in the House up to the Dissolution in 1974; as a consequence of boundary changes, the number was increased to 635 with effect from the General Election held on 28 February 1974.

3 I have frequently used these two Sessions for comparison; they were of similar length and were both early in the life of a Conservative administration.

4 Report on Ministers of the Crown and Members of Parliament, Cmnd. 4836, paras. 8–12.

5 See, for example, evidence given to the Procedure Committee in 1964–65 by the Study of Parliament Group (H.C. 1964–65, 303, p. 132).

6 See, e.g., H.C. Debs., 14 December 1966, cols. 478–80.

7 Third Report from the Select Committee on Procedure, 1964–65 (H.C. 276), p. iii.

8 First Report from the Select Committee on Procedure, 1968–69 (H.C. 410)

9 Second Report from the Select Committee on Procedure, 1970–71 (H.C. 538).

10 Second Report from the Select Committee on Procedure, 1970–71 (H.C. 538), paras. 27–29.

11 In respect of the Water Resources Bill 1968.

12 H.L. 184, H.C. 475, 1971–72.

13 See, for example, the evidence given by Mr Phillip Whitehead M.P. to the Granada Television Enquiry into the working of Parliament. He considered that the four and a half months he had spent on the Standing Committee on the Sound Broadcasting Bill in 1971–72 were 'totally wasted' and he did not believe that sort of scrutiny could possibly be effective; 'it was not . . . a detailed and informed argument' (*The State of the Nation: Parliament*, pp. 117–23).

Professor J. A. G. Griffiths expressed similar doubts about the value of scrutiny by debate alone (*ibid.*, p. 129).

14 First Report from the Select Committee on Procedure, 1970–71 (H.C. 276), paras. 27–42.

15 H.C. 1970–71, 622, and H.C. 1972–73, 341.

16 Hansard, 21 March 1972, cols. 1357–8.

17 Cmnd. 1432.

18 See, for example, my own article in *Political Quarterly*, October–December 1967.

19 See, for example, Hansard, 29 January 1974, cols. 267–8.

20 See evidence given to Select Committee on Parliamentary Questions, 1971–72 (H.C. 393) by Sir Norman Chester (co-author of *Questions in Parliament*), pp. 87–88 and Q. 495.

21 H.C. 393 (1971–72), para. 11.

22 See Erskine May, 18th edn., pp. 322–31.

23 H.C. (1971–72), 393, paras. 3–10.

24 *Ibid.*, p. 87.

25 *Ibid.*, para. 23.

26 *Ibid.*, p. 88.

27 For a full description of these facilities see *Parliamentary Services and Facilities* (eds. Rush and Shaw), Allen and Unwin, 1974.

28 Cmnd. 4836.

29 Cmnd. 4836, para. 15.

30 Hansard, 6 May 1974, col. 28.

31 H.C. 1972–73, 143 and 463, and H.L. 1972–73, 67 and 194.

Development of the Cabinet

3

G. W. Jones, M.A., D.Phil.

THE SIGNIFICANCE OF THE CABINET

The Cabinet has been belittled over the last 15 years by some commentators who have relegated it from the 'efficient' to the 'dignified' part of the British Constitution. They have discarded 'Cabinet Government', along with 'Parliamentary Government', as apt descriptions of the nature of British central government in favour of 'Party Government', 'Administrative Government', 'Prime Ministerial Government' or more subtly 'Government by Prime Minister in Cabinet'. Even some who sensibly avoid such titles and depict decision-making at the top as complex tend to denigrate the Cabinet and allege that it has become so fragmented or diluted as now to be barely an institution. It has disintegrated, they claim, into a number of other gatherings that take the important decisions: inner cabinets, partial cabinets, Cabinet committees, ministerial meetings and sessions between the Prime Minister and his ministers. For this committee system the Cabinet is a kind of holding company: its meetings keep its members informed of major policy developments, settle inter-departmental conflicts and test opinion on large policy-issues, but rarely is it an effective decision-making body. The Cabinet simply ratifies.[1]

Assessing the validity of these assertions, while Cabinet records are closed to public view under the 30-year rule, is a hazardous venture. Reliance must be placed on partial accounts in biographies and memoirs of participants, on gossip purveyed by journalists, and on scattered nuggets unearthed by academics. What emerges is that the Cabinet is alive and doing well. Of course, many decisions are not taken by the Cabinet, even decisions which have great consequences for millions of people, cost millions of pounds and alter the development of the country, especially in the long-term. But for the most politically important issues the Cabinet is the effective decision-making body. These issues may not be the most 'objectively' or 'intrinsically' important, particularly in terms of their long-run implications, but they are the most contentious at the time. The Cabinet is no university seminar: it is a meeting where divisive matters are settled. It has neither the time nor the inclination to discuss topics on which its members are agreed or about which there is unlikely to be controversy in the near future.[2] The Cabinet meets to resolve conflicts between its members, and this very purpose makes it a place of genuine collective decision-making.

31

The importance of the Cabinet is not diminished because much preliminary work is carried out before it meets; in fact, its role is strengthened. Beforehand, non-controversial points can be cleared away, so that the Cabinet can concentrate on the undetermined items. Indeed, what has enabled the Cabinet to survive into the 1970s as the central decision-making institution, while government business has increased in amount and complexity, is the elaborate network of arrangements through which government business is transacted before the meetings of the Cabinet.

The Cabinet remains the prize of the political battle. Politics in Britain involves the struggle between parties to win a majority at an election so as to be able to form a Cabinet, and once formed it is the central driving force in government, arbitrating as the final tribunal of policy and issuing authoritative directions, like the medieval monarchs whose governmental powers it has inherited. The Cabinet is now the political Crown of Britain, its supreme 'directive'. It responds to the political and administrative pressures that demand governmental decisions. Since the demands are mutually exclusive, contradictory, and seek more than resources allow, the Cabinet faces a gigantic task of satisfying, of reconciling, of persuading and of managing the conflicting forces. It can approve, reject or alter any proposal put to it; schemes carefully worked-out on prior occasions can be jettisoned.

'What does the Cabinet actually do?' is a difficult question to answer. It tries to resolve issues about which its members are divided. It considers new policies, which must include all proposed bills, since all have to be fitted into the legislative programme, and consequently their relative importance and urgency have to be assessed. It also considers items that might cause political trouble. The kinds of questions that the Cabinet is likely to ask about each item are: will it involve public controversy, especially in Parliament; who will be affected and how; will they object, and for how long and with what intensity; will it embarrass the Government at home and abroad and can it be presented to win credit for the Government? In short, is there going to be a dispute, what sort of dispute and how can it be avoided?[3] The Cabinet produces authoritative answers to such questions, since its members are specialists in politics. They have on average served for about 15 years in Parliament before reaching Cabinet office; they have held governmental positions for about $3\frac{1}{2}$ to 4 years before their first appointment to the Cabinet, and they rarely remain in one particular Cabinet position for over $2\frac{1}{2}$ years.[4] Their experience enables them to observe what sorts of matters cause trouble, who is offended and how they react, and it provides them with opportunities to handle such controversies themselves. This pattern of the careers of Cabinet members indicates that they are not expected to be primarily specialists in particular policy areas, like housing or education; nor are they expected to be departmental managers. The places for policy analysis and the mastery of departmental detail are in the departments and Cabinet committees, not in the Cabinet which requires from its members broad political expertise.

As specialists in the political costs and benefits of various courses of action Cabinet members may, after chewing over a question, reach the conclusion that there is no further decision that they might usefully take. In Cabinet some time is spent receiving reports and watching the gradual unfolding of events, especially abroad, about which it can do little. Taking no further decisions, even rubber-stamping Cabinet committee decisions which meet the Cabinet's political requirements and provoke no controversy, are themselves decisions of considerable political significance. Over the last 25 years the most politically important decisions have been taken in the Cabinet, and it could have decided other than it did. (Not ministerial appointments; perhaps not the budget, although the Prime Minister and the Chancellor of the Exchequer probably anticipate likely Cabinet reactions; and perhaps not the dissolution of Parliament, although it seems to have been discussed in Cabinet in 1974.) Its decisions were not pre-determined but were based on a genuine choice of options. In 1952 Mr R. A. Butler, the Chancellor of the Exchequer, recommended to the Cabinet the scheme, *Operation Robot*, for a floating exchange rate of the pound. Even though the Prime Minister, Sir Winston Churchill, supported him, other senior members of the Cabinet were opposed and won the Cabinet to their view.[5] Mr Butler was also unable to persuade the Cabinet to cut bread subsidies,[6] and later Mr Macmillan, when Chancellor, had to wage a vigorous campaign to win the support of the Cabinet for their abolition.[7] Mr Macmillan in his memoirs of his period as Prime Minister has shown that he submitted for Cabinet decision the major foreign policy questions—about Europe, Cyprus, Oman, Syria, Lebanon, Jordan and Nyasaland—and frequently asked each member for his views, even on subjects far removed from his department's interest. Sessions were no formalities. Discussions were lengthy, and when agreement could not be reached, the meetings were adjourned. Mr Macmillan was frequently apprehensive whether a particular measure would win Cabinet acceptance: he never took it for granted.[8]

Neither did Mr Wilson as Prime Minister.[9] He was punctilious that the Cabinet should take the crucial decisions, which it did often after long wrangling, considerable soul-searching, reservations of position and even resignations. The Cabinet took the initial economic decisions of the Labour Government in 1964 including import surcharges and the refusal to devalue; in 1966 it determined again not to devalue. It settled policy on Rhodesia and South-east Asia; it resolved to stay East of Suez and later to withdraw; it decided not to lift the ban on the sale of arms to South Africa, and to apply to join the European Economic Community after six to seven meetings devoted to that one subject. It fixed policy on the immigration of Kenyan Asians, the invasion of Anguilla and the Arab-Israeli war. It decided to exclude CS gas from a treaty banning chemical and biological weapons. It agreed in 1968, after a marathon set of meetings, on cuts in the rate of growth of public expenditure, including an increase in health service charges and the deferment of the raising of the school-leaving age. All the major decisions of the Labour Government, from prices and incomes to industrial relations, were taken by the Cabinet. It also went through White Papers line by line and vetted such important speeches as those of Mr Wilson and his Foreign Secretary, Mr Brown, on the E.E.C.

Cabinet government was, therefore, a reality. Even the Suez venture of 1956, often described as the supreme example of how important decisions could be made by the Prime Minister and a clique of cronies, was discussed and approved by the Cabinet which, if it had wished, could have adopted a totally different course of action.[10] Cabinets have obstructed Prime Ministers: Sir Winston Churchill was reluctant but had to withdraw from the Suez Canal zone in 1954;[11] the abolition of food subsidies was forced onto Sir Anthony Eden;[12] Mr Macmillan's plans for a summit meeting were checked for a long time by a hesitant Cabinet;[13] Mr Wilson failed to convince the Cabinet to appoint Lord Beeching to carry out a transport survey.[14] His suggestions for naval action in the Gulf of Akaba in 1967 were also overruled.[15] His Cabinet colleagues insisted on a Cabinet discussion of the case for devaluation in 1966 after he had tried to impose a veto on such a discussion, and it was the majority of the Cabinet, not Mr Wilson alone, that decided then not to devalue.[16] Thus from the 1950s the Cabinet has continued to perform its traditional role as the final and supreme decision-taking body in the British system of government.

THE SIZE AND COMPOSITION OF THE CABINET[17]

Table 1 shows the size of the Cabinet between 1950 and 1974. The smallest was Sir Winston Churchill's of 1951 with 16 members, but he found it necessary before long to increase the size slightly. The largest, with 23, were those of Sir Alec Douglas-Home and Mr Wilson, but the latter managed to reduce his by two during the course of his Government. The remarkable feature about the

TABLE 1   Size of Cabinet Range, 1950–74

Period	Prime Minister		Size of Cabinet: Range
		Ministers	
1950–51	Attlee	in	17–18
		out	13–14
1951–55	Churchill	in	16–19
		out	10–14
1955–57	Eden	in	18–19
		out	10–11
1957–63	Macmillan	in	18–21
		out	9–10
1963–64	Douglas-Home	in	23
		out	4–7
1964–70	Wilson	in	21–23
		out	5–10
1970–74	Heath	in	17–21
		out	6–11

size of the Cabinet, given the great increase in the work of government and in the number of departments and Ministers, is that it has remained fairly constant during this century. The usual size in peace-time between 1901 and 1914 was 19, between 1919 and 1939 20 to 22, and between 1945 and 1949 17. In normal times a Cabinet of 18 to 20 emerged.[18] Since 1950, although the size has ranged between 16 and 23, the most usual figure was between 18 and 21. (There is likely to be a difference in the working of a Cabinet of 5 from one of 17, but little difference between one of 17 and 23, or even 25.)[19]

Table 1 also shows the number of Ministers heading departments, who might possibly have been members of the Cabinet but were left out. Clearly the larger the Cabinet, the fewer Ministers will be excluded. Indeed, one pressure for enlarging Cabinets comes from Ministers who resent exclusion as a sign of their own inferior status and of the low esteem given to the work of their departments. A significant point about Mr Heath's Cabinet between 1970 and 1972 was that by merging previously separate departments he combined a smallish Cabinet with a small number of excluded Ministers.

Between 1950 and 1974 there has been a core of 12 members in all Cabinets: the Prime Minister and First Lord of the Treasury, as chairman; the Secretary of State for Foreign Affairs, now Foreign and Commonwealth Affairs; the Chancellor of the Exchequer; the Secretary of State for the Home Department; the Minister of Labour, now the Secretary of State for Employment; the Secretary of State for Scotland; the President of the Board of Trade, now the Secretary of State for Trade and Industry; the Minister of Housing and Local Government, now the Secretary of State for the Environment; the Minister, later Secretary of State, of Defence; the Lord Chancellor; the Lord President of the Council (combined briefly in 1972 with the Secretary of State for the Home Department); and the Lord Privy Seal. Close to this group are three who have been in most Cabinets: the Chancellor of the Duchy of Lancaster; and the Minister of Education, now the Secretary of State for Education and Science, and the Minister of Agriculture, Fisheries and Food, both in every Cabinet since 1953. All these 15 were in Mr Heath's (February 1974) Cabinet. It also included the Secretary of State for Social Services. His department has been in the Cabinet since 1968 when it was formed by an amalgamation of the Ministry of Health and the Ministry of Social Security, which in turn had been formed from the Ministries of Pensions and National Insurance. These separate departments had occasionally been in the Cabinet from 1950 to 1968. The Secretary of State for Wales has been a member since the creation of his department in 1964: the responsibility for Wales had previously been in the hands of the Home Secretary until 1957 and of the Minister of Housing and Local Government from 1957 to 1964. The Secretary of State for Northern Ireland has also been a member since 1972 when direct rule was imposed on Ulster and a separate department formed. The final three members of the 1974 Cabinet, to bring the total to 21, are the Minister for Trade and Consumer Affairs and the Paymaster General, who are the second Cabinet Ministers for the Department of Trade and Industry, and the Treasury respectively, and the Secretary of State for Energy, whose department was created in January 1974 from divisions of the Department of Trade and Industry. The Energy department is similar to the Ministry of Power which was in the Cabinet from 1957 to 1959 and from 1963 to 1969, when it was merged into the Ministry of Technology, which itself was in the Cabinet from 1964 to 1970, when it was merged into the Department of Trade and Industry.

Since the 1950s some other posts have been occasionally admitted to the Cabinet. The Secretaries of State for Commonwealth Relations and for the Colonies were each in every Cabinet between 1951 and 1962. Then one Cabinet Minister held both responsibilities until 1964. Between 1964 and 1967 there were again two separate Cabinet Ministers; in 1967 there was only one when the departments were merged and in 1968 the Foreign Office was amalgamated with the Commonwealth Office. The Minister of Transport was a Cabinet member from 1957 to 1969; in 1969 his department was put under the 'overlord' Secretary of State for Local Government and Regional Planning; and in 1970 was merged into the Department of the Environment. The Minister of Works was in the Cabinet 1955 to 1957, and as the Minister of Public Building and Works, 1963–64. Since 1970 he has been part of the Department of the Environment. A number of other Ministers have at times gained entry to the Cabinet: two non-departmental, the Paymaster General (1951–53, 1956, 1957–64, 1968–70, 1973–) and the Minister Without Portfolio (1961–64, 1966, 1968–70); and three departmental, the Minister of Overseas Development (1964–67), the Secretary of State for Economic Affairs (1964–69) and the Minister of Aviation (1959–62).

The number of formal members of the Cabinet is not necessarily the same as the number of people at each Cabinet meeting. Since Sir Winston Churchill's premiership (1951–55), the Chief Whip has been a constant attender. His role is to give, when invited, his assessment of the reactions of the party in the Commons to proposed measures. (The Chief Whip knows the probable forthcoming business for the week in the Commons and will have consulted the Shadow Cabinet via 'usual channels' on the Wednesday before the full Cabinet meets on Thursday morning.) At times his contribution can be crucial; in 1969, for example, Mr Mellish reported that the Industrial Relations Bill could not be pushed through and shortly afterwards the proposed legislation was dropped.[20] Also sitting in may be Ministers who are not members of the Cabinet but whose departmental responsibilities are being discussed. Prime Ministers have regularly stated, to assuage the feelings of excluded Ministers, that they would always be summoned when any issue arose which touched their department and they could always ask to attend if they had a proposal to make.[21] Normally they stay only for the items that relate to their departments. Mr Macmillan argued in 1959 that not being in the Cabinet would enable the Minister of Power to concentrate on solving some pressing fuel problems, since he would not be burdened by the general work of the Cabinet.[22] Sitting around the table, except when strictly party political matters are under discussion, would normally be the three following members of the Cabinet Secretariat: the Secretary of the Cabinet, the deputy secretary and assistant secretary responsible for the particular item under discussion, who are usually taking notes but may be occasionally asked a question about some administrative matter. A specialist adviser may also be invited to attend.[23] Thus the number of people around the Cabinet table is usually more than the formal size of the Cabinet, although illness and un-avoidable absence may reduce the figure in practice to the official size.

Cabinet Ministers consist of three types: (i) those in posts without heavy departmental duties, which are used for Ministers who may perform a co-ordinating function, or undertake special missions or just contribute wisdom to Cabinet meetings; (ii) those who head traditional executive departments cover-ing major facets of policy, like foreign affairs, defence, financial, economic and trade policies, justice and law and order; and (iii) (overlapping with ii) some who are seen as speaking for important sections of the country or society, such as Scotland and Wales, trade unions, farmers, teachers, industry, local government and the health service. Attempts to exclude departments in the last category provoke considerable opposition from the rejected interests and their depart-ments, as in 1951 when Sir Winston Churchill did not include in his Cabinet the Ministers of Agriculture and Education. Prime Ministers who are keen to reduce the size of their Cabinets soon realize that the three basic elements have to be included. It is essential to have the main fields of policy covered, to have some non-departmental Ministers, and to avoid alienating powerful interests in society, who want to feel they have a Minister in the Cabinet.[24]

Since 1950, a number of other factors have influenced the Prime Ministers' decisions about the composition of the Cabinet. Two members, at least, have to come from the House of Lords, the Lord Chancellor and the Leader of the House, who usually holds a non-departmental position like the Lord Privy Seal. Mr Wilson cut the peers down to this minimum. Mr Attlee in 1951, Mr Mac-millan in 1962, and Mr Heath in 1970 had only three; Sir Anthony Eden in 1955 and Sir Alec Douglas-Home in 1963–64 four, Mr Macmillan five in 1957; while Sir Winston Churchill had six, the most in this period, comprising over a third of his Cabinet. The Prime Minister may also want to show the country that the Government is concentrating its efforts on certain problems or areas of policy, by making a specific Cabinet Minister responsible or by creating a Cabinet post for the task. In 1959 the Minister of Aviation was included; at the time the Government was alarmed at increasing world competition and saw the need to strengthen and expand the aircraft industry and to co-ordinate its output with the needs of the airlines.[25] In 1964 Mr Wilson created the Cabinet post of Secretary of State for Economic Affairs to mark Labour's devotion to economic planning and growth. In 1972 Mr Heath showed his anxiety about price rises and the anger of consumers by bringing into the Cabinet the Minister for Trade and Consumer Affairs and in 1974 created a new Cabinet Minister, the Secretary of State for Energy, to deal with the fuel crisis. The priorities of the Government may be seen from the way the Cabinet is composed. In 1956 it was said that the inclusion of the Minister of Works but not of the Minister of Pensions and National Insurance indicated that the Government thought more of old buildings than of old people.[26]

If the Prime Minister does not want to appoint a new Cabinet Minister for some task, he may allocate it to an existing Cabinet member, usually one holding a non-departmental position. Such responsibilities have included co-ordinating Government information services, handling delicate negotiations like those for the European Free Trade Area or the European Economic Community or on Central African Affairs, sport, youth services, and science, and urgent problems like high unemployment in the North-east. At times, and more rarely, a departmental Cabinet Minister is handed a special task, as in 1973 when the Home Secretary was made responsible for co-ordinating the Government's policies towards deprived urban areas.[27] Conservative Prime Ministers have frequently given a Cabinet Minister the duty of being Chairman of the Conservative Party, responsible for good relations between the Cabinet and the party in the country. In 1974 the Secretary of State for Energy and the Lord President of the Council were the Chairman and Deputy Chairman of the Conservative Party.

When appointing Ministers, Prime Ministers have been concerned to form Cabinets that are representative of their parties. Since the very existence of the Cabinet depends on its maintenance of majority support in the Commons, Prime Ministers take care to compose their Cabinets of members who reflect the various wings, factions and tendencies in their parties. Influential personalities who have significant followings within the party have to be found Cabinet positions in order to maintain party unity and enhance party morale. (Mr Heath's exclusion of Mr Enoch Powell is perhaps a rare counter-example, but Mr Powell's strength lies more in the constituencies than in the Commons.) Prime Ministers have also been constrained by the apparent need to have within their Cabinets young members and old [the oldest Cabinet was that of Sir Winston Churchill in 1951 (average age 59 years 3 months); the youngest were those of Mr Macmillan in 1963, Sir Alec Douglas-Home in 1963 and Mr Heath in 1970 (51 years); most range between 53 and 55], males and females, who come from a range of different social, educational and geographical backgrounds. (There is need for research into the representativeness of Cabinets.) The Prime Minister has no free hand in composing his Cabinet. He may be able to include one or two personal friends, as Mr Macmillan with Lord Mills, but the constraints are formidable. [The majority of the Prime Minister's Cabinet colleagues have been selected before he comes to form his Cabinet. Of the 23 members of the 1964 Wilson Cabinet, 13 had been in the Parliamentary Committee (Shadow Cabinet) of 18; 18 Cabinet members had been Opposition spokesmen; and eight of them had Cabinet responsibilities different from those they held in opposition. Of the 18 members of the 1970 Heath Cabinet, 15 had been in the Consultative Committee (Shadow Cabinet) of 17, and eight of them had Cabinet responsibilities different from those they had held in opposition.][28]

He may want a small Cabinet to facilitate co-ordination, to speed up decision-making and to focus on the strategic issues, but the pressures on him are overwhelmingly in favour of a large, representative, Cabinet.

A Prime Minister may also calculate that a large Cabinet is to his advantage. He may be able to rely on the more junior members, just starting their Cabinet careers and eagerly dependent on him for future promotion, to support him against his more senior colleagues. Mr Wilson was scathing in 1963 about the large size, 23, of the Cabinet of Sir Alec Douglas-Home: it reflected his weakness and showed the many interests he had to buy off if he wanted to form a Government.[29] The size of Mr Wilson's first Cabinet in 1964, however, was 23, too, the majority of whom had not voted for him to be leader of the Labour Party. Initially the large Cabinet may have reflected Mr Wilson's unsureness about his personal position: later, it is more likely that he saw the large Cabinet as buttressing his influence. But he could not always rely on his protégés, some of whom failed to support him and Mrs Castle, the Secretary of State for Employment and Productivity, in 1969 over industrial relations legislation.[30]

The Prime Minister may also consider whether a person has the talents to be a Cabinet Minister. Until a man has performed that role it is hard to judge whether he is up to the responsibility, since it is such a unique position. In Britain, Cabinets are composed completely of members of the Commons or Lords: if a Prime Minister wants to bring in someone from other walks of life, like business, the trade unions or local government, he must confer on him a peerage or find him a constituency. Since 1951 there have been only nine Cabinet members appointed without substantial Parliamentary experience and five of them were the choice of Churchill in 1951: Lords Alexander, Cherwell, Ismay and Leathers and Sir Walter Monckton. Mr Macmillan appointed one, Lord Mills in 1957; Mr Wilson two, Lord Gardiner and Mr Frank Cousins in 1964; and Mr Heath one, Mr John Davies in 1970. Since Parliament impinges constantly on the work of a Minister, and since Parliament is the main arena where he has to explain and justify his department's work, the essential experience for a Minister can be obtained only in Parliament. Parliamentary expertise and the capacity to win the respect of the Commons, however, do not necessarily coincide with the capacity to be an effective departmental manager.

The convention of using the departmental titles instead of the personal names of Ministers at Cabinet meetings is intended to emphasize the departmental aspect of their identities, that they are leading members of the Government, and correspondingly to reduce personal factors. However, personal factors cannot be conjured away by formality. The members are not just departmental heads, or spokesmen of interests, or representatives of party groups; they are human beings, and are indeed some of the most ambitious people in the country, beset by compulsions that have driven them to seek the leading positions in politics.[31] Personal enmities, jealousies and rivalries are rife amongst this team who have known one another, their strengths and weaknesses, for a long time. Their debates on high policy are coloured by personal passions: Ministers think in terms of personal influence and prestige, and estimate who gets what advantage out of each decision. A Prime Minister has the difficult task of persuading the varying personalities to work together.

A Cabinet, therefore, is the product of a variety of political, administrative and personal factors. Its essence is diversity: it embodies differences of view and interest, clashes between departments, conflicts between groups within the party, and rivalries between individuals. And yet its function is to reach an agreed decision: to make unity out of diversity. The Cabinet enables a range of opinions to compete, to express themselves and to be reconciled. The Cabinet allows issues to be studied from many sides and many solutions to be considered. It also forces the members to come to a decision that they must all be prepared to defend publicly. This search for widely acceptable decisions presses the Prime Minister to compose a 'representative' Cabinet, one larger than smaller, one more heterogeneous than homogeneous, in the hope that the more the various elements are involved in making a decision, the more they will be inclined to accept the final outcome, even if it is far from their initial demand.

THE WORKING OF THE CABINET

The Cabinet can meet at any time and any place. It normally meets at No. 10 Downing Street, sometimes at the House of Commons in the Prime Minister's room, and on rare occasions at Chequers or at a party conference. In the 1950s and early 1960s Conservative Prime Ministers tried to hold regular Cabinet meetings twice a week on Tuesdays and Thursdays. Mr Wilson and Mr Heath tried to cut them down to one a week, on Thursdays, but like their predecessors found it hard to confine Cabinets to regular days of the week and had to hold extra meetings as the pressure of business demanded. Sitting in Cabinet twice a week for 2 hours from 11 a.m. till 1 p.m. is regarded by some as too great a burden on Ministers who have many other duties to perform. It is hard for them to be fully prepared, reading the voluminous papers, to make constructive contributions to twice-weekly meetings.

Over the last 25 years there was no official Deputy Prime Minister. Sir Winston Churchill tried to give the title to Anthony Eden in 1951, but the King objected that it would pre-empt the monarch's choice of a Prime Minister if the existing Prime Minister were incapacitated.[32] Unofficially deputies emerged, if only to chair Cabinet meetings in the Prime Minister's absence, as did Mr Butler for Sir Anthony Eden and Mr Macmillan. To mark Mr Butler's status, Mr Macmillan in 1962 created the title of First Secretary of State. Mr Wilson conferred this title in turn on Mr Brown, Mr Stewart and Mrs Castle. Mr Heath dropped the ascription, and until 1972 Mr Maudling was the unofficial deputy. On Mr Maudling's resignation from the Cabinet the practice evolved of having no clear deputy. If the Prime Minister were absent, the chair at Cabinet meetings would be taken by the most senior Minister present.

The major problem facing the Cabinet over the last 25 years has been how to organize itself to cope with the tremendous increase in the amount, complexity and inter-relatedness of its business. Many methods have been tried: experimenting with the number of Cabinet meetings, and instituting more formality in their proceedings, like strict adherence to the agenda, and on rare occasions voting; more use of co-ordinating Ministers; the assignment of special tasks to particular Ministers; amalgamating departments; double-banking of departments in the Cabinet; increasing the number of Cabinet committees and enhancing their authority; and expanding the staff and functions of the Cabinet Office.

(i) Co-ordinating Ministers

When Sir Winston Churchill formed his Cabinet in 1951 he sought to reproduce the system he had found useful in war-time. He wanted reporting directly to him only a few trusted Ministers, each of whom would co-ordinate a number of separate departmental Ministers. He sought a small Cabinet and an even smaller number of 'overlord' Ministers, such as Lords Woolton, Leathers, Cherwell, Swinton, Alexander and Ismay. The Prime Minister announced that Lord Woolton would co-ordinate the Ministries of Food and Agriculture, and Lord Leathers the Ministries of Transport, and Fuel and Power. A furore was unleashed. The main problem was: who was responsible for what? It looked as if the departmental Minister would not be fully responsible for his department: he would be subject to direction by the supervisory Minister who would lack the full information available to the departmental Minister. He would not have the right to present his own views to the Cabinet where the overlord might misrepresent his position or take a contrary line. The Minister, therefore, who was answerable to the House of Commons for his department, would not be fully in control of his department or able to participate fully in shaping Cabinet policy. Personal and political factors exacerbated the controversy. Ministers excluded from the Cabinet were jealous of Churchill's dependence on a group of cronies; many M.P.s were alienated because the overlords were all peers, which gave rise to the gibe that it was the 'Lord-help-us Government'; and Lord Cherwell was a figure who aroused bitter recollections of his war-time high handedness and alleged errors of judgement. Within three years the experiment of publicly announcing the specific areas of co-ordination in the Cabinet was dropped. Co-ordination continued to be carried out by Ministers, especially non-departmental ones, but their duties were hidden from public view.[33] Occasionally since the early 1950s the Government has announced that a particular Minister has some co-ordinating responsibility, as in 1964 when the Chancellor of the Duchy of Lancaster had the duty of co-ordinating 'the work of the social services',[34] or in 1973 when the Home Secretary was made responsible for co-ordinating departments' policies to deprived urban areas.[35] But no public storm arose: the departmental Ministers were felt to be fully responsible, and not subject to direction.

Non-departmental Cabinet Ministers without specific executive responsibilities are most often used for co-ordinating functions. They operate with a
small office of civil servants and through chairing Cabinet committees on which
sit members from the departments being co-ordinated: in addition, these committees are serviced by the Cabinet Office. Complaints sometimes arise from the
departments that their work is being interfered with by Ministers and civil
servants who lack the full appreciation of a situation that comes from involvement in executive responsibilities. If disagreements between participants cannot
be ironed out at committees they go up to the Cabinet for a final decision which
is binding on the departmental Minister. When co-ordinating functions are
given to a departmental Minister, he will have a strong departmental apparatus
to back and brief him, and he will have a clear status and powers, yet he will be
heavily burdened by the work of his own department, unable to take a wide and
long-term view and probably be judged biased by the other Ministers. One
advantage of the non-departmental Minister as a co-ordinator is that he appears
neutral and not ambitious to advance departmental schemes.

(ii) Amalgamating departments

By the late 1960s some people argued that the traditional methods of co-
ordination had got out-of-hand: co-ordinating Ministers and their Cabinet
committees were proliferating: inter-departmental wrangling was consuming
too much energy: paperwork mounted; delays were extended as items were
shuttled through the committees; and decisions seemed too often compromises
botched-up to take account of departmental reservations. Too many items on
which the committees could reach no agreement were pushed up to the Cabinet,
whose proceedings were clogged with trivial, yet urgent, matters, which distracted its attention from the strategic ones.[36] One solution was to amalgamate
departments so that decisions could be taken within rather than between them,
thus reducing the need for so many inter-departmental committees and for so
many appeals to the Cabinet.

Joining together previously separate departments occurred in the 1950s, as
when Pensions and National Insurance (1953) or Food and Agriculture (1955),
were merged, but it increased in the 1960s, and in a variety of forms. One way
was for one Minister to hold more than one ministerial portfolio, thus merging
the top political direction, as between 1962 and 1964 when Mr Sandys was both
Secretary of State for Commonwealth Relations and Colonial Secretary.
Another way was to have a kind of overlord Minister, backed by a small office
of civil servants and with some powers over inferior departments, as in 1969–70
when Mr Crosland, as Secretary of State for Local Government and Regional
Planning, was over the Ministries of Housing and Local Government and
Transport. Such expedients, however, still left much power to the constituent
ministries and weakened the authority of the 'over' Minister. Such drawbacks
could be eradicated only by full-scale integration into a unified department

under a single Secretary of State. Thus emerged in 1964 the Defence Department, including the three service departments and part of the old Ministry of Supply; and later the Foreign and Commonwealth Office, comprising the old Foreign, Commonwealth and Colonial Offices and the Ministry of Overseas Development; the Department of Health and Social Security; the Department of the Environment, incorporating Housing and Local Government, Transport and Public Building and Works; and the Department of Trade and Industry, comprising the Board of Trade, the Ministry of Technology, and the Ministry of Power.

One consequence of such mergers has been to strengthen the Minister in charge of the department. Wielding immense statutory powers over a huge range of functions, and supported by a vast administrative apparatus, each Secretary of State has more influence than a Cabinet Minister in the past. Decisions which might once have had to be settled in inter-departmental committees can be taken inside the department where the Secretary of State's voice is decisive. The Ministers beneath him have no statutory powers of their own and are clearly his junior Ministers unable to appeal outside the department against his view. Although they may be called to Cabinet to give their views it is hardly likely that they would use the occasion to champion a proposal to which they knew the Secretary of State was opposed.

This emergence of the 'monster' department is likely to undermine one of the values of the Cabinet system, which is to allow an issue to be considered from many perspectives, indeed to institutionalize conflict about an issue. The Department of Economic Affairs in 1964 and the Civil Service Department in 1968 were established deliberately to propound views different from those of the Treasury in which they had previously been located. The intention was to create an inter-departmental clash, so that the conflicts could be resolved in Cabinet committee or in the Cabinet itself and not just inside a single department. In this way a more general political view may prevail, against that of a narrow departmental view which may reflect the attitudes of particular civil servants and the client interests with which they have close dealings.

The power of the Prime Minister to appoint may be weakened, since in selecting the junior Ministers he will have to take into account, more than before, the views of the Secretary of State who may be able to veto a Prime Ministerial suggestion or promote a favourite. The Prime Minister is likely to defer to the Secretary's opinion, since it is important for the team at the top of a large department to be compatible. Another consequence of having fewer full Ministers is that there are fewer places for budding Cabinet Ministers to occupy as heads of departments, where they might learn how to be a Minister. Many successful Cabinet Ministers often acquired their skills from being in charge of their own non-Cabinet departments, learning by doing and then being promoted after excelling inside the department, in Cabinet committee, in Parliament and indeed in the Cabinet meetings to which they had been called.

(iii) Double-banking

It seems a paradox that while Prime Ministers have been merging departments, to reduce the size of the Cabinet, they have also on occasions resorted to having some departments represented in the Cabinet by two Ministers. For each case of such 'double-banking' there are particular explanations.[37] When Mr Macmillan appointed Lord Home as Foreign Secretary in 1960, it was felt that the House of Commons would not take kindly to hearing major foreign policy statements from a junior Minister, and the Prime Minister, despite his deep involvement in foreign policy, was not inclined to take the whole burden himself: a senior member in the Commons seemed essential. The Foreign Secretary was frequently abroad, at international conferences or on delicate negotiations, and was not always able to report in person to the Cabinet. The work of the Foreign Office was also greatly increased by the negotiations for entry into the E.E.C., which clearly entailed the attention almost whole-time of a senior Minister. The solution was to appoint for the Foreign Office a second Cabinet Minister, Mr Heath, who held the portfolio of Lord Privy Seal, 1960–63. In 1963–64 Sir Alec Douglas-Home had two Cabinet Ministers from the Foreign Office, Mr Butler, the Secretary of State, and Lord Carrington, Minister Without Portfolio.

The Treasury was another department whose burden of work was becoming too much for one Minister, especially as more attention was being paid to controlling public expenditure. Chancellors of the Exchequer found it difficult to restrain the spending propensities of the departments. Engaged in constant battles against their ministerial colleagues Chancellors soon exhausted their political credit and perhaps felt the need for a second Cabinet Minister to share or deflect the odium of opposing departmental proposals. Whatever the motive, it was increasingly felt that in the Cabinet the Chancellor needed the assistance of a Minister who would concentrate on the control of public expenditure. Hence the Chief Secretary of the Treasury became a Cabinet Minister, with Mr Brooke and Mr Boyd-Carpenter holding the post between 1961 and 1964. Mr Wilson dropped it from the Cabinet, until in 1968 it returned, occupied this time by Mr Diamond, until 1970 when Mr Heath formed his Cabinet and once again excluded the post.

In 1968 the Treasury's load was lightened when a separate Civil Service Department was established, under the headship of the Prime Minister himself, his only departmental responsibility. (There was in practice no change for the Prime Minister, since before 1968 he had been Head of the Civil Service. Between 1957 and 1959 the Prime Minister had statutory responsibilities for atomic energy.)[38] Day-to-day responsibility for the department, however, lay with another Cabinet Minister, the Lord Privy Seal, Lord Shackleton for Mr Wilson, and Lords Jellicoe and then Windlesham for Mr Heath. In 1972 Mr Heath arranged the second example of double-banking in his Cabinet: in an attempt to allay public anxiety about price rises, to bring Sir Geoffrey Howe into the Cabinet and to refurbish the image of the Department of Trade and Industry, he awarded a second Cabinet post to that department, the Minister for Trade and Consumer Affairs. In 1973 the Treasury gained another Cabinet Minister when Mr Maurice Macmillan was appointed Paymaster General. He acts as deputy to the Chancellor of the Exchequer over the whole range of Treasury work save for public expenditure on which the Chief Secretary, outside the Cabinet, reports directly to the Chancellor.

Another example of double-banking in the last 25 years was in 1964. Following the Robbins Report on Higher Education the responsibilities for science and education were merged. Lord Hailsham, previously in charge of science as Lord President of the Council, became Secretary of State of the new Department of Education and Science and the previous Minister of Education, Sir Edward Boyle, was retained in the Cabinet as Minister of State for Education and Science. (Following the merger of the Ministry of Power into the Ministry of Technology in 1969 the latter had until 1970 two Cabinet Ministers, Mr Benn, the Minister, and Mr Lever, the Paymaster General with special responsibilities for the power industries.)

Double-banking raises the possibility of a conflict between the two Ministers. There is no evidence yet that disagreement was expressed in the Cabinet. In all cases the Ministers seemed to work well together. Conflicts can be avoided if tact is displayed on both sides, if each has well-defined duties and if they regularly confer before Cabinet meetings and agree on a joint policy.

(iv) Cabinet committees

Each Government maintains secrecy about the numbers, names, chairmen and composition of its Cabinet committees,[39] although during Mr Wilson's period as Prime Minister more information was made available. The term Cabinet committee covers a wide range of meetings, including those attended by a few senior Ministers, or only by Parliamentary Secretaries, or wholly by officials. If the definition of a Cabinet committee is one serviced by the Cabinet Office then the total is around 150. But the fact that a committee exists does not necessarily mean that it is active. Probably the most important number under 15. In 1950–51 during Mr Attlee's last Government, there were at least 16 standing committees: defence (chairman Prime Minister), civil defence (Home Secretary), domestic policy not assigned to other committees (Lord President of the Council), economic policy (Prime Minister), production (Chancellor of the Exchequer), manpower (Minister of Labour), current legislation (Leader of the House of Commons), future legislation (Lord President), socialization of industries (Lord President), machinery of government (Lord President), information services (Lord President), civil aviation (Lord Privy Seal), Commonwealth affairs (Prime Minister), China and South-east Asia (Prime Minister), Middle East (Foreign Secretary) and policy towards liberated and ex-enemy countries (Foreign Secretary). And there were a number of *ad hoc* committees to deal with particular topics that arose, and with bills and crises.[40] The comprehensiveness of the above description by Lord Morrison of the Cabinet committee system of the Labour Government has never been equalled for later administrations. [The table of Cabinet committees at pp. 174–5 of Patrick Gordon Walker's *The Cabinet* (2nd edn, 1972) conveys a misleading impression of accuracy.] It is likely, however, that Mr Wilson, whose first experience as a Minister was in the Government of Mr Attlee, adopted a more elaborate committee network than his predecessors, and that Mr Heath reduced and simplified the system. Three very important committees appear to be the home affairs committee which acts as a kind of general purposes committee; the future legislation committee which plans the strategy for the forthcoming Parliamentary session; and the legislation committee which scrutinizes the drafts of bills before they are presented to Parliament.

Increasingly from the 1960s the Government has announced the existence of some Cabinet committees, largely to display its serious concern about a current problem. In 1965 when there was anxiety about power failures in a cold winter a winter emergencies committee was established.[41] In the same year an immigration committee was announced because there was public concern about coloured immigration into Britain.[42] Other committees whose existence was publicized were on the Common Market, Rhodesia, North Sea gas and the nuclear power industry. They helped formulate policy, draft White Papers and bills, and watch over and co-ordinate the performance of departments. They were used to drive on laggard departments or restrain the wayward. They might even control the Prime Minister as in 1966 when a steering committee on economic policy was apparently foisted on him by the Cabinet who felt that he and too small a group of Ministers had been taking economic decisions.[43]

The committee about which most is known is the defence and overseas policy committee, the legatee of the old Committee of Imperial Defence.[44] From 1946 to 1963 a defence committee was chaired by the Prime Minister. Its deputy chairman was the Minister of Defence, and there were eight other members, the Lord President of the Council, Foreign Secretary, Chancellor of the Exchequer, Minister of Labour, Minister of Supply, and the three service Ministers: the First Lord of the Admiralty and the Secretaries of State for War and for Air. The Chiefs of Staff, the leading military professionals, were able to advise the committee personally and directly. In the 1950s the role of the committee was weak, Ministers of Defence did not stay in office long, and their small department had little authority over the service ministries. The latter fought each other, the Ministry of Supply and the Treasury, and any co-ordination between them emerged from mutual consent. The committee did not provide general guidance or a long-term strategy; it met mainly to discuss particular urgent questions. In 1958 three new members were added, the Home Secretary, and the Commonwealth and Colonial Secretaries, in place of the Lord President, and the Prime Minister would decide which of the members would be invited to attend particular meetings. The objective was to reduce the influence of the service ministries who were no longer entitled to attend every session.

By the early 1960s it was clear that major changes in the Cabinet organization for defence were required. The Suez venture revealed grave inadequacies; the cost of weapons soared, showing that rationalization of purchasing was needed, to replace competition between the services; Britain's changed position in the world, which involved her in a network of international alliances and organizations, required more co-ordination between the services, and between defence and foreign policy; above all, it was felt that defence should be the servant of foreign policy. In 1964 the foreign affairs committee, set up in 1956 and chaired by the Prime Minister, and the defence committee were merged into the defence and overseas policy committee with a normal membership of seven: the Prime Minister (the chairman), the First Secretary of State, Foreign Secretary, Home Secretary, Commonwealth Secretary, Defence Secretary, and either the Chancellor of the Exchequer or Chief Secretary to the Treasury. The service Ministers were excluded, and during the 1960s their departments were abolished as the Department of Defence incorporated them into its structure. The Chief of the Defence Staff, the Chiefs of Staff, the Permanent Secretary of the Department of Defence and its Chief Scientific Adviser could be called into the committee when required. In addition a 'shadow' committee of senior officials was established for preliminary discussion of the main issues and to clear away departmental disagreement where possible. Both are now serviced by the Cabinet Office which contains a defence section. The defence and overseas policy committee was intended to be a kind of Ministry for National Security. It meets at least once a week and discusses matters affecting the external policy of the nation, and the effect of military decisions on its internal well-being. However, it is doubtful if it can formulate long-term policies, think through requirements or ensure sustained action to implement them, especially when the Department of Defence is in the hands of a strong Secretary of State who stays in office for a longer time than his predecessor in the 1950s.

The organization of the Cabinet for economic policy has presented many problems. The chief one seems to be how to feed into the Cabinet advice about economic policy from a source other than the Treasury. In 1953 the Treasury had acquired the Economic Section of the Cabinet from the Cabinet Office, thus eliminating an alternative source of economic advice for the Cabinet. By the end of the decade Britain's economic performance seemed to lag behind that of other industrial nations and in the 1960s a number of methods were tried to present to the Cabinet a view different from the orthodox Treasury line. The National Economic Development Council was set up in 1962, and the Department of Economic Affairs in 1964, headed by the First Secretary of State, George Brown, who took over from the Chancellor the chairmanship of the chief Cabinet committees on economic policies. One of the objectives of the Prime Minister was to set the D.E.A. against the Treasury, so that a clash of views would ensue and be settled in Cabinet. The competition also served to strengthen the political position of the Prime Minister since it pitted his two main rivals against each other. With the demise and eventual abolition of the

D.E.A. an effort was made to build up the Ministry of Technology as a ministry for industry to be a counterweight to the Treasury, and Mr Heath from 1970 seemed to continue this policy by creating the Department of Trade and Industry. The Treasury, however, seemed to have regained, and never lost, its preeminence after the collapse of the National Plan in 1966.

To inject rationality into the Cabinet's decisions on public expenditure, in place of the piecemeal system whereby the decision went to the department with the most political weight, the Plowden Committee on the Control of Public Expenditure in 1961 had recommended the establishment of a Cabinet committee of Ministers who did not head spending departments. Since they were impartial, they would arbitrate in the public interest between the contending departments. This system was tried between 1965 and 1967 and was a failure, largely because it was not a committee of vested interests and therefore carried no weight. Departments defeated by the committee simply appealed to the Cabinet and fought out the conflict in the usual way.[45] This episode further illustrates that the Cabinet is an effective decision-taking body and that it works so effectively because it is made up of contending interests who accept it as the ultimate authority. It also reveals the political naivety of those who want to replace a committee of contending interests by some unbiased brooders-on-policy above the political fray.

Mr Wilson sought to raise the status of Cabinet committees in 1967 with his ruling that an item should be sent from a committee to the Cabinet for a decision only if the chairman of the committee agreed, and he was to take into account the degree of disagreement in the committee, the importance and the political significance of the topic.[46] The objective was to cut down the amount of business coming before the Cabinet, particularly to stop only one Minister from being able to open up in Cabinet, a matter on which in committee he had been overwhelmingly defeated. The consequence would have been to give Cabinet committee decisions the same authority as those of the Cabinet. But it is doubtful if this ruling was applied rigidly, since a Minister of a major department and of political weight would have been able to raise in Cabinet his disagreement when the minutes of the committee were before it for approval. The likely effect of the ruling was probably to make the lone Minister more reluctant to raise the matter.

The pattern of Cabinet committees is basically the same for each Government, although the actual numbers, composition and subjects covered will vary according to the Prime Minister, his Ministers and the circumstances of the time. Committees enable the Cabinet to do its work more effectively. They clear away routine and obtain much agreement in the early stages, so that the Cabinet can concentrate on the points of controversy. (However, in Cabinet, Ministers may so stick to their positions that no agreement is possible and the item is sent to committee for further consideration. Cabinet committees, therefore, play an important conciliatory role.) Through their overlapping membership they facilitate co-ordination not just between the departments represented in the

Cabinet but also between those outside, since non-Cabinet Ministers can sit on Cabinet committees. The involvement of these Ministers in Cabinet committees enables them to participate in the making of Cabinet decisions and thus makes the notion of the 'collective responsibility' of the whole Government a reality. Fears are frequently expressed that such committees pre-empt many decisions, and therefore transform the Cabinet into a body which simply ratifies the decisions of Cabinet committees. The 'partial' Cabinet has, it is claimed, replaced the 'whole'. This is not the case, because a Cabinet committee realizes that its decisions will be accepted only if it has the support of the Cabinet which can reject or refer back or amend them. The authority of a Cabinet committee comes from the fact that its members might be able to influence the Cabinet on a particular item. 'Partial' Cabinets, therefore, do not detract from the authority of the Cabinet, whose existence is a constant restraint on them and whose reactions they anticipate. Nor do they add to the Prime Minister's personal power: the Prime Minister still has to carry his colleagues with him in the committee and in the Cabinet.[47]

From time to time it is asserted that some inner group dominates the Cabinet. Each Prime Minister seems to talk over Government business with a small group of Ministers, partly but not only because he finds them congenial. The inner group consists mainly of those who head the major departments and have important followings in the party and Parliament. The composition of this group changes during the life of a single Government, as the ministerial pack is shuffled, as reputations rise and fall and as different issues burst on to the political agenda. In April 1968, however, it seemed that for the first time a formal inner Cabinet had emerged, when Mr Wilson announced the establishment of a 'Parliamentary Committee of the Cabinet', responsible for 'Parliamentary and broader political aspects of the Government'. As the Government's standing in the country slumped after deflation, devaluation and the dashing of many Labour plans, it seemed that a committee was needed to consider the political usefulness of departmental proposals, especially their effects on party cohesion and the electorate. It also appears that Mr Wilson's leading colleagues felt that such a committee was needed to replace his previous reliance on an unofficial system of political confidants like the Ministers, Mr Crossman, Mr Shore and Mr Silkin, and Mrs Marcia Williams and Mr Kaufman from the personal political secretariat at No. 10 Downing Street. Its initial membership was nine or ten and it began to meet weekly, but it created a new set of difficulties. It angered those Cabinet members who were excluded and wanted a say, while the minority on the committee could always appeal to the full Cabinet. Within a year its ineffectiveness was indicated by the fiasco of the proposed industrial relations legislation, which showed scant evidence of either legislative or political planning. In May 1969 the 'inner Cabinet' was apparently re-organized and reduced to eight. Mr Callaghan, the Home Secretary, was ostentatiously excluded, supposedly for expressing opposition to the Government's industrial relations policy at the National Executive Committee of the Labour Party. By

October he was re-admitted, and the committee by then had obtained a new name—the Management Committee of the Cabinet. It continued until the end of the Wilson Government in 1970, but whether it really operated as a strategic high command for the Cabinet cannot yet be assessed.[48]

Mr Heath's smaller Cabinet had no need for any inner Cabinet, and he announced that: 'The concept of the inner Cabinet is not one known to the constitution. All decisions are taken by the Cabinet itself or by appropriate Cabinet Committees.'[49] He seemed to rely on seeing Ministers individually or in the groups which handled particular problems. Such less formal gatherings than the Cabinet help prepare and dispatch Cabinet business, concerned with perhaps a particular matter, like a bill, a specific problem or a crisis. For more long-term discussions, Mr Wilson and Mr Heath used meetings at Chequers, attended at times by the whole Cabinet and their official advisers, together with other members of the Government. Such sessions would ponder generally on the Government's strategy or else discuss areas of policy, like defence, the economy or entry into Europe. Such meetings, however, were not substitutes for the Cabinet. Mr Wilson, for instance, was scrupulous that any business transacted on such occasions should be reported to the Cabinet where the decisions were actually taken, after an opportunity had been given to re-open the discussions and even to amend or reject any proposals. Non-Cabinet meetings did not replace the Cabinet.

THE CABINET OFFICE

Supporting the Cabinet and its committees is a department that over the last 25 years has grown in size and in the specialization of its work. The Cabinet Office, containing a variety of 'offices' which provide crucial services for the Cabinet, deserves to be called the 'nerve-centre' of British Government. The Cabinet Secretariat helps the Prime Minister draw up the agenda of the Cabinet, processes departmental submissions, keeps Cabinet minutes, records its conclusions, circulates them to departments and tries to ensure they are implemented. As the general administrative co-ordinator of Government it services the Cabinet and its committees, supplying secretaries and memoranda to Cabinet committees, and 'neutral' chairmen and secretaries to the many official inter-departmental committees that shadow the ministerial committees and do their preliminary work. Mr Wilson greatly expanded the numbers and scope of such official committees on which he relied to clear away much business in order to focus the attention of Ministers on the politically significant items. For each item of business to be taken at a meeting of the Cabinet or of any Cabinet committee, the Cabinet Secretariat provides a brief for the chairman; its main aim is to help him in conducting the discussion and in ensuring that all necessary action is commissioned. Thus in practice the Cabinet Secretariat shares with the Treasury, the Civil Service Department and the Law Officers the tasks of scrutinizing and commenting on proposals before they reach the Cabinet. The

Cabinet Secretariat staff, who except for the very top levels are seconded from the departments for a term of service of about two years, specialize in policy areas like the economy, social policies and overseas affairs. In addition to their secretarial functions they may be deployed to assist Ministers with co-ordinating functions, such as the Secretary of State for Local Government and Regional Planning in 1969–70. In 1967 and 1970 the Cabinet Office served the Ministers responsible for co-ordinating the negotiations for British entry into the E.E.C., and after entry for co-ordinating departmental relations with E.E.C. institutions.

The Cabinet Office houses the Central Statistical Office. In 1966 a report from the Select Committee on Estimates criticized the inadequate use of statistics in government decision-making and urged major changes. Professor Claus Moser became the director of the C.S.O. in 1967 and was largely responsible for a more extensive and sophisticated use of statistics in government. The objective of the C.S.O. is to promote uniform standards and classification in the collection and presentation of official statistics and to co-ordinate the statistical activities of the departments.[50] Since 1966 the Cabinet Office has also housed the office of the Government's Chief Scientific Adviser and Head of the Scientific Civil Service, who had previously been the Chief Scientific Adviser at the Department of Defence. Mr Wilson felt it important to strengthen the Cabinet's resources in scientific matters and so he transferred Sir Solly Zuckerman and some of his staff to the Cabinet Office. Sir Solly was replaced as Chief Scientific Adviser in 1971 by Sir Alan Cottrell.

A further expansion in the functions of the Cabinet Office occurred in 1970 when Mr Heath established the Central Policy Review Staff, headed by Lord Rothschild. Of his group of 18, about half come from the Civil Service and half from outside, from universities, business and commerce. Together they are responsible for strategic policy thinking, for undertaking special projects of policy analysis in areas of concern and sensitivity, like regional policy, fuel policy, Concorde, population distribution, and industrial policy, and for exercising a general oversight over departmental proposals to ensure they conform to the Government's overall objectives. The role of the C.P.R.S. is to provide an analytical service to the Cabinet on subjects that cross departmental boundaries, and to put before the Cabinet a paper that considers the issue in relationship to the policy of the Government as a whole, and not just that of the department most concerned. Its objective is to provide a sounder base for collective decision-making, to make the Cabinet itself less dependent on the department initiating a proposal, and to enable Ministers not directly involved in that policy area to have more information about the issues at stake.[51] It serves the Cabinet as a whole, not one Minister. Although the Prime Minister as chairman of the Cabinet supervises the work of the C.P.R.S., and although he has regular meetings with Lord Rothschild, which may vary from one a week to one every five to seven weeks, the C.P.R.S., like the Cabinet Office as a whole, is not the Prime Minister's personal department.[52] Indeed, in September 1973 Lord Rothschild was reprimanded for making a public speech about the future prospects of the British economy, which was at variance with the Prime Minister's recent optimistic assessments. The incident indicated that Lord Rothschild, although of permanent secretary rank and with the right of direct access to the Prime Minister, was the subordinate of the official head of the Cabinet Office, the Secretary of the Cabinet, who together with the official head of the Home Civil Service issued the reprimand. Normally Lord Rothschild works through the Cabinet Secretary, because the C.P.R.S. is a specialized unit within the Cabinet Office.

When the C.P.R.S., like other parts of the Cabinet Office such as the Central Statistical office, has advice to offer to the chairman of the Cabinet or of a Cabinet committee, the Cabinet Secretariat will incorporate that advice into its brief for the chairman. In addition the C.P.R.S. may submit to Ministers its own brief, which may merely try to extract the threads of the argument and make sure that before Ministers take a decision, they are at least aware what the main themes are; sometimes the brief may recommend a specific course of action. This brief is circulated to Ministers like any other paper on the same subject for the same body. The C.P.R.S.'s function of policy analysis is an extension of the work of the Cabinet Office of advising the Cabinet about inter-departmental business. But in one important respect its role jars with that of the Cabinet Secretariat. The C.P.R.S. presents a view at times different from that of the departments: it challenges and provokes controversy, whereas the Cabinet Secretariat seeks to ensure the smooth transaction of business. The Cabinet Secretariat oils the wheels of Government; the C.P.R.S. introduces an element of friction. (To some in the departments the C.P.R.S., despite the high quality of its personnel, seems naive, meddlesome, and unable to sustain a case against the more knowledgeable departments.) The basic incompatibility of roles may mean that the functions of the C.P.R.S. will be located elsewhere in the future.

The official head of the Cabinet Office, the Secretary of the Cabinet, is one of the four most highly paid civil servants in Britain. Since 1950 three men have been Secretary of the Cabinet: Sir Norman Brook (later Lord Normanbrook) 1947–62, Sir Burke Trend (later Lord Trend) 1963–73 and Sir John Hunt (1973–   ). Between 1956 and 1962 Sir Norman Brook as joint permanent secretary at the Treasury was also the official head of the Home Civil Service. He came to be so close a confidant of the Prime Minister, Mr Macmillan, that many regarded him as the Prime Minister's permanent secretary. His successor, Sir Burke Trend, presided over a great increase in the size of the Cabinet Office. In 1951 it had 404 staff; in 1963, 379, but in 1973, 599. In 1950 the top civil personnel of the Secretariat consisted of one permanent secretary, one deputy secretary, one under secretary, three assistant secretaries and seven principals. By 1962 there was an extra under secretary, three more assistant secretaries and one less principal. But by 1973 the top administrative staff comprised one permanent secretary, one second permanent secretary, six deputy secretaries, seven under secretaries, 13 assistant secretaries and 28 principals. And if one adds the officials from the other units of the Cabinet Office, the figures become five of the rank of permanent secretary, seven deputy secretaries, 13 under secretaries, 14 assistant secretaries and 38 principals, not counting the important military, scientific and statistical staff serving there too. One of the smallest Whitehall departments is one of the most heavy at the top with staff of the highest ranks.[53] This expansion of the Cabinet Office fulfilled the promises of Sir Alec Douglas-Home, Mr Wilson and Mr Heath to build up and strengthen 'the central machinery of co-ordination'.[54] Mr Wilson and Mr Heath also located in the Cabinet Office some of their 'irregular' personal advisers, like Lord Balogh and Michael Stewart for Mr Wilson and Brian Reading for Mr Heath. But they seem not to have been fully integrated into the Cabinet Office: treated as foreign bodies they soon departed.

The influence of the Secretary of the Cabinet is rarely brought to public notice. Mrs Marcia Williams, who was Mr Wilson's personal and political secretary, however, considered in her memoirs that Sir Burke Trend was so important that she viewed him as the 'headmaster', while Sir William Armstrong, the Permanent Secretary of the Civil Service Department, was the 'deputy head'.[55] Politicians perhaps regarded Sir Burke as the most powerful civil servant because of his attendance at Cabinet meetings and because of the work of policy co-ordination of his Office, while civil servants were more aware of Sir William through his control over their careers. However, during Mr Heath's first years in office, which coincided with the last of Sir Burke's, the Prime Minister seemed to rely heavily on Sir William for advice on such sensitive issues as the Industry Act, talks with the C.B.I. and T.U.C. over prices and incomes, and over the counter-inflation legislation. Significantly Sir William sat next to Mr Heath at the press conference to announce the first stage of prices and incomes control. The Permanent Secretary of the Civil Service Department seemed to have replaced the Secretary of the Cabinet as the Prime Minister's permanent secretary.

For officials some of the most important functions of the Cabinet Office are as a storehouse and channel of information. The Cabinet Secretary, and his deputy and under secretaries, can pass on to departmental permanent secretaries news about what is 'politically active', especially what is in the Prime Minister's mind; the permanent secretaries may sometimes even give such information to their Ministers who may not be particularly close to the Prime Minister. In turn, the departmental officials can pass to the Cabinet Office views about what is administratively possible or about what is looming up. The Cabinet Office is an indispensable element of British Government, not only because of its services to the Cabinet, but also because it is the operating centre of an elaborate network of inter-departmental communications.

THE PRIME MINISTER'S PRIVATE OFFICE

The Prime Minister's own office, his private office, has scarcely changed in

3

numbers at the top levels, about five or six, over the last 25 years, although the supporting staff have nearly doubled. The total size of the office, excluding 20 or so cleaners, messengers and security staff, was 36 in 1951, 44 in 1964, 66 in 1970 and 62 in 1972. Since 1965 there have been five Private Secretaries: a Principal Private Secretary, who may be of under secretary or deputy secretary rank, a member of the diplomatic service, of counsellor rank, to look after foreign and defence affairs, an assistant secretary who deals with departments on the main current items of home affairs, and two principals, of whom one concentrates on the Parliamentary aspects of the Prime Minister's work and the other helps to deal with home affairs, general correspondence and the management of the Prime Minister's diary. Somewhat apart from the Private Secretaries, there is a Secretary for Appointments (of assistant secretary rank), who deals with ecclesiastical and other Crown appointments. On the press side, a Chief Press Secretary is supported by two Press Secretaries and four other information staff: in 1950 Mr Attlee had about three people to help him with the press.[56]

Most of the staff in the Prime Minister's Office are on loan from other departments. While at 10 Downing Street, they are on the strength of the Civil Service Department. The normal period of service for a Private Secretary at 10 Downing Street is two to three years; the Principal Private Secretary is, however, liable to serve longer than others. The Secretary for Appointments can expect to serve at least five years and often considerably longer. The Private Secretaries are assisted by a small permanent staff who provide continuity in the office and are the repositories of experience on matters of practice and procedure.

The functions of the private office have changed little since 1950. It keeps the Prime Minister's diary, briefs him on current issues and prospective developments, and through the bush telegraph of Whitehall picks up indications about events inside the departments and signals to them the views of the Prime Minister. It is an important means of communication with the private offices of Cabinet Ministers, especially those physically rather remote from Whitehall. They can receive early warnings of political trouble and can learn when is the appropriate moment to send a memorandum or a minute to the Prime Minister, or to ask for a personal appointment. The Prime Minister's private office collects in reports from departments on policy questions of the day, which are normally prepared on the departments' initiative but may also at times be specially commissioned by the Prime Minister. It checks that he has all the information and advice he needs to reach his decisions, conveys the decisions to the departments and in due course checks that instructions have been carried out. It helps him to perform his Parliamentary duties, processing his Parliamentary questions,[57] preparing his speeches and statements, and generally watching political developments so as to warn of pitfalls ahead. It is the focal point of his correspondence and the incessant flow of papers into and out of No. 10 Downing Street. It has to be alert to answer his queries, especially: 'What's the news?' Its main task is to ease the burden on the Prime Minister and smooth his way so that he can concentrate on the essentials of any matter.

It is a small private and personal office that lacks the administrative resources to compete with the Cabinet Office or other departments. It is no Prime Minister's Department. No Prime Minister over the last 25 years has tried to establish his own department, similar to those of Lloyd George or Winston Churchill in the two wars, to watch over the departments of his colleagues. The most that Prime Ministers have done is to bring an occasional personal appointee into No. 10 Downing Street. Mr Macmillan brought in John Wyndham as one of the private secretaries, Mr Wilson relied on Mrs Marcia Williams as his personal political secretary and Mr Kaufman as his political press officer, and Mr Heath brought in Mr Hurd, his political secretary. The small size and highly personal nature of the private office, and the growing size and specialization of the Cabinet Office, indicate that Prime Ministerial Government has not supplanted Cabinet Government. (It may be argued that it is easier for a Prime Minister to exercise greater influence through traditional, informal and personal practices rather than through a departmental bureaucracy.)[58]

SECRECY

Each Government thinks it essential to shroud in secrecy the workings of the Cabinet.[59] The doctrines of collective Cabinet responsibility and individual ministerial responsibility demand that each Minister is responsible for his department to Parliament and that each Minister accepts every decision of the Cabinet and defends it, even though before the Cabinet decision was taken he was opposed. Secrecy is needed so that the Minister can answer to Parliament for policies with which he may have disagreed but which were pushed on him by the Cabinet. If the disagreements were made known Ministers would be put in embarrassing situations. Further, the doctrine of collective responsibility would be destroyed, the unity of the Government imperilled, party morale diminished and opportunities provided for special interests and the Opposition to exploit the differences for their own advantage. But the differences do exist, and Cabinet secrecy is reconciled with political reality through the 'unattributable leak'.[60] Through it Ministers are able to get their views, whether genuine or fabricated, into the press, but without any ascription to them; in this way they seek to mobilize support for their own proposals or to build up opposition against those of others, or to prepare the ground for some action. The façade of unity is maintained, yet the differences are exposed.

It is often argued that the public should be told more about the numbers, scope and composition of Cabinet committees. But the arguments against are that to do so would damage collective responsibility and impair individual ministerial responsibility. It might be thought that the committees, and not the Cabinet and the individual Minister, had taken particular decisions and were responsible; also, if the membership of Cabinet committees were publicized, those Ministers not on the committee might be able to dissociate themselves from its decisions, while those on the committee might be especially associated with the decision. So far, the defence of secrecy has prevailed over the view that there should be more openness about the way the country is governed.

Up to 1968 Cabinet records were not made public until after 50 years had passed. By the Public Record Act 1967 the period was reduced to 30 years.[61] The limit is imposed so that Ministers can speak freely without any fear that their words will be used against them and damage their political careers. Former Ministers are allowed access to Cabinet papers touching their work, if they wish to refresh their memories when writing their memoirs. It is a convention that anyone who has held public office which makes him personally accountable to public opinion is entitled to put on record his own version of the events in which he played a part. It is customary in these cases to seek the advice of the Secretary of the Cabinet. (The Historical Section of the Cabinet Office watches over Cabinet records and is responsible for promoting official histories based on Cabinet records.) He is concerned to see that no disclosure could endanger national security, or have a bearing on some current policy issue or current ministerial relationships, or undermine the confidence that Ministers need to have in each other that their words will not be reported.[62]

It is often argued that in a democracy the people should have full information about how they are governed, about the opinions of their governors, and, above all, about the arguments being deployed before policy is decided. An early knowledge of such discussions might raise the standard of and widen the debate, since contributions could be made by people and groups at present excluded from the formulation of policy. The result might be greater public confidence in the decisions eventually taken. However, the present rules of secrecy are not unduly restrictive and may be necessary to preserve the conventions on which British democracy depends. The main concern of Ministers is their relationships among themselves and the exchanges they have with each other. They are divided, and yet at the end they have to present a common front. Their corporate integrity can be preserved only if they have trust and confidence in each other, and that requires that their disagreements shall not be publicized.

CONCLUSIONS

Each Cabinet is different, because its members are individuals. Just as Prime Ministers vary in their temperaments and ambitions so do their colleagues in the Cabinet. The interaction between them ensures that each Cabinet has an individuality all its own. Some Prime Ministers want to impose their imprint on a wide range of Government policies, others wish to influence only a few, and some are content to preside over their team and smooth over difficulties and arbitrate. They can be assertive or passive, in all, some or a few areas. The colleagues of the Prime Minister have varying reactions, too, to him and to each other. The same Cabinet may behave differently at different times, depending on their fortunes in the country, the circumstances of a particular occasion, and the press of events. Each meeting is quite unique: its decisions unpredictable, its decision-making process dynamic and complex. The structure of the Cabinet may remain constant but the behaviour of the participants is volatile. The initiative has to be taken by a member, usually a departmental Minister who will recommend a course of action. His proposal will be scrutinized from many angles, by the Treasury, the Law Officers, the Civil Service Department, the Cabinet Office, perhaps by the C.P.R.S., the Whips, and Ministers from other departments. On inter-departmental committees and at Cabinet committees, co-ordinating Ministers, other Ministers and civil servants from many departments will examine the suggestion. The Minister advocating a policy must fight hard to defend his proposal against contending interests and views, and the final decision lies in the Cabinet itself.

The Prime Minister as chairman of the Cabinet, the most important single member, clearly carries great weight. Ministers eagerly court his support, since his voice may tip the balance of opinion in the Cabinet. Ministers seek to draw the Prime Minister to assert himself, while Prime Ministers wish often to be uncommitted at the early stage so as to exert the maximum influence at a later more decisive moment, or else just to come out on the majority side. The Prime Minister is the supreme co-ordinator and arbitrator. The over-riding objective of the Prime Minister is to hold together the Cabinet, which is potentially fragmented. He must persuade the members to reach decisions to which all will subscribe. Mr Wilson wrote: 'The prime minister's task is to get a consensus of Cabinet, or he cannot reasonably ask for loyalty and collective responsibility . . . The difference between prime ministers lies in this: whether the consensus sought is the lowest common denominator, usually a woolly compromise, or something at, or above, the highest common factor attainable.'[63] The means adopted by Prime Ministers will vary: and Ministers will vary in what they will tolerate or endorse. The Prime Minister's role is to advise, encourage and warn his colleagues: not to do their jobs for them. He may involve himself in one or two areas of policy, which seem most important at the time or with which he is publicly associated, but he lacks the administrative resources and the knowledge to make a significant impact on a wide range of governmental responsibilities. He sets the tone of his Cabinet, propounding the general strategy, its style and philosophical approach. He is no one-man band. Although Mr Wilson said he is like the conductor of the orchestra, ensuring that his colleagues are playing the same tune and are in harmony, and not playing the instruments himself,[64] the better analogy is of the Cabinet as a chamber orchestra. The Prime Minister is conductor, but from time to time he feels like reverting to his old position as leader of one of the principal sections; yet he also knows perfectly well that a chamber orchestra has to be led, and directed, in a style which recognizes that this is a group of highly-skilled, hand-picked players some of whom may feel confident that they too could direct.[65]

Cabinet Government, not Prime Ministerial Government, is the British system.[66] And it is not Cabinet autocracy. It acts in the context of Parliamentary dominance. A Cabinet can exist only as long as it maintains a majority in the

House of Commons. The major function of the Cabinet is to manage Parliament so as to maintain the majority. The Cabinet listens closely to the shifting moods of Parliament; in framing its policies it seeks to anticipate Parliamentary reactions and to avoid or blunt the force of criticism, even from the official Opposition. (Every Cabinet meeting starts with a discussion of next week's Parliamentary business.)[67] Its activities are continually shaped by the views of its supporters in the Commons, sent to it through the Whips, party committees, and individual contacts; it observes the debates and speeches, the size of the majority, and abstentions. The Cabinet is sensitive to the ever-changing expressions of Parliamentary opinion. Britain is still governed by a Cabinet responsible to Parliament.[68]

Editor's Note

This chapter takes no account of the changes in the membership of the Cabinet as a result of Mr Wilson becoming Prime Minister in February 1974. His Cabinet included 21 members on its formation and differed from Mr Heath's outgoing Cabinet, in terms of ministerial posts, only by the exclusion of a second Treasury Minister, and the inclusion of two Ministers instead of one for Trade and Industry. It is, of course, too early to discuss the development of the internal relationships of Mr Wilson's Cabinet in this chapter although Sir Richard Clarke has been able to take account of the consequential departmental reconstruction in his chapter on the Machinery of Government.

NOTES AND REFERENCES

1 F. W. G. Benemy, *The Elected Monarch* (1965); Humphrey Berkeley, *The Power of the Prime Minister* (1968); Bernard Crick, *The Reform of Parliament* (2nd edn., 1968), esp. pp. 16–21; R. H. S. Crossman, Introduction to Walter Bagehot, *The English Constitution* (1963 edn.), and *Inside View* (1972); J. P. Mackintosh, *The British Cabinet* (2nd edn., 1968) and *The Government and Politics of Britain* (1970); Richard Rose, 'The Variability of Party Government', *Political Studies*, 1969, pp. 413–45; Colin Seymour-Ure, 'The "Disintegration" of the Cabinet and the Neglected Question of Cabinet Reform', *Parliamentary Affairs*, Summer 1971, pp. 196–207.

2 M. Kogan et al., *The Politics of Education* (1971), pp. 109, 161.

3 Lord Morrison of Lambeth, *Government and Parliament* (3rd edn., 1964), pp. 27–8, and the Earl of Swinton, *Sixty Years of Power* (1966), p. 239.

4 J. E. Alt, 'Continuity, Turnover, and Experience in the British Cabinet, 1868–1970' in V. M. Herman and J. E. Alt (eds), *Cabinet Studies* (1974), and 'How Stable a Cabinet', *New Society*, 13 December 1973, pp. 652–4; P. W. Buck, *Amateurs and Professionals in British Politics, 1918–59* (1963),

'M.P.s in Ministerial Office 1918–55 and 1955–9', *Political Studies*, 1961, pp. 300–6, and 'The Early Start to Cabinet Office 1918–55', *Western Political Quarterly*, 1963, pp. 624–32; Anthony King, 'Britain's Ministerial Turnover', *New Society*, 18 August 1966, pp. 257–8; Richard Rose, 'The Making of Cabinet Ministers', *British Journal of Political Science*, 1971, pp. 393–414; F. M. G. Willson, 'The Routes of Entry of New Members of the British Cabinet, 1868–1958', *Political Studies*, 1959, pp. 222–32, and 'Entry to the Cabinet', *Political Studies*, 1970, pp. 236–8.

5 Lord Butler, *The Art of the Possible* (1971), pp. 158–60.

6 Lord Butler, *op. cit.*, p. 180.

7 Harold Macmillan, *Riding the Storm, 1956–1959* (1971), pp. 12–14.

8 Harold Macmillan, *op. cit.*, and *Pointing the Way, 1959–1961* (1972), and *At the End of the Day, 1961–63* (1973). His earlier volumes of memoirs, *Tides of Fortune, 1945–1955* (1969) and *Riding the Storm* are useful on the Cabinets of Sir Winston Churchill and Sir Anthony Eden. Also see Sir Anthony Eden, *Full Circle* (1960), pp. 265–564, for his own period as Prime Minister and pp. 3–264 for that of Sir Winston Churchill.

9 Harold Wilson, *The Labour Government, 1964–1970* (1971); George Brown, *In My Way* (1970), Chapters 5–9; and Patrick Gordon Walker, *The Cabinet* (2nd edn., 1972).

10 Hugh Thomas, *The Suez Affair* (2nd edn., 1970).

11 Lord Moran, *Winston Churchill* (1966), pp. 482 and 580–5.

12 H. Macmillan, *Riding the Storm* (1971), pp. 12–14.

13 H. Macmillan, *op. cit.*, pp. 398, 466–7, 558.

14 H. Wilson, *op. cit.*, p. 184.

15 P. Gordon Walker, *op. cit.*, p. 93.

16 G. Brown, *op. cit.*, pp. 114–15.

17 This section is based on David Butler and Jennie Freeman, *British Political Facts, 1900–1968* (3rd edn., 1969); D. N. Chester and F. M. G. Willson, *The Organisation of British Central Government, 1914–1964* (2nd edn., 1968); H. Daalder, *Cabinet Reform in Britain, 1914–1963* (1964); *Dod's Parliamentary Companion*; *H.M. Ministers and Heads of Public Departments*; and *Keesing's Contemporary Archives*.

18 D. N. Chester, 'Development of the Cabinet, 1914–1949' in Sir Gilbert Campion *et al.*, *British Government Since 1918* (1950).

19 See R. V. Clements, 'The Cabinet', *Political Studies*, 1965, pp. 231–4.

20 Peter Jenkins, *The Battle of Downing Street* (1970), p. 153.

21 *H.C. Debs.*, vol. 493, col. 75, 6 November 1954, and vol. 516, col. 1903, 24 June 1953.

22 *H.C. Debs.*, vol. 612, cols. 853–4, 3 November 1959.

23 *Central Organisation for Defence*, Cmnd. 2097, 1963, p. 3, and H. Macmillan, *At the End of the Day* (1973), p. 152.

24 H. Macmillan, *Riding the Storm* (1971), pp. 185–92; H. Wilson, *op. cit.*, pp. 523–4.

25 *H.C. Debs.*, vol. 612, col. 74, 27 October 1959.

26 *H.C. Debs.*, vol. 548, col. 30, 24 January 1956.

27 *The Times*, 22 June 1973, p. 23.

28 I am indebted to Dr R. M. Punnett for calculations that do not appear in his book, *Front-Bench Opposition* (1973).

29 B.B.C., *Whitehall and Beyond* (1964), p. 26.

30 Peter Jenkins, *op. cit.*, p. 154.

31 See Lucille Iremonger, *The Fiery Chariot* (1970).

32 H. Daalder, *op. cit.*, pp. 248–9.

33 H. Daalder, *op. cit.*, Chapter 7.

34 *H.C. Debs.*, vol. 701, col. 65, 3 November 1964.

35 *The Times*, 22 June 1973, p. 23.

36 *The Reorganisation of Central Government*, Cmnd. 4506, 1970, and Sir Richard Clarke, *New Trends in Government* (1971). *H.C. Debs.*, vol. 805, cols. 940 and 983, 3 November 1970; for the debate on the governmental reorganization proposals in Cmnd. 4506 see cols. 871–986.

37 D. N. Chester, 'Double-Banking and Deputy Ministers', *New Society*, 11 June 1964.

38 D. N. Chester and F. M. G. Willson, *op. cit.*, p. 371.

39 *H.C. Debs.*, vol. 477, cols. 25–6, 3 July 1950.

40 Lord Morrison of Lambeth, *op. cit.*, Chapter II. Also P. Gordon Walker, *op. cit.*, pp. 38–47, and S. Brittan, *Steering the Economy* (rev. edn., 1971), p. 74.

41 *The Times*, 18 November 1965, p. 12; *H.C. Debs.*, vol. 756, cols. 208–11, 12 December 1967, and vol. 799, col. 123(WA), 9 April 1970.

42 *H.C. Debs.*, vol. 708, cols. 248–51, 9 March 1965, and vol. 763, col. 1000, 30 April 1968.

43 H. Wilson, *op. cit.*, p. 269.

44 See Michael Howard, *The Central Organisation of Defence* (1970), Chapters 1 and 2, and p. 53. Also, *Central Organisation for Defence*, Cmnd. 2097, 1963; *H.C. Debs.*, vol. 591, cols. 1010–13, 15 July 1958, and vol. 682, cols. 472–4, 31 July 1963.

45 S. Brittan, *op. cit.*, pp. 107–9.

46 P. Gordon Walker, *op. cit.*, p. 44.

47 P. Gordon Walker, *op. cit.*, pp. 37–8 and 87–101.

48 R. Butt, *The Power of Parliament* (2nd edn., 1969), pp. xii–xiii; *Financial Times*, 6 April 1968, p. 1 and 11 April 1968, p. 17; *The Times*, 6 April 1968, p. 2, 10 April 1968, pp. 2 and 11, 11 April 1968, pp. 3 and 8, 21 June 1968, p. 10, 6 May 1969, p. 2, 15 May 1969, p. 8, 18 October 1969, p. 1, 7 March 1970, p. 3;

The Guardian, 9 April 1968, pp. 1 and 8; *The Spectator*, 19 April 1968, pp. 515–16 and 16 May 1969, p. 369; *New Statesman*, 17 July 1970, p. 43.

49 *H.C. Debs.*, vol. 801, col. 198, 5 May 1970.

50 *H.C. Debs.*, vol. 762, cols. 75–6 (WA), 2 April 1968, and vol. 840, col. 748, 6 July 1972.

51 J. Fox, 'The brains behind the throne', *Sunday Times* (*Colour Supplement*), 25 March 1973; J. Gretton, 'The Think-Tank's Future', *New Society*, 1 March 1973, pp. 474–5; 'Thinking about the Think-Tank', *The Listener*, 28 December 1972, pp. 880–1.

52 *The Reorganisation of Central Government*, Cmnd. 4506, pp. 13–14; *H.C. Debs.*, vol. 805, cols. 876–7, 3 November 1970, and col. 1262, 5 November 1970; vol. 814, cols. 1668–9, 1 April 1971; vol. 822, cols. 1326–7, 3 August 1971, and vol. 854, col. 612, 5 April 1973.

53 *The British Imperial Calendar and Civil Service List*; *Dod's Parliamentary Companion*; *H.M. Ministers and Heads of Public Departments*; *Supply Estimates*, Cabinet Office, Class 1, 5; *H.C. Debs.*, vol. 825, cols. 131–2 (WA), 9 November 1971; vol. 840, cols. 171–2 (WA), 5 July 1972; vol. 864, col. 425 (WA), 21 November 1973.

54 G. W. Jones, 'The Prime Ministers' Advisers', *Political Studies*, 1973, p. 369.

55 Marcia Williams, *Inside Number 10* (1972), pp. 345–6.

56 *The British Imperial Calendar and Civil Service List*; *Dod's Parliamentary Companion*; *H.M. Ministers and Heads of Public Departments*; *H.C. Debs.*, vol. 692, cols. 33–6 (WA), 23 March 1964; vol. 847, col. 255 (WA), 1 December 1972.

57 G. W. Jones, 'The Prime Minister and Parliamentary Questions', *Parliamentary Affairs*, Summer 1973, pp. 260–73.

58 G. W. Jones, 'The Prime Ministers' Advisers', *Political Studies*, 1973, pp. 363–75.

59 *Departmental Committee on Section 2 of the Official Secrets Act 1911* (Franks Committee), Cmnd. 5104 (1972), pp. 66–70; and the written and oral evidence to the Committee of the Cabinet Office, vol. 2, pp. 9–12, and vol. 3, pp. 316–39.

60 P. Gordon Walker, *op. cit.*, pp. 27–33.

61 *H.C. Debs.*, vol. 608, cols. 62–3 (WA), 2 July 1959, and vol. 733, cols. 1706–8, 10 August 1966.

62 *H.C. Debs.*, vol. 494, col. 2386, 5 December 1951, and vol. 523, cols. 1363–5, 11 February 1954. Also oral evidence to the Franks Committee, *op. cit.*, vol. 3, pp. 329–33.

63 *New Statesman*, 5 May 1972, p. 601.

64 *The Times*, 25 January 1965, p. 13.

65 I am indebted to Lord Boyle for the elaboration on the musical image.

66 D. E. Butler, 'Ministerial Responsibility in Australia and Britain', *Parliamentary Affairs*, Autumn 1973, pp. 403–14; A. H. Brown, 'Prime Ministerial Power', *Public Law*, Spring and Summer 1968, pp. 28–51 and 96–118; I. Gilmour,

3*

62   G. W. Jones

The Body Politic (2nd edn., 1971), pp. 205–44; G. W. Jones, 'The Prime
Minister's Power', *Parliamentary Affairs*, Spring 1965, pp. 167–85, and 'Prime
Ministers and Cabinets', *Political Studies*, 1972, pp. 213–22; Anthony King (ed.),
The British Prime Minister (1969); M. Kogan *et al.*, *The Politics of Education*
(1971); P. Gordon Walker, *op. cit.*

67 R. H. S. Crossman, *Inside View* (1972), p. 59.

68 I wish to thank the following for their helpful comments on the first draft of
this chapter: Rodney Barker, Lord Boyle, Sir Norman Chester, Anthony King,
Janet Morgan, Elly Shodell, Leslie Stone and Vincent Wright. Others have to
be anonymous.

The Machinery of Government

4

Sir Richard Clarke, K.C.B., O.B.E.

The structure and articulation of government departments present a unique mixture in the study of public affairs. The machinery of government is very much the personal business of the Prime Minister, for it is the centre of his task of choosing his team of Ministers and welding them into an effective instrument to carry out the Government's policies. But even the most powerful Prime Minister must take the structure of departments as he finds it; and except in war-time, when the new problems require a new governmental apparatus, few Prime Ministers have devoted much attention to this aspect of their responsibilities. Even with the memoirs published and the public records open, it would be difficult to say which Prime Ministers had left their imprint on the peace-time machinery of government, or to distinguish those Governments whose performance has been helped by good machinery from those which have been hindered by bad.

The morphology of the structure of departments is difficult to examine. Over decades there are important changes; and looking backward one can see a kind of logic in these changes; but it is never easy to see who made these changes and why. Mr Wilson and Mr Heath have certainly devoted more attention to this subject than their predecessors ever did; so much so that machinery of government questions have sometimes become subjects of party controversy, and have impelled incoming Prime Ministers to change the structure of departments on coming into office simply in order to demonstrate the arrival of a new broom sweeping away the inefficiencies of the previous Government and ushering in a new streamlined regime. Some changes are narrowly 'political', to meet the personal problems of Cabinet-making, and to present the Government in a desired image; and these will always happen. But some (perhaps most of them in recent years) are a response to the new problems of government and the new pressures to which government is subjected.

Perhaps this process of adapting the structure of departments to the revolution in the scope and functions of democratic government since the First World War is now working through to its conclusion; and although it may be premature to signal the approach of a period of stability similar to that of the late 19th and early 20th century, it is certainly true to say that most of the present structure may be regarded as firmly established and that the area of genuine doubt about what is the best departmental layout is now smaller than it has been for many years.

SIXTY YEARS OF GOVERNMENT DEPARTMENTS

Table 1 sets out the basic structure of the major departments going back to 1914. There is no accepted definition of what is a 'department' and what is 'major': each of those included in the table, whether large or small, represents a coherent political unit of activity in the charge of a departmental Minister. For our purposes here, which relate to the political apparatus of government, there is a clear distinction between these 'major departments' and such public bodies as H.M. Stationery Office, the Ordnance Survey, the Unemployment Assistance Board (1934) and its successors until assistance was taken into the Ministry of Social Security in 1966, the Exchequer and Audit Department, the Office of Population Censuses and Surveys, the British Museum, the Law Officers' Departments, etc. These have their own links with Ministers, and some are much larger organizations than some of the 'major departments', but they are outside the main channels of direct political involvement. In the table, the titles of the 'major departments' are simplified, and I have ignored mere changes of title with no significant change in content or public impact. Where possible, the departments are arranged in groups leading towards the present structure, even where very little relationship has in the past been discerned between departments within these groups. The order has been chosen to make this group arrangement easier, and not to show relative importance.

The table shows the situation at eight dates, chosen to illustrate the structure at representative times and at times at which large changes had just taken place or were about to take place. These are:

March 1974   Mr Wilson's Government after the Election of February 1974.

Mid-1973   The situation after three years of Mr Heath's Government, embodying the final result of the changes begun in autumn 1970; and before the changes made following the energy crisis of autumn 1973.

End-1969   Mr Wilson's Government after the major changes in autumn 1969.

End-1964   Mr Wilson's first Government after the Election of October 1964.

End-1959   Mr Macmillan's Government after the Election of October 1959, from which the patterns of the 1960s developed.

Sept. 1951   The end of Mr Attlee's Government, just before the Election of October 1951, with most of the special war-time machinery disbanded, but still considerable rationing and controls.

End-1935   Mr Baldwin's Government after the Election of November 1935, a representative year of the inter-war period, with the changes following the first war fully established and before the changes made by rearmament and approaching war.

1914   Mr Asquith's Government on the eve of the First World War: the traditional structure as it had developed since the latter part of the 19th century.

TABLE 1 Major Departments, 1914 to 1974

	March 1974 Wilson (21)	Mid-1973 Heath (18)	November 1969 Wilson (21)	November 1964 Wilson (27)	November 1959 Macmillan (26)	September 1951 Attlee (30)	1935 Baldwin (23)	1914 Asquith (18)
	Treasury Civil Service	Treasury Civil Service	Treasury Civil Service	Treasury Economic Affairs	Treasury	Treasury	Treasury	Treasury
	Foreign & Commonwealth Overseas Development	Foreign & Commonwealth	Foreign & Commonwealth Overseas Development	Foreign Commonwealth Colonies Overseas Development	Foreign Commonwealth Colonies	Foreign Commonwealth Colonies	Foreign Dominions Colonies India	Foreign Colonies India
	Defence	Defence	Defence	Defence	Defence Admiralty War Air	Defence Admiralty War Air Supply	Admiralty War Air	Admiralty War
	Home Scotland Wales Northern Ireland Lord Chancellor's	Home Scotland Wales Northern Ireland Lord Chancellor's	Home Scotland Wales Lord Chancellor's	Home Scotland Wales Lord Chancellor's	Home Scotland Lord Chancellor's	Home Scotland Lord Chancellor's	Home Scotland Lord Chancellor's	Home Scotland Ireland Lord Chancellor's
	Industry Energy Trade Prices & Consumer Protection	Trade & Industry	Trade Technology	Trade Power Aviation Technology	Trade Power Aviation	Trade Fuel & Power Materials Civil Aviation	Trade	Trade
	Employment	Employment	Employment & Productivity	Labour	Labour	Labour	Labour	
	Environment	Environment	Transport Public Building & Works Housing & Local Government	Transport Public Building & Works Housing & Local Government Land & Natural Resources	Transport Works Housing & Local Government	Transport Works Local Government & Planning	Transport Works	Works
	Health & Social Security	Health & Social Security	Health & Social Security	Health, Pensions & National Insurance	Health Pensions & National Insurance	Health National Insurance War Pensions	Health Pensions (War)	Local Government
	Education & Science	Education & Science	Education & Science	Education & Science	Education Science	Education D.S.I.R.	Education D.S.I.R.	Education
	Agriculture, Fisheries & Food	Agriculture, Fisheries & Food	Agriculture, Fisheries & Food	Agriculture, Fisheries & Food	Agriculture, Fisheries & Food	Agriculture, Fisheries & Food	Agriculture & Fisheries	Agriculture & Fisheries
	Inland Revenue Customs & Excise	Inland Revenue Customs & Excise Posts & Telecommunications	Inland Revenue Customs & Excise Posts & Telecommunications	Inland Revenue Customs & Excise Post Office	Inland Revenue Customs & Excise Post Office	Inland Revenue Customs & Excise Post Office	Inland Revenue Customs & Excise Post Office	Inland Revenue Customs & Excise Post Office

We can trace the course of development by considering first the situation at each of these dates, and how the changes have taken place from each date to the next; and then by considering the course of change across the whole period, function by function. This puts the present machinery of government into a proper historical perspective, and enables us to consider realistically both its present problems and the possible pressures for future development.

1914 – 1935 – 1951 – 1959 – 1964 – 1969 – 1973 – 1974

In machinery of government, we must begin with 1914, for there is no convenient starting-point in the inter-war period, and one cannot think about the 1950s without considering the earlier structures from which the later ones were derived. In 1914, there was a firmly established set of structures. The table lists 18 departments, of which 12 were in the long-standing functions of treasury (money, taxes, government), overseas policy, defence, law and order and nationality: there were the Boards of Trade, Local Government, Education, Agriculture & Fisheries; and the Office of Works and the Post Office. This was a straightforward structure, but already creaking at the seams. The Board of Trade had had a great expansion of its activities, particularly in the creation of labour exchanges and unemployment insurance, under Mr Lloyd George and Mr Churchill: the Insurance Commissions were establishing the health insurance system (1800 staff in 1914)—an *ad hoc* organization under the Chancellor of the Exchequer (Mr Lloyd George): the Local Government Board was clearly unequipped to be the base for the expansion of social and environmental services. The 1914 system was really suitable for the Britain of 1905, not 1914, and in this as in so many other things, the outbreak of war left much unfinished business behind it.

After the proliferation and then the disbandment of war-time departments, in 1935, the total had risen from 18 to 23. The Air Ministry was by then well established; the Irish Office had gone in 1924; the Dominions Office had been separated from the Colonial Office in 1925, although they still had a common Secretary-of-State until 1930. There were five newcomers: Labour, Pensions (War) and Department of Scientific and Industrial Research (all set up in 1916); and Transport (inland) and Health, set up in 1919. The latter had absorbed the Local Government Board and the Insurance Commissions, and was the focal point for the large developments of social insurance and environmental services in the 1920s, under Mr Neville Chamberlain as Minister from 1924 to 1929.

In 1951, 16 years and another World War later, there were 30 departments against 23. The India Office had gone, making a net addition of eight departments. One was the Ministry of Defence (a small co-ordinating department). Three represented new permanent functions of government: Fuel & Power (nationalization of energy industries), Health (the national health service: the old Health had lost social insurance and had become Local Government & Planning), National Insurance (carrying out the reconstruction in the Beveridge

Report). Two were still needed to deal with physical shortages: Food and Materials. The other two, Supply and Civil Aviation, were somewhere between 'permanent' and 'temporary'—it was still thought necessary to have a Ministry of Supply for army and air equipment supply, and it was also dealing with steel nationalization and the engineering industry and with atomic energy; and the initial establishment of post-war civil aviation and the airways corporations was thought to require a separate department; but in neither case was this envisaged as permanent. The opinion of the time tended to favour setting up new departments to tackle new governmental tasks, for the pressure on all the departments of handling the new and uncharted problems of change from war to post-war was formidable, and at that stage, doing the new jobs was more important than creating a co-ordinated system.

The Conservative Administrations of the next 13 years reduced the number of departments from 30 to 22, which was about the same as Mr Baldwin's in 1935. In the first phase, Pensions (War) was joined with National Insurance (1953); Civil Aviation with Transport, which included shipping (1953); Materials disbanded (1954) and the function transferred to the Board of Trade, which also got steel and engineering from Supply (1955); Agriculture & Fisheries joined with Food (1955) creating a department with a much wider responsibility than the traditional support for the farming interest—these moves reduced the total by four. Another move for civil aviation (the third home in 14 years!) followed in 1959, when it was joined with the aircraft work of Supply to make the Ministry of Aviation, the army supply work returning to the War Office. Mr Macmillan transferred Service building to Works in 1963, and forced through the merger of the Service departments into a single Ministry of Defence (operative April 1964), one of the most constructive developments of the period. Another important move, bringing to an end a series of misty arrangements for the Government's sponsorship of civil science, brought Education (including the whole educational system from nursery schools to universities) and Science together into one department (1964).

Mr Wilson's first arrangements in October 1964 appeared to reverse this process of consolidation. He introduced five new departments, bringing the total to 27. Not all of these were unqualified successes. Land & Natural Resources lasted two years; Economic Affairs lasted five; Technology had a remarkable career, merging with Aviation in 1967 and with Power and important parts of Trade and D.E.A. in 1969, finishing in the 'giant' Department of Trade and Industry in Mr Heath's Government in 1970; Overseas Development became a federal part of the Foreign & Commonwealth Office in 1970; and only the Welsh Office remained in its initial position, now to be regarded as part of the permanent structure of government. It soon became clear, indeed, that consolidation was continuing. The departments concerned with external affairs were wholly merged by stages—a single diplomatic service in 1965, merger of Colonies and Commonwealth Relations in 1966, and of both with the Foreign Office in 1968. Health and Pensions & National Insurance were joined in the Department of Health and Social Security in 1968. The Technology mergers eliminated Power and Aviation, the civil aviation part of the latter moving to its fourth (!) home, this time in the Board of Trade, brigaded alongside shipping, which had been moved there from Transport at the previous round. At the centre, the Treasury was divided first in 1964 to make Economic Affairs, and a second time in 1968 to form the Civil Service Department, but in 1969 some of D.E.A. was returned there. So by the end of 1969, after five years of government, Mr Wilson had actually reduced the number of departments to 21, fewer than he had inherited from Sir Alec Douglas-Home; and his memoirs show (*The Labour Government 1964–70*, p. 711) that if he had continued in office after the 1970 Election, he would have reduced the numbers further.

Mr Heath, after a pause for thought and serious examination of the problems —a welcome innovation for incoming Prime Ministers—carried this process of consolidation further again. Trade and Technology were joined in the Department of Trade & Industry, the old problem of military and civil aircraft supply being eventually solved by transferring the whole research/development/production apparatus to Defence, leaving D.T.I. responsible for the Government's relationship with the aircraft industry and support for civil aircraft projects as well as for the civil aviation industry. Housing & Local Government, Transport and Works were joined in the Department of the Environment. Overseas Development was brought within the Foreign & Commonwealth Office. But it proved necessary to set up a new department for Northern Ireland. By the end of the third year of Mr Heath's Administration, the total had been reduced to 18, the same as in 1914!

This turned out to have taken the process of concentration of the industrial departments faster than could be politically managed in a period (not envisaged in 1970) of increasing Government intervention in industry. In January 1974, Mr Heath found it necessary to put a senior Cabinet Minister in charge of the energy 'crisis', and so to detach a Department of Energy from D.T.I. Two months later, Mr Wilson confirmed this, and split the rest of D.T.I. into three departments: Industry, Trade, Prices & Consumer Protection; he removed one remaining anomaly by absorbing Posts & Telecommunications into Industry, but re-established Overseas Development as a department on its own. These events brought the total back from 18 to 21, which was the figure left by Mr Wilson in 1970. However, there is some reason to believe that both Mr Heath's and Mr Wilson's moves on the industrial side were dictated more by political situations and the problems of ministerial teams than by long-term machinery of government considerations; and the structure in March 1974 looked unstable, and the numbers likely to be reduced again when suitable circumstances arose. Apart from the industrial area, each of the main functions of government now has its own department, and each new problem that arises can readily be assigned to the appropriate department, as was so in the half-century before 1914; so there are seeds of stability in the situation.

THE PROCESSES OF CHANGE

The changes from 1951 to 1974 may be summarized as follows:

	1974	1973	1951
Treasury, etc.	4	4	3
Overseas	2	1	3
Defence	1	1	5
Law, order, nationality	5	5	3
Industry, trade, etc.	6 {	3	7
Posts		1	1
Environment	1	1	3
Social services	1	1	3
Education, science	1	1	2
Total	21	18	30

Treasury

The fission at the centre of government, compared with the fusion elsewhere, is fundamental to the history of the period. From the early 1920s under the formidable Sir Warren Fisher, the Treasury was established as the leading department, controlling the departments' expenditure and staff and appointments, besides its function as the central economic and financial department. It lost ground during the Second World War, and for a considerable period the Chancellor of the Exchequer was not even a member of the War Cabinet. After the war, the Treasury recovered that part of its former authority that followed from the return to normal financial control of the departmental machine, but there was reluctance to re-establish its former ascendancy in matters of economic and financial policy; and in 1946 and 1947 attempts were made to build up economic policy co-ordination at the centre, separate from the Chancellor's responsibilities, first with Mr Herbert Morrison as Lord President (following Sir John Anderson's powerful co-ordinating role as Lord President in war-time) and then with Sir Stafford Cripps as Minister for Economic Affairs. Whether this would have succeeded will never be known, for it had lasted only for a few weeks when the Chancellor of the Exchequer (Dr Dalton) felt compelled to resign because of his inadvertent disclosure of his Budget proposals, and Sir Stafford Cripps became Chancellor, bringing with him his Economic Affairs responsibility and also Sir Edwin (now Lord) Plowden and the Central Economic Policy Staff and the management of international economic policy negotiations. So by this historical accident, the Treasury's ascendancy was restored, with even greater force than before because of the dominating position of Sir Stafford Cripps and because of the post-war centralization of the economy.

This ascendancy continued throughout the 1950s. In the dissatisfaction with the nation's economic performance in the early 1960s, which became the focus of the Labour Party's attack upon the Conservative Governments, the Treasury's hegemony was severely criticized. It was argued that the Treasury's inborn deflationism had frustrated economic expansion; and this view became widely held among academics and publicists as well as among political opponents of the Conservative Governments. It is unlikely that a fully-informed analysis of the events of the period and of Treasury officials' roles in them would substantiate this view, for the Treasury was a different kind of body in the late 1950s from what it had been in the 1920s and 1930s; and its performance could well be criticized on quite other grounds. However, the conventional wisdom of the time prevailed; and a Department of Economic Affairs was created to be an expansionist counter-weight to the Treasury in October 1964. It was never possible to establish a meaningful division of function between the two departments, for the essence of economic policy is that one cannot separate 'economic' from 'financial', or 'resources' from 'money', or 'long-term' from 'short-term', or divide the responsibility for 'planning' from the responsibility for 'execution'. In fact the Treasury and D.E.A. worked very closely together; but it became increasingly clear that the concept was faulty, and the dissolution of D.E.A. in September 1969 was generally regarded as inevitable.

The failure of the D.E.A. experiment, however, should not obscure the fact that the new policies of State intervention which were introduced by Mr Macmillan's Administration (incomes policy, 'Neddy', commitment to economic growth, regional incentives, intervention in particular industrial situations) and have been developed steadily ever since, were creating real problems of machinery of government. The Treasury machine had been reconstructed in 1962 in order to be equipped to carry out these new roles; but this was necessarily scrapped to form D.E.A. But nevertheless, by 1964 the range of the Treasury's functions and responsibilities (and the load on the Chancellor of the Exchequer), were becoming formidable; and the balance between the Treasury and the departments may have been tilting too much towards the centre with a corresponding loss of weight and initiative at the periphery. The D.E.A. experiment, by setting up another department at the centre with many of the same functions as the Treasury, did not help these real problems; and indeed made them worse. But perhaps it was impossible to deal with them at the time, while the machinery of government on the industrial side was still wholly confused.

The second fission of the Treasury, carried out on the recommendation of the Fulton Committee, was to transfer the management side of the Treasury to the new Civil Service Department. Here again, the division was not well conceived in terms of division of function, for the control of departments from the centre must include money and staff and appointments, and this control process cannot be carried out by two separate departments without the risk either of duplication and confusion for the operating departments or of ineffectiveness of the central operation because some functions fall between the two. Nor was it ever realistic to hope that the new department would be able to 'stand up to the Treasury' to improve the conditions of the Civil Service: if considerations of machinery of government are expected to alter such balances, the argument might indeed run the other way, for when the Chancellor of the Exchequer and the Treasury were responsible for the Civil Service, they necessarily gave great weight to this responsibility; and, freed from this responsibility, they would be unlikely to give the civil servants more.

There was a good argument for change, at any rate for a temporary period, to carry out the Fulton reforms; and there was permanent advantage in reducing the load on the Chancellor of the Exchequer and on the Treasury; and there were political and psychological advantages in narrowing the Treasury's hegemony. It would be difficult to argue, moreover, that the duplication of central controlling departments had cost very much in inefficiency and confusion, at any rate in the first five years, for there had been little common action between the 'economic and financial' and 'management' sides of the Treasury; and the two departments were probably as closely in touch with each other as the two sides of the one department had been in the previous five years. With the effluxion of time, however, and the physical separation of the two departments and the disappearance of the old staff, this situation will change. Moreover, in the long run one would expect the Civil Service Department to be subject to the typical difficulties of small specialized departments, with too narrow a base and too esoteric a workload for success particularly in the managerial task of controlling other departments. This particular experiment in machinery of government cannot yet be regarded as having proved itself permanently established.

The growing complexity and inter-dependence of government has steadily increased the size and importance of the co-ordinating role of the Cabinet Office. In defence and foreign affairs, this has from the beginning been done by the Secretary of the Cabinet: in economic affairs, the Treasury was the co-ordinator throughout its period of hegemony up to 1964, and after that there was something of a vacuum. But taking the government business as a whole, there has been a growing need for organization at the centre to sort out the problems and their inter-relationships. The development of the giant departments enabled more of this process to be done peripherally instead of in the central machine; but as the load on the Cabinet grows, so does the work of co-ordination.

There has been continuing experiment in finding means to give non-departmental advice to the Prime Minister (and sometimes to the Cabinet). Most Prime Ministers, except very relaxed and self-contained men like Mr Attlee, have an overwhelming need for advice from outside the normal departmental channels (which they regard as being controlled by their colleagues). Some enlist the Head of the Civil Service for this function, entirely outside his normal departmental work: Mr Baldwin and Mr Neville Chamberlain used Sir Warren Fisher and Sir Horace Wilson respectively; Mr Macmillan used Sir Norman Brook. Others have used the Secretary of the Cabinet and the Cabinet Office. Others, for example, Mr Wilson from 1964 to 1970, have preferred to have a number of advisers inside and outside the Civil Service. Some built up an organized body of independent advice: Mr Lloyd George's 'Garden Suburb', at the end of the

First World War, threatened to become an independent governmental machine: Sir Winston Churchill had Lord Cherwell and his staff, both during the Second World War and in his 1951 Administration; Mr Heath tried to establish permanent organization, with Lord Rothschild's Central Policy Review Staff, and also had his group of business men, led by Sir Richard Meyjes; Mr Wilson's first action in March 1974 was to retain C.P.R.S., to instal at No. 10 Downing Street a 'policy Unit' under Dr Bernard Donoughue, and to set up a group in the Cabinet Office under Lord Crowther-Hunt to consider constitutional questions.

In 50 years' experience, no one way of satisfying this pressing and natural need of Prime Ministers seems to have been better than another. The outcome depends upon the ability of the advisers, wherever they may be located, to work with the machine, not challenging the civil servants ignorantly where they have the real professional expertise, and thence to provide the harsh and realistic and independent advice that Prime Ministers need. In the half-century, there have been good contributions made, and many disasters too.

This provision of non-departmental advisers is the opposite of the often-canvassed idea of a Prime Minister's Department. The Prime Minister's need is for independent advice, often from people who are not professional civil servants: this calls for able sceptical people, not rooted in the organization. A Prime Minister's Department, on the other hand, must be the central department of government, with the kind of hegemony that the Treasury had at its strongest: the Head of the Civil Service would inevitably be the head of this department, whose task would be to co-ordinate the work of the departments and to distil the quintessence of the collective official advice for the Prime Minister and the Cabinet. For Prime Ministers with a Presidential style, this could have much to commend it; but it has nothing to do with organizing advice for Prime Ministers from outside the official machine.

In the review of the history of the machinery of government over the last 25 years, the changes in the role of the Treasury are fundamental. This is still unfinished business; and whilst the structure of the peripheral departments may now be moving towards long-term stability, at the centre of government there may still be changes to come.

Overseas Policy

The process of fusion went smoothly, for it was a natural machinery of government operation, and not something designed to create a desired change. By the early 1960s, the days of the Colonial Office were drawing to an end; and with the approach to Europe, the existence of a separate department to handle Commonwealth relations was no longer necessary. The first step was the unification of the diplomatic service (1965), then the creation of the Commonwealth Office (1966), and then the combination of the Foreign Office and the Commonwealth Office (October 1968). The styles of these departments were different, but this worked itself out, successfully.

The creation of the Ministry of Overseas Development from the modest Department of Technical Co-operation had been one of Mr Wilson's innovations of October 1964, less spectacular in its results than had been intended, for it was never possible to devote the additional resources to overseas aid that were needed to justify a new approach; and the absorption of the department into the Foreign and Commonwealth Office in November 1970, as a federal unit with a separate Minister and a separate title as Overseas Development Administration was straightforward. So also was the reversion to an independent Ministry of Overseas Development in Mr Wilson's 1974 Administration.

In the long run, the merging of foreign and Commonwealth affairs represents an important change in policy. Indeed, if this series of mergers could have taken place ten years earlier, our approach to Europe might have been more effective. The existence of a separate department and Secretary-of-State, dedicated to Commonwealth relations (and thus to the defence of the existing economic and commercial arrangements within the Commonwealth regardless of their value to the United Kingdom) was always a brake upon our approach to Europe. If in the 1950s we could have considered our world-wide economic relationships as one subject, with the relationships within the Commonwealth as a special element, the Governments of the day might have made up their minds more quickly and negotiated with Europe more effectively. It is hardly open to dispute that if it was right for this country to join the European Economic Community on 1 January 1973 it would have been immensely better for us to have joined on 1 January 1963, and better still to have participated in the Messina Conference of 1955 which set in motion the forces which led to the Rome Treaty in 1957. The crucial question was how fast the Government and the country could re-assess the relative weight of Europe and the Commonwealth in the formulation of British interests of all kinds. The effect of the machinery of government of the 1950s was to polarize the discussion and to obstruct rather than to stimulate the formation of objective judgments. The combination of a unified Foreign & Commonwealth Office, the Treasury and the Board of Trade could conceivably have found a course in the 1950s that would have been better than the simple endorsement of the Rome Treaty. The existence of specialized machinery of government to protect the sectional interests of Commonwealth relations (and also of agriculture) damaged these special interests as well as the national interest as a whole.

Defence

At the end of the Second World War, it was accepted that a permanent Ministry of Defence was necessary, and this was set up on 1 January 1947 after legislation. It had the task of (a) apportioning resources between the three Services in accordance with the strategic policy laid down by the Defence Committee of the Cabinet (including framing of general policy for research and development, co-ordinating manpower problems, correlating production programmes and financial Estimates, etc.); (b) settling questions of administration on which a common policy for the three Services was desirable; (c) administering various inter-Service organizations (such as the Joint Intelligence Bureau). The three Service Ministers were wholly responsible for their own departments and Services, and were not under the orders of the Minister of Defence, though they were subject to his co-ordination in the specified areas, and he was a Cabinet Minister and they were not. Broadly speaking, the Navy was responsible for its own equipment supply; and the Army and the R.A.F. depended for their equipment supply upon the Ministry of Supply (with which the Ministry of Aircraft Production had been joined in 1946) and which was subject to the co-ordination of the Minister of Defence in much the same manner as the Service departments. The post-war structure for civil defence was set up in 1948 under the Home Office (later shared with the Scottish Office).

The real issue of defence machinery of government, which occupied the next 25 years, was how 'strong' the Minister and Ministry of Defence should be. It has always been common ground that the essentials of defence policy should be centralized—the defence strategy, the allocation of budgetary and manpower resources between the Services, the shaping of the nation's defence. But it had never been accepted in peace-time that this required a Minister of Defence. Historically, it was the function of the Prime Minister, with the help of the machinery of the Committee of Imperial Defence (set up in 1904), and then the Defence Committee of the Cabinet. The Chiefs of Staff, the Board of Admiralty, the Army and Air Councils, the individual Service Ministers, all had their constitutional responsibilities, which could not be reconciled with the overlordship of a Minister or a Ministry of Defence. The establishment of N.A.T.O. and other international defence bodies, however, made it necessary for somebody to be able to speak for the nation's defence as a whole, and to negotiate for it as a continuous process—a need which could not easily be accommodated within a structure of independent Services and Service departments, co-ordinated from time to time by the decisions of Cabinet committees. At one end of the spectrum was the concept of a defence 'overlord', with little more than a private office, dependent wholly upon the Services for facts, with responsibility for carrying out the minimum of co-ordination imposed by the political, financial, technological and international considerations. At the other end was the concept of one single Defence department, and even ultimately one single Service. In 1946 we started at the 'narrow' end; and the next 25 years has been a progression along this spectrum by a series of jumps to the present situation. The three Services are still distinct, and the ideas which were strongly and authoritatively pressed earlier for the unification of the top echelons of the Services have dropped out of sight at any rate for the present. But we are not far from unification in those areas in which Government decisions are often needed.

The fundamental change was announced by Mr Macmillan in March 1963, to take place on 1 April 1964. This established a single Ministry of Defence, with a single Minister, and the Services under three Ministers of State. This reform was the result of many years' initiative and pressure by Mr Macmillan, who had had a traumatic experience as Minister of the 'weak' Ministry of Defence in the period from October 1954 to April 1955 (*Tides of Fortune*, the third volume of Mr Macmillan's political memoirs, pp. 560–2); and he had powerful support both from the Services, notably Lord Mountbatten, and from the Civil Service. There were great controversies at the time, but looking back at the period from January 1947 to March 1963, one would find it difficult to justify the defence machinery that was allowed to exist for so many years. The 'weak' Ministry was in fact unable to carry out those minimum functions of central formulation of defence policy which required to be carried out on any concept of government: all that the Minister could do was to negotiate compromises and allocate 'fair shares' between the Services. Minor reforms were made: at the end of 1955, a permanent chairman was appointed to the Chiefs of Staff Committee, additional to the three Chiefs; when Mr Macmillan became Prime Minister he sought to increase the Minister's authority, without changing the legislation, and gave him the authority for the new permanent chairman of the Chiefs of Staff; but none of these changes made fundamental impact upon the situation. Those Ministers who were best at overriding the Services were not always the best at deciding the best course for defence policy; and in the 16 years from January 1947 there were no less than 11 Ministers of Defence, which reflects the weight that successive Prime Ministers (some of whom preferred their individual access to the Chiefs of Staff and the Service departments) placed upon this post. In the end Mr Macmillan carried out the re-organization, with Mr Thorneycroft as the Minister at the crucial time. The new structure came into being on 1 April 1964; and was just finding its feet when Mr Healey became Minister in Mr Wilson's Government in the following October. He stayed there until the end of the Labour Government in June 1970; and this was another personal factor of great importance.

There have been three major developments since then. One has been the centralization of all defence procurement within the department, under a Procurement Executive. Navy procurement had been with the Admiralty all along; Army procurement reverted to the War Office when the Ministry of Supply was replaced by the Ministry of Aviation in October 1959; the future of military aviation procurement, which had been one of the most intractable problems of machinery of government (because of the close links between civil and military aircraft production and between both and the aircraft industry) was resolved in 1971 by its inclusion within the new Procurement Executive, which also has responsibilities for the civil aerospace programme on an agency basis for the Department of Industry. The consolidation of defence procurement is a fundamental change, not only by bringing all weapon supply into the Ministry of Defence, but by organizing supply as a separate function there. The only supply which is not included in the Defence Department is the works services, which were transferred from the individual Service departments to the Ministry of Public Buildings and Works in April 1963 (a mysterious move by

Mr Macmillan at the time) and later to the Department of the Environment where it is now part of the duties of the Property Services Agency.

The second major development has been the concentration of the control and management of the defence budget. From the mid-1950s onward, during the period of the 'weak' Ministries of Defence, the Treasury pressed hard to develop a 10-year forward defence budget, and to use this to strengthen the Ministry of Defence and to force discussion of the crucial issues of defence planning. This was strengthened further by the prompt introduction of the techniques of pro-gramme budgetting developed by Mr McNamara in the U.S. Department of Defense in the early 1960s—changes which made it possible, for example, for the first time (and with great effect) to make an authoritative estimate of the cost of the defence effort East of Suez. So from the start of the new Defence Department in 1963–64, great emphasis was placed upon the central control of the budget and programme; and this turned out to be important, not only for the integration of the new department, but also in providing the apparatus for discussing the fundamentals of defence policy in the second half of the 1960s.

Third has been the change at the top level of the department. In the 1963–64 structure, below the Secretary-of-State, there were three Ministers-of-State, each responsible for one of the three Services (plus other broader responsi-bilities); so that there were still Ministers for the Navy, the Army and the Air Force. The defence policy controversy in 1965–66, which led to Mr Mayhew's resignation from 'Minister of the Navy', led in January 1967 to the replacement of these three Ministers-of-State by two, both free of Service responsibilities; with the individual Services put under the charge of Parliamentary Under-Secretaries. There are now the Secretary-of-State, one Minister-of-State, and three Parliamentary Secretaries. The top organization of the department is not now Service-orientated; and in terms of government, defence is treated as one subject—and certainly not fragmented between three Services.

On any reckoning, these are very large and successful reforms in machinery of government.

Law, Order, Nationality

In the last 25 years there have been many transfers of function between the Home Office and other departments, but with the possible exception of the ruling of 1946 which permanently transferred the administration of the Factories Acts to what is now the Department of Employment, these are of secondary impor-tance. For the long-term machinery of government, the significant changes have been the completion of the transfer of the social and environmental services to the Scottish departments in the mid-1950s, the establishment of the Welsh Office in the 1960s, and the reversion to direct rule of Northern Ireland in 1972.

Before the First World War, the administration of services in Scotland was carried out by boards, which were generally answerable to the Secretary for

Scotland. In 1926, the Secretary became a Secretary-of-State, and gradually the boards became departments in Edinburgh under him—Home, Health, Agriculture and Education—with a small parliamentary and liaison Scottish Office in London (1939). This apparatus was welded together into one organization under a Permanent Secretary; and after the Second World War took on other responsibilities, e.g. for roads and harbours in 1956. By the end of the 1950s, virtually all social and environmental services (except for national insurance) were under Scottish management and control. In 1962, the organization was remoulded, with a Scottish Development Department aimed at improving the infrastructure, and fostering industrial development in order to check the southward loss of population, a Scottish Home & Health Department, and the Scottish Education Department and the Department of Agriculture & Fisheries.

There has been a great consolidation and strengthening of Scottish administration, and a framework has been provided for economic development. The structure is under political criticism in Scotland, for it is not independent Scottish Government; however, the extent to which the Scottish electorate would favour the risks and responsibilities of greater political independence is always in doubt, for a rational appraisal of Scotland's interests is bound to give great weight to the integration with England and Wales. Indeed, the present arrangements are vulnerable to the opposite criticism, that the Scottish administration has great independence in the expenditure of public money on the social and environmental services—and has indeed established a kind of dual standard, by which Scotland is 'entitled' to at least equal treatment with England where there is no specific Scottish difficulty but special treatment wherever a colourable argument can be made—without having to limit this expenditure in accordance with Scottish resources as it would do under conditions of greater political independence. The responsibility for handling formidable economic and political problems such as Upper Clyde Shipbuilders was seen as a responsibility for London, with Edinburgh's role as one of bringing pressure to bear on London; in the whole problem of the development areas, indeed, the Scottish administration's function is to press the Government, both to organize the action and provide the financial support in general, and to allocate to Scotland as much as Scotland's political pressure can extract. This mixture of independence and clamorous importunity has had practical benefits in the building of Scotland's services and in the handling of Scotland's economic problems: but it may have weakened the fibre of responsibility both in private enterprise and in public life; and it must be hoped that no steps will be taken towards greater Scottish autonomy without including responsibility for finding the financial and economic resources as well as for distributing grants from the United Kingdom Government.

In the same period, the emphasis on action in Wales has been towards setting up a separate administration. This began in October 1951, when Sir Winston Churchill's Government gave the Home Secretary the additional function of Minister for Welsh Affairs. Mr Macmillan in January 1957 transferred this office to the Minister of Housing & Local Government, with a Minister-of-State who would be available to spend most of his time in Wales. In Mr Wilson's Government of October 1964, Welsh Affairs were specifically represented in the Cabinet by a Secretary-of-State for Wales, with an office in Cardiff, and this was followed up by a series of transfers of executive functions for roads, housing, new towns, town and country planning, local government, water (1965), health and welfare and some agriculture (1969), child care, primary and secondary education (1970). The present Welsh administration therefore has much the same scope as the Scottish administration's: the apparatus at Cathays Park, Cardiff, is still very small compared with that at St Andrew's House, Edinburgh, and will probably remain so; but the change in a few years is remarkable, and it can no longer be regarded as just a political move designed to assuage nationalist political feeling.

From one point of view, to have a separate administration for Wales, with only about $5\frac{1}{2}\%$ of the population of England & Wales, and no past tradition of separate legal or administrative principles, is difficult to justify in terms of efficiency; and the institution of a special Cabinet representation for this part of the community (hardly more than half of Yorkshire or Lancashire) is not easy to defend in democratic principle. However, the experience so far is not disturbing, for there has not been unduly large allocation of resources to Wales or unreasonable sensitivity by government to Welsh interests; and the political advantage for the cohesion of the whole community resulting from this specific representation may well offset any disadvantages of a more theoretical character that could result.

Lastly, we now have a Secretary-of-State for Northern Ireland, and a Northern Ireland Office in London and Belfast—back to the Irish Office which had been abolished in 1924, and its Northern Ireland functions bequeathed to the Home Office. This is not the place to consider the rights and wrongs; but there may be a bearing on machinery of government. The striking fact in retrospect is that Westminster and Whitehall wasted nearly half a century of 'peace' in Ireland, doing nothing either to ensure that Northern Ireland could stand on its own feet as a viable democratic political entity, or to draw it more closely towards Great Britain, or to prepare the way towards a united Ireland. It is worth pondering whether a different allocation of responsibility for the relationship with Northern Ireland from 1924 onwards might have led to constructive initiatives over the decades. Was putting it as an appendage in the Home Office (together with the Isle of Man and the Channel Isles), a department with a huge involvement in the social and political issues of our time, really the wise course? Is it conceivable that if the health of the Northern Ireland relationship had been made the personal responsibility of the Lord President, rather like his earlier responsibility for Government science, there might occasionally in 50 years have been some recognition that all was not well in the Ulster political system, and that Westminster had some responsibility to intervene?

Industry, Agriculture, Employment

From the First World War there were three industrial departments—the Board of Trade, the Ministry of Labour and the Ministry of Agriculture. At the end of the Attlee administration in 1951, there was a whole family of departments in the industrial field. These had been built up in the creation of the war economy, and were retained to guide the process of reconversion of industry and the dismantling of war-time controls. Some of the new war-time departments were now seen as permanent departments, such as Fuel & Power, and the Ministry of Food; and the Ministry of Labour was still a Ministry of Labour and National Service; there was a new Ministry of Materials to deal with the crisis created by the Korean war; there was a new Civil Aviation department. The Ministry of Supply was combining its responsibilities for army and aviation procurement and for promoting and controlling the development of atomic energy with responsibility for the control of steel, non-ferrous and light metals and for the 'sponsorship' of the engineering industries. In this immediate post-war period, the departments in charge of the war-time economy, which had acquired great knowledge of the various sectors of industry, remained to tackle these sectors' post-war problems. So the concept of 'sponsorship', which had been a necessary part of the war-time controls—to maintain as tight a control and as effective a system of allocation as had been developed, e.g. for steel, re-quired a 'sponsoring department' to speak for the interests of every consumer of steel—continued during the post-war period.

As the war-time controls disappeared one by one in the late 1940s and early 1950s, this original idea of 'sponsorship' related to allocation withered away, but the word remained (and still remains), and every part of the national economy continued to be 'sponsored' by a government department. As usually happens in public affairs when words are used in a slovenly way, however, a misunderstanding of purpose followed. There are still parts of Whitehall where it is thought that the duty of the 'sponsoring department' is to be the advocate for 'its' industry, just as it did in speaking for its raw material or labour alloca-tion during the war. But this is out of date. The industrial department is now the focus of Whitehall's expertise about an industry, and provides the channel through which government policy is created and transmitted to industry, and industry's views communicated to government; and this is a far cry indeed from the departmental 'sponsor'. There have been industrial departments (e.g. Agriculture and Aviation at certain times and under certain Ministers) which have regarded themselves as 'sponsors' in the narrow sense. But the words 'sponsorship' and 'link' would not normally be regarded as synonymous; and the continued use of the word 'sponsorship' in the Whitehall vocabulary must take its share of odium for the lack of clarity in the relationship between government and industry in the last 20 years.

Moreover, the retention of the war-time concept led to fragmentation in Whitehall's thought about industry, and in the relationship between government and industry. In war-time the Government was dictating end-uses, and controlling both by direct contract and by regulation virtually all of industry's output. It was natural for the Admiralty to control merchant shipbuilding (to be its 'sponsor'), the Ministry of Food the food and drink industries, the Ministry of Works the building materials industries, and so on; and this continued. After the war, on the same formula, when the National Health Service was set up, the Ministry of Health became the 'sponsor' for the pharmaceutical industries; the Ministry of Aviation for the electronics industries; the Post Office for the telecommunication equipment industries, etc. Thus the relationship between the Government and these industries became dominated by the Government's customer interests in their output; and they fell outside the normal stream of government–industry dialogue on commercial policy, export development, monopoly policy and so on.

The fuel and power industries—nationalized coal, electricity and gas, and also the private oil industry—came under the Ministry of Fuel and Power (Scottish electricity was separate again). In 1957, the iron and steel industry was brought under this department from the Board of Trade (to which it had been transferred from the Ministry of Supply in 1955 with the engineering industries, except for aircraft and electronics and light metals, 'to associate the Board of Trade more closely with certain major industries which are of great importance to our export trade'). Here were two more large parts of industry—iron and steel and oil—which were again separated from the main stream of government–industry dialogue. Rail and road transport (some nationalized and some privately-owned but under government control) was under the Ministry of Transport: 'sponsorship' of the shipping industry was transferred from there to the Board of Trade in 1965; and merchant shipbuilding, which had been transferred from the Admiralty to Ministry of Transport by 1959, was transferred to the Board of Trade with shipping. Civil aviation was merged with the Ministry of Transport in 1953; left in 1959, when the Ministry of Aviation was formed; and reverted to the Board of Trade in July 1966.

The point to be emphasized is both the frequency of change, which led to confusion of the industries and services which were being 'sponsored' and of the loyalties and careers of the departmental staffs which were supposed to deal with them, and also the fragmentation among many government departments of responsibilities for important industries and services which tended to be dealt with as separate enclaves. The responsibility for these relationships was separated from the responsibility for government's policy towards industry as a whole.

As we have seen, the 'sponsorship' of the engineering industry was allocated to the Ministry of Supply in 1945, and in 1955 this was transferred to the Board of Trade. The rest of manufacturing industry—textiles, chemicals, boots and shoes, and so on—was with the Board of Trade throughout. The last great series of changes was brought about by the expansion of the Ministry of Technology in 1966, which transferred the engineering industry (this time with the shipbuilding industry) to this department; and this was followed in 1969 by the transfer there of virtually all the rest of the manufacturing industries from the Board of Trade and also the Ministry of Power. So the responsibilities for specific industries were brought into one department—the Ministry of Technology. The general functions of regulation of industry were retained (with shipping and civil aviation) in the Board of Trade (apart from control of monopolies and mergers, which in 1969 went to the Department of Employment, then with the soubriquet 'and Productivity').

This all cleared the way in the end for the creation of the Department of Trade and Industry in October 1970, bringing all this together, room being found for this by the transfer of aviation procurement to the Defence Department. But in three years, the parcel came apart, with the Department of Energy separated in January 1974, followed by Mr Wilson's division of the rest into three—the responsibility for specific industries (plus the Post Office) going to the Industry Department, the regulatory functions (plus shipping and civil aviation) to the Trade Department, and a miscellany of functions (including monopolies and mergers) to the Department of Prices and Consumer Protection. This kind of situation has in the past proved so unstable that further changes are to be expected, though it is not yet entirely clear whether the most practical course is to have one industrial department or two.

The main conclusion which emerges from this narrative is that throughout this period of 25 years, there was no stable or satisfactory organizational situation. There was a continuous process of change, sometimes well-conceived and sometimes less so; and it is difficult in retrospect to recognize any of these changes from which a clear national benefit can be said to have resulted. The two leading thoughts of the period, one to pick out particular industries for special departmental treatment, and the other to regard general industrial policy as being distinct from the responsibility for the Government's relationships with individual industries, both appear as having been unconstructive. It may now be regarded as demonstrated that to put particular industries into special departmental enclaves provides no solution for their problems (this is as likely to be as true of energy in the future as it has been in the past); and most people would agree that the consideration of general industrial and commercial policy may become theoretical and academic if those who are responsible for it are not confronted with the day-to-day industrial problems across the whole range of industry, whilst those who are concerned with individual industries will become unduly opportunist if they are not simultaneously responsible for general policy. After 25 years, this conflict was momentarily solved by the creation of the Department of Trade & Industry. There were problems about the D.T.I. and although this has been split up again, it would be unwise to neglect the solid reasons that led to it; and there is no stable alternative at present in sight.

The amalgamation of the Ministry of Agriculture & Fisheries and the Ministry of Food in 1955 has been a success. The Ministry of Agriculture had always been a narrow enclave, and neither in manpower nor in income is the agricultural industry nearly large enough to justify a separate department: agriculture, forestry and fishing are less than 3% of gross national product, less than one-tenth of manufacturing industry. But bringing in the Government's responsibility for food (one-quarter of consumers' expenditure and about one-fifth of imports) changes the subject altogether. The widening of the scope of the traditional Ministry of Agriculture has certainly been beneficial. It was reported with some circumstantial evidence, however (*The Times*, 22 March 1974), that in the formation of Mr Wilson's Administration, the possibility of transferring some or all of the 'Food' function to the new Prices & Consumer Protection Department was seriously considered. It can legitimately be argued indeed that the problems of food prices and consumer protection in food, and the problems of the food and drink industries and of food imports should be dealt with as part of the normal national industrial policies; and the problems of the Common Agricultural Policy in Europe are for Britain much more important in terms of food and money than in terms of agriculture. On the other hand, the restoration of the narrow and specialized Agriculture Department, with no counterweight to the farmers' lobby, is entirely contrary to the trend of government in recent years; and such a department could clearly not justify having a Cabinet Minister at its head. In the event, it appears that Mrs Shirley Williams's authority will extend only to retail food prices; and M.A.F.F. will continue to handle the C.A.P. negotiations in Brussels. But a situation in which one Minister is fixing bakers' prices and another is fixing millers' prices is not likely to be readily manageable and there is another unstable situation here. It may be that at the next round, some reshaping of the four ex-D.T.I. departments and M.A.F.F. into two (or conceivably even three) great industrial departments could be a promising line of approach.

The transition from Ministry of Labour to Department of Employment has been administratively uneventful. The problem of the department through the post-war period has been in policy. The original purpose of the Ministry of Labour was to be the friend of labour within government; to see fair play in collective bargaining; to defend the interests of the lower-paid workers; to administer unemployment insurance and organize the labour exchanges, etc. The Ministry was the point of contact between government and trade unions, and the conciliation service was a support for the weaker party in labour disputes.

But the increased power of the trade unions after the Second World War meant that this original function was changing; and when the first positive governmental incomes policy arrived in 1961, the role of the department as mediator, conciliator, organizer of arbitration became increasingly difficult to reconcile with the current needs of government. The natural course would have been for the Ministry of Labour to be the department in charge of incomes policy; but this was impossible for these traditional and psychological reasons, and this responsibility fell to the Treasury under Mr Selwyn Lloyd and then

Mr Maudling. In Mr Wilson's Government, this was one of the main functions of the new Department of Economic Affairs, and not until April 1966 was the day-to-day administration of incomes policy passed to the Ministry of Labour.

In May 1968 came a fundamental political change, with the Ministry given a new title of Department of Employment and Productivity, under Mrs Barbara Castle, combining both the D.E.A.'s responsibilities for overall prices and incomes policy and the old Ministry of Labour's functions; and in the new structure of industrial departments in October 1969 the department received the responsibility for monopolies and mergers and restrictive practices in anticipation of the combination of the Monopolies Commission and the National Board for Prices & Incomes. At the same time, the department's responsibilities for training, productivity, etc. were strengthened. The traditional role had been reversed; and the department was now a major instrument of government regulation of industry.

In the reforms of 1970, this widening of authority was retracted, as the monopolies work was restored to the D.T.I., and the previous incomes policy was disbanded and the N.B.P.I. abolished. But nevertheless compared with ten years ago, it is now the Department of Employment that is operating incomes policy, and the traditional role of the Ministry of Labour has been transformed, probably permanently. The management of the employment and training services is now under the Manpower Services Commission, a non-departmental body responsible to the Secretary of State for Employment; and if the attitude of government to incomes policy were to change again, it is conceivable that the functions of the department might be integrated further with the rest of the industrial administration.

Environmental and social services

In the early 1900s, the central government's responsibilities in England and Wales for the environmental and social services were in general combined with those for local government in the Local Government Board. The administration of the Poor Law and the public health legislation of the 19th century were part of the same subject as the successive reforms of local government. Education (here treated separately) was of course under the Board of Education; and the Home Office had child care and mental illness; but otherwise it was a unified departmental operation. But the social programme of the 1906 Liberal Government created a new situation. The introduction of non-contributory old age pensions (1908), health insurance (1911), unemployment insurance (1911, following labour exchanges) required new nation-wide apparatus, provided by Customs & Excise, Insurance Commissions (under the Treasury) and the Board of Trade respectively. None of these new functions went to local government: and here began the division of this area of government into three—local government and environment, health, social security, which occupied the next decades.

After the First World War, the Local Government Board was replaced by the

Ministry of Health (which also took health insurance): the Labour Department of the Board of Trade had become the Ministry of Labour, with unemployment insurance: a new Ministry of Pensions to look after war pensions. Mr Neville Chamberlain produced his succession of reforming Acts of Parliament, ranging from the introduction of contributory old age and widows pensions (1925) to the Local Government Act of 1929 (replacement of Poor Law Guardians by county councils' Public Assistance Committees; derating of industry; reform of highway administration). Unemployment insurance could not cope with the huge assistance needs of the unemployed, which were ultimately removed (1934) from both the Ministry of Labour's insurance system and from the local authorities' administration, with a new Unemployment Assistance Board 'outside politics'—another great long-term landmark. Throughout this period, the Ministry of Health was the great department of local government, housing, public health, health insurance: unemployment insurance was becoming separated from unemployment: a new nation-wide assistance system had been established for unemployment assistance, nation-wide and separate from public assistance: Customs & Excise continued to distribute to the aged and the Home Office to handle workmen's compensation. These had been 20 years of rapid development of the social services, but the administrative structure, both of these and of the local government, behind them, was a patchwork quilt, much in need of reform.

The Second World War brought with it a need for centralization, and the preparation for post-war reconstruction brought with it the acceptance of major reform in four related fields: (i) physical reconstruction, especially housing; (ii) town and country planning and control of land use; (iii) unification of social security (Beveridge Report); (iv) national health service (in effect, nationalization of municipal and private hospitals and free medical treatment). In terms of machinery of government, after some false starts, the functions were sorted out in 1951–53 between three departments—Housing & Local Government, which did (i) and (ii), Pensions & National Insurance (taking in war pensions too, and with the National Assistance Board in a part-independent situation linking together the old Unemployment Assistance Board, the old Public Assistance Committees, and the non-contributory pensions), and Health (predominantly the national health service). The Home Office continued with child care. These operations by successive Governments had good administrative logic.

Through the 1950s and 1960s two difficulties developed. One was that the new Ministry of Health was too small a unit: its Minister was often outside the Cabinet; and the career prospects and variety of work for the officials were too narrow. In the end, this was settled by Mr Wilson (1968) by joining it with what had earlier been Pensions & National Insurance (likewise too small), and the merger became the Department of Health & Social Security. The positive arguments have never been thought convincing, for most people like to think of the national health service as a great constructive service for the whole community (like education) and not related fundamentally to welfare, and the two sides of the merged department have little overlap. Nevertheless, the political-administrative argument, which ensures that there will always be a powerful Cabinet Minister in charge of the social services has great weight. The consolidation has gone further by the transfer (1970) of child care from the Home Office; and it may be that eventually the consideration of these services as a whole could lead to concepts of health and welfare involving a closer integration than had earlier been thought likely to be fruitful.

The second difficulty was more fundamental. In the early 1950s, under Mr Macmillan's regime at the Ministry of Housing & Local Government, there had been a great burst of house-building, which had taken priority over other public construction. The Ministry had been successful too (and so had the Scots) in starting a series of new towns (in England, mainly to reduce congestion in London). Successive Governments had provided substantial incentives to industry to expand in the old depressed areas and had introduced restraints against development in the congested areas of the South-East and Midlands. But in the early 1960s came a much clearer realization that more comprehensive policies were needed, both for physical modernization of the industrial areas of the North and for a more effectively planned development of the South; and this was bound to lead to a series of machinery of government questions.

One question was that of the primacy in responsibility for regional development between the Board of Trade (responsible for the industrial end) and Housing & Local Government (responsible for the local government and infrastructure end). Which sets the pattern? When Mr Heath became Secretary of State for Industry, Trade & Regional Development in October 1963, it seemed to be the former. In Mr Wilson's Government a year later, the main strategic responsibility was given to D.E.A., but most of the activity there was in setting up regional planning councils and boards; the 'overlord' role is difficult without control of the administration at either end, and when Mr Crosland became 'overlord' on D.E.A.'s demise, exactly the same difficulty persisted. In the end it has become clear that there can be no primacy of the industrial or the infrastructure department.

Another problem was housing and transport. How could Housing & Local Government plan development while Transport was responsible for planning roads? There were attempts to set up joint planning units; and then Mr Crosland was a 'co-ordinating Minister'. But in 1970 it was decided to merge the departments, so that all these things could be brought together.

Another was the difficulty arising from the separation of the Housing department's responsibilities from the responsibility for much public sector building and for relations with the construction industry, held by the Ministry of Public Building & Works. This too was settled by merger.

So the Department of the Environment came into being, another of the 'giant' departments; and this was sustained by Mr Wilson's 1974 Administration. The name has been relevant, for it has given a sign to give a fresh illumination to a wide variety of tasks which were not formerly regarded as having anything in

4

common. It has also become the home for several laboratories, which will help the application of science to its problems. It has succeeded in reducing the load of day-to-day administration on its Ministers by setting up the Property Services Agency as a non-Departmental body to carry out the old Ministry of Works functions for Whitehall. Looking from the outside, it is difficult to detect improvements of performance which can be attributed to the new departmental structure. But the comparison must be with what would have happened under the old machinery; and there is no sign anywhere of any desire to revert to previous patterns.

Education, Arts, Science

The Education Department was born in 1856, to take charge of the educational establishment of the Privy Council and the Science & Art Department (formerly the Department of Practical Art) of the Board of Trade. It became the Board of Education in 1900, and the Ministry of Education in 1944, and the Department of Education & Science in April 1964. For universities, arts and science, there has been considerable change in machinery of government since the Second World War; but the main body of the department has had a long history of stability.

It is historically the department of the national education service rather than the department of education: its task has been to provide the legislative framework within which the local education authorities provide the education, and to exercise the necessary minimum of central supervision and control. The landmarks have been the changes of framework—new leaving ages, status of denominational schools, changes of local authority units, the grant system for L.E.A.'s, provision for new facilities for technical education, etc.—rather than changes in the concept and content of education in the schools. In recent decades, there have been moves towards a greater central control (e.g. grammar v. comprehensive education) but this has not called for such changes of system as would lead into changes in machinery of government. So the dimensions of the department's task have remained.

For machinery of government, the most interesting development has been the change in the governmental handling of universities (and also arts and science). Twenty-five years ago, these areas of society enjoyed a very special relationship with government. These intellectual activities were believed to present a fundamental problem to government. Their development in the community called for public money on a significant and increasing scale: but it was deemed to be essential that they should be free to pursue their own course of development without interference from the Government. There was an intractable political dilemma here, for the principle of accountability for the expenditure of public money requires that a Minister and his department must accept responsibility for this expenditure, and that Parliament (through its apparatus of the Public Accounts Committee and the Comptroller-and-Auditor-General) should be able to investigate the way in which this responsibility has been exercised: but this process at once brings in both Whitehall and Westminster, which inevitably frustrates the objective of these intellectual institutions' freedom in the use of the public money.

For the universities, the elements of a solution had been found in 1919 in the establishment of the University Grants Committee (U.G.C.) by the Chancellor of the Exchequer. This Committee, appointed by the Chancellor, with a full-time chairman and secretariat on the Treasury pay-roll and with part-time academic and other members, had the responsibility of recommending what public funds were needed by the universities, and for allocating these funds between the universities.

In this system as it had developed by the early 1950s, there was an equilibrium between the conflicting objectives of public policy. The crucial point was that the U.G.C. was under the aegis of the Treasury. University policy and requirements were therefore handled in government in complete separation from the national education service (i.e. from the local authorities); and the Chancellor of the Exchequer (and the Treasury) was of all Ministers (and departments) the least likely to have the time or inclination to impose his wishes upon or to interfere with the universities: moreover, the Treasury was the only body that could persuade Parliament that the U.G.C. (and behind it, the universities) should be free from the jurisdiction of the Comptroller-and-Auditor-General and thence the Public Accounts Committee. This issue of the universities' freedom from the normal processes of accountability to Parliament was stubbornly and success-fully fought by the Treasury against the Public Accounts Committee in the early 1950s. So for a long period of great importance for the universities' develop-ment, the irreconcilables of public policy were in practice reconciled.

The immense university expansion of the 1950s brought this system to an end. It was admirably devised for dealing with genuinely independent universities making their own policies for their own development, and seeking public money as a component—essential, but only a component—in carrying out their own plans. But as the concept developed in the university world and in the U.G.C. of a great expansion of the universities as a national need, the situation changed in kind. Instead of each university saying 'this is our plan, can we have £X to carry it out?', and the U.G.C. collecting these into a package for a quinquennial grant, the Government was confronted with proposals from the U.G.C. saying in effect 'if the nation's need for an expansion of university-trained people is to be met, then the universities will need £Y'.

This approach opened new questions for government. Did the Government accept the objective in numbers? Could the objective be achieved more cheaply in staff–student ratios, use of buildings, etc.? What were the implications for local authority awards to university students (handled through the Ministry of Education)? What should be the relationship and priorities between university expansion and the expansion of other higher education; and between both and the national education service? By the end of the 1950s it had become clear to the

Treasury that the system (which was based on there being no Government policy for the universities with the Treasury providing money for carrying out the U.G.C.'s policy) could not survive in its present form. [These problems were no obstacle to university expansion. The number of full-time university students increased from the pre-war 50,000 to 119,000 in 1962–63, on a plan of growth to about 150,000 (for these institutions) in 1966–67. The U.G.C. Vote rose from £10m in 1947–48 and £24m in 1952–53 to £90m in 1962–63.]

When the Robbins Committee was set up in February 1961 to review the pattern of full-time higher education and to advise on the principles of its long-term development, it was common ground that in the next phase of development, particularly with the extension of university status to colleges of advanced technology and other higher education institutions, the Chancellor of the Exchequer and the Treasury could no longer continue in their previous role. [See Treasury evidence to Robbins Committee (Cmnd. 2154—XI, pp. 1956–2000). This consisted of three memoranda in answer to the Committee's questions. 'A' dealt with the economic and financial issues involved in expansion of higher education, and a re-reading finds some of this more topical than it seemed to the Committee at the time. 'B' deals with the problems of unified administration. 'C' is a history of the argument between the Treasury and the Public Accounts Committee about accountability.] The Committee recommended that the U.G.C. should be under a new Minister of Arts & Science, and rejected its being brought under the Education Ministers. As so often happens in public affairs, the case was made for a tidy change in machinery of government that would have well fitted the situation ten years earlier, but in terms of the political realities (in universities, arts and science) was already outmoded.

Sir Alec Douglas-Home set up (April 1964) a new department covering all education and all science, with the former Lord Hailsham, Mr Quintin Hogg (the Lord President) as Secretary of State. In its initial stages, the new department was set up in two parts, with two permanent secretaries, one for 'education' and one for 'universities and science'. (To unite the responsibility for universities and the Research Councils always made sense, because of the very important role of the latter in financing university research.) This proved temporary, however, and under Mr Wilson's 1964 Government, the Department of Education & Science (D.E.S.) became a single integrated unit, which appears to be the ultimate solution, with suitable arrangements for co-ordination with the Scots and the Welsh. Immediately after this had been done, the Public Accounts Committee once more raised the question of accountability, and this time Parliament's view was accepted and the Comptroller-and-Auditor-General was given access to the relevant accounts.

Ten years later, it is difficult to argue that the brigading of U.G.C. with what is in effect the old Ministry of Education, and the access of the C. & A.-G., have created the kind of troubles for the universities that had been feared. The growth of the universities and the extension of university status to several other institutions, and the immense increase in numbers and public expenditure have

changed the standing and independence of the universities, but this is the inevitable result of the impact of taxpayers' money and cannot be attributed to new
machinery of government.

In the arts, the same tendency has happened. Twenty-five years ago, the
Treasury dealt directly with the museums and art galleries (except where, like
the Victoria & Albert, they were already under the Ministry of Education), and
when the Arts Council was set up in 1946, it was put under the Treasury. The
principle here was the same as for the universities: the best way to prevent the
Government from interfering with the policy of these bodies was to give them
direct access to the Treasury, with no Minister (except the Chancellor, who was
much too busy) to seek to establish a Government policy in the field.

The case for change happened here because Mr Wilson's Government wanted
to have a policy of progressive increase in the Government's support for the
arts. This was clearly incompatible with the system of Treasury sponsorship,
so in February 1965 this was transferred to the Department of Education &
Science, with Miss Jennie Lee as a junior Minister with special responsibilities
in this field; this arrangement has continued.

The same process has taken place in civil science. When the first steps were
taken to set up government support for scientific research (Department of
Scientific & Industrial Research 1916: Medical Research Council 1920, and in
1931 Agricultural Research Council, and in 1949 Nature Conservancy) care was
taken to ensure that the control of these bodies was separated from the departments which could be expected to use their work. The purpose of this was not,
as has sometimes been alleged in argument about machinery of government in
this field, to preserve the 'academic freedom' of scientific research (on an analogy
with universities) or to enable public money to be used for scientific research
with no practical application. The Haldane Report (Cd. 9230 of 1918) which is
the source of the philosophy of the Research Councils, made no mention of such
considerations. The whole purpose of Research Councils was to get practical
applications of science in the work of government. They were to be under
separate control (under the Lord President) because the Haldane Committee
feared that if they were under the user departments, the latter would suppress
those results that were politically or administratively inconvenient. So there
began the isolation of the Government civil science organization from the
practical responsibilities of the departments.

Science's prestige stood high after the Second World War, with rapid growth
of expenditure for civil aircraft and nuclear research as well as for D.S.I.R.
and the Research Councils. The doctrine of non-intervention by Ministers was
maintained: the Lord President was the Government's link with the Government
civil science, with a very small scientific secretariat, an Advisory Council on
Scientific Policy (1947) and a general oversight over the D.S.I.R. and the
Research Councils (and in 1954 over the new Atomic Energy Authority). Each
body arranged its own money with the Treasury, each with a relationship
analogous to that with the U.G.C. in an atmosphere of strong Government

commitment to rapid expansion of Government civil science, for purposes determined by the bodies themselves.

After the 1959 Election, Mr Macmillan created a formal Ministry of Science to which these functions were transferred, but the Minister (Lord Hailsham) had many other responsibilities, and no fundamental change took place. In April 1964, as we have seen, came the merger into the Department of Education & Science, which did mark the beginning of a real change. It was intended to accompany the merger by major reforms of organization; but this did not happen until Mr Wilson's Government, which had the task of both dismantling D.S.I.R. and constituting two new Research Councils (for Science and for Natural Environment) and of dividing this whole civil science apparatus between the 'applied' Ministry of Technology and the 'pure science' D.E.S. The amalgamation of the Ministry of Aviation with the Ministry of Technology in 1967 led to the creation of an uniquely powerful scientific apparatus, which was subsequently divided again between the Department of Trade & Industry, the Defence Procurement Executive and the Department of the Environment.

The effect of the machinery of government changes of the 1960s has been to alter irrevocably the structure and ideas of the 1950s. There are the four Research Councils under D.E.S., in a structure that considers them (and particularly their money) as a whole, and must negotiate with the Treasury as a block, in competition with other expenditure blocks: the rest of the civil science organization is within the user departments, though with varying degrees of autonomy (with the A.E.A., so to speak, at one end and perhaps the M.A.F.F. laboratories at the other). The reforms (Cmnd. 5046 of July 1972) following Lord Rothschild's report have put a major emphasis within the Research Councils on the creation of an effective customer-contractor relationship with user departments; matching in this area the analogous developments in the Ministry of Technology departmental and A.E.A. laboratories a few years earlier. These processes are not yet complete; and many old ideas survive of the 'independence' of publicly-financed laboratories from the responsibility to meet users' needs. But there is now no doubt that the course of the 1970s in science as in the universities and the arts has been transformed by the changes in machinery of government from the organization of the 1950s.

MISCELLANEOUS

It is impossible in this chapter to cover all the important machinery of government changes in recent years. But there have been three developments of an importance that cannot be left unmentioned.

The first to come into effect was the setting-up (April 1967) of the Parliamentary Commissioner for Administration, or 'Ombudsman'. The original idea was to protect the public against injustices suffered as a result of maladministration by departments. It became necessary to exclude from the field for complaint a number of areas, such as actions by the Government as an employer or as a contractor, by the police and by the local authorities and by the hospitals: similar machinery was set up later to investigate National Health Service complaints; and Mr Heath's Government announced their intention to set up similar machinery in local government. In general it can be said that on the one hand the new institution has served a useful purpose in drawing attention to certain cases, whilst on the other hand it has provided no evidence whatever of any significant amount of maladministration by departments. Whether these results, positive and negative, are enough to justify the heavy expenditure of time and effort in the departments in handling the cases (and the greater time and effort still in doing their normal work in order to avoid the risk of a charge) is more debatable. All the departments are working under conditions of great pressure and if more time and effort is devoted to some things, the rest of the work will inevitably suffer equally.

Next is the change in the Post Office from a government department to a public corporation (1969). The arguments for and against this course are outside the scope of this chapter; and the experience is difficult to assess, for very soon after the corporation came into being, Mr Heath's Government reversed previous successive Governments' policies towards the nationalized industries (from which the benefits from the change in the Post Office were expected to flow). In terms of machinery of government, for the old Postmaster General was substituted a Minister of Posts & Telecommunications, responsible for 'sponsorship' of the Post Office and the supervision of broadcasting. But this was the last case of a very small department with a very limited scope; and Mr Wilson transferred the sponsorship work to the Department of Industry and the responsibility for broadcasting to the Home Office. This may be regarded as another permanently established move.

Finally, within the last two years, a number of departmental agencies have been set up to provide services previously provided within the normal departmental structures. One is the Manpower Services Commission to manage the employment and training services for the Department of Employment: another is the Property Services Agency, in effect to carry out the old Office of Works function for the Department of the Environment: another is the Central Computer Agency within the Civil Service Department. It is much too early to express any view of the contribution that they are likely to make. They cannot reduce the pressure on Ministers or top departmental officials; for these subjects previously contributed little to the pressure at the top (and if the pressure existed the new organization could not reduce it, for the same problems will have to go to Ministers in any case). The judgment will turn on whether the new agencies are able to develop personnel and financial systems and policies which increase the efficiency and return on resources employed. The presumption underlying the establishment of these agencies is that they will, and that the personnel and financial systems of the civil service are deficient in running services of this kind, and that the new structure of accountability will give better value for money than the old. This is still to be proved, and it is to be hoped that the new agencies will be able to make their reports in a form which permits some assessment to be made of the experience under these heads.

CONCLUSIONS

What conclusions can be drawn from the 25 years' experience? Looking within this time-scale, one gets the impression of an inexorable development from Mr Attlee's 30 major departments to Mr Heath's (back to Mr Asquith's) 18, and Mr Wilson's 21. But those who were following the subject from day to day did not recognize such forces at work. Nor can the seven Prime Ministers and four heads of the civil service who participated in these events be regarded as having planned it: indeed, the trend often seemed to be moving in the opposite direction, sometimes in Conservative and sometimes in Labour administrations. It is hardly credible that these great changes have been fortuitous, the outcome of a stochastic process, a random walk from Government to Government. There have surely been persuasive underlying forces at work, that have led successive Prime Ministers in this direction even though their immediate political problems (like Mr Wilson's in October 1964 and March 1974) temporarily pointed the other way.

(1) One is the advantage of matching the number of major departments to the practical size of a Cabinet, and avoiding the unsatisfactory situation (both political and administrative) of having some departments in the charge of Ministers not in the Cabinet.

(2) Another is the experience of the burden on the time and effort of senior Ministers and officials which is involved in inter-departmental co-ordination. The devices to overcome this—'overlords', Ministers without departments to do co-ordination, etc.—have never been successful in peace-time; and they take top-class Ministers away from work in the departments.

(3) A third is that the work of government falls naturally into a few big sets of functions—overseas, defence, economic, environmental, social services and so on. Experience has shown that to set up small departments for small specialized tasks is not effective in the long run even for doing the small tasks, for the problems of government are too inter-dependent both within the big functional areas and between them to enable the small units to work on their own.

(4) Experience has shown both Ministers and civil servants that it is practicable to run efficiently much larger departments than were hitherto thought manageable in peace-time. (See Appendix, for which I am obliged to the Civil Service Department. The problems are discussed in my *New Trends in Government*, H.M.S.O., 1971, and in 'The Number and Size of Government Departments', in *Political Quarterly*, 1972, pp. 169–86.) The critical problem is in brigading senior and junior Ministers (and top-level officials correspondingly) in teams together. This involves selecting them in teams, and also changes in the technique of operation at the top of the department, with the Cabinet Minister

acting as the chairman and leader of the team, just as the Prime Minister does in Cabinet. This does not come easily or automatically; and in my opinion the explanation should be sought in this critical area when a 'giant' department's performance comes under criticism. In most cases, the experience has been favourable; and there is no reason in my opinion to doubt that the 'giant' department has come to stay; though at the next round of re-organization on the industrial side it will be necessary to take the constraints outlined in this paragraph very carefully.

All these considerations suggest that the changes have come about as a result of gradual realization that it was practicable to reduce the number of major departments radically (4), that there were strong practical reasons for pushing in this direction because of experience with (2) and (3), and that there were positive political advantages (1) from a Prime Minister's point of view. In short, a consensus has gradually come into being that a structure with a few very large departments is more effective than one with many smaller departments.

The narrative of the course of events in each of the big sectors shows the importance of time. In my opinion the present arrangements (except on the industrial side) are good, but in many instances years have been spent with unsatisfactory arrangements, which must have done some damage to the quality of government, before it was possible to move to better systems. It would in my opinion be unfair to be critical of the timing of the consolidations in overseas policy and defence, for it must be doubted whether the weight of professional opinion (very important in both of these fields) could have been moved to accept this very much earlier. In the social services, the record has been continuously good, thanks to the war-time work of Sir William Beveridge and his Civil Service assessors in working through the administrative tangle of the 1930s and arriving at a sound administrative concept. It seems likely in retrospect that the separation throughout the 1950s of the U.G.C. from the Education department must have distorted the priorities in educational expansion; and that the separation of civil science from the industrial departments must have weakened the impact on industry: but hardly anybody was pressing these opinions at the time. Again, it is only comparatively recently that the concept of a consolidated development of environmental services has become clear, and it could never have been practical for the machinery of government to anticipate this. There is no doubt in my opinion, however, that a great deal of time was lost under successive governments in establishing effective machinery for handling industry (and industrial technology) and trade; and more is likely to be lost in future: this was partly a lack of clear objectives in industrial policy in relation to both the private and the public sector, but weakness in machinery of government may have contributed to this; and this is still not settled. Finally it can hardly be denied in 1974 that there were serious inadequacies under successive governments, both in omission and in commission, in developing the central machinery of government in economic and financial affairs: this series of problems was always the most intractable, and may not have yet reached its long-term solution.

4*

Looking ahead, there are two formidable problems which primarily concern systems of government rather than machinery of government in the sense described in this chapter. One is the public sector, which now appears to be established at about 50% of the gross national product, and involving the direct employment of about one-quarter of the labour force (and probably 60% of the highly educated manpower), half of new construction, half of scientific research, and a long list of industries which have been termed 'the commanding heights' of the economy, and the products of which are so pervasive to the whole economy that they are crucial to the nation's economic performance—coal, steel, electricity, gas, railways, telecommunications, airlines and so on—together with the great education and health services spending resources of some £7000 million a year. Can the strategy of the deployment and development of this immense agglomeration of resources be effectively handled by the decisions, in the last analysis (and in addition to all their other preoccupations) of the score of men and women who constitute the Cabinet? Can new constitutional systems be devised to do this better?

The other great problem ahead is Europe. At the present stage of the development of the European Economic Communities and of member-countries' relations with them, the pressure on our system of government may become intolerable. Her Majesty's Government must make up its mind on thousands of individual questions (taking just as much care and time as if the problems were to be decided by H.M.G.) and then negotiate them for the ultimate decisions through the Council and the Commission and the other institutions of the Communities. If the Community was a much simpler concept, like a customs union, this could be readily accommodated. If it were a much deeper concept, like an economic and financial union, it would inevitably have strong federal institutions, and the role of national governments would change accordingly. But the situation as it can be seen for some years ahead is neither of these, and the implications for the governments of the member-countries (especially one with a public sector and load on government of our size) are formidable, and the answer difficult to envisage.

It may be, indeed, that a cycle of machinery of government in the sense in which it is normally discussed, is now working towards its end; and that the real problem for the future may be becoming the much wider one of finding systems of government which can accommodate the centralization of decisions across the whole national life, both in our own institutions and in those of Europe.

APPENDIX   Ministers and Staff of Government Departments (1 April 1973)

	(1) Ministers*		(2) Senior Staff			(3) Total Staff (000s)		Notes
	Secretaries of State/Ministers/Ministers of State	Parly Secs and Under Secs	Perm and Second Perm Secs	Deputy Secs and Above ‡	Under Secs and Above ‡	Total Staff	of which Central Administration	
Foreign & Commonwealth	5	2	15	50	187	12·6	4·6	Includes O.D.A.
Defence	2	3	5	25	121	272·7	16·8†	
Trade & Industry	5	4	5	25	106	20·4	5·7	Includes E.C.G.D.
Environment	4	4	3	20	92	74·7	6·1	Includes Ordnance Survey
Social Services	2	2	3	16	70	81·3	7·3	Includes O.P.C.S.
Scotland	2	3	1	7	38	11·3	4·2	Includes Scottish Courts Admin.
Agriculture, Fisheries & Food	2	1	1	7	34	15·7	3·6	
Home Office	3	1	1	7	35	28·8	3·8	
Employment	2	1	2	7	26	34·9	1·7	
Education & Science	1	2	1	8	27	4·3	2·1	Includes V. & A. and Science, Museums
Lord Chancellor's Dept.	1	—	1	8	29	14·9	0·2	Includes Land Registry, Public Trustee and Public Record Office
Wales	2	—	—	1	8	1·0	0·9	
Posts & Telecommunications	1	—	—	1	4	0·5	0·3	
Chancellor of the Exchequer's Depts	4	—	8	29	94	111·6	5·8	Includes Treasury, Inland Revenue, Customs & Excise, National Savings, etc.
Civil Service Department	1	1	1	7	27	13·4	1·9	Includes H.M.S.O. and C.O.I.
Cabinet Office	—	1	5	12	25	0·6	0·6	

* Includes only Ministers with responsibilities within departments.
† Headquarters staff.
‡ The numbers in these columns are cumulative of those in the columns above.

The Civil Service

Sir Philip Allen, G.C.B.

5

This chapter is concerned with the management of some 500,000 Crown employees who make up the non-industrial Civil Service. There have been more changes here during the later part of the period covered by this book than for very many years.

Later sub-sections in the chapter discuss various aspects of management, but there are some preliminary general points to be borne in mind.

To begin with, it must not be forgotten that there are, in addition to these half million non-industrial civil servants, some 200,000 industrial civil servants, for example in the ordnance factories and the dockyards. Although there is an increasing tendency to bring some of their conditions of service more into line with those of the non-industrials, the basic problems of management are not so unlike those affecting industrial employees elsewhere.

Secondly, the Civil Service, large though it is, comprises only quite a small proportion of the total number of employees in the public sector. In 1971, that total amounted to some 6·3 million.

The next point is that public discussion tends to concentrate on the top managers and policy advisers in and around Whitehall. It is sometimes overlooked how complex the service is and what a wide variety of functions it carries out. The immigration officer at the ports, the social security officer who assesses need for supplementary benefit, the prison officer, the factory inspector, the driving examiner, the Yeoman Warders at the Tower—these are all civil servants. It is also sometimes overlooked that most of the service is outside London. The 1973 Hardman report on dispersal of government work from London (which aimed at still more dispersal) recorded that, on 1 October 1972, 346,418 civil servants, out of a total of 500,200, were already at regional or local offices; and that of the remaining headquarters staff of all grades, not many more than half (85,774) were within 16 miles of Charing Cross. As regards make-up of the service, considerably less than half the total (209,000) were in the 'administrative group', which included the big battalions of the former executive and clerical classes. The 300,000 other civil servants included a wide variety of specialized departmental classes and experts from pretty well all the professions.

Then, the management of the service has been greatly affected by changes in the role of government. This chapter is primarily concerned with the management of people, rather than with their work, but the two are not completely separable. The traditional responsibilities of government, such as defence, and law and order, have grown no simpler; but, in addition, the central government has taken on, and keeps taking on, new positive responsibilities for social services of various kinds in the community; for environmental issues; for projects so costly or of such national significance that only government can fund or manage them; for overall policies where executive power rests elsewhere, whether in local government (housing, education) or in the nationalized industries (coal, steel, posts); and for formulating policies and objectives for the economy as a whole. There are some issues too which transcend the lifetime of any one government or any one Parliament. All this means that new skills and expertise have been called for from those who advise on policies and carry out ministerial decisions.

Both political parties came to the conclusion in the late 1960s that some of the functions of government, as they had developed, were best carried out by merging a number of Ministries to create giant departments—Defence, Health and Social Security, Environment, Trade and Industry. This development has had direct consequences for management. It is obviously a very different proposition to manage, say, the Department of Environment on the one hand and on the other, a small department in which those at headquarters at any rate know most of their colleagues and carry on their work in a distinctly collegiate atmosphere; and those responsible for these giant departments, although they have the advantages of large resources, must guard against the risk that, to the individual civil servant, the management may seem more anonymous, more impersonal, more remote.

Some aspects of the management problems of the Civil Service are unique. It is not just its size and complexity. There are certainly considerable parts of the service where the problems would be familiar enough to any outside industrialist. Many of the responsibilities of management in the giant departments for example are of the same order as those in the big concerns in the private sector. But there remains the basic fact that the Civil Service exists, in essence, to meet political aims. There are many areas where there can be no test of profitability and where it will be impossible ever to quantify, or perhaps not for many years, the results of current decisions. The official, anyway, is not the person who takes the final policy decision. This is for Ministers, who may import political considerations. There is nothing wrong about this. But, for the civil servant, it may mean that the policy he has been working on turns out not to be acceptable for reasons which he is not equipped to judge; and it may mean too that he finds himself faced with a significant change in policies overnight, not only following a general election and a change of government, but perhaps also because of a change of Ministers, or because of a row in the House of Commons.

Right down the line there is a lively appreciation of the reality of Parliamentary accountability. There are plenty of watchdogs ready to spot mistakes. Any officer knows that his Permanent Secretary, as Accounting Officer, may be hauled before the Public Accounts Committee, or that the Parliamentary Commissioner for Administration may come enquiring into some constituent's complaint of maladministration; and every civil servant knows that the smallest of errors can well lead to much publicity and embarrassment for his Minister.

The last point in this preliminary recital is that individual civil servants are, many of them, proud of their service and anxious to take part in working out any changes affecting their own profession. For over 50 years, there has been, under the Whitley system, a record of collective bargaining and joint negotiation which has by no means been restricted to narrow issues of pay and conditions of service. There have been rough passages, but over the years the management has in general refrained from decreeing changes from on high and simply handing them out for implementation. A price has to be paid. There is some restriction on the speed of change and freedom of manœuvre of the management; but the rewards, in the way of getting agreement on change and securing its effective implementation, have been considerable.

At the beginning of the period covered by this book, the service still clearly harked back to the main principles of the Northcote-Trevelyan report of 1854 and to the re-organization carried out, consistently with those principles, at the end of the First World War. Looking back, it seems that an opportunity was missed after the Second World War, when the army of temporary war-time entrants had mostly gone, of carrying out an appraisal of the service in the light of the very considerable changes in the community which it served. There was considerable progress in some areas. In training, as will be seen later, and in 'O and M' and technical aids to management, the service had a very creditable record. Also, a Royal Commission on the Civil Service sat from 1953 to 1955, concerned almost entirely with pay. But it was not until some time after this that things really began to move over a wide front. In 1962, for the first time, there was appointed a Head of the Service who did not have to combine this appointment with other responsibilities; and he and others within the service, as well as a number of observers outside, felt increasing doubt whether the service was adapted to the needs of government as they themselves were developing. It was a symptom of this unease that in 1965, a sub-committee of the House of Commons Select Committee on Estimates questioned whether recruitment policies had kept pace with changing social and educational conditions and whether indeed the time was not coming for a Royal Commission to look into the service as a whole. These recommendations fell on fruitful ground. The Government had themselves been coming to the conclusion that a fundamental review was called for, and in the end decided to set up a committee composed both of outsiders and of serving civil servants, the latter being in a minority.

The report of that committee, which sat under the chairmanship of Lord Fulton, was published in 1968. It was an important document. It can easily be criticized. It exaggerated some of the faults it found in the service; it dressed up, as new and drastic recommendations for change, policies which the Treasury was already carrying out; and some of its conclusions were blurred and others were superficial. A number of issues too have come into prominence since the committee sat on which its report was silent. But the committee carried out its main purpose. It brought most of the main issues into the forefront and stirred them up. Things could never be quite the same again.

One of the committee's recommendations was promptly implemented. The Treasury gave up its management functions for the service, and a separate Civil Service Department came into being on 1 November 1968. The Department was directly under the Prime Minister and, although the Prime Minister of the day has since then always been helped by a Cabinet Minister in day-to-day charge, he has retained both a general responsibility for the department and a particular responsibility for certain issues, such as higher appointments, on which the official head of the service works to him directly. The setting up of this separate department established the management of the service as a separate central function in its own right, and ensured the continued existence of the means of keeping up the impetus for change. (What would happen if the Prime Minister of the day happened to have no taste for management is something one can only speculate about.)

In some ways, the programme in these early days was allowed to become somewhat unbalanced. The new department was generously staffed; but as a result of the tight control on manpower and the new policy burdens which were being put on departments, the allocation to this work of resources within departments, on whom fell the main burden of carrying out changes, did not altogether keep pace. But a good deal has been achieved; and as the story of change is described in more detail in the sub-sections that follow, the report of the Fulton committee (except for pay, which was not within its remit), and the setting up of the new Civil Service Department, can be seen as significant landmarks.

RECRUITMENT

Recruitment to the Civil Service is in the main in the hands of a body independent of, and separate from, the departments where the recruits work. The Northcote-Trevelyan report laid it down as a basic principle that recruitment should take place through open and independently conducted competition, and this principle has remained. The Civil Service Commission came into being to implement it; and, although the Commissioners became part of the new Civil Service Department when it was created, their independence in selection was left unimpaired.

It is obvious that recruitment at any given time is affected both by economic and social conditions outside, and by the needs of the service and what it can offer. The employment situation in the area where recruits are being sought can be relevant. So can public attitudes towards the service; this is a far from simple consideration, but it is pretty clear that when for example the service was beginning to need executive recruits of high quality to run a vast computer programme, some potential recruits were still being put off by the dusty and old-fashioned image of the service. Then there are such factors as the national scarcities in some of the professions, for example lawyers; a greater readiness for people to move around from job to job; the increase in the numbers going to universities, which has particularly affected the numbers of sixth-form leavers prepared to come in as executives; the competition from other employers, including the universities themselves; the decline in status of clerical work, and the raising of the school leaving age, which itself has had a direct effect on clerical recruitment; and the demands of the service itself for an increasing number of skills and for more high quality manpower.

At the beginning of the period covered by this book, the post-war reconstruction examinations were coming to an end and 'normal' recruitment was being resumed. But, as a result of some of the factors referred to, it was already becoming plain that the climate for recruitment had greatly altered and that drastic changes were called for. It was no longer enough for the Commission to function as an academic examining body. It had to go out into the marketplace, and to experiment with new ideas and new methods.

The numbers of recruits to what was then the administrative class were falling below what was needed. Of the steps taken, two were particularly significant.

Under the old procedure, most recruits were graduates from Oxford or Cambridge who came in after sitting a degree-type examination (Method I). Experiments were now made for up to a quarter of the vacancies to be filled under a new procedure (Method II) based on the War Department officer selection board. In 1957 the proportion of vacancies which could be filled by this method was upped to one-half. The restriction subsequently went altogether.

The second development worthy of special mention was the holding of regular competitions for direct entry at the level of Principal. The precise field of eligibility has since varied from time to time, but the principle of direct recruitment at other than the basic level became firmly established as part of the accepted order, and was extended to some of the specialist appointments. In 1965 and 1966 there was a modest attempt to recruit direct at Assistant Secretary level, but this experiment was then abandoned.

During this time, the upper age limits were raised for executive and clerical appointments, and the Commission took on new commitments for centralized recruitment to some of the technical groups—for example, it became its concern to recruit psychologists when they were created a separate class in 1950.

But the sub-committee of the Select Committee on Estimates, to which reference has already been made, was critical, in its 1965 report, of what was being done. Why was there such a shortage of recruits from the redbrick universities? Had enough contact been established with the universities? Why was there such high wastage? Why were there so few economists?

It was doubts of this kind about recruitment which, in effect, led up to the appointment of the Fulton committee; and that committee, for all the width of its terms of reference, devoted a good deal of attention to issues of recruitment.

In its report, it proposed that the Commission should become part of the new Civil Service Department it was recommending, so as to make sure that recruitment issues were brought into the main stream of thinking about the service; and it proposed too that there should be an enquiry by management consultants into the speeding up of recruitment procedures. Both proposals were adopted.

The Fulton committee also thought, although in each instance only by a majority, first that Method I should be retained, and secondly that, in recruiting graduates, preference should be given to the relevance to civil service work of the academic studies of the candidate.

Method I, however, attracted fewer and fewer candidates and after consulting the universities the government decided to abolish it. It had lasted a century. The Method II procedure was thoroughly overhauled by an expert committee and given a clean bill of health.

The Government decided too not to accept the majority recommendation for 'preference for relevance'. They could not persuade themselves that the study of certain subjects at university was a reliable guide to knowing whether an individual had a practical interest in contemporary problems within the purview of those subjects; they thought that it would be pretty well impossible to define 'relevant' courses in a way that would not end by distorting academic courses at universities—and in a way which would be acceptable to the universities; and they had also in mind the practical consideration that, when there was so much competition for able graduates, the result of creating a bias in favour of certain academic disciplines might result in fewer, rather than more, acceptable candidates. The Government thought that it would obviously be right to try and select people with the potential for developing the right kind of qualities and expertise; but they decided that to insist on formal academic relevance was not the way.

In 1971, as will be described below, the administration group was formed by merging the administrative, executive and clerical classes. This meant the end of the old-style assistant principal recruitment. Method II was used for the new-style administration trainees. In 1970, 90 assistant principals were recruited. In 1971, the first year of the new scheme, 195 administration trainees took up appointment, including 56 from within the service. Of the external recruits, Oxford and Cambridge still contributed a majority (57%). But, ten years previously, the Oxbridge proportion in the assistant principal entry had been 85%. Perhaps in another ten years a fresh social survey would convey a very different picture of the top generalist from that given in the survey prepared for the Fulton committee by Dr Halsey and Mr Crewe. They found that, until very recently, the administrative class had tended to become more, rather than less, socially exclusive.

The demand for executive officers continued to rise. In 1971, some 4300 recruits, 23% of them graduates, were just about enough to meet the declared needs. In the following year, although the number of successful candidates rose to 6800, 25% of them graduates, there were still 400 unfilled vacancies at the end of the year.

There were geographical problems in getting clerical recruits; there was a shortage in London, but a plentiful supply in some other areas.

For both executives and clericals the traditional academic examinations were abandoned, and instead reliance was placed on interviews and quick non-academic tests.

There continued to be difficulties in a number of the specialist groups—lawyers, economists and scientists, for example—and in some of the departmental classes. It had become a common pattern for the individual department itself to recruit scarce specialists on a temporary basis, and in due course to submit the candidate to the Commissioners for establishment. But all this was changed by the adoption of a new pensions scheme for the service in June 1972 which meant that the old-style temporary civil servant pretty well disappeared. The new recruit became pensionable from the outset. Pension no longer depended on 'establishment', which had in turn depended on the issue of a certificate of qualification by the Commissioners. The breaking of this chain did not greatly affect the general administrators at executive level and above, who had normally been recruited on established terms from the outset. But it did affect large numbers of staff in the specialist and clerical fields, where recruitment was increasingly in the hands of the Departments; and new procedures had to be devised to test each applicant against the appropriate standard on initial recruitment.

The Commission handles 120,000 or more applications from candidates in a year. It is not surprising that so big a machine creaks a little from time to time, that delays occur, and that sometimes the frustrated candidate thinks that it is all a bit too rigid. But let not this conceal the far-reaching changes that have taken place. The Commission are not responsible for pay and other conditions of employment which directly affect recruitment. But they have in these 25 years done a good deal within their own province. They have altered their publicity out of all recognition; they have increased their contacts with the schools and universities; they have speeded up their procedures; they have organized more frequent, and in some areas continuous, competitions; they have got away from pure academic testing; they have extended or abolished age limits; they have gone in for recruitment at above basic levels; the scope of recruitment by departments has been enlarged; and starting pay arrangements have been improved. But the Commission would be the last to claim that they have solved all the problems and reached the end of the road. Shortages in a good many grades persist, and constant effort, and a readiness to change, will continue to be needed.

There is underlying all this the question whether the bids which the Commission make on behalf of the service represent the right and proper share of the total national resources which should be devoted to the Civil Service. Happily, this is not a question to be answered in this chapter.

STRUCTURE

By 'structure' in this context is meant the system by which civil servants are paid, graded and grouped for management purposes.

Inevitably, it is necessary to go back to the Northcote-Trevelyan report. They thought that a proper division of labour depended on the separation of intellectual from routine work, and the way in which the service was organized up to the 1960s still looked back to this basic approach. It was entirely consistent with it that, after the First World War, three separate service-wide classes were set up—administrative, executive, clerical—with separate recruitment, based on appropriate educational standards, to each. In the 1930s, service-wide classes were created for scientists, and other specialists followed suit. When the Fulton committee sat, it found that there were 47 general service-wide classes, including, to take random examples, machine operators, typists, and photoprinters. As for the generalists, so too there were sometimes hierarchies of classes for the specialists—three for example for the scientists. In addition, there was a large number of departmental classes; the estimate then was that they totalled 1400. Some were big, like the tax inspectors and prison officers. Some comprised only a handful, like the alkali inspectors.

The Fulton committee strongly criticized this system. It said that it was based on out-moded distinctions, created horizontal and vertical barriers to movement within the service and to promotion on merit, and made it impossible to adopt the simple principle of selecting the best man for the job. The committee's solution was to plump for a single grading structure for the whole service. Within this structure there would be a series of 'occupational groups' for the purposes of recruitment, training and career management. (Whatever resemblance these groups might have to the existing classes was just coincidence, and certainly the particular title of 'class' with all its social connotations, should go.)

The picture which some of the critics painted of a service made up of a vast number of pigeon holes with impenetrable barriers preventing the occupants from ever moving from one hole to another was considerably exaggerated. Some 40% of the administrative class (although not 40% of the very top posts), consisted of people from within the service who had managed to cross the barriers surrounding the class. Nevertheless, there was force in the criticisms made by the committee, and by some of the outside commentators. On the day the Fulton report was published, the Prime Minister (Mr Wilson) announced that the government accepted the abolition of classes within the service.

A joint committee of the National Whitley Council then went into ways and means of achieving the implementation of this decision (as part of a wider remit). In the event, it turned out that classes were not to be abolished as easily as all that. But nevertheless this review led to significant changes.

On 1 January 1972 a system of unified grading was introduced down to and including Under Secretary level. For the top 900 or so posts in the service, all the specialisms and disciplines were brought together in an open structure. The Whitley enquiry thought that the Fulton committee had gone a little astray in regarding all these people as a homogeneous group carrying a collective responsibility for management and for advising on policy, but nevertheless concluded that in practice it made good sense to regard the posts as making up a single group which should be filled individually and on a service-wide basis. They believed that this open structure would make it possible for each post to be filled by the person best fitted for it, irrespective of his profession, discipline and previous history within the service. Although the immediate practical consequences of this change should not be exaggerated into an expectation of something really dramatic, it could prove to be an important development in the longer term.

The Whitley committee did a great deal of work on the possibilities of common grading lower down, but found the difficulties too formidable. They concluded that a more realistic way of going for the Fulton objectives would be to concentrate on new arrangements for personnel management and on a major restructuring of the class system by developing a new and different system of 'categories' and 'occupational groups'.

A 'category' in this new system is basically a grading and pay structure. Each has a continuous series of grades from bottom to top, although entrants may join at different points and need not necessarily go through every grade on the way up. Within the categories, there are 'occupational groups' which are essentially units for recruitment and management and vary greatly in size.

The biggest single category so far is the 'general category'. The biggest group within this category is the 'administration group', numbering over 200,000. The administration group came into being on 1 January 1971 when the administrative, executive and clerical classes were merged (as the Treasury had itself recommended to the Fulton committee); and this group, together with the economists' and statisticians' groups, made up the new 'general category' which began life on the same day.

This is the moment which, as has already been noted, marked the end of the assistant principal. Instead, there was introduced the new grade of 'administration trainee'. It was a grade open both to graduates from outside and to people already in the service. Special training was to be given to the members of this new grade. The best third of the total (or thereabouts—and it has not worked out with mathematical precision) were to be selected for promotion to another new grade, that of Higher Executive Officer (A), after between two and four years, with a view to their receiving more training and achieving promotion direct to principal within another two or three years. The hope was that, in this way, a fast stream of the most promising candidates from outside and inside would be identified in good time and given special training; and that also there would be a second stream of candidates who would strengthen the middle management of the service in the years ahead. How the later careers of the young men and women starting in this way will compare with those of the young men and women who spend their early years as specialists but would wish to blossom out later as managers remains to be seen.

In September 1971 the 'science category' came into existence. In January 1972 the works group and associated classes were merged into the 'professional and technology category'. An architect recruited to the service, for example, will be paid and graded as a member of the 'professional and technology category', but he will be a member of the architects' 'group' within that category, and those responsible for managing the group will be concerned with his postings as an architect and with his acquiring suitably wide experience as a government architect. Later on, when he has climbed some way up the hierarchy, he will be considered as a member of a wider category, with those from other professions, when the best man is being selected for a job for which other than purely technical qualifications are required.

In the main, the new 'categories' were made up, to begin with, of service-wide general classes, but the intention is to go as far as possible with bringing into the categories those departmental classes which bear some family resemblance to those already in the category. The total disappearance of the departmental classes is, however, likely to prove to be a gradual affair.

One feature of this post-Fulton structure is the intention that there should be no impediment to 'lateral' movement within the service, either for a temporary period or for keeps. Members of the staff who would themselves like to take the initiative and ask to be considered for a lateral move are encouraged to do so. An attempt has been made also, throughout the service, to identify 'opportunity posts', that is to say posts which can be filled by persons of varying disciplines.

These are more complicated matters than might appear from a brief summary, and a lot of money can be involved. Bringing differently paid groups into a common pay structure, life being what it is, means that some people get more money, and that no-one gets less. At the end of the day, too, structure is not an end in itself, and it is important not to exaggerate what can be achieved by altering it. But structure provides a framework which helps, or hinders, as the case may be, the best deployment of staff; and although not every detail of the Fulton committee's conclusions has stood up, the committee was right in stressing the need for more flexibility, more opportunity for movement, more chances for the right individual to be chosen for a job.

PERSONNEL MANAGEMENT

It was not enough, post-Fulton, to contrive a more flexible structure. It was essential too to try and equip the service to take advantage of this structure—to recognize ability, to allocate staff to the work which suited them best and to deal with the human resources of the service in an understanding way. Before Fulton, the Treasury had a central role in regard to pay and numbers; advised the Prime Minister about the top appointments in the service; and had increasingly been giving guidance on service-wide issues. Appraisal interviews for junior executive and clerical staff were started in 1965. Management committees for some of the specialist classes were set up, for example for lawyers and economists, and advised the Treasury about problems affecting the class as a whole, such as recruitment, mobility and promotion procedures.

But Fulton thought that neither the Treasury nor the departments, on whom the main burden fell, devoted nearly enough effort, or allocated nearly enough suitable staff, to personnel work.

This was a main reason for the committee's conclusion that management should be taken from the Treasury and given to a new department. But the pace of change depended also on what could be done in the departments, and as has been pointed out earlier, they had to share out their resources among a number of competing demands. Even so, considerably more people have been put on to personnel work since the Fulton report, and a number of the top posts in this area have been upgraded. Just as important, the status of personnel work within the service has undoubtedly gone up. 'Establishments man' has effectively been replaced by the personnel manager.

If the right decisions are to be taken about posting and promoting people, it is necessary to have up-to-date and well-directed information about them. In the discussions with the staff side about changes in the light of the Fulton report, agreement was reached to use right across the service a basically standard annual report form. This may sound a modest achievement. But it is really of considerable significance, since over the years it should provide a picture of each individual's past achievement and experience, and a guide to his future needs and potential. There have been other developments in this area. The use of appraisal interviews with the line manager (not the individual's immediate boss) is being steadily extended. The interview centres on performance of the current job. A lot of effort is being put into training staff in how to make reports and conduct appraisal interviews, and explaining to those being interviewed what the purpose of the exercise is. In addition, as a complement to appraisal reviews, career interviews are being developed. At these, the individual can discuss with someone from the personnel branch his own career aspirations and prospects.

Computers are now making it possible to build up comprehensive staff records within the departments, and these computers are being linked to provide, for the first time, a comprehensive pay and personnel record system for the whole of the non-industrial civil service. This system, rejoicing in the name of P.R.I.S.M. (Personnel Record Information System for Management), should be operative by 1975, and will be used both centrally and departmentally.

All this improved management information is intended to make for better career planning, including sensible lateral moves and appointments to 'opportunity' posts.

For top appointments, the Head of the Civil Service is now assisted by a committee drawn from permanent secretaries and senior professionals (but not persons from outside the service, as Fulton recommended). All appointments at the level of deputy secretary and above require the approval of the Prime Minister. The senior appointments selection committee reviews periodically the career prospects of senior officers, and is assisted by a number of specialist panels, also chaired by the Head of the Service, which keep under review the career prospects of the various senior specialists.

The Civil Service Department now has to be consulted about any promotion to Under Secretary in any department, and is building up its knowledge about those below this level who may eventually be in the running for senior posts.

The management committees for specialists have been given a new lease of life and extended to other professions. In some instances, for scientists and accountants for instance, they have been supplemented by central career development panels.

The Fulton committee was particularly critical of the 'amateur' status of the administrator, and his haphazard and frequent moves from job to job. Much thought has been given to ways and means of achieving greater administrative specialization, but there is no easy answer. The most hopeful line is to develop positive planning to secure that those of highest potential secure a breadth of experience in spheres which complement each other, and to secure also that those whose potential is less clear have time to acquire depth of knowledge in particular areas of work and that new postings are related to the type of job for which they have shown aptitude. But, anyway, the Fulton description of the 'amateur' was overdone. Many generalists acquire an expertise, for example in Parliamentary legislation, which is unique to the service; and while more can profitably be done by intelligent career planning, a number of generalists are already, and indeed have always been, specialists of a kind—specialists in some field of administration.

For the senior appointments, and for some of the professional appointments, the tendency since Fulton, then, has been for increasing central management across the service. For the lower and middle grades, on the contrary, there has been felt the need for personnel management to be increasingly devolved. There are large numbers here, many of them away from London, and they should not be left to be managed by some remote and distant central branch of which they know little. There has been increasing emphasis also on the need for the line manager to take a close interest in his staff, and not just to leave it all to the personnel branch.

But there are problems. There is first the fact that the line manager cannot hire and fire, cannot settle pay, cannot give financial rewards for meritorious work. He has no responsibility even for the building in which he operates. (For that matter, neither has his parent department, which is dependent on the Property Services Agency of the Department of the Environment.)

Then behind all this is the even bigger problem of how to reconcile accountable management within the service with the twin doctrines of ministerial responsibility and Parliamentary accountability.

For some time now, the service has been experimenting with various techniques. Multi-discipline teams, under one clearly designated leader, have been assembled to handle especially complicated projects, such as Concorde, or the review of planning issues affecting a whole region. Model-building and simulation studies of a complex nature have been carried out by teams made up of senior management, operational research specialists, economists, statisticians and automatic data-processing staff. And the development of P.E.S.C. (Public Expenditure Survey Committee) and P.A.R. (Programme Analysis Review), experiments with management by objectives and in a limited way with P.P.B. (Planning Programming Budgeting) and, indeed, the setting up of the large executive agencies, such as the Property Services Agency of the Department of the Environment and the Procurement Executive of the Ministry of Defence, have all in their own way been aimed at improving financial control and balanced policy-making, and at making those in charge of units more conscious of what the aim of that unit should be and more clearly responsible for success or failure in achieving those aims.

But there are limits to the distance one can travel on this road. It is sometimes (but not invariably) difficult to devise adequate performance criteria; and there is the special problem of how far it is possible to go in putting responsibility on to an individual civil servant when it will not fall to him to defend the policy in a Parliamentary debate. This is a very difficult area indeed.

There are one or two other rather more straightforward aspects of personnel policy which should be briefly mentioned. First, the Service has a good record in the use of management services. Its O and M work has long been widely recognized as being of outstanding quality and it has been among the leaders in this country in making intelligent use of computers and in applying operational research and the social sciences to management problems.

The service too has a good record as an enlightened employer of women. At the risk of seeming frivolous for treating so important a topic so cursorily, it is right at least to record that, in addition to equal pay and generous maternity leave, the service has recently devoted much effort to giving women more part-time employment in positions of responsibility, to making it easier for married women to combine looking after a family with a Civil Service career, and to re-training women who come back into the service after a lengthy period of absence.

Next in this rather miscellaneous list are the attempts made over the years for a greater interchange of experience between the service and outside industry. This is not as easy as it might at first seem. Although there are clear advantages in a promising individual obtaining experience of the philosophy and practice of management in another sphere, it is not worthwhile unless the individual can be given, not just a Cook's tour, but a real job to do. Attachments of staff, in both directions, have been managed on a fairly modest scale. In mid-1970 there were 57 of them, most of them for two years' duration.

To maintain a properly balanced structure in each group of officials requires manpower planning, and the collection of statistical information which will enable potential promotion blockages or particular shortages of staff to be foreseen in good time. Work has been done on this, although the programme depends to some extent on the development, aimed for completion in 1975, of the P.R.I.S.M. computer facilities.

Last in this somewhat miscellaneous list is the help which has been sought from the behavioural scientists. A good deal has been said earlier about the need to spot and look after the officer of potential. But there are a lot of members of the service who cannot expect, or for various reasons do not wish, to rise very far, and on whom the service depends for its day to day functioning. They must not be forgotten, and experiments which have been made in job enrichment could turn out to be of some significance.

TRAINING

The Treasury had put a lot of effort into training before the Fulton committee was set up. It had a specialized training and education division, and although the great bulk of training was (and is) a matter for the departments, the Treasury provided four elements which were later brought together to provide the basis for the Civil Service college. These four were the courses run for executive officers; those for assistant secretaries; the specialized training organized by the management services division; and, perhaps most important, the centre for administrative studies set up at Regent's Park in 1963. This centre at first provided a longish course in economics for assistant principals. Its clientele was later enlarged by the introduction of some principals; and its teaching programme was extended to include statistics, public administration and social administration.

In 1965 an important working party was appointed by the Chancellor of the Exchequer, with representation from the service and from outside, to review management training in the service. The working party's report was fed into the Fulton committee, who printed it and endorsed, and extended, most of the conclusions.

The Fulton committee was impressed by the evidence in this report and elsewhere of the efforts that had been made to improve training, especially vocational training. But it thought that not nearly enough was done to train in techniques of modern management. It also thought (going rather beyond the working party's findings) that the time had come to set up a full-blown Civil Service college.

This last recommendation was one of those immediately accepted by the government.

The new college came into being in 1970. It brought together, as a start, the four elements of Treasury-provided training referred to above. The college was organized in three parts. Two of them were residential, one at Sunningdale (in the former civil defence college) and the other in Edinburgh; and one was non-residential, in central London.

The college is still in its early days, it is still being expanded, and the shape and content of the courses have not reached finality. It has, however, provided, and will clearly continue to provide, a wide variety of instruction for a wide variety of needs. Heed has been paid to the criticisms of Fulton about the inadequacy of management training. In 1968–69 something of the order of 4800 student course weeks were provided in centrally provided management training. By 1970–71 this figure exceeded 11,000. The courses include long courses for administration trainees, and a variety of courses for middle management. The early 1970s also saw the beginning of general management training for specialist staff. Various seminars are arranged for the top civil servants, not excluding Permanent Secretaries. Non-civil servants attend some of the courses, if not on quite the scale envisaged by Fulton. An Advisory Council, including outside academics and industrialists, advises the Principal.

The college has established itself, and as it expands and comes to its full capacity by the mid 1970s should meet a need in the service which perhaps ought to have been met earlier. There have been growing pains. Sometimes, for example, those attending a course have not had it clearly explained to them what the purpose of the course was. But these are still early days, and although it will be a long time before it is possible to make a worthwhile assessment of the effect of college training on the service as a whole (just as for the police college, which preceded it by a few years), it is to be hoped that it will come to fulfil the vision which the Fulton committee had of it.

In one respect, however, the college has not so far developed as the committee thought it would. The academic members of the staff have done quite a bit of research, for example for case-studies for courses, and have published some interesting books and articles. But the Fulton committee saw the college as becoming a centre for research in problems of government, and being used by the departments for these purposes. In the event, in the first few years, precious little in the way of research projects has been fed into the college by departments; and the staff themselves have had their hands pretty full in devising the various courses and catering for the steady expansion of the college. Whether it will eventually grow into an important academic centre of research has still to be seen.

Specialist instruction on a fairly modest scale is also arranged for the service in other academic institutions—for example, courses in systems analysis have been arranged with the City University; and the service has continued to send people to outside bodies such as the business schools and the administrative staff college at Henley. Over 1000 student course weeks are taken up each year in external management training of this kind.

The new college is the most dramatic of the developments in the field of training in this period. But over 90% of the total training still rests with the departments; and good though the record of the departments was before the Fulton committee, there has been a noticeable increase since then in the skills and resources devoted by departments to this vital function. In 1966–67, the first year for which detailed figures were collected, just under 145,000 people were given formal training by departments. Three years later, the total had gone to almost 240,000. In 1972–73, the figure was something like 257,000. Most of the training was still vocational and specialist; but there was more refresher training, more induction training for new entrants, more management and supervisory training. The National Whitley Council has continued to keep a close eye on the development of training, and so have the departmental Whitley Councils; and it is with the full co-operation of the staff side that arrangements have been developed, for example, to provide courses in job-related management training for the full annual flow of all higher executive officers and of all executive officers with significant supervisory responsibilities. Limitations of resources mean that not everything can be done at once and that the pace may differ from department to department. But in general the service can claim, on training, to be pretty well in the forefront in this country.

CONDITIONS OF SERVICE

It is impossible to write a chapter about the management of the service without some reference to pay, but, at the time of writing, national incomes policy is still in the making and in view of the impossibility of foreseeing what impact that policy will have on service pay, it would be pointless here to go into this topic in any depth.

The Royal Commission on the Civil Service, 1953–55 (the Priestley Commission), was concerned primarily with pay. Their conclusion was that the primary factor in determining the pay of the service should be a fair comparison with the rates paid for broadly comparable work outside. In 1956, a Pay Research Unit was set up to establish fair comparisons for the main classes. This Unit, working at first on a three-year cycle and then later over shorter periods, has tackled the complicated task of preparing factual reports after a study of suitably selected outside analogues. These reports, which are inevitably open to argument, then form the basis for negotiation with the staff representatives— who have not hesitated to claim, and have been awarded, interim increases in the middle of the cycle of the Unit's researches.

Unlike local government, separate arrangements were made for the pay of the higher Civil Service. At first there was an outside committee to advise just on this topic, but in 1970 higher civil servants were brought, alongside Ministers, Members of Parliament, chairmen of the boards of nationalized industries and the higher judiciary, within the ambit of the Top Salaries Review Body.

When the Statutory Pay Board was set up in 1973, it reached the conclusion at quite an early stage that the Civil Service merited an immediate pay increase to remove the anomalies resulting from their having been left too far behind comparable employees outside. Once the anomalies were corrected, then civil servants stood to be dealt with like everyone else, but how it will all work out cannot be foreseen at the time of writing. The staff are at any rate well aware that the full rigours of any governmental incomes policy are bound to be applied to the Civil Service.

There has been one development of a novel kind. There have been bitter enough disputes about service pay in the past, but in the end negotiation and arbitration have settled the issues, even though the staff have sometimes been left feeling aggrieved. But the system has been showing increasing signs of strain, and in 1973, for the first time, civil servants were to be seen resorting to industrial action over pay disputes.

In the period under review, there has been much new thinking in the country about pensions, and the service has played its full part. The service was a pioneer as a good employer in introducing terms which, by contemporary standards, were generous. Since then, many in the outside world have caught up and in some respects passed the civil servant—who still has to do 40 years to earn a full pension. But a number of important improvements have been made in the 1970s, in addition to stepping up pensions for widows to half the rate of the husband's pension, and meeting the new statutory requirements put on to employers about preservation. Those who cannot complete 40 years' service have been enabled to buy in additional years; the pensions scheme has been extended to cover unestablished full-time staff; sanction has been obtained to alter the pensions scheme in future without the need each time to seek fresh legislation; and, even though the Civil Service scheme has continued in the main to be non-contributory, it has been made much easier for people to move in and out while continuing their pension entitlement. This last development is not limited to moves between the Civil Service and the rest of the public sector; and the Civil Service Department is ready to welcome into 'the club' private employers who are prepared to accept the payment to and from their pension schemes of transfer values in respect of people moving in and out.

It had become the practice since the Second World War to pass legislation every three years or so providing for the pensions of civil and other public servants to be increased to take account of the increases in the cost of living. Under an Act passed in 1971 power was taken to carry out regular reviews, without the need for fresh legislation each time, to protect public service pensions against inflation. Starting in December 1972 these reviews were to be made annually.

New powers were taken, going beyond the existing powers to retire those who were inefficient, making it possible to retire individuals prematurely when performance no longer adequately measures up to requirements, and also for structural reasons where for example bad age distribution in a particular grade might lead to serious management difficulties because of a serious promotion blockage. Fair compensation is given in such cases; and an appeal board has been set up to hear representations from anyone who thinks that he is being unfairly dismissed, whether under the old or under the new powers.

In 1973, the first year for which figures under the new rules were circulated, something of the order of 950 civil servants were prematurely retired. During that year, 37 appeals were heard by the Civil Service Appeal Board. Twenty-two per cent were successful.

Of other conditions of employment, two can perhaps be singled out. The first was the introduction of a five-day working week following the recommendation of the Royal Commission which reported in 1955. In view of the changes in the social pattern of the community as a whole, this is now almost forgotten, but it seemed important enough at the time.

The second is the attempt being made to improve the working environment. The Fulton committee was critical of the conditions in which a lot of civil servants had to work and thought that the bad physical surroundings adversely affected morale and efficiency. The official and staff sides accepted that there was force in these criticisms. As a result, training courses have been introduced for departmental accommodation officers; there has been a drive to improve cleaning and maintenance standards; there has been a campaign against clutter and untidiness in offices; and there has been experimenting with open plan offices.

Something has been achieved. A good many government offices are not as shabby inside as they were. The outsides of buildings have been cleaned. Automatic roller towels and liquid soap dispensers have become rather more common. Furniture is not quite so standardized. Some typing pools have been carpeted and curtained. These may seem trivial points, but they represent an important aspect of management—and there is still some way to go, even if the service at the end of the day can never afford to give the impression to the public that it is being housed in unnecessary luxury.

CONCLUSION

It has been convenient to discuss various aspects of management in separate sub-sections. But they are not subjects which are completely separate and self-contained. On the contrary, they closely interlock and are but different aspects of one large, complex, but unified, service.

There are a number of issues which bear to some extent on management which have hardly been touched on. They include the long-term impact on the service of our joining the E.E.C.; 'open' government and the relevance (not very great, probably) of the Official Secrets Acts; the part played by business men or political advisers brought in from outside; the repercussions of more dispersal; and the tendencies towards making the service a little less isolated from the rest of the community, for example by civil servants appearing in public more than they used to, whether on television, or addressing local meetings, or giving evidence at public enquiries. But to discuss these issues and others like them would need another long chapter to do them anything like justice, and it is time to try and bring together a few concluding remarks.

The service must clearly bear its share of responsibility for the failures (as well as the successes) of government since the Second World War, and for its contribution to the policies followed by this country in a period which has seen such a decline in its role in the world. The service was certainly slow to begin reforming itself after the war to reflect changes in society and in the role of government, and no-one would claim that since then it has completely solved the very real management problems touched on in this chapter. It is not just discontent about pay; and it is not to be wondered at that, at the end of 1973, it was decided to hold an inquiry into why so many civil servants—for reasons other than pay—felt frustrated and discontented.

But it would be wrong to end on too gloomy a note. The excellences of the service, which are sometimes taken a little for granted, still exist. Not every country can boast of a government service which is characterized by incorruptibility and a strong sense of equity, which has a very fair share of people with a strong sense of vocation and with a readiness to work extremely hard, and which includes individuals of high calibre, in a wide variety of professions, who can hold their own in any company. It is often assumed that, whatever the service's other merits, it must be inefficient and overstaffed, but there is plenty of informed comment from outside to demonstrate that this is grotesquely untrue. Merely in the field covered by this chapter the service has pioneered a number of management practices which can be found only in some of the largest industrial firms, and not always then; and it can claim a considerable success in evolving its own solutions, or substantially amending practice followed elsewhere, to meet management problems which are indeed different in kind from those of any other organization in the country. As this chapter has tried to show, a considerable effort has been put into remoulding the service since the 1960s, and although there are still plenty of gaps and evidences of frustration, and although the story of change is still at a comparatively early stage, a chapter on the Civil Service fits appropriately into a book about the modernization of government in this country.

There are, though, moments when one wonders whether the nature of the work has changed all that much. Samuel Pepys, a civil servant long before the period covered by this book, concluded his entry for 10 April 1662 in a way which still strikes a familiar note:

> *'Late at the office. Home, with my mind*
> *full of business, and so to bed.'*

The Redress of Grievances   6

Professor J. F. Garner, LL.D.

THE IMMEDIATE POST-WAR YEARS

Traditionally, the Englishman has looked to the Royal Courts for assistance in any time of trouble at the hands of an over-mighty subject, and especially those most mighty subjects of all, the Ministers of the Crown. Whenever a citizen has a grievance against some other person, the law should (and probably will) provide an adequate remedy; a means of redress for his grievance by the machinery of the courts. And this attitude of mind applies equally to a grievance suffered at the hand of some agency of the administration, including a local authority or a public corporation,[1] as it does to a grievance suffered at the hand of the citizen's neighbour. Traditionally also this right of a citizen to have recourse to the courts, has been jealously guarded by Her Majesty's judges. As Lord Denning, that robust upholder of the rights of the 'little man', said in 1952:[2]

> 'If parties should seek by agreement to take the law out of the hands of the courts and into the hands of a private tribunal, without any recourse at all to the courts in the case of error of law, then the agreement is to that extent contrary to public policy and void.'

In a later case Viscount Simmonds said,[3]

> 'It is a principle not by any means to be whittled down that the subject's recourse to Her Majesty's Courts for the determination of his rights is not to be excluded except by clear words' (of an Act of Parliament).

But in spite of these strong words, the fact was that at the end of the Second World War this inalienable remedy of 'Her Majesty's subjects to seek redress in her courts',[4] was being alienated, or at least eroded, by the twin action of express statutory provisions and the current attitude of the courts in interpreting those provisions. Express statutory provisions were for the most part concerned with processes involving the taking of decisions necessary in the course of administration of the newly established Welfare State, removing them from the courts and giving them to new and specially created tribunals. Such were the tribunals created to determine disputed claims arising out of the State system of insurance for industrial injuries[5] and those dealing with closely related

5

117

national pensions[6] and family allowances.[7] Rents for furnished houses could be determined by another group of tribunals,[8] while the new system of control over land use introduced by the revolutionary Town and Country Planning Act, 1947, and entrusted at the first instance to local authorities, was subjected to the overall supervision of a Minister acting through a corps of permanent civil servants whose duty it was, and is, to hold inquiries against the refusal of planning permission by local authorities.[9]

In some of these instances the relevant statute made provision for a right of appeal on a point of law to the courts,[10] but in others the decision of the tribunal was said to be 'final'.[11] In either case, no express provision was made for supervision by the courts, except in the most general terms,[12] over the procedure that was to be followed by these tribunals. Frequently, the statutes were hurriedly drafted, and omitted to make adequate provision for procedural matters, these either being omitted altogether, or left to be covered by Departmental Regulations, which were themselves subject to but the most haphazard scrutiny in the House of Commons.[13] In at least one case regulations governing the procedure to be followed by a hierarchy of tribunals expressly prohibited parties appearing before the tribunals from engaging legal assistance.[14] Every time a new form of statutory control was proposed which would require administrative decisions to be taken affecting the rights of individuals, a new tribunal or, in some instances, an appeal to a Minister involving an inquiry was established, and no attempt was made either to co-ordinate the new tribunal with existing ones or even to follow a common pattern of constitution, appointment of members, etc.[15]

Some substantial statutory reforms in our administrative law were, however, made in the period 1946–50; thus, the *lacuna* in the law which was a disgrace to any civilized country, whereby a subject could not sue the Crown in tort or for breach of contract, was abolished by the Crown Proceedings Act 1947, and the procedure for the making of most forms[16] of subordinate legislation was improved by the Statutory Instruments Act 1946. But these reforms did not in any way affect tribunal procedure.

Almost more serious than the abdication by Parliament of any effective controls over administrative adjudication, was the less conscious attitude of the courts towards these same and similar statutes. If Parliament appeared to give a discretion to a Minister, the courts were only too ready to interpret this in such a manner as to exclude any supervision by the Courts. Thus, in *Liversidge v. Anderson*[17] the Home Secretary was empowered by war-time legislation to intern without trial any person whom he had 'reasonable cause to believe to be of hostile origin or associations,' if he considered that, by reason thereof, 'it was necessary to exercise control' over that person. In *habeas corpus* proceedings taken by an applicant who had been so interned, the House of Lords were prepared to consider whether there were grounds on which a reasonable man could 'believe some at least of the facts', but, in spite of an outspoken dissenting judgment from Lord Atkin, the majority of their Lordships were content to accept without question the certificate of the Home Secretary to the effect that in his opinion it was 'necessary' to exercise control over the applicant. This was an executive discretion not subject to discussion or control by a judge in a court of law. Much the same attitude was adopted in *Duncan v. Cammel Laird & Co. Ltd.*,[18] when the House of Lords accepted without question a certificate of a Minister claiming privilege from production in court proceedings between two private litigants of a public document[19] vital to those proceedings, on the ground that it would be contrary to the public interest that such a document should be disclosed. The Minister, not the court, was the sole judge of what was in the public interest.

Of perhaps even greater significance was the Privy Council decision in *Nakkuda Ali v. Jayaratne*,[20] on appeal from Ceylon. In this case, the plaintiff, a dealer in textiles, had had his licence to export goods from Ceylon revoked by the Controller, a government official, under a statutory power enabling him so to act when he had reasonable grounds to believe that a dealer was unfit to be allowed to continue as a dealer. The plaintiff complained that he should have been given a hearing by the Controller before the decision against him had been taken. The Privy Council, however, decided that this was an executive, not a quasi-judicial decision, and that therefore it was not liable to be reviewed in the courts. Although it was agreed that the courts could satisfy themselves in such a case that the Controller in fact had reasonable grounds on which to base his decision, this did not mean that the Controller was obliged to follow 'a course of conduct analogous to the judicial process'.

These cases, therefore, showed that in the 1950 era the courts were prepared to ensure that a Minister[21] or a tribunal[22] did not exceed the powers given by Parliament; nevertheless they would not insist on the observance of any special procedure. Where the Minister was given by statute an administrative discretion, this did not necessarily have to be exercised in a judicial manner, nor was it necessary for the well established[23] common law principles of natural justice to be applied. Even in a case like *Nakkuda Ali* (*supra*) where the plaintiff was being deprived of a right to continue in his chosen line of business, or one like *Liversidge v. Anderson*, where the plaintiff was being deprived of his personal liberty, it was not considered necessary to require compliance with the procedures of natural justice.

The same line of thinking was followed a few years later, in *ex parte Fry*,[24] concerning disciplinary proceedings taken against a member of a fire brigade because he had refused to clean a senior officer's uniform, and also in *re Parker*,[25] where the Commissioner of the Metropolitan Police had revoked the licence of a taxicab driver. In both of these cases the decision was categorized by the court as being of an administrative nature, and that, therefore, neither appellant was entitled to a hearing before the decision was taken against him.

The years from, say 1946 to 1952, may be described therefore as a period of rapid expansion of adjudication by tribunal and by a Minister of the Crown (after the holding of an inquiry), and a certain awareness on the part of the legislature of the need for reform in administrative procedures, modified by the lack of time in a Parliament which was preoccupied with what were considered to be more fundamental issues, such as the nationalization of gas, electricity and rail transport. There was also a marked hesitancy on the part of the courts to exert any very close controls, procedural or otherwise, over the wide discretions entrusted by Parliament to the executive.

THE CHANGING ATMOSPHERE OF THE 1950s

By 1952 or 1953 the country was tiring of the post-war administrative shortages and controls. The Korean War was over and rationing had finished, and with these changes the unpopular development charge of the town and country planning legislation of 1947 also disappeared.[26] Then two *affaires scandales* were to alert the nation to shortcomings of administrative justice.[27] The first of these was the 'Pilgrim affair'. Mr Pilgrim had purchased a plot of land for £500 (financing the purchase by a mortgage) on which he had intended to build a house for himself when he could afford it. The local authority compulsorily acquired the plot from him in 1952 and he was paid compensation of £65, this representing the then existing use value of the land—all that Mr Pilgrim was entitled to under the then existing law. Mr Pilgrim appealed for a larger sum to the Ministry, and to his Member of Parliament, without success, and ultimately committed suicide.[28] The affair created a considerable stir, it being argued that the local authority should have taken more care in explaining the position to Mr Pilgrim, and also that the law should have given them discretion to pay more than existing use value for land in a hard luck case of this kind. Future cases of Mr Pilgrim's kind were in fact met rapidly by Section 35 of the Town and Country Planning Act 1954, but the case left in the public mind a sense of unfair behaviour by 'them', the administration generally, which was not altogether justified by the facts of the case.

'Crichel Down' was a much more serious case, which considerably aggravated the critical atmosphere generated by Pilgrim. In this famous affair, land in Dorset had been acquired compulsorily on behalf of one of the Service departments during the 1939–45 War, and the then owner had been given an undertaking that when the Government no longer had use for the land he would be given an opportunity of buying it back. However, when it eventually became redundant in the 1950s, the land by then having come under the control of the Ministry of Agriculture and Fisheries, it was sold to a private purchaser without first being offered to the original owner. He, being a former serving officer and a person of considerable pertinacity, complained vehemently and questions were asked on his behalf in the House of Commons. A departmental enquiry was held, and the Minister resigned, although he was not personally responsible. As a consequence of the very considerable publicity that the case attracted and the outspoken criticisms made of the administrative procedures generally, a special committee (subsequently to be known as the 'Franks Committee')[29] was set up, charged with the duty of considering the question of tribunals and inquiries generally. Crichel Down was certainly the spark that set alight the current smouldering discontent over these administrative procedures, but actually that affair had nothing to do with tribunals or inquiries; no tribunal or inquiry could have been seised with the subject matter in issue over Crichel Down.[30] Nevertheless, the Committee, with commendable expedition, produced a report some 18 months later, in which they made a number of very important recommendations. Many of these were too detailed to be listed here, but among the most important were:

(a) recognition that the supervision by the courts over the conduct of administrative tribunals, mainly confined to ensuring that the principles of natural justice were observed, was not sufficient; all tribunals should follow three general and linked procedural characteristics, which were, in the words of the Committee, 'openness, fairness and impartiality';

(b) whilst leaving the courts to keep the tribunals within the limits set them by the law, and making sure that this would be so, by providing for a right of appeal on a point of law from any tribunal decision,[31] there should be a body in permanent session, 'the advice of which would be sought whenever it was proposed to establish a new type of tribunal, and which would also keep under review the constitution and procedure of existing tribunals.'[32]

The Report of the Franks Committee was, mercifully, *not* pigeon-holed, as has so often been the case with reports of similar bodies convened as a consequence of a national bru-haha such as Crichel Down.[33] In this case the Tribunals and Inquiries Act 1958[34] followed very shortly on the heels of the Report itself.

This important statute established the Council on Tribunals, the standing body recommended by Franks, with a standing sub-committee to deal with Scottish affairs,[35] and the Council was given the duty of keeping under review the working of a number of tribunals listed in the Act,[36] to report on such matters, and also on matters involving statutory inquiries;[37] it was also provided that the Council must be consulted before procedural rules were made for tribunals or statutory inquiries. Provision was also made in the Act for appeals to lie from certain tribunals to the courts on a point of law, and for tribunals and Ministers (after the holding of a statutory inquiry) to be required to give reasons for their decisions on request. A section was introduced overriding provisions in the then existing legislation that purported to exclude the right of an aggrieved litigant before a tribunal to seek one of the prerogative orders from the court, so as to query the legality of the decision.

The Town and Country Planning Act 1959 reflected the same desire to implement the Franks recommendations of fairness, and a reversion to supervision by the courts of administrative procedures. This Act made provision for appeals to the courts on a point of law from a number of planning decisions and orders, and also reversed the principles on which compensation for the compulsory acquisition of land were to be assessed, departing from the existing use value of the 1947 Act and approximating to market value.[38]

Since its establishment by this Act, the Council on Tribunals, consisting of some 16 members[39] (all except the chairman serving part time and without salary) and with a very small staff of civil servants, has been able to achieve very considerable improvements in tribunal and inquiry procedures. It has secured recognition in Whitehall, in that it is regularly consulted over these procedural matters, not only in cases where its constituent Act insists that it must be consulted, namely where procedural rules are made by a Government Department by way of subordinate legislation, but also in cases where the Government Department concerned is proposing to create a new tribunal or hierarchy of tribunals in a Bill which it proposes to place before Parliament.[40] Its supervision over inquiries was considerably extended by the wider definition of the expression 'statutory inquiry' given by the Tribunals and Inquiries Act 1966.[41] Indeed, the work of the Council on procedural rules had by the mid 1960s achieved such success that a standard pattern could be seen emerging. Also, as a result of visits by its members to individual tribunal or inquiry hearings, the Council has been able to achieve improvements of detail in particular cases, although its work in this regard has perforce been of a somewhat haphazard character.

All this work of the Council on Tribunals was, and is, concerned only with procedures before formally constituted tribunals and inquiries; it is not concerned with the more informal administrative discretions of Ministers of the Crown, local authorities or public corporations. In so far as these were subject to control at all, the controls were confined to the restricted controls of the courts and the more insubstantial and indirect, in many cases, control of the House of Commons.

Controls by the courts over administrative authorities during the period under review remained of a procedural nature, being concerned to ensure that the agency concerned did not exceed its jurisdiction or act in an *ultra vires* manner (these two expressions are really synonymous); but where the court considered the law required the agency to act in a judicial (or 'quasi-judicial': another near synonym) manner, then the court would insist on the rather rudimentary procedure of the rules of natural justice being observed.

By the end of the 1950s we can see the newly established Council on Tribunals ready for action, and a few minor reforms were being undertaken in central government departments as a consequence of the Franks Report, but the courts were much where we had left them in 1952. This is subject to the exception that statutory provisions excluding the right of the courts to supervise the legality of tribunal decisions in existing legislation were overruled by the Act of 1958, and they would, it was hoped, not be used in the future; much as the Donoughmore Committee in 1932 had condemned the so-called 'Henry VIII' clause of their day. Certainly these hopes were realized in the next decade; clauses expressly excluding the supervisory jurisdiction of the courts no longer appear in the statute book.

THE ACHIEVEMENTS OF THE 1960s

Four main new threads in the texture of our administrative law can be detected in the period 1960–70. These are the work of the Council on Tribunals, which has already been discussed; the creation of new tribunals; an increasing activity by the courts in the direction of controlling the administration; and the establishment of a new means for the redress of grievances, the Parliamentary Commissioner for Administration or 'Ombudsman'. We will deal with the last three named separately.

New Tribunals

As the immediate post-war years could be characterized as the age of the creation of new inquiries procedures (town and country planning, compulsory purchase, the national health service, etc.) so the 1960s saw the creation of a considerable number of important new administrative tribunals. These included the mental health review tribunals,[42] the rent assessment committees charged with determining disputes about the fair rent for unfurnished dwellings subject to regulated tenancies,[43] the Betting Levy Appeal Tribunal,[44] the 'dividend stripping' tribunal established under the Finance Act 1960, and right at the end of the period under review the Immigration Appeals Tribunal.[45] The Plant Varieties Tribunal was another newcomer,[46] but perhaps most important of all were the industrial tribunals. Established originally with a comparatively minor jurisdiction to determine appeals by persons assessed to a levy made by an industrial training board towards meeting its expenses,[47] they were soon to be given additional work, as follows:

(a) matters arising in connection with claims to redundancy payments;[48]

(b) references as to particulars of terms of a contract of employment;[49]

(c) determinations of compensation for loss of office under specified statutes;[50]

(d) disputes as to the meaning of 'dock work';[51]

(e) determination of complaints of alleged unfair dismissal (perhaps the most considerable of the tribunal's several headings of jurisdiction);[52]

(f) when the Equal Pay Act 1970 comes into force in 1975, the determination of questions arising thereunder.

All these tribunals have been made subject to the supervision of the Council of Tribunals and detailed rules of procedure observing the 'Franks' standards apply to them. The Annual Reports of the Council on Tribunals have raised several important matters connected with the organization of tribunals. In particular, the value of the 'Presidential' system (first developed in the National Insurance tribunals and followed by the industrial tribunals) was recognized, whereby a President is appointed as the nominal head of a hierarchy of tribunals and made responsible for arranging the business and personnel for particular hearings. This type of organization has obvious advantages over the older uncoordinated tribunals, where each tribunal is a separate unity, such as the furnished houses rent tribunals and the local valuation courts. Other problems that came to light in this period, most of which have not yet been satisfactorily resolved, include the staffing of tribunals, methods of recruitment, and the accommodation provided.[53]

The Criminal Injuries Compensation Board, created in 1963, is an unusual kind of administrative tribunal, in that it has no statutory constitution. It was established under the Royal Prerogative and has the duty of adjudicating upon claims for compensation, payable out of Exchequer funds, from members of the public who have suffered physical injuries of some kind as a consequence of some crime of violence, either as victims of a crime such as robbery or rape, or because they have attempted to apprehend a criminal or assisted in an arrest, etc. The terms under which compensation may be awarded are set out in a Royal Warrant, and the Board (which is not, in spite of its title, a public corporation), being a public body, is susceptible to correction by an order of *certiorari* from the court, should they make an error of law in interpreting and applying the terms of the scheme.[54]

It is perhaps strange that the Board has never been put on a statutory basis, but its existence is clearly necessary; in the first six months of 1972 over £1½ million was paid out in compensation on some 4000 cases. The establishment of the Board was the result of agitation over several years by such bodies as 'Justice', and the Howard League for Penal Reform, and followed on the successful institution of similar schemes in New York State and in New Zealand, in each case on a statutory basis.

Activity of the Courts

During the 1940s and 1950s, as we have seen, the courts showed a distinct reluctance to require observance of the principles of natural justice, in spite of quite outspoken comments in such well known earlier cases as *Board of Education v. Rice*.[55] *Liversidge v. Anderson*[56] and the other cases referred to above had shown a similar reluctance to question the exercise of a statutory discretion by a Minister of the Crown. A change of heart was foreshadowed in *Ross-Clunis v. Papadopoullos*[57] where the Privy Council said they would have been prepared to quash an administrative decision if it could be shown that no reasonable official could properly have come to that decision; in such circumstances it would not be necessary to establish that the official had acted *ultra vires*. But the real break came with *Ridge v. Baldwin*.[58] In this seminal decision, the House of Lords held that a local watch committee acting under powers given them under Police Regulations had acted illegally when they dismissed a chief constable without first giving him the opportunity of being heard before them. Whether they were acting 'quasi-judicially' or 'administratively', as had been said to be the case in the Court of Appeal[59] they were dealing with a case of dismissal from office for cause, in which event he was entitled to an opportunity of first explaining his conduct.

The ideas of natural justice have been further developed in later cases. Thus, the person 'accused' must be given reasonable notice of the time and place of the hearing,[60] of the nature of the case he has to meet,[61] and in certain circumstances, admittedly at present ill-defined, he must have an opportunity of being represented by a lawyer of his choice.[62] The right to be heard has been recognized in the context of dismissal from a trade union,[63] disciplinary proceedings against students at a University or college,[64] dismissal from an office protected by statute,[65] and cases where a person's 'right to work' is in issue.[66]

The other branch of the natural justice rule, the requirement of freedom from bias, was also applied by the courts in this period. Thus, a trade union official was not allowed to initiate disciplinary proceedings against a member of the union and then act as a member of the committee having jurisdiction to determine the proceedings.[67] When it was alleged that a police officer was medically unfit to continue in his office, it was held that there had been a breach of natural justice when the same medical officer was allowed to give evidence as to his mental state at two different stages of the proceedings; especially when it was also established that the medical officer's reports had not been made available to the police officer or his own medical adviser.[68] 'If he [the medical officer] was to decide the matter, justice would not be seen to be done.' In this branch of natural justice, another case decided in 1967[69] made it clear that it was not necessary, in order to establish a breach of natural justice, that the court was actually biased; it is sufficient to show that there is a reasonable likelihood of bias, or that a litigant could reasonably suspect that the judge in question was or would be biased.

On a quite different subject it is significant that the first scholarly study of a central theme in administrative law, *The Judicial Review of Administrative Action*, was published by Professor S. A. de Smith under that title in 1959, and that the first substantial students' textbook on Administrative Law, by the present author, followed in 1963.

Following the line of thought revived, if not initiated, by *Ridge v. Baldwin* (*supra*) the courts have also in the period under review evolved a duty to act 'fairly' in circumstances where the full panoply of the rules of natural justice would not be considered to be applicable. Thus, in *re H(K)*[70] an immigration officer was required to act fairly in considering the allegations made by a young would-be immigrant; before rejecting out of hand his application to enter this country the officer should have made certain simple enquiries by way of verification of the case put forward. Similarly, when a magistrate took advice privately from a public analyst as to the fitness for human consumption of certain potatoes that he was asked to condemn under the Food and Drugs Act 1955, it was held that he was not acting 'fairly'; whether it could be said the decision was administrative or judicial, the nature of the advice given should have been made known to the owner of the potatoes.[71]

Again, a trade union committee must act fairly when considering whether or not to confirm the election by his workmates of a member of the union as a shop steward.[72] However, when a tribunal convened under S.28 of the Finance Act 1960 failed to disclose the whole of the Inland Revenue's case to the

5*

taxpayer, the House of Lords refused to intervene, but it is significant that they based their decision on the argument that as the tribunal was seised of only a preliminary matter, and an outline of the case had been given to the taxpayer, the tribunal had acted 'fairly'.[73]

It is still by no means clear as to what is meant by the duty to act 'fairly', but apparently the courts will insist on it being observed in cases of discretionary decisions. A specialized example of this may be seen in several cases where the courts have struck down the decisions of local authorities, because they have prejudged the issue, either following an established line of policy, or by binding themselves in advance by contract with a third party to take a particular line of conduct.[74] Administrative bodies may follow 'house rules' and take decisions in accordance with pre-determined policies, but they must always be prepared to consider individual applications and take into account any special considerations that may, or should, persuade them to depart from their established policy in that particular case.[75]

Academic writers have been concerned with the problem whether a failure to observe the principles of natural justice, or to act fairly, in a case where such a duty can be shown to exist, has the effect of avoiding the decision, *ab initio*, or whether the decision stands as valid until such time as its validity is challenged by proceedings in the courts. There are many *dicta* in the cases suggesting that the former is the correct position, but it is also true that the courts will not necessarily give a remedy quashing a decision arrived at contrary to natural justice where no injustice has been caused.[76] Certain complicating factors have to be taken into account, namely the fact that the plaintiff in a particular case must have 'standing' and so be entitled to sue, i.e. to have *locus standi*[77] and also he must ask for the particular remedy that fits the circumstances of the case in issue.[78] It is these procedural factors that have given rise to the void/voidable argument; the true answer to that argument seems to be that a decision arrived at contrary to natural justice will be declared void by any court having jurisdiction, on the application of a plaintiff entitled to bring the proceedings. Until, however, the validity of the order or decision has been challenged in such proceedings, it will be presumed to be valid and enforceable. These procedural difficulties, only outlined here, are one of the most substantial blemishes on our administrative law, illustrated but not cured by the decisions of the courts in the 1960s.

To return to the notion of reasonableness raised in *Ross-Clunis v. Papadopoullos (supra)*, this remained dormant until the important decision in *Padfield v. Minister of Agriculture and Fisheries*.[79] In this case, the Minister was empowered by statute to refer questions arising in the course of operating a milk marketing scheme for the advice of a specially constituted committee; but the determination of any such questions was entrusted to him. The Minister received a substantial complaint about the operation of the scheme, but refused to refer the matter to the committee as, so he alleged, he had made up his mind and did not need the advice of the committee. Nevertheless, in proceedings for a *man-*

damus to require the Minister to refer the matter to the committee, the House of Lords construed the power to refer to the committee as a duty, in any circumstances except a frivolous or vexatious case. The court construed the statute as a whole and expressed the view that as Parliament had created an advisory committee with the sole object of considering such questions, it must have been the intention of Parliament that the committee should be used whenever possible. Although the Act provided that the Minister 'may' refer questions to the advisory committee, the Lords decided that it meant that he *must* refer such questions to the committee.

In *Anisminic* v. *Foreign Compensation Commission*,[80] the House of Lords showed themselves reluctant to accept an apparent exclusion of judicial review by the terms of a statute. The Act in question had provided that a determination of the Commission should not be capable of being questioned in any legal proceedings. Instead of staying outside what appeared to be a closed door,[81] the court pushed open the door and investigated the validity of an apparent determination of the Commission, by saying that as the Commission had erred to such an extent that they had acted outside their jurisdiction, the 'determination' was no determination at all, and so could be declared void by the court.

This method of interpreting legislation was a novelty for an English court, although it would have been by no means strange to a French administrative court. At present the case remains a solitary example in modern decisions; when the House of Lords was asked to adopt a similar kind of broad interpretation in two later cases, in each case the House declined to do so.[82]

The Parliamentary Commissioner for Administration

The idea of an Ombudsman, in the English guise of an Inspector-General of Administration, was introduced to the thinking English public at the time when the Franks Committee were considering the evidence given before them, by a letter published in *Public Law* in 1957 from a much revered Oxford comparative lawyer, Professor F. H. Lawson. This suggestion was inspired by the Swedish and Danish institution of the 'Ombudsman', who in his home countries is seised with the duty of receiving complaints from members of the public alleging injustice or hardship suffered as the consequence of some discretionary action of a government agency which could not be made the subject of proceedings in the courts of law. The Scandinavian Ombudsman has full powers to investigate the complaints, and he is then required to make a report to his Parliament, which report is at the same time made public. No redress of the grievance follows automatically, although if a criminal offence has been brought to light the Ombudsman or some public official will normally institute legal proceedings. Criminal cases apart, the Ombudsman is content to rely on the good sense of Ministers and the pressure of political and public opinion as a means of obtaining an improvement of any errors revealed in the administrative machine as a consequence of his investigations.

Professor Lawson's letter attracted considerable interest, and this was followed in 1958 by visits to English universities by the Danish Ombudsman, Professor Hurwitz, the idea of an Ombudsman for Britain having been sponsored by the then newly founded all-party association of lawyers known as 'Justice' (the British section of the International Commission of Jurists). Later, 'Justice' commissioned Sir John Wyatt to prepare a report on the proposal, and this was published in 1961 under the title 'The Citizen and the Administration.'

In spite of the favourable atmosphere in many quarters created by the Franks Report and the passing of the Tribunals and Inquiries Act, 1958, the Wyatt Report was not at once taken up by either political party.[83] However, after some vicissitudes, the project was adopted by the Labour Government that came to power in 1964, and the Parliamentary Commissioner Act 1967 eventually became law on 1 April 1967.

This Act established the office of Parliamentary Commissioner for Administration (P.C.A.), an office given the same security of tenure, salary, and conditions of service as that of a High Court Judge. The Commissioner is appointed by H.M. The Queen on the recommendation of the Prime Minister, and he is answerable only to Parliament. A Select Committee of the House of Commons has been appointed to give him general advice on the performance of his functions, but the Select Committee does not consider individual cases, and is in no sense a court of appeal from the Commissioner.

Any person in the United Kingdom who considers himself aggrieved by some injustice occasioned to him as the consequence of an act of maladministration[84] at the hands of a Government Department subject to the jurisdiction of the P.C.A., may complain to a Member of Parliament (not necessarily his own constituency Member) and if the Member is satisfied that the matter appears to fall within the Commissioner's jurisdiction, he may with the complainant's consent send the complaint on to the P.C.A. The P.C.A. will then investigate the complaint, having first decided whether the case falls within his jurisdiction, as to which matter he is the sole judge.[85] In the course of his investigations he has very wide powers; he can call for the production of documents in the custody of a Minister of the Crown or any government department within his jurisdiction, with the sole exception of Cabinet documents. He can summon persons to appear before him and he can afford the complainant a hearing, although he is not obliged to do so. When his investigation is complete he will prepare a report in which he will state whether he finds there has been maladministration, and if so whether it has resulted in injustice to the complainant. He may also include a recommendation suggesting how any such injustice may be remedied, but in that event the government department concerned is not obliged to act on the recommendation.

The report will be sent to the Member of Parliament originating the complaint, and a copy sent to the government department concerned. Absolute privilege against proceedings in defamation will attach to these publications of the report, but not to any further occasions. Normally the Member of Parliament will forward the P.C.A.'s report to the complainant, but he is not obliged to do so. There is no procedure provided for in the Act whereby the press is notified of these reports, but the Member of Parliament or the complainant may inform the press, and the Commissioner now issues a quarterly summary of the cases he has decided, which is generally available to the public through H.M. Stationery Office.

It is difficult to appraise the work of the P.C.A. In the first place it must be appreciated that there are considerable limitations on his jurisdiction. He is concerned only with acts of maladministration, which in itself excludes judicial acts,[86] and not with discretionary decisions arrived at in a proper manner.[87] The act complained of must have been committed within the United Kingdom,[88] there must be no right of appeal to a court of law or to an administrative tribunal,[89] and the act must be the act of a department listed in the Second Schedule of the Act of 1967 and not specifically excluded by the Third Schedule thereto. Thus, the P.C.A. is concerned only with the departments of the central Government, not with public corporations,[90] or local authorities, and he is excluded from such matters as concern the Armed Forces of the Crown, the pay and conditions of service of civil servants, commercial contracts and the administration of the criminal law.

These are serious limitations on the Commissioner's activities. It is also sometimes considered a defect that a complainant should be obliged to route his complaint through a Member of Parliament, but perhaps this defect does not seem so serious when it is remembered that he may apply to any one or all of the 635 Members. What is more serious is the lack of effective publicity for the reports of the Commissioner. He claims that his existence has in itself improved the general standard of administration in Whitehall, but the press does not take any very considerable notice of his activities, and it may well be that many members of the public are not aware of his existence. Even after five years of operation many Members of Parliament were not aware of the limits of the jurisdiction of the P.C.A. and this is evidenced by the fact that according to the P.C.A.'s Annual Report for 1972, in that year no less than 318 complaints received by the Commissioner, out of a total of 596, were found by him to be outside his jurisdiction.

However, there is no doubt but that the institution has established itself in this country. In 1969 the P.C.A.'s jurisdiction was extended to include Northern Ireland,[91] and in the same year a separate officer, the Complaints Commissioner,[92] was established in Northern Ireland to investigate complaints against local authorities and other local bodies in that Province. The National Health Service was re-organized in Scotland in 1973[93] and in England in 1974,[94] and in each case a Commissioner was established to deal with complaints concerning the National Health Service.[95] H.M. Government has also announced that there are to be Commissioners for Local Administration seised with the duty of investigating complaints against local authorities in England and Wales (and, presumably, also in Scotland).

THE 1970s — PRESENT AND FUTURE

To continue our historical account, we must first note the developments of the early years of the 1970s, which in general took further the trends of the previous decade.

The Courts

The courts continued the process of defining and elaborating the doctrine of natural justice. The Privy Council had decided in 1964 that natural justice need not be observed in an ordinary employment situation where an employer was dismissing an employee, because the employee's appropriate remedy lay in contract;[96] nevertheless in 1971 the House of Lords held that where the employment was 'reinforced' by statute, as for example when dismissal can only be for cause laid down by statute, or where the statute prescribed a procedure that must be followed,[97] the principles of natural justice must be observed. The notion of 'fair play', a requirement of something less than natural justice, in circumstances when an administrative agency is deciding some matter affecting the interests of a citizen, to be detected in several cases decided in the latter years of the 1960s and referred to above, was taken further in the case of *re Liverpool Taxi Owners' Association*.[98] In this case, the Court of Appeal granted an order of prohibition against a local authority who proposed to exercise their discretionary licensing powers under the Town Police Clauses Act, 1847, to increase substantially the number of hackney carriages operating in the city. As a promise had been given to the effect that the number would not be increased until certain other action had been taken, it was held that the authority were not acting 'fairly' when they proposed to increase the number before that event had taken effect. If this case is followed, it may have a considerable effect on the manner in which local authorities exercise their discretionary powers.

Another decision in a very different field also may have far reaching effects for the future. In *Dutton v. Bognor Regis Building Co. Ltd.*[99] a builder had erected a house on what subsequently proved to have been insecure foundations; the house subsequently commenced to subside, and the then owner of the house sued the builder and also, of greater interest for present purposes, the local authority. The local authority were held liable in damages for the tort of negligence, because their building inspector had inspected the building work when it was in progress and had failed to prevent the construction of the building on unsatisfactory foundations, as the authority had power to do under the building by-laws then in force. It was argued that the authority could not be liable for failure to exercise a *power*, but the Court of Appeal held that the process of building work was under their *control* by virtue of the by-laws,[100] and they must therefore exercise that control with due care. Therefore they would be liable to any potential plaintiff who suffered damage as a consequence of a breach of that duty of care.

Statute law

As already mentioned, the Ombudsman principle has been extended by Acts of 1972 and 1973 to the National Health Service, and by the Local Government Act 1974 to local government. The jurisdiction of the industrial tribunals has been considerably extended by the Industrial Relations Act, 1971, and new tribunals organized on the presidential system have been established for the administration of Value Added Tax.[101] The tribunals hearing matters concerned with civil aviation were re-organized by the Civil Aviation Act, 1971.

Planning law

The turn of the decade has seen several developments in the rights of the individual to seek redress of grievances suffered as a consequence of some action by the local planning authority. These may be summarized as follows:

(a) Whilst the system of appeals to the Minister against a refusal of planning permission or the imposition of unpalatable conditions in a permission established by the Town and Country Planning Act 1947 remains virtually unchanged, the Act of the same name of 1968[102] and regulations made later thereunder, have modified the scheme in some respects. In a considerable number of such appeals the decision may now be taken by the inspector who conducted the hearing, on behalf of the Secretary of State (as he has now become). In important matters the Secretary of State may refer the appeal for the consideration of a specially constituted body of highly qualified experts, known as a Planning Inquiry Commission.[103]

(b) Largely as the result of a report of a Departmental Committee[104] issued in 1969 recent legislation has made more ample provision for public participation in the processes of planning. This particularly applies to the preparation of development plans,[105] and also to the specialized control over buildings of special architectural or historic interest and conservation areas.[106]

As the new style development plans introduced by the Act of 1968 have not yet been prepared by many authorities, the full effect of some of these provisions for public participation have not yet fully come into effect.

Consumer Protection

When shortly after the Second World War gas and electricity distribution were taken away from the administration of local authorities and private companies, and entrusted to new public corporations,[107] it was evidently considered desirable by the legislature to provide machinery for dealing with complaints from consumers. For this purpose, and so as to provide some continuing interest in these two industries for local authority members, the constituent statutes established consultation councils for each gas and electricity board, consisting partly of members of the relevant area boards and partly of members of local authorities, chambers of commerce and other local bodies, but all appointed by the Minister. These bodies acted in an advisory capacity, receiving complaints from members of the public and advising their respective boards on matters of current interest. As a means of ventilating or redressing grievances these bodies were never very satisfactory; they were, and still are, closely identified with the boards, their business was not sufficiently interesting to attract members of the highest calibre and very little publicity was given to their activities. Other consultative councils on a national basis were established for air transport,[108] for the railways[109] and for the coal industry.[110]

Nevertheless, in spite of the shortcomings of these bodies there has recently been renewed interest in the device. When the Post Office was turned into a public corporation in 1969, consumer councils were established on a country basis.[111] The Fair Trading Act 1973, following this trend and perhaps also the current popularity of the Ombudsman institution, and further fortified by the move for public participation in town and country planning already discussed, will establish customer advice centres, where members of the public will be able to take their enquiries and complaints about prices and quality of goods on retail sale in local shops.

The European Communities

The early years of the 1970 decade has seen the entry of the United Kingdom into the European Economic Communities. Within the present context this means that in a number of fields the validity of English legislation will fall to be measured against the Treaties and the legislation of the Commission and the Council of Ministers made thereunder. Moreover, any question of interpretation of the Treaty or legislation thereunder may be referred by any English court to the Court of the European Communities at Luxembourg and a court of 'last resort' (one from which no appeal will lie under English law)[112] is obliged to refer such a question of interpretation to Luxembourg. An individual can in certain circumstances take proceedings before the Luxembourg court. In the case of the Treaty of Rome, such a right of action is available to an individual or a corporate body if the proceedings challenge the validity of a decision of an institution of the Community which is directed to him or which is of direct concern to him;[113] in the case of the Coal and Steel Treaty the test of *locus standi* is somewhat wider.[114] Perhaps even more important, the existence of the Luxembourg court and its procedure, very considerably affected by French administrative law, will inevitably have some influence on the development of English law and may well make such proposals as those of the Law Commission and 'Justice' hereafter to be referred to, more likely to be readily acceptable.

Even before the entry into Europe, however, the United Kingdom had acceded to and ratified the European Convention on Human Rights. This entitles any British subject to appeal to the Commission and ultimately the Court at Strasbourg if any of his 'human rights', as defined in the Convention (for example, if he contends that he has been subjected to inhumane punishment or has not received a fair trial) have been infringed by the administration; but in any such proceedings the plaintiff must be able to establish that he has exhausted all domestic remedies available to him within the United Kingdom.

The Future

In 1971 the society known as 'Justice'[115] published a report entitled 'Administration under Law.'[116] This contained three principal recommendations for the reform of English administrative law and procedure, which may be summarized as follows:

(a) Parliament should enact 'principles of good administration', which should be observed as a framework for all government departments, local authorities, statutory undertakers and nationalized industries. These principles would expand and clarify the common law principles of natural justice,[117] and would be of general application.

(b) All administrative litigation should be concentrated into an Administrative Division of the High Court, which should develop a procedure whereby the Registrar would have power to investigate the facts and merits of the case and, in the absence of the plaintiff, to examine files.[118]

(c) There should also be a simple procedure for initiating proceedings by way of an originating summons, 'thereby obviating the need for the plaintiff to specify the remedy sought.'

This Report was shortly followed by a Working Paper from the Law Commission entitled 'Remedies in Administrative Law.'[119] By the terms of reference given by the Lord Chancellor, the Law Commission were not concerned to consider the matters covered by the first two recommendations of 'Justice' above mentioned, but their principal proposal was very similar to 'Justice's' third recommendation. This suggested that there should be 'a single remedy for judicial review of administrative action and orders,' to be known as an 'application for review.'[120]

At the time of writing it is impossible to say whether this or any other suggested reforms will be enacted in the near future, but the need for reform is obvious. The procedure of the courts in administrative matters follows that of ordinary civil actions, and the following disadvantages (among others) exist:

(a) it is very largely an accident of litigation which determines the forum of any particular dispute; proceedings may arise in the Chancery Division, before a Queen's Bench Divisional Court, on appeal from the Lands Tribunal in the Court of Appeal, before local magistrates, or before a County Court judge;

(b) the success or failure of a litigant taking proceedings against an administrative agency may turn on the type of proceedings (*certiorari*, declaration, injunction, action for damages, etc.) he has chosen to bring;

(c) the grounds on which proceedings may be brought are by no means clear; it is not even clear precisely when the principles of natural justice must be observed;

(d) a plaintiff seeking redress against the administration may well have difficulty in assessing the strength and nature of the case against him, perhaps owing to ignorance of administrative procedures generally.

The courts have on occasion adopted a broad interpretation of legislation,[121] but it is by no means certain that they will always be able to do this,[122] and most of the matters here discussed are clearly beyond the powers of the courts to reform, and must wait on legislation.

NOTES AND REFERENCES

1 For example the hospital, gas, electricity, or railway boards or the air corporations, the creation of which were one of the principal features of the period of post-war re-organization from 1945–50.

2 In *Lee v. Showman's Guild of Great Britain* [1952] 1 All E.R. 1175, at p. 1181.

3 *Pyx Granite Co. v. Minister of Housing and Local Government* [1959] 3 All E.R. 1, at p. 6.

4 *Ibid.*

5 National Insurance (Industrial Injuries) Act, 1946 (replacing the old law of 'Workmen's compensation').

6 National Insurance Act 1946.

7 Family Allowances Act, 1945.

8 Furnished Houses (Rent Control) Act, 1946.

9 In these cases the decision remained that of the Minister, arrived at after considering a report on the inquiry held by his inspector. Under the Town and Country Planning Act 1968, the inspector was, in a number of specified cases, required to make the decision on behalf of and in the name of the Minister. See now Town and Country Planning Act, 1971, Sched. 9.

10 For example, in national insurance and industrial injuries insurance.

11 For example, the decision of a Minister on a planning appeal; see now 1971 Act, section 36(6).

12 See, for example, the skeletal rules of procedure contained in the Schedule to the Furnished Houses (Rent Control) Act, 1946.

13 The Scrutiny Committee in the House of Commons, established in 1945 largely as a result of the recommendations of the Donoughmore Committee (1932), has never had time to examine more than a small proportion of the many statutory instruments made every year.

14 National Health Service Act, 1946, subsequently amended by the National Health Service Reorganisation Act 1973.

15 Statutory inquiries for planning appeal and objections to compulsory purchase orders, local valuation courts and the Lands Tribunal for valuation for rating, local insurance tribunals, furnished houses rent tribunals, the National Assistance Board, the licensing authority for road service vehicles and the Transport Tribunal, may be quoted as examples of the statutory activity of the period under review.

16 But this procedure would be avoided if the draftsman of the relevant enabling statute did not include a provision to the effect that the subordinate law making power was to be exercisable by 'statutory' instrument. Sub-delegated legislation also is not subject to the procedure of the 1946 Act: see *Patchett v. Leatham* [1949] 65 T.L.R. 69.

17 [1942] A.C. 206; later to be characterized by Lord Reid in *Ridge v. Baldwin* [1963] 2 All E.R. 66, at p. 76, as a 'very peculiar decision'.

18 [1942] 1 All E.R. 587; the law was subsequently changed by *Conway v. Rimmer* [1968] A.C. 910.

19 The blueprint for a new design of submarine.

20 [1951] A.C. 66.

21 As, for example, in *R. v. Minister of Transport, ex parte Upminster Services Ltd.* [1934] 1 K.B. 277.

22 *R. v. Agricultural Land Tribunal for Wales and Monmouth ex parte Davies* [1953] 1 All E.R. 1182, where the tribunal was not properly constituted.

23 See, for example, such old cases as *Cooper v. Wandsworth Board of Works* [1863] 14 C.B.N.S. 180, and *Osgood v. Nelson* [1872] L.R. 5 H.L. 636.

24 [1954] 2 All E.R. 118.

25 *R. v. Metropolitan Police Commissioner, ex parte Parker* [1953] 2 All E.R. 717.

26 Town and Country Planning Act, 1953.

27 Much in the way the publication of Lord Chief Justice Hewart's book, *The New Despotism* caused an outcry in 1929, and led to the Donoughmore Committee of 1930–32.

28 See account at [1954] J.P.L. 785.

29 After its chairman, Sir Oliver Franks, later Lord Franks.

30 The Crichel Down affair was really a better argument in favour of the establishment of an Ombudsman, but this institution was not to come for another ten years.

31 Provided for by s.9 of the Tribunals and Enquiries Act, 1958, and provisions in particular statutes, such as the Town and Country Planning Act, 1959.

32 Franks Report, paragraph 128.

33 Cmnd. 218.

34 Subsequently replaced by the consolidating Tribunals and Inquiries Act, 1971.

35 And an office in Edinburgh. The Franks Committee had recommended a separate Council for Scotland.

36 And subsequently added to by Order in Council; for an up to date list, see the Annual Reports of the Council on Tribunals.

37 An item added by the Town and Country Planning Act, 1959.

38 It was still only an approximation, as the method of valuation was (and is) based on existing use value, but in assessing that value the Lands Tribunal is entitled to take into account certain planning 'assumptions', which virtually bring the existing use up to the optimum use permissible under planning legislation (see now Land Compensation Acts, 1961 and 1973).

39 Including, since 1967, the Parliamentary Commissioner for Administration, *ex officio*.

40 See Annual Reports of the Council, and article by the present writer at [1965] P.L. 321.

41 The Tribunals and Inquiries (Discretionary Inquiries) Order, 1967 (S.I., 1967, No. 451) has been made under this Act, bringing a considerable number of inquiries which are discretionary, in the sense that the Minister has a discretion whether or not to hold one in particular circumstances, within the supervision of the Council on Tribunals.

42 Mental Health Act 1969.

43 Rent Act, 1965, later consolidated with earlier legislation in the Rent Act, 1968.

44 Betting, Gaming and Lotteries Act, 1963.

45 Immigration Act, 1971.

46 Plant Varieties and Seeds Act, 1964.

47 Industrial Training Act, 1964.

48 Redundancy Payments Act, 1965.

49 Contracts of Employment Acts, 1964 and 1971.

50 Redundancy Payments Act, 1965, s.44, and Seventh Schedule.

51 Docks and Harbours Act, 1966.

52 Industrial Relations Act, 1971.

53 See *Administrative Law*, by the present author (4th edn.), Ch. VII.

54 *R. v. Criminal Injuries Compensation Board, ex parte Lain* [1967] 2 All E.R. 770.

55 [1911] A.C. 179.

56 [1942] A.C. 206; *ante*, para. 1.

57 [1958] 2 All E.R. 23 (on appeal from Cyprus).

58 [1964] A.C. 40.

59 [1963] 1 Q.B. 539.

60 *Lee v. Secretary of State for Education and Science* [1967] 111 Sol. Jo. 756.

61 *Kanda v. Government of Federation of Malaya* [1962] A.C. 322; *Maradana Mosque Trustees v. Mahmud* [1966] 1 All E.R. 545.

62 *Pett v. Greyhound Racing Association (No. 1)* [1968] 2 All E.R. 545; *Pett v. Greyhound Racing Association (No. 2)* [1969] 2 All E.R. 221; *Enderby Town Football Club v. Football Association* [1971] 1 All E.R. 215.

63 *Taylor v. National Union of Seamen* [1967] 1 All E.R. 767; and see *Breen v. Amalgamated Engineering Union* [1971] 1 All E.R. 1148.

64 *R. v. Senate of University of Aston, ex parte Roffey* [1969] 2 All E.R. 964; *Glyn v. Keele University* [1971] 2 All E.R. 89.

65 *Ridge v. Baldwin* (*supra*), but contrast *Vidyodaya University of Ceylon v. Silva* [1964] 3 All E.R. 865.

66 *Nagle v. Fielden* [1966] 1 All E.R. 689; but see now Industrial Relations Act, 1971, s.65.

67 *Taylor v. National Union of Seamen* (*supra*).

68 *re Godden* [1971] 3 All E.R. 20.

69 *Metropolitan Properties Co. v. Lannon* [1968] 3 All E.R. 304.

70 [1967] 1 All E.R. 226.

71 *R. v. Birmingham City Justice, ex parte Chris Foreign Foods (Wholesalers) Ltd.* [1970] 3 All E.R. 945.

72 *Breen v. Amalgamated Engineering Union* [1971] 1 All E.R. 1148.

73 *Wiseman v. Bornemann* [1969] 3 All E.R. 275.

74 *Stringer v. Minister of Housing and Local Government* [1971] 1 All E.R. 65.

75 See the judgment of Devlin, L. J., in *Merchandise Transport v. British Transport Commission* [1961] 3 All E.R. 495, and *British Oxygen Co. Ltd. v. Minister of Technology* [1970] 3 All E.R. 165.

76 See the remarks of their Lordships in the House of Lords in *Malloch v. Aberdeen Corporation* [1971] 2 All E.R. 1278; but Lord Denning argued to the contrary in the Privy Council case of *Amnamunthudo v. Oilfield Workers Trade Union* [1961] 3 All E.R. 621.

77 See *Durayappah v. Fernando* [1967] 2 A.C. 337, where the Privy Council refused a remedy in a clear case of breach of natural justice, solely on the ground of the plaintiff's lack of *locus standi*.

78 Thus, in *Punton v. Ministry of National Insurance (No. 2)* [1964] 1 All E.R. 448, the plaintiff was refused a declaration in a case where the court held that a *certiorari* would have been more appropriate.

79 [1968] 1 All E.R. 694.

80 [1969] 1 All E.R. 208.

81 Contrast *Smith v. East Elloe R.D.C.* [1956] A.C. 736.

82 See *British Oxygen Co. Ltd. v. Minister of Technology* [1970] 3 All E.R. 165, and *Westminster Bank Ltd. v. Minister of Housing and Local Government* [1970] 1 All E.R. 734.

83 For a full account of the history of the Ombudsman idea in Britain, see F. A. Stacey, *The British Ombudsman*, Oxford, 1971.

84 An expression not defined in the Act, but which has come to be understood in the terms used in the House of Commons by Mr. Richard Crossman, M.P., as 'bias, neglect, inattention, delay, incompetence, ineptitude, perversity, turpitude, arbitrariness and so on'.

85 Parliamentary Commissioner Act, 1967, s.5(2).

86 Of, for example, a tribunal. As the P.C.A. is an *ex officio* member of the Council on Tribunals, there is a link between the respective jurisdictions of the two institutions.

87 Parliamentary Commissioner Act, 1967, section 12(3).

88 *Ibid.*, section 6(4).

89 *Ibid.*, section 5(2), unless the Commissioner considers it would be unreasonable to have expected the complainant to pursue such a right.

90 Except for the Decimal Currency Board and the Intervention Board of Agricultural Produce, which have been expressly brought within his jurisdiction.

91 Parliamentary Commissioner Act (N.I.) 1969.

92 Commissioner for Complaints Act (N.I.) 1969. This statute went further than the English prototype, in that it authorizes a member of the public whom the Commissioner has found to have been the victim of injustice caused by some act of maladministration, to sue the offending local authority, etc., for damages and/or an injunction.

93 National Health Service (Scotland) Act, 1972.

94 National Health Service Reorganisation Act, 1973.

95 It has been announced that the existing P.C.A. (Sir Alan Marre) is to hold his office in plurality with those of Health Service Commissioners for England and Wales and for Scotland.

96 *Vidyodaya University v. Silva* [1964] 3 All E.R. 865.

97 *Malloch v. Aberdeen Corporation* [1971] 2 All E.R. 1278.

98 [1972] 2 All E.R. 589.

99 [1972] 1 Q.B. 373.

100 See now Building Regulations, 1972, made under the Public Health Acts, 1936 and 1961.

101 Finance Act 1972.

102 Now replaced by the consolidating Town and Country Planning Act, 1971.

103 Town and Country Planning Act, 1971, s. 47.

104 The Report of the Skeffington Committee, *People and Planning*.

105 Town and Country Planning Act, 1971, Part II.

106 Provisions dealing with these matters are to be found in the Civic Amenities Act, 1968, the Town and Country Planning Act, 1968, and the Town and Country Planning (Amendment) Act, 1972.

107 Electricity Act, 1947; Gas Act, 1948.

108 Civil Aviation Act, 1949.

109 Transport Act, 1948.

110 Coal Industry Nationalization Act, 1948.

111 Post Office Act, 1969, establishing a National 'Users' council', and country Councils for Scotland, for Wales and Monmouthshire and for Northern Ireland.

112 Treaty of Rome, article 177.

113 *Ibid.*, article 173; Euratom Treaty, art. 146.

114 Coal and Steel Community Treaty, arts. 33 and 80.

115 An all-party organization of lawyers, affiliated to the International Commission of Jurists.

116 Published by Stevens.

117 The suggested Principles are set out as a Code in the Report, and owe something for their origin to the French *principes generaux du droit.*

118 This idea also is borrowed in part from the procedure of the French administrative courts, also followed by the Court of the European Communities at Luxembourg.

119 Published Working Paper No. 40, issued 11 October 1971.

120 This again has similarities with the procedure of the French administrative courts.

121 As in *Padfield v. Minister of Agriculture, Fisheries and Food*, and *Anisminic v. Foreign Compensation Commission* (*supra*).

122 See, for example, *Westminster Bank Ltd. v. Minister of Housing and Local Government*, and *British Oxygen Co. Ltd. v. Minister of Technology* (*supra*).

The Nationalized Industries   7

W. Thornhill, M.Sc. (Econ.)

The nationalized industries constituted a new element in post-war British government. Although there were some forms of national public enterprise before 1939, such as the British Broadcasting Corporation, the Central Electricity Board, the London Passenger Transport Board and Imperial Airways, in the immediate post-war years the nationalization programme of the Labour Government brought the Bank of England into public ownership and created vast undertakings for whole industries which were taken over from their existing proprietors. These were managed by new bodies created on the conceptual model embodied in the B.B.C., which had been described by Lord Reith as the public corporation.[1]

The National Coal Board took over the coal mines and a large number of other activities, some ancillary to coal production, others not, in 1947. The generation and distribution of electricity became the responsibility of the British Electricity Authority and 14 area boards in 1948. The North of Scotland Hydro-Electric Board which had been established in 1944 remained as a separate body, but the two area boards established in 1948 in southern Scotland, and their associated generating facilities, were re-organized into a new South of Scotland Electricity Board in 1955. The British Transport Commission and its operating Executives for Railways, Docks and Inland Waterways, Road Transport (soon separated into Road Haulage and Road Passenger services), London Transport and Hotels, took over on 1 January 1948 the entire railway and canal systems, most of the docks, the London passenger transport system, many road passenger undertakings and most of the road freight industry operating for hire. A large number of gas undertakings were taken over in 1949 by 12 area gas boards, supported by a central Gas Council. The final element in the Labour Government's programme was the creation of the Iron and Steel Corporation of Great Britain in 1950 to take over the ownership of the major steel producing companies; this had a short but controversial life and all but one of the companies were resold to private ownership by the Conservative Government which took office in 1951.

The nationalization programme of the Labour Government between 1945 and 1951 was largely a political jamboree, in which the noisy celebrations obscured the serious problems of the country's primary industrial base: energy, transport and communications. The impact of the new form of administration

141

on these problems is discussed in the later parts of this chapter, but before doing so the concentrated activity of this period of six years and three months must be examined in its historical perspective. The Labour Government, and the Labour Party which motivated it, invented neither public enterprise nor the particular form of organization, the public corporation, which they used for the nationalized industries. Nor did the return of a Conservative Government in 1951 lead to a wholesale reversion to private enterprise. Its attempt to de-nationalize the publicly owned iron and steel companies was never completed, whilst the attempt to sell the road freight transport undertakings was abortive. On the other hand, in addition to restructuring the inland transport and the electricity industries, Conservative governments have added Independent Television (now renamed Independent Broadcasting, to embrace local radio as well as television) and the aero-engine side of the former Rolls-Royce company. The Labour Government of 1964–70 was less venturesome. It re-nationalized iron and steel; transformed our second oldest public enterprise, the Post Office, from a government department to a public corporation; and set up the British Airports Authority to take over the already government owned international airports at Heathrow, Gatwick, Prestwich and Stansted.

This list of undertakings shows a remarkable concentration on activities concerned with energy and communications. These have for many decades been described as public utilities, and they are now regarded almost axiomatically as services essential to the daily conduct of a complex industrial society. On the fringes there are undertakings in which the state has either a controlling or a significant minority interest, which either do not fall into the energy/communications group or are not managed by the public corporation type of organization. British Petroleum, and a large number of relatively small companies in which the Government has shareholdings, are examples. So were the State Management Districts which owned and managed the public houses in the areas around Carlisle, Gretna and Cromarty for over 60 years from the First World War. The nationalized iron and steel undertaking has been a more marginal case, owing more to socialist dogma than any of the others. Yet even here there is the beginning of a new strain of public enterprise, also exhibited in the takeover of the aero-engine side of Rolls-Royce as well as in the countless forms of financial aid provided by successive governments, Conservative and Labour alike, to privately owned industries in all fields to encourage modernization, relocation into development areas, or production for export. The latter development seems to indicate that there is no longer any particularly desirable advantage in public ownership and management of the public corporation variety.

Such a conclusion can well be reached by another route. The Acts of Parliament which provided for nationalization and created the new institutions subscribed to a concept which was never adequately defined, and never understood by the architects of the legislation nor by the politicians and administrators who were subsequently engaged in running the new institutions. The idea of the public corporation was expressed by John Reith to the Crawford Committee on

Broadcasting in 1926 as a body 'acting as a trustee for the national interest'. Herbert Morrison, who is generally regarded as the mastermind behind the Labour Government's nationalization activities, saw the public corporation as a means of combining public responsibility with freedom for commercial administration. These crude views were inadequate as a basis for the translation of the concept of the public corporation into accepted and effective practices. The first difficulties in applying the concept came to light with the struggles over Parliamentary control which began in the late 1940s and were only eased, but not solved, by the setting up of the Select Committee on Nationalized Industries in 1956. Confirmation of the inadequacy of the original ideas came with the development from 1961 onwards of methods of control and appraisal as checks on the efficiency and performance of the undertakings. Indeed, writing in *The Times* on 26 March 1966 Reith recognized that his original trusteeship concept had not developed in the post-war institutions, and he called for the creation of a Royal Commission to examine 'the public corporation system of management' and to promulgate 'a common administrative doctrine'.

There can be no doubt that in the two decades since 1955 the nationalized industries have been subjected to many interventions by governments concerned to ensure that these large undertakings, whether measured in terms of workers employed or capital invested, pursue their business in a manner which does not rock the Government boat. Successively, governments have extended and improved the controls which they exercise over the capital borrowing, investment, pricing policies and, more recently, wages policies of the industries. At the same time, within the parameters set by these controls, the managing boards have been continually pressed to act in a normal commercial manner in those matters of trading which are still left to them. During this period, privately owned industry has also been increasingly subjected to governmental influence in the same areas. As a result, the nationalized industries have lost much of their conceptual difference from private industry, and it has become difficult to see them as anything other than large firms which happen to be owned by the Government.

It is this fact of public ownership which gives rise to one of the major difficulties. The Reith/Morrison concept seemed to imply an area of non-intervention by governments in the affairs of the public industries, and a somewhat idealized regard for public responsibility on the part of the industry managers. This idyllic state has not been attained, primarily because the industries are too large and essential to escape being a political football. The ideological differences between the Labour and Conservative Parties have been of less significance than the views taken of the social and economic roles of the industries. There is much evidence to show that politicians in general, and the members of the House of Commons in particular, have not been willing to let the nationalized industries escape the full ramifications of public scrutiny which are normally applied to ordinary governmental functions. Governments of both parties have been quite ready to exert their powers over the industries to further what they have regarded as legitimate political objectives. The management of the economy has been the most plausible reason for governments to use to justify their activities in this regard, and it has been difficult to gainsay the fact that these industries are significant economically. Yet the wisdom of individual actions, whether for political or economic purposes, has sometimes been questionable; and public doubts on this score have often been reinforced by the secretive manner in which the Government has exerted its influence.

Most of the developments of the nationalized industries over the past quarter of a century owe more to pragmatism than to principle. There is practically nothing in the achievements of this period which can be said to have been derived from Reith's original concept of the public corporation as a trustee acting in the public interest. This view will become obvious as we examine the main developments of the period.

ORGANIZATION

None of the major industries has escaped structural re-organization since the original nationalization structure was established. There has been no single cause, each reconstruction having been due to the particular circumstances of the industry involved.

The coal industry has sustained the least institutional change, since only the National Coal Board itself was created by statute. The 980 coal mines which were taken over from more than 800 colliery companies, together with a wide range of ancillary activities, were grouped into 48 areas, and these in turn were supervised by eight divisional coal boards. Although there were subsequent alterations at area level, this basic structure continued in existence until March 1967. By this date, the number of collieries in operation had been reduced to 438 as a result of rationalization and the falling demand for coal. The National Coal Board then adopted a simplified structure. The divisional coal boards were abolished, and so were the posts of area general manager. A new post of Divisional Chairman was created, to form a link between the National Coal Board and the areas. The latter, which numbered 38 in 1966, were re-organized into 17 new areas, each in charge of a Director accountable to the Board.

In the electricity industry, in addition to the North of Scotland Hydro-Electric Board which had been established in 1944, the nationalized industry consisted of a central body called the British (later renamed Central) Electricity Authority, which was responsible for the generating stations and the main transmission lines, and 14 area electricity boards which were responsible for distribution to consumers. Together they took over 558 separate undertakings. The two area boards which operated in Scotland were reconstituted in 1955 as the South of Scotland Electricity Board and joined the North of Scotland Hydro-Electric Board as the responsibility of the Secretary of State for Scotland. The Central Authority also had overall control over the development and finances of the industry in England, but the Herbert Committee[2] which investigated the industry in 1954/6 thought that the Authority's supervisory activity should be separated from its executive responsibility for the generation of electricity. To give effect to this view, the Electricity Act 1957 abolished the Central Electricity Authority as from 1 January 1958 and transferred responsibility for the generating stations and the national 'grid' to a new body, the Central Electricity Generating Board. The advisory role and the task of co-ordinating and supervising the industry was placed in the hands of a new Electricity Council. Ten years later there was much support, on grounds of improving technical efficiency, for the idea of abolishing the Generating Board and transferring the generating stations to the area boards. Though it once seemed likely that this further change would be achieved, it failed to get implemented due to the lack of Parliamentary time for the necessary legislation.

The gas industry's structure on nationalization bore a superficial resemblance to that of the electricity industry, and consisted of a central Gas Council and 12 area gas boards which took over 1037 gas undertakings from 991 proprietors. Unlike the situation in electricity, the area gas boards were responsible both for the production of gas and its distribution, whilst the Gas Council had a very limited role of advising the Minister, securing co-ordination between the area boards and dealing with capital borrowing and wage negotiations for the industry as a whole. Given the state of gas technology at that time, there was little for the industry to look forward to beyond a rationalization of its system in a climate in which its prospects in the fuel market were not rosy. After a decade of consolidating the undertakings which had been taken over, techno-logical progress changed the industry's outlook remarkably. The development of long-distance transmission systems made it possible to concentrate gas manufac-ture into larger and more efficient units just in time for the industry to break away from coal as its major, if not sole, raw material, by making use of oil feedstocks and imported liquefied natural gas. The industry had just begun to deal with these developments when natural gas was discovered under the North Sea. The new production techniques required for this had to be accommodated into the industry's organization; there were three alternatives—leaving the area boards to cope with the new sources, creating a 13th board specially for this purpose, or allowing the Gas Council to deal with the problem. The third course was chosen, and the Gas Act 1965 gave powers to the Gas Council to enable it to produce, distribute and store gas on a national scale. In 1973, the next logical step was taken of abolishing the separate area boards and the Gas Council, and creating a single organization known as the British Gas Corporation for the whole industry.

Inland transport has had the most tortured organizational history. Originally, the industry was managed by a two-tier structure consisting of the British Trans-port Commission, responsible for high level policy, the creation of an integrated transport system, and the co-ordination and control of the second tier of Executives, created by statute and responsible for the operation of different transport activities: railways, docks and inland waterways, road haulage, road passenger services, hotels and London transport. The creation of an integrated transport system proved to be an impossible task; it had been assumed to be the answer to the inter-war competition between road and rail, but post-war the effective competition was between public transport and the privately-owned vehicle, whether for freight or persons. 'Integration' was of limited application, anyway; it was irrelevant, for example, to the services for London commuters and freight traffic on the canals. Another difficulty arose from the failure of the Commission to continue with the progressive takeover of road passenger undertakings after the original nationalization date. Although the Transport Commission acquired the road passenger undertakings which were subsidiaries of the nationalized electricity companies, it encountered some brisk opposition in local areas to the early schemes which it promoted for the acquisition of further undertakings and these were not proceeded with. Soon afterwards, a Conservative Government came to power with the electoral promise to return to private ownership the road haulage services. When the attempt to do this turned out to be abortive, because of a dearth of prospective buyers at acceptable prices, the Government decided to simplify the organization. The Transport Act 1953 abolished all the operating Executives except that for London Transport, and the Commission assumed full management responsibility. It was under a statutory duty to operate the railways through area railway boards, but was free to establish its own management units for the other activities.

This reconstruction served at least to demonstrate that the railways were to be the Achilles' heel of a single inland transport organization. Far from the Commission being able to create an integrated inland transport system, it soon became clear that the problems of the railways were dominating the work of the Commission to the disadvantage of other services. The railway modernization plan published in 1954,[3] which was aided by generous financial help authorized in 1957 and supplemented in 1959, failed to achieve the hoped-for goal of financial viability, and it became clear that the structure of the industry needed radical revision. This was achieved by the Transport Act 1962, which disbanded the British Transport Commission and distributed its services to five new organizations. The railways together with the hotels and catering services became the responsibility of the British Railways Board; docks and harbour undertakings were transferred to the British Transport Docks Board; canals and navigable waters, with some associated harbours, to the British Waterways Board; London transport to the London Transport Board; and the wide variety of road haulage, shipping, travel and road passenger services to the Transport Holding Company. The London Transport Board was abolished in 1972 when the London transport undertaking was transferred to the Greater London Council. The Transport Holding Company has also been abolished: the road haulage and shipping activities, and the road passenger services having their own separate organizations—British Road Services, the National Bus Company and the Scottish Bus Group. Thomas Cook and Son Ltd., into which the various travel services were consolidated, has now been sold to private enterprise.

Civil aviation has suffered less organizational change than inland transport.

When civil aviation was resumed after the Second World War it was managed by three separate operating bodies as from 1946. British European Airways was established to operate services to Europe and within the British Isles; British South American Airways operated to the South American continent; and British Overseas Airways Corporation operated services throughout the remainder of the world, having been established in 1940 as successor to the former Imperial Airways and British Airways. Largely because of trading difficulties, the viability of the South American line soon became questionable, and the undertaking was merged with B.O.A.C. at the end of July 1949. The two remaining airlines continued to enjoy their separate existence for the next two decades before the desirability of their merger was raised. The creation of a major 'second force' airline in the private sector in 1970 as part of the effort to improve British competitiveness in the international sphere; the desirability of meeting passenger convenience by the two state-owned lines providing continuous services; and the likely economic and management advantages to be obtained from a single organization, were the basic arguments supporting the case for a merger. This was achieved in two stages. The first was the creation of a new body, the British Airways Corporation, to act as a holding company and to promote a joint trading image. The second was in 1974 when B.E.A. and B.O.A.C. were wound up so as to leave the new British Airways Corporation as the sole state-owned airline.

The two remaining major industries need only a brief mention. The conversion of the Post Office from a government department to a public corporation had no statutory organizational consequences below the level of top management. On the other hand, the renationalization of the steel industry produced internal organizational problems, the original territorial grouping of the companies which were taken over giving way to a structure based on product groups.

REVENUE FINANCE

Few people have questioned the implicit assumption that the nationalized industries should *sell* their products or services, as distinct from a system in which their costs would be met out of taxation and their products would be distributed free of charge to consumers on some form of assessment of need. Though such a totalitarian arrangement might appeal to an ultra socialist, 'nationalization' as we know it has been supported by those who, following the mild concepts of Fabian public enterprise, saw advantages flowing from the removal of the capitalist owners of public utility services, rather than by those who appreciated the greater socialist virtue of government control of basic industries as a means of managing the economy and of securing distributive justice. Consequently, most nationalization statutes were primarily concerned with replacing the private shareholder, or in some cases a local authority, by the state as the owner. Another important objective in some cases, was the creation of a new unified organizational structure to replace the large number of previously separate undertakings; such was the case with coal, electricity and gas. Thirdly, there was the other major problem of bringing an industry within the ambit of governmental and Parliamentary control in order to secure the 'public responsibility' element of the public corporation concept. Most of the remaining provisions in the statutes were subsidiary to these major aims. This is true of the financial provisions, both capital and revenue. Experience in this area during the last 25 years has shown how the absence of any accepted principle has exposed the industries to the expediency of government action, denied to the managing boards adequate opportunities for the practice of the skills of financial management, and has gone a long way towards the use of political processes rather than customer relations to influence price movements and investment activities.

Most of the industries have been subject to a common formula which requires them to arrange their finances so that their income is not less than their outgoings properly chargeable to revenue, taking one year with another. Outgoings chargeable to revenue include interest on and provision for the redemption of capital loans, as well as provision for the depreciation of assets. In some cases, too, there have been additional financial requirements, such as to establish a reserve fund and, in the case of the gas industry an additional central guarantee fund. Though there are some financial and economic questions which might be raised about these provisions, it is the general implication of the basic formula which has had the greatest significance. First of all, it is necessary to dispel some popular misconceptions about the formula, which have at times affected political attitudes towards the industries. It is not a 'break-even' formula and it does not proscribe the making of a profit. The break-even or non-profitmaking view was firmly dispelled when the 1961 White Paper *The Financial and Economic Obligations of the Nationalized Industries* (Cmnd. 1337) introduced the financial targets as objectives for the earning of a surplus related to the capital employed in the industries. What the formula does imply is that over a sequence of years there shall be no deficit on revenue account, and the presumption is that if a deficit does occur then remedial action will be taken to make it up.

Unfortunately, this theory of the financial formula has not worked very well. The scope for continuous improvements in efficiency is not unlimited, and their attainment is often difficult in practice even when the potentiality clearly exists. The Herbert Committee which examined the electricity industry pointed out that in spite of having attained a regular annual surplus, the electricity industry still showed scope for improved efficiency. In the coal industry, in spite of frequent deficits, efficiency as measured in terms of output per man-shift has continually improved over the years, due to new capital investment and the concentration of production into the more productive mines. The circumstances of the individual industries have differed—coal has experienced a huge contraction (though in 1974 it looks as though there is to be some re-expansion); the railways have lost a lot of track mileage, much of it little used; gas has encountered two technological revolutions in quick succession; and electricity has enjoyed a widening of its sources of power from coal alone (with a little water power) to oil, natural

gas and atomic energy as well. Yet all of them have experienced the almost
continuous inflation of the post-war years and this, coupled with the political
environment in which the financial practices of the industries have been
conducted, has made nonsense of the general formula.

Once the advantages of increased efficiency have been exploited, industries in
an inflationary situation must increase prices in order to avoid lapsing into
deficit. Some industries have encountered particular restraints against price
increases. The National Coal Board encountered difficulties in a number of
attempts to increase coal prices because it was held to be bound by an agreement,
made during the Second World War between the Government and the colliery
owners, not to increase coal prices without the consent of the Government. In
consequence, the Board sustained a deficit on its operations in some years. The
British Transport Commission was originally under an obligation to charge
fares and freight rates in accordance with a scheme which had to be approved
by a judicial body known as the Transport Tribunal. The fact that the Tribunal
spent nearly two years investigating the Commission's proposals and hearing
objections to them, did not save the Government from embarrassment nor the
country from a political fracas when the increased railway fares were put into
operation in the spring of 1953. The functions of the Tribunal were later
amended to the fixing of maximum charges and, except for passenger fares in
the London area, its controlling role over transport charges to the public was
abolished at the end of 1962.

Some general restraints have affected all industries. Firstly, the consumers'
consultative councils have had a watchdog role but, except for the one moment
of glory when the council for the area of the South Western Gas Board temporarily upset a price increase because of an alleged defect in the procedure used
by the Board, these bodies have not generally been able to exercise any restraint.
Exceptionally, the Post Office Users' National Council has been successful in
this area; in 1970 it managed to secure a letter of direction from the Minister
of Posts and Telecommunications to prevent the Post Office from making some
increases in postal rates which the Council considered to be unjustified. Over the
last ten years, however, with the country suffering price increases at an ever
increasing rate, all the nationalized industries have encountered a general
political concern, expressed both in Parliament and in the country, at their
attempts to increase prices. Apart from attempting to cover increases in their
production and other costs, they encountered suspicion when it became apparent
that a part of their case for price increases was the necessity placed upon them,
as a consequence of the policy expressed in the 1961 White Paper, to attain their
'target' earnings. The immediate consequence was the Labour Government's
decision in 1967 to refer applications from the nationalized industries for price
increases to the National Board for Prices and Incomes; but the Board was also
requested to review the efficiency of the industries when considering such applications, a power which it did not possess in regard to the private sector. The
Select Committee on Nationalized Industries, which was at the time of this
6

decision conducting its inquiry into ministerial control[4] of the industries, expressed caution about the wisdom of this additional investigation of the industries. It seemed likely that the Board's new role would be subject to increasing criticism, not least from the industries themselves. In the event, the Board only had the opportunity to make a few investigations, and did not have the time to make a serious attempt at the efficiency problem, before it was abolished by the Conservative Government which took office in 1970. The respite from price supervision was, however, only temporary, as the industries were brought within the jurisdiction of the Prices Commission which was set up towards the end of 1972. By this time, the Government had already prevailed upon the nationalized industries in general to refrain during an indefinite period of 'price restraint' from seeking the full extent of price increases they might otherwise have done. Some of the industries which incurred deficits as a consequence —electricity, gas, and the Post Office—were recompensed by special payments from the Exchequer in respect of the five-year period from 1970/71 to 1974/75.

Revenue financing has also been affected by a number of other decisions taken since the 1961 White Paper was published. Another White Paper was published in 1967, *Nationalized Industries: A Review of Economic and Financial Objectives* (Cmnd. 3437), to meet some of the defects attributable to the earlier document, especially that of attaining financial targets by raising prices. This tightened the financial framework, by requiring the application of discounted cash flow techniques to major investment programmes. In regard to pricing policy, the principle was laid down that revenues should normally cover their accounting costs in full, and additionally that pricing policies should be related to the actual costs of goods and services in order to avoid hidden cross-subsidization and the consequent misallocation of resources. The aim was to ensure that consumers generally should pay the true costs of providing the goods and services to be enjoyed. The White Paper then went on to advocate the advantages of marginal costing in some circumstances; but the subsequent inflationary spiral produced unpropitious circumstances for this aspect of the new policy to be followed to any great extent.

The principle of relating prices to the actual costs of particular goods and services had wider significance, especially for the railways which had for many decades worked on the principle of average pricing. The Select Committee on Nationalized Industries had repeatedly criticized the inadequacy of the accounting systems in some industries, and in particular in the railways, as a result of which it was impossible to identify the costs attributable to particular groups of customers. This was a serious problem when the possibility of government subsidization of revenues was discussed. The Select Committee, and many other critics, were not in favour of blanket subsidies to cover annual deficits, principally because these would make it difficult to assess efficiency because of the impossibility of separating the ordinary commercial activities which paid their way from those uneconomic activities which were kept on for social and public reasons. The Select Committee's discussion of these ideas in the course of its inquiry into ministerial control coincided with the Labour Government's activity in shaping a new public transport policy, which was eventually enshrined in the Transport Act 1968. This Act introduced the policy of fixed Exchequer subsidies, provided for limited periods and then subject to review with regard to renewal or revision, for specific railway services which operated at a loss but were considered to be necessary on social grounds. The basic idea is that the cost of the social element is evaluated and used as the prime element in the calculation of the subsidy; in this way, assessment of the efficiency of the remaining commerical element in the operation of the service becomes more of a possibility.

The statutory financial formula has thus ceased to have any purpose. Its original intent was vague in any case; the proscription of regular and unredeemed deficits, considered over an unspecified number of years, was the only point which was clear. Financial out-turn has now been relegated to the role of a residual calculation whose only purpose is to provide the final component in a clearing-up operation in which the Government periodically wipes the slate clean, as it has done for example with the railway and coal industries by cancelling accumulated deficits and, more rarely, by taking out for the benefit of the Exchequer a regular surplus, as with Independent Television. What is now significant for the management of revenue financing is the use of devices such as the financial targets and capital investment appraisal techniques, which might be termed 'substitute-market' factors, with the aim of improving the measurement of commercial activity. Equally important also, are the revenue subsidies which, by taking the public service factor out of the argument, free the commercial tests from complication by social considerations.

CAPITAL FINANCE

With the exception of the National Coal Board, all the major industries were endowed at nationalization with the power to raise capital on long-term borrowing by public issues of stock. Their original capital was the stock issued to satisfy the compensation provisions of the nationalization statutes (there were some exceptions to this general rule as, for example, in the case of the Bank of England whose shareholders were recompensed by Treasury Stock whilst the Government, through the Treasury Solicitor, became the legal owner of the Bank of England Stock). Short-term borrowing was also permitted by various means, including bank overdrafts. The latter have been used extensively, not only to meet requirements for working capital, but also as the immediate source of funds for investment programmes; the overdrafts are from time to time repaid from the proceeds of the periodic long-term issues.

The National Coal Board was never given the right to make public stock issues, presumably because it was considered at the time of nationalization to have too gloomy a future. All its capital for both long- and short-term purposes was provided by the Exchequer. The Board had a limited ability to borrow on bank overdraft. The Exchequer provided the compensation payments and the capital moneys needed for new investment out of its ordinary transactions and did not issue any stock specifically related to the National Coal Board.

In 1956 the Chancellor of the Exchequer decided that the transport, electricity, gas and airways corporations would be barred from raising new capital by public stock issues for a period of two years. Instead, their long-term capital would be provided by the Exchequer through the appropriate Minister. The temporary embargo received the approbation of the Radcliffe Committee on the Working of the Monetary System in 1959 and was renewed from time to time. It still continues in operation, modified only by the innovation, first begun in 1969, of allowing (and later encouraging) the raising of loans in overseas markets. The cessation of public stock issues was considered necessary by the Chancellor in order to maintain 'discipline' in the capital market. There were two possible causes of indiscipline. The first concerned the mechanics of the market in handling these stock issues. The Bank of England regulated access to the market by would-be borrowers, but the requirements of the nationalized industries were so extensive that they could not be kept in the queue indefinitely; their need for capital was determined by the rate of their capital investment, not by the state of the capital market. They could not be allowed to run up bank overdrafts excessively. The scale of the stock issues, however, and the subsequent repayment of the overdrafts produced technical problems of their own for the monetary system. The other cause of indiscipline arose from the status of the securities issued by the industries. The statutes which authorized the public issues of stock also enabled the Treasury, if it thought fit, to guarantee the stock as to payment of interest and repayment of capital. All the public stock issues were in fact so guaranteed. The effect was not only to remove the normal commercial test that an industry should be able to raise new capital on the strength of the market rating of its own credit-worthiness, but it also elevated the stocks to the status of gilt-edged securities. The consequence was to improve their marketability; and although the funding of the bank overdrafts by long-term securities was theoretically deflationary, the status of the stocks was such as to return an inflationary element to the system because they were regarded by the money market institutions which held them as part of their 'near cash' assets, thus increasing the credit base.

The transfer of capital borrowing to the Exchequer had its own consequences. Though the provision of capital funds did not in theory have any effect on the capital investment programmes, since these were approved at an earlier stage in the time scale and involved different officials, one cannot be entirely certain that in the long run decisions on capital investment programmes were taken without any regard for the economic significance of the eventual financial transactions. The more certain result of borrowing from the Exchequer was the inability of the boards of the industries to exercise any financial expertise in providing for their capital needs, due to the rigidity of the loan arrangements and the repayment processes. A number of boards complained to the Select Committee about the laborious and inflexible arrangements associated with capital advances from the Exchequer. Not only did the inflexibility of the Exchequer loan arrangements make it difficult for the industries to practise good financial administration, but they were prevented, by being tied to the Exchequer as the sole external source of capital finance, from shopping around for capital on the most advantageous terms.

Whatever case there might have been for the 1956 decision to transfer borrowing to the Exchequer—and in retrospect it is doubtful whether the reasons then put forward were soundly based—there was no such case ten years later. Yet the Treasury was still wedded to Exchequer financing, largely one suspects for the added influence, if not control, which it enabled the Government to exercise over the industries. The system came under fire from the Conservatives on the simple argument that, since advances to the industries were met out of normal Exchequer financing, and not from earmarked loans raised from the public, the ultimate source of the funds was taxation. If Exchequer advances to the nationalized industries were abandoned, then taxation could be reduced. This line was pursued by the Conservatives during their period in opposition from 1964 to 1970, and they actively canvassed other methods of providing capital finance, such as some form of investment by private lenders, but before a policy was evolved they found themselves in office as a consequence of the 1970 election.

A step towards capital finance on the analogy with the private sector had been taken in a rather different form in 1965–66 with the introduction of a tranche of 'equity' capital into the B.O.A.C. financial structure. About half the Corporation's capital (£35 million out of a total of £66 million) was converted into non-redeemable Exchequer Dividend capital on which a 'dividend' would be paid instead of an annual payment of interest at a fixed rate. The argument was that the existing system of providing capital by fixed-interest stocks, whether the public stock issues prior to 1956 or the subsequent advances from the Exchequer, meant that a nationalized industry was loaded with capital charges whether there were any trading profits or not. Joint stock companies in the private sector were under no such disadvantage since they could omit to pay a dividend on their equity capital when their profits were inadequate or when losses were sustained, and unlike the situation in the nationalized industries, capital costs were not accumulated by being carried forward as an element in a deficit. B.O.A.C., which had to compete in an international market, was subject to fluctuating returns which were more often a reflection of the state of international competition than its own management efficiency, and it was able to sustain the argument for having part of its capital freed from regular annual interest payments but made subject to the declaration of a dividend in the light of the trading results. The amount of the dividend is fixed after consultation with the Minister and the Treasury, though the latter have compulsory powers in reserve. In its evidence to the Select Committee in 1967/68, B.O.A.C. contended that the dividend of 10% paid for 1965–66 and that of 15% for 1966–67, amounted to more than would have been paid on fixed interest loans.

It is difficult to quarrel with the view expressed by the Select Committee that this form of capital has psychological rather than economic or administrative advantages. Its principal effect is to prevent the accumulation of a deficit, and the accompanying depressive effect on the workers, in an industry whose results fluctuate over good and bad periods. As the B.O.A.C. comment referred to above indicates, it does not necessarily lighten the long-run capital cost of an industry, but it concentrates the payments for the use of capital into those years when trading can bear it. Dividend capital is of no use to an industry which is in regular deficit, nor would it help the Government in its relations with such an industry. Thus, the railways got nowhere with their wish, expressed in evidence to the Select Committee, to have some form of equity capital. On the other hand, the British Steel Corporation was allowed to experiment with this sort of capital again because of the competitive situation in which they operated. By this time, the term Public Dividend Capital was being used to describe this type of finance.

B.O.A.C. also pioneered another development in capital finance. It secured permission from the Treasury to raise capital overseas, mainly for the purpose of meeting the cost of American aircraft and capital projects such as premises which were being undertaken overseas. Shortly afterwards, the Electricity and Gas Councils were also permitted to borrow abroad, and the power was later extended to the Post Office when it was established as a public corporation. It is a matter for computation and the exercise of financial acumen to decide whether to meet overseas expenditure by borrowing overseas and to use the foreign exchange mechanism to deal with the annual servicing of the loan and its eventual repayment, or whether to borrow at home in sterling and to handle the servicing and repayment in sterling, using the foreign exchange mechanism to handle only the one transaction of the original purchase. The B.O.A.C. transaction had the further justification from a foreign exchange point of view of creating overseas earnings out of which the loan could be serviced and repaid. However, these events coincided with the existence of lower rates of interest in overseas capital markets than in London. Other corporations sought the facility to borrow overseas, partly because of the lower interest rates and partly to escape the rigidities of borrowing from the Exchequer. The Government was amenable to this, and probably encouraged the idea. It certainly created the suspicion on the part of some observers that it was anxious to obtain the benefit accruing to the balance of payments and the foreign exchange reserves from the influx of foreign money when the proceeds of the loan operation were realized. It is also doubtful whether, after taking account of the exchange guarantee premium which was imposed on the operations by the Treasury and the other costs involved, there was any great advantage to the borrowers in terms of the costs of servicing the loans. Overseas borrowing has continued despite these misgivings, and in 1974 the right to borrow overseas was extended to all the nationalized industries which had not already acquired the power in their own legislation.

Mention must also be made of the growing importance of internal funds as sources of capital finance. Most of the industries had been able to use some internal funds for capital purposes, but the 1961 White Paper emphasized the need for the industries to make substantial contributions out of their own earnings towards the cost of capital development. A figure of about 48% was mentioned for the electricity industry; from nationalization to the end of March 1966, it had met about 41·4% of its capital requirements from internal sources. The 1967 White Paper also reaffirmed the need for the industries to generate a substantial proportion of their capital needs, though by this time the emphasis was placed on the techniques for investment appraisal and the economic consequences of differing pricing policies rather than on the significance of the annual out-turn. Indeed, adequate investment appraisal is all the more necessary if resort is to be had to internal funds since there is thereby no external evaluation of the operation.

MINISTERIAL CONTROL

The weakest aspect of the nationalization statutes was their failure to provide a clear allocation of responsibilities between the supervising Ministers and the boards. The statutes laid upon the Ministers various duties in respect of the industries for which they were responsible. These commonly extended to a power to vary the territorial jurisdiction and the number of any subsidiary bodies in those industries where there was some form of statutory devolution; the power to approve capital expenditure programmes and the raising of loans for capital expenditure; the approval of pensions arrangements for employees; the power to approve programmes of research and schemes of education and training for staff; the duty to take decisions on matters raised by a consumers' consultative council; the power to call for returns, accounts and information; the appointment of auditors; the prescription of the form of the annual accounts and matters to be included in the annual report, and the duty to prescribe the manner of repayment of capital loans. Additionally there were particular powers and duties related to individual industries. There were two other general powers, that of appointing the members of the board, and the ability to give directions to a board 'on the exercise and performance of its functions in relation to matters which appear to the Minister to affect the national interest'. These might be regarded as the first and the last powers, and in the first decade of the post-1945 nationalization era they were generally regarded as the most significant of the ministerial powers. The absence of any accepted doctrine about the public corporation encouraged the general assumption that, apart from the statutorily prescribed duties of Ministers, the board of the corporation was free to run the industry in its own way. The ability of the Minister to issue a general direction in the national interest was regarded as his reserve power to ensure that the industry was conducted in a manner which was politically acceptable. Events have disproved these early beliefs.

The division of functions between Minister and board developed in a different manner, and the hypothetical relationships explained in the previous paragraph have remained an unattained ideal. In the first place, the political environment inhibited the growth of any extensive area of independence for the boards. Nationalization remained a politically contentious subject throughout the life of the Labour Government from 1945 to 1951 and for some years afterwards. Once the nationalization statutes had been enacted, formal Parliamentary procedures relating to the industries provided little scope for the House of Commons to discuss their affairs, although the daily question time gave individual Members the chance to bring the industries under Parliamentary scrutiny. Many questions put down in this period related to matters within the daily competence of the boards and were disallowed, and as a result Members were uneasy. There were two sides to the problem. On the one hand, Members were trying to exact the same kind of accountability from the nationalized industries that they had over Government departments. They were unappreciative (perhaps unaware) of the fact that they had, in Mr Morrison's words to the Select Committee which inquired into methods of Parliamentary review in 1952–53,[5] passed a self-denying ordinance and 'did deliberately decide in place of a State Department ... to set up public corporations and to leave them a good deal of freedom'. On the other hand, there was a strong suspicion that many things were happening between Ministers and their nationalized industries which were not altogether in conformity with the division of responsibility implied in the statutes, and which some Members thought that Parliament ought to know about. In face of the restlessness of Members of the House of Commons about the difficulties in putting down questions concerning the nationalized industries, the rules were relaxed slightly in 1948 to allow the Speaker to have a wider discretion to accept questions on matters of sufficient public importance even if an answer had previously been refused to a similar question. By this time, too, the House had begun the practice, which still continues, of having annual debates on the annual reports of the major industries—the lesser industries hardly get noticed in this way. In the early years, however, there was a tendency for these debates to retrace the arguments for and against nationalization; they have rarely dealt with the significant problems affecting the organization and operation of the industries.

The situation was further confused by the manner in which normal Parliamentary procedure was applied to the industries. As a consequence of the way in which the Standing Orders of the House of Commons were worded, the annual accounts of most of the nationalized industries came within the purview of the Public Accounts Committee. In the six sessions from 1946 to 1952, that Committee examined the accounts of 16 public corporations, but it did not have the advantage, as it did with its examination of the accounts of Government departments, of the Comptroller and Auditor-General's assistance since he had no jurisdiction in the audit of the accounts of the public corporations. The Select Committee on Estimates also had a right of examination, though this was much more limited than that of the Public Accounts Committee, and its investigations were few in number. The activities of these two Committees gave rise to some animosity on the part of the industries which had been examined, and their representatives made clear to the Select Committee, already referred to, that they thought that Parliamentary investigation of this kind was an infringement of what might be called their management area. In this they were supported by Herbert Morrison. But the pressure for some form of Parliamentary review had been growing, especially amongst Conservatives, and the return of a Conservative Government in October 1951 created a more sympathetic climate for these claims. In spite of opposition from Morrison and Reith, and from some representatives of the major industries, the Select Committee reported in favour of establishing a regular Parliamentary committee to investigate the nationalized industries.

Such a committee was eventually established in 1956—its role and activities are discussed later—and in the course of the successive inquiries into most of the nationalized industries enough evidence has been produced to show that the division of responsibility between Ministers and boards which appeared to be implicit in the statutes has had no basis in reality. It is quite clear that over the years Ministers have never been restrained by the absence of specific statutory powers from actions which have usurped or restrained the managerial function of the boards. Various explanations have been offered to account for this. The power which Ministers have to appoint board members is also a power not to renew a member's tenure (all appointments are for fixed periods); and a Minister can, if he wishes, bring a member's appointment to an end before the expiry of his contractual tenure. There is no evidence to support the view that this power of patronage has weakened the resistance of boards to the encroachment of Ministers on their managerial domain. Most ministerial encroachments can be accounted for by other factors, such as the power to approve capital expenditure programmes; and most board members whose tenure has not been renewed or who have been dismissed have had other characteristics rather than antipathy towards the extension of ministerial power.

The nationalized industries as a whole form an important sector of the economy. In an age when government management of the economy is not only thought desirable throughout the greater part of the political spectrum, but is also practically unavoidable, no Government Minister can forgo his influence over the industries if economic management is to have even a partial chance of success. Moreover, it is quite clear that Ministers will not hesitate to use their powers, whether *de jure* or *de facto*, over the nationalized industries in order to assist them with other aspects of their ministerial activities. This has been seen throughout the post-war period in successive attempts by Governments to exercise control over prices; in the pressure on the aircraft corporations to buy aircraft different from that which they would have preferred to buy on commercial grounds; and in the special duty on oil used by the electricity industry in order to make coal financially more attractive. There is, indeed, a standing temptation for Ministers to use their powers over the nationalized industries to secure courses of action which the industries would not follow of their own free

6*

will, but which avoid or help to solve awkward problems in other sectors for which the Minister is responsible. The Select Committee in its report on ministerial control was anxious that ministerial interventions should be brought out into the open, and it condemned what it called the 'lunchtable directive'.

There are two good reasons why ministerial control and influence should generally be made public, always accepting of course that there are times and matters on which secrecy should be preserved. In general, however, it is necessary for the adequate and rational public appraisal of the work of Ministers and the boards that the respective responsibilities of each should be known. If it is not, there can be no proper allocation of praise or blame—a situation which may well suit the political predilections of Ministers but which has undoubtedly adversely affected the willingness of first-rate people to serve on the boards. The other reason is a financial one. The Select Committee frequently argued that where the board of an industry acted otherwise than in a commercial manner, either to meet matters of high level public policy or to provide uneconomic services for social reasons, the financial consequences should be costed and a grant made by the appropriate Minister. The making of the grant from public funds will in itself bring the action into public review, but it will also provide a sounder basis on which to make judgments about the efficiency of the industry concerned. There is no reason to believe that Ministers accept the first of these arguments; as politicians of the first order it is probably too idealistic to expect them to expose themselves unnecessarily to public scrutiny. However, the financial argument has been accepted and is firmly enshrined in the provisions of the Transport Act 1968 for the subsidization of uneconomic railway services, in the payments to the National Coal Board in respect of certain social costs incurred as a result of pit closures, and in the payments authorized in 1974 to various industries affected by the Government's policy of price restraint.

The ministerial power to issue a general direction on matters affecting the national interest is, perhaps, the most abortive element of ministerial control. A general direction has been issued on only three occasions:[6] in 1947 to deal with a legal problem relating to the transfer of property in France from B.O.A.C. to B.E.A.; in 1951 to forbid the Iron and Steel Corporation from continuing with the re-organization of the individual steel companies; and in 1952 to stop the British Transport Commission from putting increased railway charges into effect. We shall never know whether the insidious development of the 'lunchtable directive', with the chance that a Minister would not have to account in Parliament for his action, was deliberately preferred by a long line of Ministers to the general direction, which would most certainly need to be at least explained in Parliament. Yet it is certain that the former ousted the latter. It is most unlikely that the reason for the disuse of the general direction was that suggested by some constitutional lawyers, namely that a 'general direction' was a legal impossibility because any direction would in the nature of things refer to specific actions. It was surely not beyond the ingenuity of lawyers to get round that difficulty. The real reasons why the concept of the general direction failed were, firstly, because its issue would always result in sharp political controversy, since it was regarded both as the remedy of last resort and, as the three instances in which it was used show, it was set in the midst of some wider political controversy. Secondly, as a remedy of last resort it had all the appearances of being the final stage in a dispute between a Minister and a board. The wider political controversy referred to could only aggravate the situation and, in two of the three cases, had nothing to do with the relations between the Minister and the board. On the other hand, there is no reason why the general direction should be seen as the last stage in the settlement of a dispute between Minister and board.

It is a pity that the idea of the general direction has fallen out of favour without its proper use having been adequately explored. It could serve a more positive purpose than its previous impedimentary use. My own view, which was expressed in evidence to the Select Committee,[7] is that the direction should be used to share and define the respective responsibilities of Minister and board for policies based on social and economic grounds on the one hand and on commercial considerations on the other. A direction issued on regular occasions would be the means whereby a Minister established the social and economic objectives for the industry; it could be debated in Parliament on its merits so that ministerial actions would be brought into the open. In this way, the boards would be working within a more certain framework than they have ever enjoyed.

The Select Committee accepted the underlying argument when it referred to 'this lack of clarity, this confusion of responsibilities and this breakdown of confidence'. Its own solution was a separate Ministry of Nationalized Industries to take responsibility for the institutional aspects of the industries, leaving the service responsibilities with the appropriate functional Ministers. In this way the Government's oversight of the working of the industries, including their efficiency, could be kept separate from their responsibilities for the wider industrial problems and developments, and the nationalized industries could thereby be protected from influences determined by the wider interests of government. Unfortunately, this solution has not found favour in the Government. Perhaps in a future re-organization of the machinery of government, the concept of control embodied in the idea of a Ministry of Nationalized Industries will be subsumed within a Department of the Interior endowed with supervising duties over the subordinate institutions of government.

THE MANAGING BOARDS

It has already been explained that the role of the managing boards is inadequately identified in the nationalization statutes. It is also the case that the statutes provide little guidance as to the kind of persons who should compose the boards. The statutory provisions are mainly concerned with mechanical matters, giving to Ministers the power to make appointments and to fix their terms and conditions, prescribing disqualification from appointment in various specified conditions, and establishing some procedures for the formalities of board meetings.

There is usually a prescription of numbers, always a maximum and sometimes a minimum, and often a requirement that some appointments should be on a part-time basis. The power to make appointments is usually qualified by the requirement that the appointments shall include persons with experience in various fields, generally finance, commerce, industry and industrial relations. This qualification is of little significance; the specified fields are so broad that it would be practically impossible to collect a board of six or more members, of the right calibre for board membership, who did not between them possess the range of talents required. Neither does the numerical requirement amount to any real limitation, since it is relatively easy for a Minister to secure amending legislation, and this has frequently been done.

The type of board embodied in Reith's original public corporation concept was a body of men appointed by the State to conduct the industry on the nation's behalf. The limited experience of elected boards was gathered in undertakings, the Port of London Authority and the Mersey Docks and Harbours, where an electoral process was easily organized. The electoral principle was obviously not applicable to the large national service industries of the post-war era. Moreover, the electoral basis implied a measure of independence, but the newer nationalized industries were clearly intended to be subject, theoretically at least in the areas of social and economic policy, to governmental influence. The appointment of board members by Ministers was the most obvious way of securing this influence; it also had the additional advantage that it was more effective than an electoral process in securing members with adequate training and experience, and was the only way in which a board could be composed of members able to work together as a team.

The system which has evolved[8] is that the chairmen and board members are appointed for limited periods, usually of five years, rarely longer, but often for shorter periods. At the end of each person's tenure the Minister can either renew the appointment for a further period or appoint a new person. In this way it is relatively easy to drop a member who has either been ineffective or has developed undesirable qualities. It is popularly believed that it is by the threat of non-renewal that Ministers have been able to increase their influence over the boards beyond the powers with which they are endowed by statute. There is little real evidence of this, however, but the practice of making appointments of limited tenure has nevertheless had disadvantages. In the first place, it has often been difficult to find a younger person who was willing to give up a promising career for a board post which might abruptly come to an end well before he was ready for retirement. This has meant that Ministers have sometimes been forced to appoint a person nearing the end of his working life, although a younger person would have been preferable. This is quite apart from the general predisposition of Ministers in the period up to 1955 to prefer persons at the upper end of the age scale anyway. In the 25 years from 1945 to 1970 nearly 10% of all persons appointed as board chairmen or members were over 65 years of age, and a further 20% were aged between 60 and 65. Secondly, the principle of limited tenure has sometimes led to board members not wishing to have their appointments renewed, or Ministers deciding not to renew them, mainly because the industry was experiencing a bad time and thereby encountered a hostile political environment. In such circumstances a good record is easily forgotten by the public and politicians alike, but industrial managers are not used to working in such situations and generally dislike being involved in them. This has been a factor accounting for the reluctance of many people in private industry to accept board appointments in the nationalized industries. It has been aggravated by the comparatively low level of salaries paid to the chairmen and members of the boards in the nationalized field.

In the period since about 1960 there has been an increasing tendency to appoint as board members, and in one or two cases as chairmen, persons who have had a long career in the industry. This was partly due to the coming to fruition of management development programmes within the industries; and partly to a recognition of the important incentive effect that would ensue from opening up board membership to persons inside an industry as the apex of their career development. It seems likely that this process was helped by a greater willingness on the part of Ministers to appoint people at younger ages and to renew appointments more readily. It was, perhaps, not entirely a coincidence either that two industries, B.E.A. and gas, in which there was stability of board membership over a long period and more than an average number of appointments from within the industry, were also amongst those which gained public regard for their overall efficiency and technological progress.

In looking at the methods by which Ministers have carried out their task of finding and selecting board members and chairmen, one is struck by the haphazard nature of the process. Too much has depended on personal recommendation without adequate verification and appraisal. Too often, elderly men have been appointed on the basis of their past record, and sometimes on a very inadequate assessment of that, at a time in their working lives when there has been little chance that they could repeat their achievements in a new sphere. There have been few instances of Ministers appointing their political friends for political reasons (rather surprisingly there are rather more instances of Ministers making appointments from amongst their political opponents), but equally it is quite clear that until about 1970 little real attempt was made by Ministers or their Departments to make appointments on the basis of an effective appraisal of the potentialities of possible candidates. This is an area which is sorely in need of improvement; far more care is taken in making appointments to the Civil Service than in seeking members for the boards of the nationalized industries.

SELECT COMMITTEE ON NATIONALIZED INDUSTRIES

The genesis of this Committee has already been described. Its purpose was to make Parliament better informed about the nationalized industries, and although

it has never been given any powers of supervision and control over these industries, nor over the activities of Ministers in relation to them, it has undoubtedly
had an influence. This has, perhaps, been most obvious in the sphere of activity
officially denied to the Committee when it was established. When the first Committee was set up in 1955 it was given terms of reference which so restricted its
scope that there was little of practical use which it could do. Another Committee was established late in 1956 with simpler terms of reference, and though
these allowed wide scope for investigation the Government made it clear that it
did not intend that the Committee should deal with matters either of day-to-day
administration or of 'major government as distinct from commercial policy'.
Yet it is by invading the latter field that the Select Committee has been most
useful.

During its first ten years, the Committee was largely concerned with the
investigation of individual industries, and although these have continued up to
the present time it has, in the last ten years, done what is probably its most
significant work in its 'across the board' investigations, those into ministerial
control, relations with the public, and its own terms of reference.[9] As a result of
the latter, it has been able to include the Bank of England, the Independent
Broadcasting Authority, Cable and Wireless Ltd. and the Horserace Totalisator
Board within its jurisdiction. The Post Office was brought in earlier in 1956,
even before its status was changed from a government department to a public
corporation; the Select Committee had the unique opportunity of being able to
publish its views as to the manner in which this change might be accomplished.

This is not the place to review in detail the many reports which the Select
Committee has presented to Parliament. It is sufficient to recount its accom-
plishments, some of which have already been discussed. Firstly, it has uncovered
the extent of the non-statutory ministerial controls over the industries; some of
these have now been covered by appropriate authority in amending statutes.
The repeated criticisms of the inadequacies of departmental and Treasury
controls over capital investment by the industries are generally regarded as the
motivating factor behind the 1961 White Paper on financial and economic
obligations. Repeated criticisms of inadequate accounting procedures and the
undesirable effects of internal cross subsidies were reflected in the 1967 White
Paper and in those provisions of the Transport Act 1968 which allowed operating subsidies to British Railways for the maintenance of uneconomic services.
The statutory provisions relating to consumer consultative councils are also
gradually being changed so as to make these bodies obviously independent of
their respective industries; this action is in response to the report on consumer
relations.

In spite of these achievements, and a host of improvements in operating and
administrative procedures in individual industries, an air of unfulfilment hangs
over the Committee. Rather surprisingly, having regard to the animosity with
which the major industries viewed the idea of such an investigatory committee
in the early 1950s, it has emerged as the main champion of the industries. It

has sought to protect them from the capricious interventions and influences of Ministers and Departments, and it has advocated the need to establish a certainty and clarity in the wider political environment so that the industries can enjoy a determinate scope for the attainment of efficiency and commercial objectives. It may have provided Parliament with more information about the industries, but this does not appear to have had any obvious effect on Parliament and its attitude and procedures relating to the nationalized industries. Whatever success it has achieved derives from its ability to influence either the industries which it investigates or the Ministers who are responsible for them. Some observers, the present author included, took the view in evidence to the Select Committee in its inquiry into ministerial control that the Committee would be more effective in its investigatory role if it were backed by the services of a small public audit board, working on similar lines to the Comptroller and Auditor General in his examination of the accounts of government departments. An examination of the Minutes of Evidence of the Select Committee over the years will show many occasions when questions about the evidence or information presented to it might have been pursued by the Committee if it had been aided by expert assistance. A supporting body of the kind described would be essential if the Select Committee were to be endowed with any supervisory or controlling powers over the nationalized industries. Until that stage is reached, the Select Committee will continue to be a watch-dog which barks but which cannot bite.

CONSUMER RELATIONS

It has been said that one consequence of the establishment of the nationalized industries has been the replacement of the consumer by the citizen. There is some truth in this in the sense that the industries respond more to political pressures, political in the wider sense rather than in the party sense, than to transaction-based pressures exerted by consumers. Enough has been said in this chapter to show that the environmental pressures to which the industries are exposed are most significant; consumers tend to regard the political machinery as the most obvious method of approach to the industries. There is a considerable amount of belief in the idea that the consumer is impotent because nationalized industries are monopolies, and because the consumer is trapped by the necessity to purchase his essential services. This is true only in a superficial sense. There is much competition between electricity, gas and coal, as well as atomic power and oil, as sources of energy. The same sort of competition exists amongst the different bodies in the transport field. In the long run, consumers are free to move from one service to another, but it is the short run in which the individual consumer, as distinct from consumers as a whole, faces difficulties. For most consumers do not find it easy to change to another source of supply, partly because of the capital costs involved and partly because of the technical difficulties which may be involved in making the change. In this respect, the nationalization process has not worsened the position of the individual consumer, who was in precisely similar difficulties when public utilities were run by municipal corporations and statutory undertakers, all with local monopolies. Yet the predominance given to political processes of control over the nationalized industries, probably does mean that the consumer is in a weaker position for the rectification of his commercial grievances than his predecessors were in pre-nationalization days.

The nationalization statutes relating to most of the industries created what are generally termed consumer consultative councils. Their function is to 'represent' the consumers and to make representations on their behalf to the managing boards. In some cases they have to be consulted over changes in tariffs, though they have no power of veto. These bodies are the most useless part of the nationalization machinery. Their consultative role in respect of tariff changes has been of no practical effect in dealing with the general problems of rising prices and of pricing policy. The running in this field has been made by the Select Committee on Nationalized Industries, the former National Board for Prices and Incomes, and the present Prices Commission. As sounding boards for consumer relations and development, their record is unobtrusive and they are no adequate substitute for an effective industry-based consumer relations activity.

The consumer consultative councils have suffered from two other defects. The first is that the public as a whole is largely ignorant of their existence; this is partly due to the fact that complaints about specific defects in consumer services must go to the management of the industries. The other is that some of them have been staffed and provided with office facilities by their respective industries. As a consequence, the few people who have known about these councils have suspected a lack of independence from the industries. The Select Committee investigated the area of consumer relations in 1970/71,[10] and its only practical suggestions were for a separation of the administration of the councils from the industries and for the improvement of the advisory facilities at the disposal of the councils. These recommendations are being implemented as amending legislation is enacted for individual industries, but they are not likely to promote any marked improvement in the role and effectiveness of the consumer councils. With so much emphasis now being given to the development of consumer services generally, through the machinery stemming down from the Minister for Consumer Affairs and the Fair Trading Practices Registrar at national level to the local authority consumer services departments, and with prices and pricing policy also in the hands of separate national machinery, the consumer consultative councils for individual industries are now redundant.

After three decades it is perhaps time to abandon the phrase 'nationalized industries' and to adopt instead the term 'public industries'. Quite apart from the fact that the description 'nationalized' implies a takeover from private ownership which is not strictly true in some cases, the concept of nationalization seems irrelevant to the contemporary situation. There are few features of the current administration of these industries which can be derived directly and solely from the aims and ideals implied in the original nationalization proposals.

This is no doubt due to the ambiguities inherent in those ideas and in the statutory provisions which endeavoured to give effect to them. It is also in part due to the fact that amongst the community generally, and amongst socialists in particular, there are no generally accepted principles about the public corporation concept of organization. It is also worth pointing out that, whatever doctrines they may have preached from time to time against the nationalization doctrine, the Conservatives began to take industries into public ownership years before the Labour Party was established and has continued to do so right down to its latest period of office. But whether they have been motivated by pragmatic or ideological considerations, none of the governments of the last century has given any serious attention to the task of devising a satisfactory code for the management of the public industries and for the regulation of the relations between the Government and the industries.

In the period since the end of the Second World War during which the public corporation has been used as the main form of organization for the public industries, enterprises in the private sector have gradually been subjected to more and more governmental influence and control. In addition to control over prices and influences over capital investment, successive governments have provided massive financial aid, either by loans or grants, to a large number and a wide variety of firms. There have been changes in company law and in the regulation and control of monopolies, both of which have had important effects on the management, structure and control of firms in the private sector, particularly the large joint-stock companies. These developments in the private sector, alongside of those which have affected the management of the public industries, raise the question of what has really been gained by the acts of nationalization. There have been some advantages, such as the rationalization and re-organization which have flowed from unified management and ownership, but these are only marginal in time and effect. The significant developments in technology and economic management owe little to the fact of nationalization since many similar developments can be found elsewhere in the world in private enterprise.

What then is the future of the public corporation? It is no more a determinate form of organization now than it was in 1945. It would be out of place here to speculate what it might be in the future, but before it becomes a unique aspect of British government a good deal more thought must be given to the development of the ideas formulated by John Reith 50 years ago and to their practical application.

NOTES AND REFERENCES

1 Report of the Broadcasting Committee, Cmd. 2599, 1926.

2 Committee of Enquiry into the Electricity Supply Industry, Cmd. 9762, 1956.

3 Railway Reorganization Scheme, Cmd. 9191, 1954.

4 See First Report from the Select Committee on Nationalized Industries: Ministerial Control of the Nationalized Industries. H.C.P. No. 371—I, 1967–68.

5 Report of the Select Committee on Nationalized Industries, H.C.P. No. 235, 1952–53.

6 The 'letter of general direction' issued in September 1970 to the Post Office Corporation by the Minister of Posts and Telecommunications does not appear technically to have been a formal 'general direction', but the intent was the same.

7 See pp. 539–40, vol. II, Minutes of Evidence, First Report from the Select Committee on Nationalized Industries: Ministerial Control of the Nationalized Industries. H.C.P. No. 371—II, 1967–68.

8 The author bases the information and comment in this section on the study he has made of the methods of selecting and appointing members of the boards of the public corporations. He wishes to acknowledge the research grant from the Social Science Research Council which made this study possible.

9 Special Report from the Select Committee on Nationalized Industries: the Committee's Order of Reference. H.C.P. No. 298, 1967–68.

10 Report from the Select Committee on Nationalized Industries: Relations with the Public. H.C.P. No. 514, 1970–71.

The Local Government System

8

C. A. Cross, M.A., LL.B., Barrister-at-Law

DEVELOPMENTS IN STRUCTURE

The structure of local government in England and Wales, excluding Greater London, was changed in April 1974, almost 30 years after the first significant steps were taken towards reform. Continuously throughout this period the nature and extent of change was under discussion in local government itself, in Parliament, before Royal Commissions and statutory commissions, in White Papers and consultative documents, in conferences of local authority representatives and conferences between the associations of local authorities, and in academic research. Plans were conceived, publicized, adopted, modified and finally dropped. There were strongly held differences of opinion among leading personalities, there were changes in government, and, above all else, an absence of unanimity among the governors in local government, elected and professional. Indeed, there were very few areas of agreement.

Many possibilities were examined throughout the period but three lines of thought were pursued in depth. First, that the existing structure should be retained and improved by greater use of the devices of joint committees and joint boards for those services which required the larger unit, and with a power given to a Minister, with Parliamentary consent, to create joint boards where the authorities concerned were reluctant. A power of this kind is currently available in the fire service[1] and the education service.[2] Secondly there was much support for, and much opposition to, the extension to all parts of the system of two-tier government, with provincial or regional organizations of government to provide some services and to undertake over-all economic and physical planning. Thirdly, there was much support for, and opposition to, a system of large one-tier government.

The movement towards reform in the immediate post-war period began with a general criticism of a system which had remained unchanged for decades. Many authorities, it was said, were small and their resources too limited to sustain the quality of service required of them.[3] Physical boundaries had not been altered though conditions had drastically changed, and they bore, in many cases, no relation to any community of interest—commercial, historic or cultural. Two-tier government had necessarily involved the allocation of services by reference to type of authority, but the allocation had not been settled as a whole. It had

167

emerged through the years and consequently the split was not always sensible. Services which ought properly to be administered by the same authority were administered by different authorities. Criticisms of this kind found common acceptance, but a commonly accepted solution never emerged.

TOWARDS REFORM — THE FIRST ABORTIVE MOVES

In January 1945 the Government presented to Parliament the White Paper 'Local Government in England and Wales During the Period of Reconstruction'.[4] The Government had reached the conclusion that a fundamental alteration of the structure of local government was neither necessary nor desirable at that time, and in their view the needs of the post-war period could best be met by an adaptation within the existing framework of local authorities and by advancing co-operation between them. It was proposed to establish a Local Government Boundary Commission, a body of not more than five members, to review the areas of local authorities and to make any necessary adjustments in status and boundaries. It was to be concerned solely with status and boundaries and with nothing else. The view was expressed that there was no general desire in local government for a disruption of the existing system, nor was there any consensus of opinion as to what should take its place. The making of a change of any magnitude, which would by common consent have to be preceded by a full-dress inquiry, would be a process occupying several years, and would, as a result, delay the establishment of the extended housing, educational, health and other services which formed part of the Government's post-war programme. Though there was a case for wider administrative areas, in planning, for example, it was no part of the Government's policy in dealing with post-war reconstruction to perpetuate the system of Regional Commissioners which had been a feature of war-time administration.

The Local Government (Boundary Commission) Act 1945 reflected these proposals and established the Local Government Boundary Commission, charged with the duty of reviewing areas (excluding the administrative county of London) and of introducing change and any consequential alteration in status. Boundaries could be altered, authorities joined one with the other or divided, a borough could be constituted a county borough, either by itself or together with the whole or a part of another county district, a county borough could be made a non-county borough, a new urban or rural district could be created or changed from one type to the other. Its chairman was Sir Malcolm Trustram Eve.

The Commission produced reports in 1946, 1947 and 1948. The report for 1947 proposed the division of England into 20 one-tier counties and 47 two-tier counties. Within the two-tier counties were included most of the existing county boroughs and these boroughs, with the larger non-county boroughs, would have been 'most-purpose authorities'. Their major recommendations were summarized at paragraph 41 of the report as follows:

'(a) In future there should be three main types of local government units—counties, county boroughs and county districts. To distinguish the first two from existing units we refer to them as "new counties" and "new County boroughs".

(b) The whole of England and Wales, including the areas of the existing county boroughs, would be divided into new counties. The bulk of these would be the existing counties, with some combined and some divided, and they would be administered, as now, on the two-tier system. The remainder of the new counties would be large cities and towns (with suitable alterations of boundaries where necessary) administered, as now, on the one-tier system. The general aim would be to secure a population in each new two-tier county of between 200,000 and 1,000,000, and in each one-tier county of between 200,000 and 500,000.

(c) The new county boroughs would consist broadly of the middle-size towns—boroughs with populations between 60,000 and 200,000. They would also include the Cities of Liverpool and Manchester which would form the centres of two new counties. The new county boroughs would be part of the administrative county and would look to the county for certain services (including police and fire). But they would form a new and middle rank of authority with important autonomous functions—in particular, all education, health, and care of the old and disabled services, and parts of town and country planning and highways—in addition to all those of an ordinary second-tier authority.

(d) County districts would include all non-county boroughs (except those which would become new county boroughs), urban districts and rural districts. They would be responsible for all existing second-tier functions and, in suitable cases, for functions delegated by county councils. The distinction in title between Urban and Rural Districts would be abolished and all county districts would, after their boundaries had been reviewed, have similar autonomous functions.

(e) Delegation of functions by county councils would be effected by means of "county schemes" prepared in accordance with general principles approved by Parliament. The schemes would take into account the nature of the function to be delegated and the circumstances of the county and of each second-tier authority.'

The report for 1948 began with the following comment:

'We may be asked why the Commission after two years of existence have made no single Order altering the status or boundaries of any local authority . . . It would have been possible for us to make some Orders in accordance with the terms of the Local Government (Boundary Commission) Act 1945 and the regulations made thereunder, which would, in our view, have resulted—to quote the words of the general principles laid down by Parliament for our guidance (these general principles appeared in the schedule to the regulations)—in "effective and convenient units of local government administration" . . . But we have definitely reached the conclusion that in many areas—and these cover the great bulk of the population—our present powers and instructions do not permit the formation of local government units as effective and convenient as in our opinion they should be. Thus the alternatives before us were to make orders which would in many cases have resulted in second best arrangements or, taking the opportunity presented to us by our statutory duty to make an annual report, to set out our views. We have chosen the latter course, and, if our recommendations commend themselves, some legislative action and some amendment of the general principles will be necessary ... Our experience amply confirms the statement made recently in Parliament by the Minister of Health:[5] "Everyone who knows about local government feels that it is nonsense to talk about functions and boundaries separately. They have to be taken together." ... We have no jurisdiction over functions.'

The Minister of Health did not accept the Commission's plea. He made the following statement in the House of Commons on 27 June 1949:

'The Government have come to the conclusion that, in present conditions, it is difficult for the Commission to proceed with their work and they have accordingly decided to repeal the Act of 1945, which will involve the winding up of the Commission. This will restore the position substantially to what it was before the passing of that Act, until such time as the Government have had an opportunity of reviewing the structure and functions of local government.'

The Local Government Boundary Commission was dissolved in 1949.

As noted in an earlier paragraph the local authority associations have never appeared able to take a detached view of reform. They have at all times reflected the views and argued the interests of their constituent authorities. So it was in the Trustram Eve period, in the first spasm of reform. The County Councils' Association considered that the two-tier system should continue, strengthened by integrating county districts into larger units wherever possible, and extended by converting into second-tier units all the existing county boroughs with populations below 200,000. The Association of Municipal Corporations expressed no collective view, but their constituent groups, the county boroughs and non-county boroughs, submitted separate statements. The county boroughs as a class urged that the county borough system should be maintained unimpaired and extended where appropriate. Though there might be areas where for a variety of reasons it might not be practicable to establish a one-tier system they were convinced that the purposes of local self-government were in general less well served in two-tier than in one-tier authorities and that the standard of local government administration was in general higher in a one-tier system. The upper-tier authority, they said, had a remoteness from the electorate which weakened local self-government.

The non-county boroughs argued for a two-tier system, subject to proper delegation to effective second-tier authorities. The second tier should be given direct responsibility for services sufficient in number and importance to attract the right type of public representative and officers. The Urban District Councils'

Association were strongly opposed to large extensions of county boroughs and deprecated limited extensions into built-up urban areas. In areas of continuous urban development they considered that new county areas should be formed in which there would be no county boroughs and in which administration would be divided between county councils and district councils. The Rural District Councils' Association also supported the two-tier system and opposed the disruption of rural authorities near the borders of county boroughs and other municipalities. They supported the merger of the smaller authority to facilitate a considerable degree of delegation of county functions to the second tier.

So began a conflict of view within the local authority associations which continued unresolved and unabated through the following years.

THE SECOND PHASE—THE LONG DEBATE

Soon after the dissolution of the Local Government Boundary Commission the associations of local authorities entered into discussion in an effort to produce an agreed scheme for submission to the Government. In March 1950 a meeting was held to consider proposals prepared by the County Councils' Association and further meetings were held throughout the following year. But agreement could not be reached and in May 1952 at a final meeting of the series it became apparent that a common view could not be settled. The County Councils' Association, the Urban District Councils' Association and the Rural District Councils' Association, joined later by the Association of Parish Councils, accordingly produced their own proposals. They agreed that the two-tier system of government in administrative counties and single tier government elsewhere should continue, and that parish councils should be retained as a third tier in the areas of rural districts. Existing county boroughs with a population of not less than 75,000 should retain their present title and functions and all other existing county boroughs should cease to be county boroughs yet retaining borough status and any special charter privileges. Existing non-county boroughs and urban districts with a population of not less than 100,000 should be entitled to seek county borough status by private bill. The conurbations should be subject to a review by the Minister of Housing and Local Government with a two-tier form of government in mind. The Minister should undertake the review of counties and the county councils should thereafter undertake the review of county districts. A considerable degree of delegation within the administrative counties was urged.

These proposals were resisted by the Association of Municipal Corporations on the grounds that they did no more than offer suggestions for the re-adjustment of existing areas to meet the requirement of existing functions: it perpetuated the frustrations of the current system. It gave no consideration to what functions an elected council should perform and what a suitable unit of local government should be to perform those functions. It sought to maintain the existing unsatisfactory structure of county government and the continuance of areas which, in many cases, were constituted to meet conditions existing half a century ago. The Association placed on record that the growing complications and disharmony arising from the forms of delegation and devolution of powers then in use had, over recent years, helped to produce a feeling of frustration without parallel in the history of local government. Any scheme of re-organization which should have enduring value must have two basic features. First, that areas are suitable for the administration of the functions which authorities are called on to perform; secondly, that financial resources are adequate to enable those functions to be performed without undue reliance upon government grants with consequential central supervision. Areas and finance must, therefore, be considered at one and the same time. The joint document, said the Association of Municipal Corporations, sought also to perpetuate the existing artificial severance of urban and rural communities, a wholly unacceptable situation.

The next significant step was taken in 1954, when the Association of Municipal Corporations, on the one hand, and the other four Associations jointly, on the other, submitted memoranda to the Minister of Housing and Local Government, but again there was a deep divergence of view. The Association of Municipal Corporations argued for the one-tier system of all-purpose authorities and recommended its extension as far as possible. The other Associations pressed for a reduction in the number of county boroughs and the possible creation of a two-tier system in the conurbations. Other differences emerged, amongst other things on the distribution of functions between county councils and district councils.

Towards the end of that year the Minister met the Associations and told them that, in his view, it would not be fruitful to embark upon any extensive reform unless there existed some broad measure of agreement among local authorities themselves. He was not prepared to contemplate the elimination either of the two-tier system in the counties or the one-tier system in the big towns. The Associations, in the light of that statement, decided to make a fresh attempt to find a basis for agreement within the framework of the existing structure. A measure of agreement was in fact reached. On 25 March 1955 the Minister made a statement in the House of Commons in which he referred to the talks he had had with the representatives of the Associations, as a result of which there was general agreement 'upon common proposals covering a number of the main issues upon which they had previously been divided'. The statement continued:

'These proposals, while not involving any change in the basic structure, contain important recommendations for the improvement of local government organization. The proposals also include a general recommendation that there should be some redistribution of functions between county councils and county district councils; but the Associations are not as yet agreed on what changes should be proposed. In any case, since most of the services concerned are the responsibility of other Ministers, those questions will have to be discussed between the Association and my right hon. friends.

When these talks on functions have been held, the Government will examine the proposals as a whole and consider its attitude towards them. A further statement will then be made to the House.'

The proposals which emerged from the agreement appear in the Appendix to the White Paper 'Areas and Status of Local Authorities in England and Wales'.[6] As might be expected the proposals had no novelty and evoked little enthusiasm. It should be permissible for an authority to apply for an extension of its boundaries and for promotion to county borough status, and there should be a presumption that an authority with a population of 100,000 or more was able to discharge effectively and conveniently the functions of a county borough. An application by a county borough to extend its boundaries should be considered in the light of all the relevant factors, including the effect on the administrative county. Certain functions then exercisable by county councils should be conferred as of right on county districts with a population of more than a specified figure—these functions included domiciliary and certain other health and welfare services, education and planning. Two further White Papers were issued 'Functions of Local Authorities in England and Wales',[7] and 'Local Government Finance (England and Wales)'.[8]

THE COMMISSIONS OF 1958

Out of all this came the Local Government Act 1958. In broad terms it provided for a review of the organization of local government in England and Wales (excluding the London area) by two Commissions, one for England and the other for Wales including Monmouthshire, and for the review of county districts by county councils. The Commissions were under a duty to make proposals for change 'in the interests of effective and convenient local government' and a similar obligation was put on county councils in respect of county districts. The whole country (apart from the London area) was the subject of review, but certain areas were dealt with differently—they were described in the Act as 'special review areas' and corresponded to what are generally known as the conurbations, those areas where a number of towns and cities are situated in close proximity. The primary responsibility for the review of the special areas (including the county districts in them) fell to the Commissions.

The terms of reference of the Commissions were in some respects narrower than those available to the Trustram Eve Commission, and in some respects broader. They were narrower in the sense that the Commissions were required to concentrate on the pattern of counties and county boroughs—it was for the counties at a later stage to undertake the review of districts within them. But they were wider in relation to the special review areas—the conurbations of Merseyside, South-east Lancashire and North-east Cheshire, the West Midlands, West Yorkshire and Tyneside. In these areas the Commissions were obliged to take account of all authorities including districts, and they were able, if they thought fit, to propose the creation of a 'continuous county', a county containing no county boroughs. Here the Commission could recommend the pattern of areas and the distribution of functions between the resulting tiers. Except in the special review areas the Commissions were not empowered to deal with the allocation of functions as between tiers.

Parliament devised a most elaborate procedure within which the Commissions were obliged to work. It was expensive, tedious, time-consuming and friction causing. It involved consultation—widespread consultation—the publication of draft proposals, fresh consultations and conferences, local inquiries and finally an affirmative resolution of both Houses.

Certain changes did emerge from the Commissions' work, including two new counties, Huntingdonshire and the Soke of Peterborough, and Cambridgeshire and the Isle of Ely, and the new county boroughs of Luton, Solihull and Torbay. New county boroughs were created at Teesside (taking in the former county borough of Middlesbrough), and Hartlepool (taking in the former county borough of West Hartlepool) and, in the Midlands, Warley, which incorporated the county borough of Smethwick. The Commission's solution for the West Midlands special review area was a series of contiguous county boroughs, and after exceedingly lengthy public inquiries, effect was given to these proposals. In the West Yorkshire special review area they proposed a new pattern of county boroughs and county districts, and for Tyneside a continuous county with four 'most purpose' second-tier boroughs. The Minister would not accept the Commission's proposals for Tyneside and he made an alternative proposal for a single Tyneside county borough. But no effective action was taken in relation to West Yorkshire and Tyneside for in 1966 the Government decided to dissolve the Commission and to appoint in its place a Royal Commission on Local Government in England under the Chairmanship of Sir John Maud, later Lord Redcliffe-Maud.

The Act of 1958 dealt with Wales. It may therefore be convenient to note here the moves towards the reform of Welsh local government. A Commission for Wales was established, and it reported in 1962 recommending that 13 counties and four county boroughs in Wales and Monmouthshire should be reduced in number to seven counties and three county boroughs. Again there was the strongest resistance from local authorities and in February 1964 the Government undertook to prepare proposals themselves. They established an interdepartmental working party to examine functions and boundaries of local authorities in Wales and in due course a White Paper 'Local Government in Wales'[9] was published. It proposed five new administrative counties in Wales and a reduction in the number of county boroughs from four to three. Thirty-six new districts should be created in place of the existing 164 county districts and one county borough (Merthyr Tydfil) should become a non-county borough. Discussions followed on the White Paper, and in October 1969 the Government announced that they proposed to undertake a further review to see if a satisfactory pattern of local government could be established for the geographical counties of Glamorgan and Monmouthshire which would avoid the division between county boroughs and administrative counties. This was followed by a further White Paper 'Local Government Reorganisation in Glamorgan and Monmouthshire'[10] published in March 1970—the view was here expressed that in Glamorgan and Monmouthshire a system of unitary authorities would be more satisfactory than a two-tier system. That paper proposed three unitary authorities, two comprising the area of the existing geographical county of Glamorgan and one the area of Monmouthshire. These authorities would include respectively Swansea, Cardiff and Newport. But with the change of Government nothing was done and a further document, a consultative document, 'The Reform of Local Government in Wales', was issued in February 1971.

THE COMMISSION OF 1966

The Royal Commission on Local Government in England began its work in 1966. The Chairman invited written evidence from Government Departments and local authority associations, and gave an open invitation to the Press. 2156 witnesses submitted evidence. It came from individual local authorities, professional organizations, private persons, Government Departments, the local authority associations, the Association of Education Committees and the National and Local Government Officers Association and other groups and individuals. The Commission's work lasted until 1969.

The Commission (with one dissentient) in its final report[11] recommended that England (outside London) should be divided into 61 new local government areas, each covering town and country. In 58 of them a single authority would be responsible for all services. In three metropolitan areas, those around Birmingham, Liverpool and Manchester, responsibility for services should be divided in each case between a metropolitan authority whose key functions would be planning, transportation and major development, and a number of metropolitan district authorities whose key functions would be education, the personal social services, health and housing. These authorities would replace 79 county boroughs and 49 counties.

The 61 areas proposed would be grouped, together with Greater London, into eight provinces, each with its own provincial council. These councils would be elected by the authorities for the unitary and metropolitan areas (including the Greater London authorities) and they would include co-opted members. The principal function of these councils would be to settle a provincial strategy and planning framework within which the main authorities would operate. They would replace the regional economic planning councils and collaborate with central government in the economic and social development of each province.

Within the unitary areas, and wherever they were wanted within the metropolitan areas, local councils would be elected to represent and communicate the wishes of cities, towns and villages in all matters of concern to the inhabitants, with a right to be consulted on matters of special interest to its inhabitants.

The report of the Commission was based on a most thorough review of local

government administration and a scrutiny of an immense amount of evidence. It appointed a Director of Intelligence, with the status of Assistant Commissioner, to undertake its own research, including the analysis and assessment of the mass of information available about economic, social and geographical conditions in all parts of the country. In addition, ten research studies were undertaken for the Commission by outside persons and organizations. But despite the authority with which it spoke its recommendations were widely challenged. They 'provoked considerable debate and discussion'.[12] The Association of Municipal Corporations accepted the diagnosis made by the Commission and the principles on which reform should be based. But they took the view that many of the unitary authorities and some of the metropolitan districts were too large, yet local councils could detract from the standing of the unitary authorities. They urged a more realistic pattern of unitary authorities. The County Councils' Association, the Urban District Councils' Association and the Rural District Councils' Association again asserted their preference for two-tier government. Within the unitary areas there should be district authorities of 100,000 or more, perhaps less in sparsely populated areas. The professional organizations were broadly in agreement with the Commission's proposals— this was to be expected since the large unitary authority would provide the more satisfactory career structure. The National and Local Government Officers Association though favouring unitary government were against local councils, 'mini-councils with minimal powers'. The Institution of Municipal Engineers, too, were against local councils and they thought that some of the new units were not large enough. The Institute of Municipal Treasurers and Accountants supported the principle that local government in each area should be a unity. The Town Planning Institute preferred the unitary principle in all places, including the metropolitan areas. The Liberal Party, alone amongst the political parties, rejected completely the proposals because they made no provision for transferring powers from the centre to the regions, and individual participation in government would be impossible in the system proposed. They urged a structure of 12 provincial assemblies, single tier district councils, and neighbourhood councils.

The Government broadly accepted the Commission's proposals and issued its White Paper 'Reform of Local Government in England'.[13] A change of government followed the General Election in 1970 and yet one further fresh start was made. The Redcliffe-Maud proposals were wholly rejected. The new Government produced the White Paper 'Local Government in England: Government Proposals for Reorganisation'[14] and a consultative document on Wales. These proposals bore no relationship to those of the Redcliffe-Maude Commission.

THE FINAL PROSPECT

The White Paper's conclusions (paras. 59 to 62) are set out below.

'In preparing their proposals for the first comprehensive local government reform of this century, the Government have sought to balance complementary and conflicting factors. Decisions will be taken by those most directly affected and every encouragement will be given to local democracy. Services must be organized on a scale sufficient to command the skilled administration and the concentration of resources that produce the quality which the nation expects. The boundaries must be accepted as sensible by people on the spot. These long-term policies can be introduced only after many detailed decisions have been taken; to give them effect will require application, energy and dedication.

The proposals set out in this White Paper constitute a major reform of local government in England, ambitious beyond anything attempted this century—but one which retains and improves the essential elements of the present system.

The Government are firm in their resolve that reorganization should be centred on two tiers of local government throughout the country. They are initiating further consultations on the boundaries and will consult the appropriate associations on details of the final distribution of functions.

In putting forward the changes set out in this White Paper, the Government have several linked objectives:

(a) they will establish a new pattern of areas within which the major services can be efficiently administered and developed in the future;
(b) by retaining important responsibilities at the more local level, too, they will give powers of decision and action to those who will be immediately affected;
(c) the total number of authorities is to be reduced, but the new and rationalized system will be founded upon the organizations of the existing authorities and will preserve wherever possible the loyalties attaching to ancient units of local government; the reduced number of authorities will permit the effective transfer of responsibility and power from central to local authorities;
(d) they accept the need for the operational authorities to be complemented at provincial and parish level.'

A new debate began. 'These long term policies,' said the White Paper, 'can be introduced only after many detailed decisions have been taken; to give them effect would require application, energy and dedication.' This promise was fulfilled. There followed an incredible number of consultations between the government and local authorities acting through their associations and between the government and professional societies and other representative groups, and out of all this came the Local Government Act 1972.

ACHIEVEMENT—THE ACT OF 1972

This measure is the culmination of a quarter of a century of discussion. Leaving aside the reform of London government, it is the only identifiable result. What, then, did it do? First, it created a wholly new set of authorities and made provision for a fresh distribution of functions. Secondly, it perpetuated, though with slight modification, the doctrine of *ultra vires* in its application to local authorities. Thirdly, it introduced a new system of audit of local authorities. Fourthly, it gave authorities greater freedom in the way in which they undertake their business. Fifthly, it set up permanent machinery for change in areas and status. Each of these features is now considered in turn.

The new structure

The Act creates a two-level system of government, each level independent of the other. England and Wales (excluding Greater London) is divided into 53 counties and 369 districts. Six of the counties are metropolitan counties and the 36 districts within them are metropolitan districts. It is open to a district council to petition Her Majesty for the grant of a charter conferring upon the district the status of borough, but this has no legal significance. It does little more than to turn the chairman of the council into the mayor of the borough, with accompanying style, dignity and ceremony. The argument as between the unitary authority of the Redcliffe-Maud type and the two-tier system so much favoured by the County Councils' Association and its associates is finally settled. Two-tier becomes two-level, with provision for joint working but not tutelage. The district is not a *county* district.

This broadly is the system—counties, and districts within counties. But there is a complicated pattern of other authorities and units of government. Rural parishes in England which were in existence before 1 April 1974, continued to exist by the name of parishes, and rural boroughs created under section 28 of the Local Government Act 1958 ceased to be boroughs but continued in the status of parish. Provision was made in the 1972 Act for a further category of parish. The Local Government Commission for England (referred to later) was required in 1973 to make proposals to the Secretary of State for the constitution of parishes by reference to the areas of the then existing boroughs and urban districts, areas which were to be merged with other units in local government reorganization. The recommendations of the Commission were accepted by the government and promulgated by Order, and the councils of these authorities became successor parish councils and the members of the existing councils became parish councillors. In Wales the districts were divided into communities; these are the areas of what were formerly boroughs, urban districts and rural parishes.

The council of a parish or community may resolve to adopt the status of town, and then the council becomes the town council and the chairman and vice-chairman are known as the town mayor and deputy mayor respectively.

The Act makes specific provision for the retention of the privileges and dignities of former authorities.[15] It abolished boroughs and cities as units of government but their charters were not abrogated. The rights and privileges belonging to a borough or city were specifically preserved, subject to any contrary provision appearing in the charter granted to the district of which the city or borough was part and subject to any contrary provision in the Act. Privilege and dignity survived in three ways. First, where former boroughs and cities virtually became the new districts those districts were able to incorporate within the new charter many of the historic rights and privileges. Secondly, many smaller boroughs became successor parishes in the way described above and their councils adopted the status of town, and the chairman of the council became town mayor. Thirdly, the Act made provision to enable a former borough, in a district which did not petition for a charter for borough status, to retain an identity through charter trustees, a body consisting of district councillors representing the borough. These charter trustees are enabled to elect one of their number as city mayor or town mayor as the case may be. The Act of 1972 achieved much, but not amongst its achievements is simplicity in style and nomenclature of authorities.

The restructuring of authorities naturally brought with it a fundamental redistribution of functions. A simple formula was given:[16] the functions of the former county councils became those of the new county councils, the functions of former boroughs and urban district councils became the functions of new district councils, functions of parishes became the functions, in England, of the new parishes, and in Wales, of the new community councils. This broadly expressed formula is subject to the specific allocations of functions throughout the Act, more particularly in Part IX and the relevant schedules, and when these provisions are examined in detail one discovers that there are few services in which there is a clear-cut definition: in some of the services there is a division between the county and district, and in some cases (as in planning, highways, consumer protection) there is a complicated division, certainly complicated so far as the public is concerned.

The following table (drawn from Circular No. 121/72 of the Department of the Environment) sets out the broad division of functions.

County Councils (Outside Metropolitan Areas) and Metropolitan District Councils

Education
Youth employment
Personal social services
Libraries

All County Councils	All District Councils
Museums and art galleries (a)	Museums and art galleries (a)
Housing—	Housing—
Certain reserve powers	Provision
	Management
	Slum clearance
	House and area improvement

180   C. A. Cross

All County Councils	All District Councils
Town Development (a)	Town Development (a)
Planning—	Planning—
Structure plans	Local plans (c)
Development plan schemes (b)	
Development Control (d)	Development Control (d)
	Advertisement Control
Derelict land (a)	Derelict land (a)
National parks	
Country parks (a)	Country parks (a)
Conservation areas (a)	Conservation areas (a)
Building preservation notices (a)	Building preservation notices (a)
	Listed building control
Tree preservation (a)	Tree preservation (a)
Acquisition and disposal of land for planning purposes, development or redevelopment (a)	Acquisition and disposal of land for planning purposes, development or redevelopment (a)
Footpaths and Bridleways—	Footpaths and Bridleways—
Surveys	
Creation, diversion and extinguishment Orders (a)	Creation, diversion and extinguishment Orders (a)
Maintenance (e)	
Protection (a)	Protection (a)
Signposting	
Transportation—	Transportation—
Transport planning	
Highways (e)	
Traffic	
All parking	Off-street parking (f)
Public transport (g)	Public Transport Undertakings (h)
Road safety	
Highway lighting	
Footway lighting (a)	Footway lighting (a)
Environmental Health—	Environmental Health—
Animal diseases	Food safety and hygiene
	Communicable disease
	Slaughterhouses
	Offices, shops and railway premises (j)
	Factories
	Home safety
	Water and Sewerage (k)
Refuse disposal	Refuse collection
Consumer protection (e.g. weights and measures, trade descriptions, explosives, food and drugs)	Clean air
	Building regulations
	Coast protection
Police (l)	Cemeteries and crematoria
Fire (l)	Markets and fairs
	By-laws
Swimming baths (a)	Swimming baths (a)
Physical training and recreation (a)	Physical training and recreation (a)
Parks and open spaces (a)	Parks and open spaces (a)
Small holdings	Allotments
	Local licensing
Airports (a)	Airports (a)

Parish Councils

Parish councils retained their former functional responsibilities. In relation to the functions listed above they have powers in connection with:

Footpaths and Bridleways—
Maintenance
Signposting
Transportation—
Off-street parking (f)
Footway lighting
Cemeteries and crematoria
Swimming baths
Physical training and recreation
Parks and open spaces
Allotments

The Act provides parish councils with a right to be consulted about planning applications affecting land in their areas.

NOTES
(a) Concurrent powers exercisable by county and district councils.
(b) In consultation with district councils.
(c) Except in national parks where counties would be responsible. Responsibility for local plans subject to development plan schemes or structure plan.
(d) Primarily a district council function except in the case of a national park or of 'county matters' as defined in Schedule 16 to the Act.
(e) District councils may claim maintenance powers for footpaths, bridleways, and urban roads which are neither trunk roads nor classified roads.
(f) In accordance with the county transportation plan.
(g) Metropolitan counties are Passenger Transport Authorities, non-metropolitan counties have co-ordination functions.
(h) Some non-metropolitan districts under local act powers.
(j) Fire precautions under the Offices, Shops and Railway Premises Act are a county council responsibility.
(k) Under agency arrangements with water authorities.
(l) Subject to amalgamation schemes.

Allocation of Functions in Wales

The distribution of functions in Wales broadly follows the distribution of functions in England, except that the following fall to district councils or may in certain circumstances be exercised by them: refuse disposal, disposal of abandoned vehicles, libraries, on and off-street car parking, food and drugs, weights and measures, and certain functions relating to agriculture.

The functions of parish councils in England are exercisable in Wales by community councils.

The 25-year-long debate on reform had as a main purpose an allocation of functions which not merely had regard to appropriate areas and adequate resources but to simplicity and intelligibility, and, not least, to clear gravitation of whole responsibility to each administering authority. It is too early to judge whether the division just described can satisfy this requirement.

The ultra vires rule

There has been debate throughout the years of reform as to the nature and effect of the doctrine of *ultra vires* on local authority administration and as to whether it might usefully be removed or modified. All councils, being corporate bodies, are subject to this doctrine: a statutory corporation can do only those things which it is authorized to do by statute, directly or by implication.[17] But the

7

courts have held that a corporation may do not only those things for which there is express or implied authority, but also whatever is reasonably incidental to the doing of those things.[18] It has been variously argued that the *ultra vires* rule should be replaced by a general competence clause, but this was never seriously pressed. The Royal Commission on Local Government[19] took the view that all the main authorities which they proposed should have a general power to spend money for the benefit of their areas and inhabitants, additional to their expenditure on services for which they would have statutory responsibility. They put the view that the only limit on the use of the new power should be the wishes of the electors and such restrictions as have to be placed on local government expenditure in the interests of national economic and financial policy. The White Paper 'Reform of Local Government in England'[20] expressed some sympathy in principle, but noted that there were practical difficulties in it. Unconditional powers, not restricted by any financial limit, might lead to wasteful duplication or to local action which would conflict with national objectives in important fields of policy.

In the event the doctrine remained, with slight modification. First, the common law rule as to incidental powers was given statutory force in section 111 of the Local Government Act 1972, so that an authority is now empowered by statute to do anything which is calculated to facilitate, or is conducive or incidental to, the discharge of any of its functions. This provision does not appreciably change the situation. An authority when challenged may more easily point to statute rather than to case law. Secondly, the 'free penny' provisions of section 6 of the Local Government (Financial Provisions) Act 1963 were re-enacted and slightly broadened. Up to the product of a 2p rate may be spent for the benefit of the area or a part of it or for the benefit of all or some of the inhabitants. The 1963 Act provision was the first appreciable inroad into the doctrine of *ultra vires*, the first provision to enable an authority to spend money as it chose, provided that the purpose was not one in which there was already some statutory provision. This proviso might well have been dropped in the process of re-enactment. It was designed to prevent the provision of the same kind of service by an authority with statutory power and by an authority without statutory power. Thirdly, the Act conferred several other widely expressed powers but of marginal significance in relation to the doctrine of *ultra vires*. Authorities may spend money on gifts donated for the benefit of the inhabitants of the area, and a gift may be unrelated to a statutory purpose. Expenditure may be incurred in dealing with actual or imminent or apprehended disasters and emergencies affecting an area or its inhabitants. Authorities may purchase land for the benefit, improvement or development of their areas, an extension to the powers contained in section 2 of the Local Authorities (Land) Act 1963 which enabled authorities, for the benefit or improvement of their areas, to erect buildings or to construct or carry out works on land. These statutory powers are exercisable for the benefit of an area generally and in that sense modify the strict rigidity of the *ultra vires* doctrine.

It is of some interest to note that the investigators who prepared the material for volume 2 of the Report of the Committee on the Management of Local Government (the Maud Committee, to which reference is later made) enquired into the extent of dissatisfaction and frustration with council work arising from statutory limitations on the activities of councils. In answer to the question 'Does your council make full use of its power and authority?', 78% of those questioned answered in the affirmative. In answer to the question 'Does your council need more powers of any sort than it now has?' 53% said 'no'.[21] This documented evidence is not very conclusive either way. Less documented debate has argued that the doctrine has had a continuing inhibiting influence on local administration. There has been no room for adventurous administration and experiment in service and it has given an undue dominance to legal thinking in management. The doctrine is here to stay, but those who complain about it might note the extent to which existing powers available to local authorities remain unused.

Audit

The doctrine of *ultra vires* is in practice closely linked with the rules of statutory audit, and here the Act of 1972 has sensibly rationalized the system. Under the Local Government Act 1933 all authorities except borough councils were subject to district audit. Borough councils could by resolution adopt the system of district audit or a system of professional audit. Where district audit or professional audit had not been adopted a borough council was subject to elective audit. In this case there were three auditors, two elected by local government electors for the borough called 'elective auditors', and one chosen by the mayor from amongst members of the council, called the 'mayor's auditor'.

The district auditor had far-reaching powers. It was his duty, *inter alia*, to disallow every item of account which was contrary to law, to surcharge the amount of any expenditure disallowed upon the person responsible for incurring or authorizing the expenditure, and to surcharge any loss or deficiency upon any person by whose negligence or misconduct the loss or deficiency had occurred. Expenditure has been held as 'contrary to law' if it is unreasonable in its extent or excessive even though the objects of the expenditure are lawful.[22]

The Act of 1972 made drastic changes.[23] Compulsory district audit disappeared, together with the power of surcharge. Instead, the accounts of local authorities are now subject to audit by a district auditor or by an 'approved' auditor—one belonging to a professional body named in the Act and whose appointment by a particular authority has been approved by the Secretary of State. If a district auditor considers an item of expenditure to be *ultra vires* his duty is to apply to the court for a declaration to this effect, unless the expenditure has been sanctioned by the Secretary of State. Where a declaration is made the court may order repayment and in certain cases disqualification from local authority membership may follow.

An approved auditor has no sanctions at his disposal. He reports to the Secretary of State, who may then direct the holding of an extra-ordinary audit by the district auditor. If an application is to be made to the court it will be by the district auditor. But the power of surcharge has gone.

There are provisions enabling an authority to change from one type of audit to the other.

It is not without significance that at the end of 1973, at a time when most authorities had exercised an option, the vast majority of them had chosen district audit, including many which formerly had been subject to professional audit. It is also significant that at that time it was estimated that some 130 private auditors were engaged in local government audit, yet only about 30 of these audited the accounts of more than one local authority. There was clearly no great specialism in municipal auditing. On the matter of approval the Minister said 'it will be very difficult for a firm that does not specialise . . . to satisfy the Secretary of State that it is capable of doing the work'.[24]

The bill as originally proposed had a highly controversial provision in it. It enabled the district auditor to judge the merit of local authority expenditure. The provision as finally enacted puts a duty on an auditor to consider whether, in the public interest, he should make a report on any matters arising out of or in connection with the accounts in order that those matters may be considered by the body concerned or brought to the attention of the public. This is an extension of the auditor's powers. He is seen now to have a duty to the public, a statutory duty in place of what was regarded as a conventional duty.

Procedural reform

The Act of 1972 gave greater flexibility in administration. The former law prescribed in much detail how the work of local authorities should be carried out. It laid down that certain officers were to be appointed and in some cases their qualifications were prescribed and there were safeguards as to tenure, and certain named committees were to be appointed. The Act of 1972 removed some of these restraints and made easier the adoption of more convenient management structures.[25] It provides that an authority may discharge its functions through a variety of internal arrangements (through committees, sub-committee and officers) and through the use of agency arrangements with other authorities. The term 'delegation' in earlier statutes is replaced by the more general phrase 'arrangements for the discharge of functions'. The power generally to delegate decision making to officers is of particular significance. It replaces a conventional practice that was open to legal challenge.

This provision takes account of the recommendations of the Committee on the Management of Local Government (the Maud Committee, 1967), the Committee on Local Authority and Allied Personal Social Services (the Seebohm Committee, 1968), the Royal Commission on Local Government in England (the Redcliffe-Maud Commission, 1971) and the Interim Report of the Working

Group on Local Authority Management which became the New Local Authorities—Management and Structure (the Bains Report, 1972). In drafting the provision the Government had available a mass of comment in response to a Consultative Paper which had the widest circulation.

Review of areas

The Act of 1972 provides permanent machinery for the review of areas. This is one of the more significant reforms: it remedied what has been a constant weakness. Authorities which in the past would have been prepared for change have been discouraged by the cost and difficulty of Private Bill procedure.

The Act established two Commissions, the Local Government Boundary Commission for England and the Local Government Boundary Commission for Wales. The English Commission is under a duty to undertake a regular review of certain areas at intervals of not less than ten years and not more than 15 years, subject to directions given by the Secretary of State. These are the counties in England, all metropolitan districts, all London boroughs, and the boundaries between Greater London and the counties adjoining it and between the City of London and adjacent London boroughs. It is open to the Secretary of State to vary the interval between reviews either for a whole review or for a particular case or class of case. A variation is made simply by a direction of the Secretary of State. Between periodic reviews the Commission may carry out an *ad hoc* review of any particular area. In the case of non-metropolitan districts there is a broad duty to keep them under review and no timings are given. Any local authority or parish meeting may invite the Commission to undertake a review.

It is the continuing duty of the Welsh Commission to keep under review all counties and districts in Wales. It is not related to specified periods of time. The Secretary of State for Wales may give directions as to the holding of reviews, but, unlike the arrangement in England, he is not empowered to give directions not to undertake reviews during a specified period. As is the case in England, the Secretary of State for Wales may give directions to the Welsh Commission for their guidance in conducting reviews. If a direction concerns all reviews, or reviews of any class or a single review of all or any class of the principal areas in Wales, the Secretary of State must first consult the appropriate local authority associations. A local authority may ask for a review to be carried out.

The object of all reviews is to consider if change is called for and, if it is, to formulate proposals. The proposals may be far reaching. The Commission is to have in mind 'the interests of effective and convenient local government', a phrase drawn from Part II of the Local Government Act 1958. There is a wide variety of means by which change may come about, including the alteration of a local government area or the constitution of a new local government area of any description outside Greater London by the amalgamation of two or more areas. Authorities may be converted from one type to another.

The Commissions are basically advisory bodies. Their recommendations are submitted to the Secretary of State and become effective when contained in an order made by him.

LONDON REFORMS

As noted earlier, the area of London had been excluded from the terms of reference of the Local Government Boundary Commission established under the Local Government (Boundary Commission) Act 1945, and subsequent White Papers on reform did not deal with London. An earlier Commission, the Royal Commission on the Local Government of Greater London (the Ullswater Commission) had reported in 1923[26] more particularly on the question of the establishment of a central local authority for Greater London but it made no recommendation.

In 1957 the Royal Commission on Local Government in Greater London was set up under the chairmanship of Sir Edwin Herbert and it produced a unanimous report in 1960.[27] It recommended the abolition of all existing local authorities in a defined area of Greater London (except the City of London and the Temples) and the setting up of an authority for Greater London as a whole and 51 new borough authorities. The recommendations of the Herbert Commission were embodied in the London Government Act 1963 but with some modifications. The number of London boroughs was reduced to 32 and the Commission's recommendations as to education were accepted with some change. The 12 London boroughs whose areas, together with the City of London, formed the former administrative county of London, became known as inner London boroughs. Education in that part of Greater London comprising the inner London boroughs became the responsibility of the Inner London Education Authority, a special committee of the Greater London Council comprising the councillors of the Greater London Council for inner London and one representative from each of the 12 inner London boroughs and from the City and Corporation of London. With the exception of these modifications the proposals of the Herbert Commission were generally accepted. The London County Council and the Middlesex County Council disappeared: the counties of Surrey, Hertfordshire, Essex and Kent were reduced in area; 70 of the existing metropolitan boroughs, non-county boroughs and urban districts lost their separate identity by amalgamation. West Ham, East Ham and Croydon ceased to be county boroughs.

The Greater London Council was given responsibility for metropolitan roads, traffic management and fire protection. It was given a shared responsibility in planning, refuse disposal and housing matters with London boroughs and the Common Council of the City of London, and provision was made for the delegation of functions (with specified exceptions) by the Greater London Council to London borough councils and the Common Council.

London government has been the subject of innumerable Royal Commissions, Select Committees of the House of Commons, departmental committees and other investigations, but the Herbert Commission was unique in that it produced comprehensive proposals for reform. The Commission was unusual in another sense in that it included no one drawn from local government, and this was a matter of critical comment at the time. A third and somewhat unique feature of the investigation was its reliance as much on 'independent evidence' as on the official evidence given by local authorities—in fact the Commission appeared to accept that evidence with caution since those who sought change 'consisted of certain authorities who hoped to improve their status or powers'.

MOVEMENTS AWAY—THE PERSONAL HEALTH AND THE WATER SERVICES

The Local Government Act 1972 made provision for changes with respect to the administration of the personal health services and the water services, but this was overtaken by subsequent measures. The National Health Service Reorganisation Act 1973 gave effect to the proposals contained in the White Papers 'National Health Service Reorganisation: England'[28] and 'National Health Service Reorganisation: Wales'.[29] It brought together under one unified administration: (a) the hospital and specialist services formerly administered by the Regional Hospital Boards, Hospital Management Committees and Boards of Governors; (b) the family practitioner services formerly administered by executive councils; (c) the personal health services formerly administered by local authorities; (d) the school health service formerly administered by local education authorities. The new arrangements came into operation on 1 April 1974. England is divided, for the purposes of the Act, into 14 regions, and the regions are divided into areas. Regional health authorities administer the first and area health authorities the second. In Wales the area health authorities are in direct relationship with the Welsh Office.

The Water Act 1973[30] transferred responsibility for sewers and sewerage from local authorities to the newly created water authorities. This Act unified under nine regional water authorities and the Welsh National Water Development Authority the responsibilities of statutory water undertakers (there were 198 in England and Wales), sewerage and sewage disposal authorities (there were 1300 authorities in England and Wales), and river authorities (of which there were 29, responsible for water conservation, land drainage, fisheries, the control of pollution and in some cases navigation). There was accordingly in April 1974 a redistribution of functions and a loss of functions to local authorities.

CENTRAL CONTROL AND LOCAL AUTHORITY FINANCE

Throughout the period under review there have been persistent pressures from local authority associations upon the government to reduce the extent and degree of central control, and there have been declarations on behalf of the government that central control should and would be modified. Since 1949 attempts have been made in this direction and some progress towards achievement is to be seen in the Local Government Acts of 1972 and 1974. In 1949 the Local Government Manpower Committee was set up to examine the possibility of simplifying administrative procedures involved in central control of local authority work. It was charged with the duty of examining the possibility of relaxing departmental supervision of local authority activities. This Committee, made up of representatives of government departments and local authority associations, took the view that 'local authorities are responsible bodies competent to discharge their functions and that . . . they exercise their responsibilities in their own right'. The Committee drew this conclusion—'the objective should be to leave as much as possible of the detailed management of a scheme or service to the local authority and to concentrate the department's control at key points where it can most effectively discharge its responsibilities for government policy and financial administration'. Similar declarations have been made from time to time. In 'The Future Shape of Local Government Finance',[31] it was said 'The government wish to give greater freedom to local authorities, but they cannot evade their own responsibility for management of the national economy, nor can they evade their duty to ensure minimum standards for essential services throughout the country. The problem for central government is how to resolve this dilemma within these constraints.'

The White Paper 'Reform of Local Government in England'[32] contains the following paragraph:

> 'The government believe unequivocally in greater freedom for local authorities within the framework of national policies laid down by Parliament. The re-organization of local government creates an opportunity, which the government intend to seize, for achieving this aim.'

The topics of central control and local authority finance are considered together for they are interrelated—it is not without significance that one of the passages just quoted is taken from the Green Paper on Local Government Finance. Without doubt the most significant control is exercised through the system of grants and the control of borrowing. Nor is this surprising, for local authority spending is so great a part of public sector spending. This point is taken in the Report of the Radcliffe Committee on the working of the monetary system.[33] The Report recommended that all local authority borrowing should be through the Public Works Loans Board for reasons which in this context are significant, namely, that the sums involved are large and that the method of borrowing influences the market in a way which may not suit Treasury policy, that the fragmentation of demand increases costs, and that the bulk of capital requirements is largely determined by the Government's policies on social legislation. The Radcliffe Committee took the view that the way in which short-term debt had been built up by local authorities was 'clearly contrary to the funding policy of the monetary authorities'. This Report led to the imposition of restrictions by the Treasury on local authority short-term borrowing.

It manifests a recognition that the operation of local authority finance, more especially in its capital aspects, has a significant influence on the national economy. If that be the case it follows that overall central control in this area will not and cannot diminish.

The Plowden Committee on the Control of Public Expenditure[34] dealt with the theory and practice of Treasury control of expenditure. It dealt with all public service expenditure including local government expenditure. It recommended that regular surveys should be made of public expenditure as a whole, over a period of years ahead, and in relation to prospective resources. Here again central government expenditure, local government expenditure and expenditure in the nationalized industries, were linked together for long-term planning purposes, a situation which inevitably leads, in the field of local government finance, to greater dependence on government decisions.

Since 1961, White Papers have been regularly published on public investment. These papers dealt, among many other things, with the levels to which certain local authority services were expected to develop.

The Green Paper 'Public Expenditure: A New Presentation'[35] further recognized the interdependence of public expenditure. It said:

'Decisions about public expenditure cannot be taken in isolation but must be related both to the whole range of government's objectives, and to the other instruments of policy available to the government for achieving them.'

Local government is essentially one of these 'other instruments'. The Paper said that:

'The manifold objectives of government interlock. Some are concerned with general economic management . . . other objectives are concerned with meeting the need of the community for particular services—education, health and so on . . . to achieve these objectives there are many instruments which can be used. Among them are fiscal policy, monetary policy, and prices and incomes policy as well as the management of public expenditure programmes, separately and in total.'

The projection of public expenditure over a period of years on the lines suggested by the Plowden Committee—a projection which includes a very appreciable element of capital expenditure of local authorities—has understandably set limits to local authority expenditure, and since the overall limit is the sum of limits in functional areas (some functional areas include both central and local activity) it is clear that the scope of central control through finance is not likely to diminish. These basic and fundamental points are made before the grant system and borrowing procedures are examined.

FINANCIAL CONTROLS

The grant system

Exchequer aid has been a constant feature in local authority administration. It

7*

began in 1835 with a contribution towards the cost of transporting prisoners to Assize and Quarter Sessions. It has grown over the years and is now in the order of 60% of all local authority expenditure. The grant system has been used to stimulate new services, to encourage the growth of existing services and to ensure minimum standards; it has been used to meet local authority costs in services which some regard as national rather than local, for example, the education and police services, and to compensate authorities with inadequate local resources.

There have at all times been two basic arguments, whether grants should be specific or in aid of services generally, and the total amount of the subvention. The general movement has been away from specific grants towards grants in aid of expenditure generally, and there has been a steady increase in the proportion borne by the central government. Prior to 1888 all grants were specific grants and were in fact percentage grants. In 1888, in addition to specific grants, there were created 'assigned revenues'—the proceeds of certain local licences and a proportion of the net proceeds of probate duty were paid to local authorities. Assigned revenues from time to time changed into fixed payments and they ceased altogether in 1929.

From 1929 specific grants were supplemented by block grants, grants in aid of expenditure generally. The allocation of a block grant between authorities depended on the weighted population—the actual population was varied by factors related to rateable value, number of children, number of unemployed. The grant was thus related in some respects to need.

The Local Government Act 1948 introduced the Exchequer equalization grant, based on resources instead of needs. It was payable only to those authorities whose rate resources were below the average of authorities.

The Local Government Act 1958 created two new grants in aid of local authority services—the whole range of services—namely, a rate deficiency grant and a general grant;[36] the Exchequer equalization grant and many specific grants disappeared.

The rate deficiency grant was payable to any authority (the council of a county, county borough, county district, London borough and the Common Council of the City of London) where the *actual* product of a rate of one penny in the £ for the area of the authority was less than the *standard* penny rate product for the area—resources were measured in terms of the rate product, not in terms of rateable value per head of population as in the case of the Exchequer equalization grant.

The general grant was payable to all counties and county boroughs and replaced a large number of specific grants—those in respect of education, health services, fire services, child care, were the more important ones. The aggregate amount available for distribution was prescribed in a general grant order made by the Minister. The amount which any authority received was calculated under a formula contained in the First Schedule to the 1958 Act and was related to population and not (as in the case of specific grants) to the expenditure of the receiving authorities.

The Local Government Act 1966 continued the trend contained in the Act of 1958 with certain extensions and simplication. The reasons for change were set out in a White Paper[37] presented to Parliament in February 1966. The main purpose of the revised system was to give further relief to the ratepayer and this was done by means of an earmarked grant for domestic ratepayers coupled with a progressive increase in the proportion of local authority expenditure to be met from grants. The grant under the Act of 1966 was termed the rate support grant, and it continues, in modified form, under the Local Government Act 1974.[38]

In order to determine the aggregate amount of the rate support grant, the Secretary of State for the Environment decides on the total sum which shall be paid to local authorities by way of Exchequer grants, excluding housing subsidies and grants in respect of rate rebates and of mandatory awards and grants to students.[39] From this total is deducted the amount which he estimates will be paid out in specific grants towards the revenue expenditure of the services which still attract other specific grants, and supplementary grants towards expenditure with respect to National Parks.[40] The sum which remains is the aggregate rate support grant.

Before reaching a decision on the total sum payable by way of grants and before making his estimate of the amount which will be allocated from that sum to specific services the Secretary of State must consult the local authority associations and must take into account:

(a) the latest information available to him as to the rate of relevant expenditure;
(b) any probable fluctuation in the demand for services giving rise to relevant expenditure, so far as the fluctuation is attributable to circumstances prevailing in England and Wales as a whole which are not under the control of local authorities;
(c) the need for developing those services and the extent to which, having regard to general economic conditions, it is reasonable to develop those services; and
(d) the current level of prices, costs and remuneration and any future variation in that level which in the opinion of the Secretary of State will result from decisions which appear to him to be final and which will have the effect of increasing or decreasing any particular prices, costs or remuneration.

The relevant expenditure of a local authority in general comprises expenditure out of the rate fund.

The rate support grant contains three elements, the needs element, the domestic element, and the resources element. The domestic element is intended to make good the loss of income from the reduction required to be made in the rates in the pound levied on domestic ratepayers. The needs element and resources element have regard to the needs of an authority to incur expenditure and to the resources available for that purpose.

The White Paper 'Rate Support Grant 1974–75'[41] set out the Government's decision on the rate support grants made to local authorities in 1974–75 under the provisions of the Local Government Act 1974. It said:[42]

'The prospects for the British economy in 1974 are dominated by energy problems—the price and quantity of oil supplies, and, in the immediate future, the availability of coal. In these circumstances it is more than ever necessary to safeguard the balance of payments. The Government therefore took action just before Christmas to restrict the growth of domestic demand, principally by imposing controls on consumer credit and, above all, by reducing the public sector's use of goods and services.

The share local authorities will need to bear of these reductions on their current expenditure is £111 million at November 1972 prices. This is in addition to the reductions of 21 May 1973 which included £81 million in local government current expenditure in 1974/75. Local authorities were then formally told that there would have to be restraint in the growth of local authority expenditure, and that this year's rate support grant negotiations would proceed on the basis that these reductions would be achieved.

*   *   *

In arriving at their forecasts of relevant expenditure for 1974–75, the Government have given careful consideration to the reports of joint Working Groups of officials of local authorities and Government departments. These Working Groups were invited to prepare detailed forecasts of the expenditure that might be incurred by local authorities as a whole on individual services, bearing in mind past trends in expenditure and on the basis that existing policies would continue uninterrupted. They were also asked to consider what changes would be feasible in order to obtain the required reductions in the rate of growth of expenditure to which the Chancellor of the Exchequer referred in his statement of 21 May. The Working Group forecasts were based on the level of prices, costs and remuneration current at November 1972 and take into account demographic and other factors not under the control of local authorities. In addition the forecasts include allowances, as appropriate, for changes in expenditure expected to arise in the first year of local government reorganization and for improvements in services under relevant legislation and in accordance with announced policies.

The Government took note of the views expressed by the Working Groups about the difficulties of achieving the required reductions in expenditure, and have accepted as estimates of relevant expenditure the figures set out in Annex B. These revised forecasts produce a total of £192 million below the Working Groups' forecasts for 1974–75 (figures at November 1972 prices). This will require local authorities to make the specific savings identified in the Working Group discussions together with a further £10 million of unspecified savings representing in part the continuing effect of the efficiency reductions which the Government included in its forecasts for the current year. These savings total £81 million. In addition the revised figures also incorporate savings of £111 million (at November 1972 prices) which represent the share local government is being asked to bear of the reductions announced by the Chancellor on 17 December 1973. The basis for the forecasts for individual services is given in Annex B.

The Government will therefore be basing the rate support grant for 1974–75 on a relevant expenditure figure on the new definition, and at November 1972 prices, of £5148 million. Adjusted to November 1973 prices the figure of relevant expenditure becomes £5671 million. Nothing is included for possible future increases, but in the event of an unforeseen increase taking place in the level of prices, costs and remuneration which has a substantial effect on the relevant expenditure of local authorities, the Secretary of State may by order increase the amount of rate support grants.

The Government attach the greatest importance to expenditure being kept within the total stated above. To that end they will be issuing a circular to all local authorities in England and Wales spelling out the nature of the total reductions.'

The paragraphs indicate the nature of central direction and the place of the grant system in government control of local authority expenditure.

The White Paper 'Rate Support Grant 1974–75'[43] accepted a need to adjust the distribution formula to provide for the difficult situation in the large cities and areas of urban stress. This change of emphasis was foreshadowed in the Green Paper 'The Future Shape of Local Government Finance'.[44]

The grant system understandably brings with it a measure of central control—where money passes there must be accountability. It is an invariable rule that a specific grant is payable only if the appropriate Minister is broadly satisfied with the service in respect of which the grant is claimed, and in most cases grant-earning expenditure must first have been approved by the appropriate Minister. It is a rare thing for a grant to be withheld—it is essentially a reserve power. The general grant—the rate support grant—may be reduced if a Minister is satisfied that an authority has failed to achieve or to maintain reasonable standards in the discharge of any of its functions, and he may reduce the amount of the grant as he thinks just.[45] The Secretary of State in reaching his decision must have regard to standards maintained in other authorities, and his decision is not effective until a report from him is approved by the House of Commons. Regulations prescribing the standards to which the services must conform are made by the appropriate Ministers and are subject to a negative resolution of either House. These again are reserve powers, there but never used.

Borrowing

All major local authority activity involves capital expenditure and the borrowing of money, and sanction to borrow must first be obtained from a Minister. It had been the practice of Ministers, in the exercise of this sanctioning power, to examine the merits of every capital scheme, ensuring that it was technically sound, adequate for its purpose, and within the resources of the authority seeking the sanction.

The Secretary of State for the Environment introduced, from April 1971, a new kind of loan sanction procedure intended to provide greater freedom to local authorities in planning their capital expenditure, to simplify administrative procedures, in particular by restricting the need for individual loan consents, and to improve the Government's ability to monitor the total level and main trends of expenditure while reducing its detailed control of individual projects.

Under Circulars No. 2/70 and 66/71 four types of capital expenditure are distinguished and a general consent is given.

> (a) Key sector schemes. Included in this category are schemes relating to education; principal roads; police; social services; advances for house purchase and improvement; derelict land reclamation; coast protection works.
> (b) Acquisition of land for education, principal roads, or for most of the purposes of Part V of the Housing Act 1957 and for personal social services.
> (c) Improvements under Parts I and II of the Housing Act 1969, and expenditure on slum clearance.
> (d) Locally determined schemes.

The circular itself formally gives consent to borrowing within its terms, provided that in the case of (a) the appropriate Department has approved the project, in the case of (b) the price of the land is not more than the district valuer's valuation, and in the case of (d) the amount does not exceed the total allocated to the authority. The capital expenditure in group (d) is determined for the country as a whole by an annual allocation fixed by the Secretary of State after consultation with the local authority associations. The amounts from the total available to authorities are notified to them by the Department.

This arrangement reduced the need for the individual sanction of the Secretary of State in many situations, and within the amount allocated to individual local authorities there is some freedom in the choice of capital schemes.

OTHER FORMS OF CONTROL

Emphasis has been laid on the extent and degree of financial controls for these controls are the more important. There are, of course, other statutory provisions. First, there is control through regulation. Ministers have wide regulation making powers in many areas of local administration. The authorizing statute is in fairly general terms. Detailed administrative rules are contained in statutory instruments made by the Minister. An interesting example of this—interesting in its nature rather than in its importance—is seen in the changes in the law relating to burials and cremation made by the Local Government Act 1972.[46] Under earlier legislation authorities outside of London provided burial grounds under the Burial Acts 1852 to 1906—there were 16 of them—or alternatively under adoptive provisions in the Public Health (Interments) Act 1879. The Act of 1972 established one code in place of the two. The earlier Acts were largely repealed and replaced but for the most part temporarily. The significant point, in this context, is the power given to the Secretary of State by order to make provision with respect to the management, regulation and control of cemeteries, and such an order may amend or repeal other statutory provisions. The management powers of authorities may be wholly recast by order of the Minister. There is the customary safeguard. Before making an order the Secretary of State is required to consult local authority associations and other interested bodies, and an order so made requires an affirmative resolution of each House of Parliament. This is a sensible device to use in a complicated area of law, and its use here illustrates a current tendency.

More practical examples are seen in the Town and Country Planning Act 1971—in very many sections authority is given to the Secretary of State to make regulations setting out the way in which the Act is to be administered. Control through regulation has undoubtedly increased in the period under review. It has been inevitable. The services which authorities administer have become more and more complex and Parliamentary time has become more and more restricted.

Secondly, there is control through inspection, more particularly in the education, police and fire services. There has been no discernible movement one way or the other. The inspectorates exercise a considerable influence by way of advice, the interchange of ideas and the pooling of experience. It is not normally regarded as a link in a chain of command.

Thirdly, there are powers in relation to authorities in default. Several examples are given—default powers are available to the Secretary of State where a planning authority has failed to carry out its functions in connection with the preparation and submission of a structure or local plan.[47] The Secretary of State for Education and Science may declare a local education authority to be in default and may issue appropriate directions, enforceable by mandamus.[48] There are similarly expressed powers in the Housing Finance Act 1972.[49] The Local Government Acts of 1972 and 1974 have made some modest changes away from the use of this power.

Fourthly, Ministers have a minimal control in relation to officers of local authorities. A number of earlier statutory provisions had required the appointment of specified officers. Some provisions had set down the work which particular officers were required to undertake; in some cases qualifications were specified, in some there were controls over appointment and dismissal, in others a short list of candidates for appointment had to be submitted to the Minister and he had the power of veto. Each provision in the circumstances of its enactment had some justification—the need perhaps to ensure the appointment of a person competent to discharge a duty or perform a service, or to have an identifiable person upon whom a particular responsibility could rest, or to specify minimum standards of qualification or to safeguard officers against local pressures.

The situation was reviewed during the passage of the Local Government Bill in 1971. Authorities were in general to be larger and would accordingly have greater financial resources. There had grown up over the years a high degree of professionalism in the local government service with its built-in safeguards.

Thinking in regard to management structures in more recent times had encouraged experiment and change and there had been a tendency to devise structures to meet particular local authority situations rather than to accept traditional patterns.

It was to be expected, therefore, that the requirement to appoint particular officers should be minimized and that central control over the appointment, tenure and qualification of officers should be reduced. With a very few exceptions all existing statutory requirements as to the appointment of officers ceased to have effect.[50] It is still obligatory to appoint chief education officers, chief fire officers, chief constables, directors of social services and a few others, and there remains a veto power in the Secretary of State for Social Services in regard to the appointment of directors of social services. The reason for the retention of this minimal control might well be linked with the statutory responsibilities which in some cases fall to Ministers in connection with local authority services. But the control retained is not in any way significant. Authorities would not do other than appoint the officers named. Where in any statute a named officer is required or authorized to carry out some activity the power or duty now falls to what is called the 'proper officer' appointed by the authority.[51]

Fifthly, there is a measure of control through the confirmation of by-laws. This is to be expected for by-laws in the main create penal offences. The Government Department concerned examines proposed by-laws to see whether they are likely to be held to be *intra vires* if challenged in the courts. The Department will wish to satisfy itself that a need exists in the particular locality for the by-law proposed, for departmental thinking is against the making of by-laws except where the need for them is proven. The control here has little significance though in recent years discussion has taken place on the simplification of procedures.

Sixthly, in the immediate post-war years it became increasingly common for statutes to impose on local authorities a duty to prepare 'schemes' or 'proposals' or 'plans' setting out how local authorities proposed to undertake duties which statute had put upon them. When the scheme or proposal or plan had been approved by the appropriate Minister it became binding upon the authority. The Education Act 1944[52] required each local education authority to estimate the immediate and prospective needs of its area in relation to primary and secondary education and to submit to the Department a development plan showing the action which the authority proposed should be taken for securing sufficient primary and secondary schools in its area and the successive measures to accomplish this purpose. A further example of control through scheme making is seen in the Town and Country Planning Act 1971[53] which requires every county planning authority to survey its area and to submit to the Secretary of State a report of its survey and a structure plan, formulating the authority's policy and general proposals in respect of the development and other use of land in its area. The Secretary of State is enabled, through this procedure, to exercise influence over the manner in which and extent to which the statutory powers of planning control may be employed. This kind of control has the merit of elasticity. General statutory obligations can be turned into precisely stated obligations which have regard to local needs. Before a plan or proposal is submitted to the Minister for approval there has generally been a good deal of consultation between the Department and the officers of the local authority and in these discussions some measure of agreement will already have been reached before submission is made.

Lastly, scattered throughout statute are numerous provisions which enable a Minister to issue directions to a local authority or to local authorities generally or which require the consent of a Minister to individual acts. A few are of significance, not because of their use but simply because they are there. If the Secretary of State for Education and Science is satisfied that a local education authority, or the managers or governors of any county or voluntary school, have acted or are proposing to act unreasonably in the exercise of any power or the performance of any duty, he may give such directions as to the exercise of the power or the performance of the duty as he considers expedient.[54] It is open to him to take action under this provision even though what the authority or managers or governors have done or propose to do lies wholly within their discretion, and the Secretary of State is the judge of reasonableness. But there have been many powers which have had no importance at all and discussions took place over a number of years between government departments and local authority associations concerning their removal. This was effected in the Local Government Act 1972 and the Local Government Act 1974. The following is one of many controls removed by the Act of 1972—the Secretary of State was deprived of his power to require local authorities to make by-laws with respect to fish frying![55] The Act of 1974 amends a large number of statutory provisions so as to remove or relax central control over particular issues or transactions and, what is of greater significance, the Secretary of State is empowered by order to make further amendments from time to time to achieve this purpose.[56]

RATES—THE STALEMATE

A substantial part of local authority income (some 40%) comes from local rates, a local system of taxes first introduced by the Poor Relief Act of 1601—commonly referred to as the statute of Elizabeth. There have been constant arguments against the system, more particularly in recent years, but it has survived them all. The advantages and disadvantages of the system are sum-marized in the Green Paper 'The Future Shape of Local Government Finance'.[57]

> 'Despite the criticisms frequently levelled at them rates have many positive merits as a local tax. Their yield is substantial, certain and predictable; and straightforward increases in poundages secure proportionate increases in yield. They are a tax on fixed property which is unambiguously related to one particular area and cannot be transferred to another area to take advantage of a lower level of taxation. Their burden falls, to a large extent,

on local electors—though not all local electors pay rates—and the need to raise poundages to finance increases in expenditure provides a direct link between what the local electorate demands in terms of local services and what it must pay to finance them. There is virtually no scope for evasion, and local variations present no difficulty. The cost of collection and administration including the cost of valuation—at less than 2% of yield— is low by comparison with the costs that would be entailed in local operation of other possible taxes. In short, rates satisfy very well the main tests of local tax . . .

But rates also have disadvantages. For the domestic ratepayer at the lower income levels rates tend to be regressive—that is to say, the lower the householder's income the greater the proportion that will be taken by his rates—although at average income levels and above rates are no more regressive than the other main taxes on expenditure. Moreover rates are the largest tax which is demanded in substantial amounts from those of average means or less. In the commercial and industrial sectors, rates fall relatively heavily on those whose operations depend upon substantial investment in fixed property and plant—and anomalies in the rating of plant and machinery aggravate this effect. Periodic revaluations are needed to ensure that rateable values maintain their relationship with current rental values, and, between revaluations, poundage increases are necessary simply to offset the effects of inflation. In addition, valuation of dwellings has become increasingly difficult because there is at present a growing scarcity of evidence of open market rentals, on which rateable values are based, in large parts of the domestic sector.'

The Government, in the Green Paper, considered the alternatives—a local income tax, a local sales tax or value added tax, a local employment or payroll tax, motor fuel duty, motor vehicle duties, lotteries—and finally concluded in favour of the traditional system of rating, with some improvements to it, more particularly in relation to the rate rebate scheme. The General Rate Act 1967 introduced rate rebates and granted widespread relief to domestic ratepayers with low incomes. The Local Government Act 1974 continues this relief. The Secretary of State may by regulation prescribe the terms of a statutory rate rebate scheme and may vary its terms. A rating authority may by resolution make a local rebate scheme for its area. It may be distinct from the statutory scheme or it may differ from it only in certain respects, but in any event it must be so drawn that no ratepayer receives a rebate which would be less than that to which he would have been entitled under the statutory scheme.

The system is likely to remain, modified to lessen the harshness of its operation on poorer people, and tinkered with to give particular reliefs more especially in the area of charity operations.

MOVEMENTS TOWARDS THE 'MANAGEMENT' ERA

The way in which local authorities have conducted their business has undergone appreciable change in recent years. The movement towards reform began in the middle of the 1960s—until then one found a uniform pattern of administration differing only in scale according to the size of authority. There was a neat matching of committees and departments and a professionalism within each department. The clerk of the authority headed the legal and secretarial department and acted in a co-ordinative role as the officer *primus inter pares*. It was customary for the finance committee of each authority to exercise a measure of co-ordination more particularly through the budgeting process. There was a general inclination on the part of members of authorities to be concerned with the more detailed matters of administration and to suffer much from a multiplicity of committees and agenda material. It was from this situation, necessarily described here in the most general terms, that movement began. There had of course been experiment before this time and individual authorities had adopted systems which gave greater flexibility in administration and greater cohesion in the planning and execution of their policies. Co-ordinating committees were established during the 1920s in a number of the larger authorities, including Birmingham, Edinburgh, Liverpool, Manchester and Salford,[58] but it does not appear that these committees exercised any dramatic influence. In the early 1960s the Coventry County Borough Council had a Policy Advisory Committee under a duty

> 'to consider generally the future development of existing services or the introduction of new services, and (as may seem desirable in the Committee's judgment) either to advise the council thereon or to bring such matters to the notice of the appropriate controlling committees for their examination.'[59]

Manchester City Council had a General and Parliamentary Committee under a duty to report to the council upon questions of policy in connection with the following:

(1) New projects of a substantial character not previously approved in principle by the council.
(2) Proposed extension of a service already in operation or programme of development where, in either case, the proposals are of a substantial character.
(3) Periodic forecasts of expenditure.
(4) Matters referred to them by the Finance Committee.

THE COMMITTEE ON THE MANAGEMENT OF LOCAL GOVERNMENT

A thorough review of the internal organization of local authorities was undertaken by the Committee on the Management of Local Government. That Committee was appointed by the Minister of Housing and Local Government at the request of the local authority associations on 3 March 1964

> 'to consider in the light of modern conditions how local government might best continue to attract and retain people (both elected representatives and

principal officers) of the calibre necessary to ensure its maximum effectiveness'.

Its Chairman was Sir John Maud (later Lord Redcliffe-Maud), and its report, with three of its four associated volumes, was submitted to the Minister on 23 March 1967. The report was unanimous, subject to several notes of dissent on certain points from three of the Committee members.

The Committee did not limit itself strictly to its terms of reference. It produced far-reaching recommendations for change in internal structures and working practices, and urged a number of other changes, including a re-adjustment of relations between central government and local authorities. The Committee's recommendations as to internal organization were stated as follows:[60]

'Without waiting for any change in the structure of local government, each authority should therefore forthwith review its internal organization, with the following points in mind:

(i) There should be a clearer division of labour between council-member and officer.

(ii) Council-members must exercise sovereign power within the authority and accept responsibility for everything done in the council's name. But having settled the policy they must delegate to officers the taking of all but the most important decisions.

(iii) Committees should cease to be executive or administrative bodies, save for some exceptional purposes. Their main functions should be deliberative.

(iv) There should be as few committees as possible, perhaps not more than half-a-dozen even in large authorities. Each committee should concern itself with a group of subjects: for example child care, personal health and welfare might be the concern of a single 'social work' committee.

(v) There should be as few sub-committees as possible.

(vi) All but the smallest authorities should appoint a management board, of between 5 and 9 council-members, and delegate wide powers to it.

(vii) This board should be the sole channel through which business done in the committees reaches the council. It would itself formulate and present proposals requiring council approval. It would also propose the establishment and dis-establishment of committees. It would serve as the focal point for management of the authority's affairs and supervise the work of the authority as a whole.

(viii) If the council is organized on party political lines, the minority party should be offered representation on the management board; thus knowledge of council business would be shared, and the experience gained by minority-party members would prove valuable if, after an election, their party secured a majority of council seats.

(ix) A council should be free to pay the members of its management board a part-time salary (say, £1000 a year in the largest authorities), additional to any allowances payable to ordinary council-members.

Each authority should appoint a Clerk as undisputed head of the whole paid service of the council. He should not necessarily be a qualified lawyer but should be chosen for qualities of leadership and managerial ability. He would be chief officer to the management board.

The other principal officers should form a team under the Clerk's leadership and report to the council through him.

Departments should be grouped under not more than, say, half-a-dozen principal officers.

The full council would debate and decide questions put to it by the management board, which would sometimes circulate before debate 'white papers' on important issues of policy. Full opportunity should also be given in council for members to ask questions and table motions for debate.'

One member of the Committee found himself in disagreement with his colleagues as to the functions of the management board. Sir Andrew Wheatley took the view that the proposals would vest far too much power in the small number of members who would be members of the management board and would deprive the great majority of council members of the opportunity of participating effectively in the formulation of policy and the development of services. The committee system, he said, is characteristic of local government, and indeed by far the greater part of the work of local government is done in committees. Without that system local government could not work and there was much in it that was excellent. He accepted the need for a strong management board to co-ordinate the whole range of activities of the council, something which had hitherto been lacking in many authorities, but it seemed to him essential that the board should not usurp the functions of committees. He recommended the retention of standing committees, investing them with executive powers to manage the services for which they were responsible (but not to authorize every item involving revenue expenditure), with a duty to report to the council on the discharge of their functions. But on any major issue, policy or new scheme involving capital expenditure the committees should first report to the management board. It would be the responsibility of the board to ensure that any new proposal of this sort did not conflict with the activities of the council in other directions.

It was in fact the dissentient view which more readily won the approval of local authorities.[61] Most if not all authorities rejected the Committee's view of the management board on several grounds: it was argued that members of a board could not possibly absorb all the information they would require to carry out their functions properly; it would gravely discourage spirited people from joining local authorities, or staying with them, if they were to serve merely on advisory and deliberative bodies; in any event the devolution of all executive responsibility upon five to nine members of a management board was basically undemocratic. These were the kinds of criticisms made. But the policy committee principle, though under a variety of names, was widely accepted. At the end of 1969, 23 county councils had established a central committee with prime responsibility for the co-ordination of policy, and most of them were constituted on the lines of the Wheatley dissent. Nine of the authorities referred to made their co-ordinating committee also responsible for financial matters: in the remaining authorities separate policy and financial committees had been set up. All London boroughs and county boroughs which had applied their minds to the issue rejected the management board principle but most adopted some form of policy committee.

Most if not all authorities accepted as a principle the need to reduce the number of committees but few if any went so far as to adopt the Maud suggestion of 'about six'. County councils tended to have more committees than county borough councils, and county councils tended to perpetuate their sub-committees—several of them at the end of 1969 had 30 or more, though many of these were area committees. Thirty-four county boroughs at the end of 1969 had 10 to 15 committees instead of appreciably more. One council only achieved the Maud target—the number was reduced from 25 to 6. The reduction was generally achieved through grouping. To take one example, Bury County Borough Council had identical memberships for three groups of three committees:

Group A: Health, Welfare, and Children's Committees
Group B: Transport, Cleansing and Sewage and Watch, Fire Services and Civil Defence Committees
Group C: Art Gallery and Library, Markets and Baths, and Recreation Grounds and Cemetery Committees.

Three other recommendations of the Maud Committee gained widespread acceptance. First, the principle of delegation to officers. What had formerly been accepted on a conventional basis was extended and codified. Secondly, many authorities gave greater emphasis to the chief executive role of their Clerk or Town Clerk, though in many cases this was merely a codification of existing practices. Thirdly, there was a consistent move to restructure departments, though certainly not to the suggested 'half a dozen or so'. Sheffield City Council, for example, adopted a structure having group administrative officers with the specific responsibility, under group chief officers, for ensuring the effective and economical administration of departments within the group. The group chief officers ensure the best use of the resources of their groups, both in planning and performance, and control common services to the group where appropriate. Departmental chief officers operate on separate budgets.

The Maud Report contained 79 recommendations: 56 of them could have been put into effect without a change in the law; the balance required legislative action. And much of this appears in the Local Government Act 1972. The Committee recommended that those provisions in the law which require authorities to establish certain committees should be repealed. This in part was done.[62] It became no longer necessary for a county council to appoint a finance committee, but a number of statutory committees were retained, police committees and social service committees, to take two examples. There should be a statutory power to delegate decision making to officers of local authorities. This again was done.[63] An authority is authorized to arrange for the discharge of any of its functions by an officer of the authority. The committee recommended that authorities should be enabled to pay management board members part-time salaries in addition to fixed expense allowances for all members. The fixed expense allowance is authorized in the Local Government Act 1974.[64] The Committee recommended that principal officer posts should lie within the discretion of local authorities and should not be subject to consent, veto or sanction of a Minister, nor should tenure of office be subject to ministerial control. The Act of 1972 gave authorities a much wider discretion in the appointment of staff[65]—they may appoint such officers as they think necessary for the proper discharge of their functions. But certain officers must still be appointed, chief education officers and directors of social services, for example, and in the second case there remains a power of veto in the Minister. The Committee recommended the abolition of the aldermanic system, and this was done by the omission of provisions for the election of aldermen in the Act of 1972. The Committee recommended that there should be an additional alternative qualification for election to a local authority, namely, that a person should have had a principal place of work within the area of the authority during the whole of the twelve months preceding the election. This provision first appeared in the Local Authorities (Qualification of Members) Act 1971 and is re-enacted in the Act of 1972.[66] The Committee recommended that the law relating to pecuniary interest should be consolidated and simplified. It was consolidated in the Act of 1972[67] and at the end of 1973 the Government had entered into consultation with the local authority associations as to the matter generally.

COMMITTEE ON THE STAFFING OF LOCAL GOVERNMENT

On 3 March 1964 the Minister of Housing and Local Government appointed a committee at the request of the local authority associations 'to consider the existing methods of recruiting local government officers and of using them; and what changes might help local authorities to get the best possible service and help their officers to give it'. The Committee is generally known as the Mallaby Committee after its chairman. The Committee made an exhaustive study into the recruitment, training and career prospects of officers. So far as internal organization of local authorities was concerned the Committee recommended that the Clerk be recognized as the head of the council's paid service and that he should have authority over all other heads of departments so far as this was necessary for the efficient management and execution of the council's functions.[68] All clerkships should be open to people of all professions and occupations.[69] Authorities should consider reducing the number of separate departments by placing under one officer a group of departments which could be shown to have related functions.[70] Authorities should devolve much wider administrative responsibility to principal officers and there should be a central establishment organization in each authority.[71] These recommendations, it will be seen, run parallel with those of the Maud Committee.

The recommendations of the Committee raised little dissent. They were, to some extent, a codification of the existing practice in many progressive authorities.

MANAGEMENT IN THE NEWLY CREATED AUTHORITIES

A Study Group on local authority management structures was set up by the Secretary of State for the Environment and the local authority associations to produce advice for the new local authorities on management structures at both member and officer level. The Group reported in August 1972 in a publication *The New Local Authorities Management and Structure* (commonly called the Bains Report, after its chairman, Mr M. A. Bains, Clerk of the Kent County Council). The main feature of the Report was its stress on corporate management. It said:[72]

'Local government is not, in our view, limited to the narrow provision of a series of services to the local community, though we do not intend in any way to suggest that these services are not important. It has within its purview the overall economic, cultural and physical well-being of that community, and for this reason its decisions impinge with increasing frequency upon the individual lives of its citizens.

Because of this overall responsibility and because of the inter-relationship of problems in the environment within which it is set, the traditional departmental attitude within much of local government must give way to a wider-ranging corporate outlook. This corporate approach should be displayed not only within the authority itself but also in its relations with other spheres of local government and with public bodies such as the proposed Area Health Boards and Regional Water Authorities. The allocation of functions to the different local authorities and the freedom given to them to create organizations which are appropriate to local needs only serve to emphasize the need for close co-ordination at all levels for the benefit of the community.'

The Group recommended that each authority should appoint a chief executive to act as leader of the officers of the authority and principal adviser to the council on matters of general policy. He should be free from specific departmental responsibility. A management team of principal officers should be appointed to each authority whose corporate identity should be recognized formally within the management structure. That team should be responsible, under the chief executive's leadership, for the preparation of plans and programmes in connection with the long-term objectives of the council and for the general co-ordination of the carrying into effect of those plans.

Each authority should also establish a policy and resources committee to provide co-ordinated advice to the council in the settling of its plans, objectives and priorities. The Committee should also exercise overall control over the major resources of the authority and co-ordinate and control the carrying into effect of the council's programme. Sub-committees of the policy and resources committee should exercise day-to-day control over staff, finance and land. A fourth sub-committee should operate as a performance review body with a power to investigate any project, department or area of activity.

How far the newly created authorities really give effect to these recommendations is something which only future observers will be able to determine.

NOTES AND REFERENCES

1 Fire Services Act 1947, s. 6.

2 Education Act 1944, s. 6.

3 Ten counties and twenty county boroughs had populations of less than 75,000 in 1947.

4 Cmd. 6579.

5 House of Commons, Standing Committee B, Official Report 16 December 1947, col. 157.

6 Cmd. 9831.

7 Cmnd. 161.

8 Cmnd. 209.

9 Cmnd. 3340.

10 Cmnd. 4310.

11 Cmnd. 4040.

12 Cmnd. 4584, para. 2.

13 Cmnd. 4276.

14 Cmnd. 4584.

15 Part XII.

16 s. 179.

17 *Ashbury Railway Carriage Co. v. Riche* [1875] L.R. 7, H.L. 653 and *Attorney-General v. Fulham Corporation* [1921] 1 Ch. 440.

18 *Attorney-General v. Great Eastern Railway* (1880) 5 App. Cas. 473 *per* Lord Selborne at p. 478.

19 Vol. I, para. 323.

20 Cmnd. 4276.

21 p. 155.

22 *Roberts v. Hopwood* [1925] AC 578.

23 ss. 154 *et seq.*

24 House of Commons Standing Committee D, 15 February 1972, col. 1680.

25 Part VI.

26 Cmd. 1830.

27 Report of the Royal Commission on Local Government in Greater London, 1960 (Cmnd. 1164).

28 Cmnd. 5055.

29 Cmnd. 5057.

30 s. 14.

31 Cmnd. 4741, para. 40.

32 Cmnd. 4276, para. 60.

33 Cmnd. 827.

34 Cmnd. 1432.

35 Cmnd. 4017.

36 ss. 1, 2 and 3, and Sched. 1.

37 Cmnd. 2923.

38 ss. 1 to 5 and Sched. 2.

39 Local Government Act 1974, s. 8.

40 ss. 6 and 7.

41 Cmnd. 5532.

42 At paras. 4 and 5 and 8 to 11.

43 Cmnd. 5532.

44 Cmnd. 4741.

45 Local Government Act 1974, s. 5.

46 s. 314 and Sched. 26.

47 Town and Country Planning Act 1971, s. 17.

48 Education Act 1944, s. 99.

49 s. 95. These powers were invoked in 1973 against the Clay Cross Urban District Council.

50 s. 112.

51 Sched. 29, para. 4.

52 s. 11.

53 s. 6.

54 Education Act 1944, s. 68.

55 Sched. 14, para. 12.

56 s. 35 and Sched. 8.

57 Cmnd. 4741, Appendix 3.

58 See *Co-ordination and Planning in the Local Authority*, by H. R. Page, Manchester University Press, 1936, at p. 352.

59 These examples are quoted in *The Town Clerk in English Local Government*, by T. E. Headrick, 1962, George Allen and Unwin Ltd.

60 paras. 8 to 12.

61 See hereon the Occasional Papers published by the Institute of Local Government Studies, University of Birmingham, entitled 'Recent Reforms in the Management Arrangements of County Boroughs in England and Wales', 'Recent Reforms in the Management Structure of Local Authorities—The London Boroughs'; 'Recent Reforms in the Management Structure of Local Authorities—The County Councils'.

62 s. 101.

63 s. 101.

64 s. 172.

65 s. 112.

66 s. 79.

67 s. 94.

68 para. 490.

69 para. 493.

70 para. 498.

71 para. 499.

72 at paras. 2.10 and 2.11.

The Local Government Service

9

K. S. Carter, M.A., LL.B., D.P.A.

INTRODUCTION

As from 1 April 1974, local government in England and Wales became the responsibility of some 400 local authorities, as compared with 1400 or more prior to that date. From the local government officer's viewpoint, although a member of the local government service, his position will be unaltered—he will remain the employee of one of the many local authorities. This is not the place to debate the definition of the term 'local government service' and whether or not there can be a service where there is no common employer. The arguments were well put by Warren in 1952 in his *Local Government Service*. It is, however, the place to define the scope of this survey and Warren's definition will suffice. We are considering, he wrote, 'those who participate in the administration and management of local authority services and whose duties are of an administrative, professional, technical or clerical nature'. Teachers, police and manual workers are excluded.

At the end of 1972, the officers within our definition numbered some 500,000 of whom about 440,000 were full-time—just over half of them men. Some 340,000 were in the administrative, professional and technical grades or were undertaking responsible clerical work. They were supported by about 160,000 clerks undertaking more routine duties, typists, machine operators and others working at a similar level. This work force is by no means homogeneous; it performs a wide variety of functions. The National Scheme of Conditions of Service makes specific reference for grading purposes to administrators, architects, careers officers, chemists, education welfare officers, engineers, finance staff, inspectors of weights and measures, laboratory technicians, land agents, librarians, planning staff, public analysts, public health inspectors, solicitors, social workers, surveyors, traffic controllers, typists and valuers—and this list is far from exhaustive.

To mention the National Scheme of Conditions of Service is to draw attention to one common characteristic of all occupational groups within local government—their terms and conditions of employment are determined directly through the negotiating machinery of the National Joint Council for Local Authorities' Services or one of its related committees. Some of the issues dealt with, however, are the subject of recommendation rather than rule and local variation can be quite significant. Local variation must in fact be the keynote in any consideration of the local government service. No two authorities are alike in every respect. Furthermore, their characteristics as employers can change significantly over a period of time. The local authority consists of elected representatives, who individually and collectively have personal influence, and whose election on a party basis may well bring significant policy changes between one election and another. Apart from personalities and politics, each authority has some discretion in the extent and nature of the services provided and in methods of administration. There are, therefore, significant factors at work to give each local authority its distinct 'profile' as an employer as well as a provider of services to the community.

As between one authority and another, staffing will differ according to the range of services provided to the public. In any one case, this will depend not only whether under the 1972 Local Government Act it is a county or district and within or without a metropolitan area, but on the variety of relationships which can develop, under the Act, between authorities for agency working, particularly where counties and districts are involved in closely related functions. Size is another factor in which even after re-organization major differences arise, whether measured in terms of population, geographical area or rateable value. The size of the unit must have its effect on management and departmental patterns and hence on staffing structures.

Management and departmental structures will also differ according to the relationships between elected members and their officers. Delegation to directors or chief officers may be more or less extensive and each will have his own style of management. Furthermore, some local councils have been, and are still, in the forefront of the modern management movement. They effectively operate forward looking personnel and other management practices, whilst others remain not only sceptical, but determined to live in the past, if by so doing they can nominally keep costs down, regardless of benefits foregone. These are internal factors but external ones also have their influence. The calibre of officers, for example, as well as the proportion of established posts which are filled, vary according to the local employment situation or the attractiveness of the area.

The above is not a comprehensive list of the ways in which local authorities can differ from one another, but even these factors can create innumerable variations. All too often generalizations are made from overall figures which disguise the fact that the 'average' authority may be just one which happens to be at the median point, whilst a fair number of the others are scattered at the extremes. This may be one reason why there has been no regular and systematic collection of data about the local government service as a whole. Another is that such collection may well be regarded as a trend towards centralization—which draws attention to another characteristic of British local authorities—they are not only local, they still have a high degree of autonomy. This autonomy is jealously guarded and its voluntary surrender, for example in decisions to provide services jointly with neighbouring authorities, has never been taken lightly, usually taken reluctantly and frequently deferred year after year.

One important area of local autonomy is in respect of staff. It is natural and reasonable that whatever organization is responsible for getting something done, it should have the power to appoint and control those who are to do it. This is true of local government, despite the fact that historically local government appointments were associated with patronage and nepotism—but local government is not unique in that.

Because local authorities are concerned with local needs and tend to apply local value judgements, it calls for Parliamentary edict, for trade union persuasion, or even for the threat of national emergency to turn the attentions of local authorities to national considerations. These have all stimulated trends towards centralization and a measure of standardization. In response, the local authorities have recognized the need to act together to promote and protect their interests through the several local authority associations. However, there has always been an uneasy relationship even between these, since the protection of local autonomy has generally been interpreted as including the protection of the interest of one type of authority as against another. It is possible to argue that the main motivation of local councils in joining together in associations is, paradoxically, to retain their individuality *vis-à-vis* the central government rather than a desire to standardize practices by voluntary agreement.

The natural reluctance of local authorities to move towards national standards was mirrored earlier on by the attitude of the trade unions. This is vividly described by Alec Spoor in *White Collar Union*, which covers the history of N.A.L.G.O. from 1905 to 1965. He shows that local government officers, too, had reservations about national movements, but overcame them quicker and to such good effect that N.A.L.G.O. was, and still is, one of the major underlying influences at work in the move towards national standards.

It is, however, Parliamentary and government department influence towards standardization which is well known, immeasurably significant, and exercised in a variety of ways. Apart from the obvious impact of legislation, debates in Parliament can draw public attention to local affairs, royal commissions and departmental committees are set up and, in the fullness of time, their investigations and recommendations can affect legislation and practice. Under existing legislation, the Government has various powers of control and supervision of standards in some services, and in others can still influence the short list for appointments of certain officers although the number of posts whose occupancy is now legally subject to central government approval or interdict has declined.

Neither Parliament nor N.A.L.G.O., however, could influence local government as much as did the 1939–45 War. A national emergency focuses the mind on national problems. During the Second World War there was a clear choice—between 'guns' and 'butter'. The choice being made, everything could be related to it. Town Clerks could be defined as 'workmen' by the High Court. Local authorities as employers could be forced to toe the line under war-time legislation, and local issues could be seen in their national contexts. The Second World War played its part in bringing local authorities together to establish a National Joint (Whitley) Council—for the first time operating over the whole of England and Wales. The consequences of this have been very significant because not only did the Council agree the previously mentioned National Scheme of Conditions of Service in 1946, it also created the Local Government Examinations Board, which has had a continuous influence on qualification and promotion policies. Publication of the National Scheme—usually called the 'Charter', as it will now be in this chapter—was important, because for the first time attention was focused on *national* recommendations affecting the local government service; salary scales were specified and a very comprehensive range of employment issues dealt with in the scheme. It presented difficulties for both sides—difficulties of principle, of interpretation, and of detailed application. But because it marked a period when local councils and their staffs began to think in national rather than local terms, in considering the changes which have taken place in the local government service the end of the last war has been taken as a starting point, and the 1946 Charter as a basis for comparison.

NEGOTIATING AND ALLIED BODIES

As the various negotiating bodies which determine the grading structures and other employment conditions in the local government service will be mentioned frequently in this chapter, it may be helpful to identify them here. The National Joint Council for Local Authorities' Administrative, Professional, Technical and Clerical Services (N.J.C.) covers the majority of non-manual employees in local government, other than specified chief officers. It consisted prior to reorganization in 1974 of 63 members. Thirty-two of them were appointed to represent the employers: 16 drawn from the Employers' Sides of the Provincial Councils (see below) and 16 from the four local authority associations—Association of Municipal Corporations, County Councils Association, Urban District Councils Association, and Rural District Councils Association. The Officers had 31 representatives, 16 drawn from the Staff Sides of the Provincial Councils and 15 appointed nationally by trade unions—National Association of Local Government Officers (N.A.L.G.O. 8), General and Municipal Workers Union (G.M.W.U. 3), National Union of Public Employees (N.U.P.E. 2), Transport and General Workers Union (T.G.W.U. 1) and Confederation of Health Service Employees (C.O.H.S.E. 1). Its functions were described in general terms in the Charter as being 'to secure the largest possible measure of joint action for the consideration of salaries, wages and service conditions of officers within the scope of the Council and to consider such proposals in reference to these matters as are submitted to them from time to time by the Provincial Councils'.

Following re-organization in 1974 the constitution of the N.J.C. remains in principle the same but it is the three reconstituted local authority associations which will be representing the employers, i.e. the Association of Metropolitan Authorities (A.M.A.), the County Councils Association (C.C.A.) and the District Councils Association (D.C.A.). The Provincial Councils (P.C.s) referred to are also joint negotiating (Whitley) bodies. Before re-organization there were 13 Provincial Councils between them covering England and Wales on an area basis. After re-organization the number remains the same but some of the titles and boundaries have changed. Provincial Councils are similarly constituted to the N.J.C. Their function is to assist the implementation of national agreements and recommendations by local authorities within their area, and to resolve local disputes or difficulties. However, if they cannot do so they refer them to the N.J.C.

The salaries and conditions of service of certain specified chief officers (e.g. clerks of councils and chief executives, treasurers, engineers and chief education officers) and their designated deputies are dealt with by a Joint Negotiating Committee for chief officers (J.N.C.) on which the employers are represented by the Local Authority Associations (13 members) and the officers by their various professional associations (14 members) as well as N.A.L.G.O. (2 members).

At the level of the individual local authority the Charter in its preamble enjoins employing authorities to 'afford facilities for regular consultation with representatives of their staff on all questions affecting their conditions of service through the medium of Local Joint Committees' (L.J.C.s). These can be joint negotiating bodies in their own right and will be constituted of roughly equal numbers of representatives of the local council concerned and the union or unions representing the staff. Under the aegis of the N.J.C. and responsible to it was set up in 1946 the Local Government Examinations Board (L.G.E.B.). The Board's functions were: (a) to devise and manage promotion examinations for clerical and administrative staff; (b) to advise the N.J.C. on qualifications to be recognized for appointment and to keep under review examinations relevant to the local government service; (c) to advise the N.J.C. on recruitment to the service; and (d) to advise on post entry training. In many ways the constitution of the L.G.E.B. foreshadowed not only that of the Local Government Training Board which it later became, but that of training boards set up under the Industrial Training Act 1964. It had an independent chairman and of its ten other members two represented the staff side of the N.J.C., three were educationalists co-opted by the N.J.C., and one was the independent Chairman of the N.J.C. itself. When the Local Government Training Board (L.G.T.B.) replaced the Examinations Board in 1970 it had 30 members. In addition to the independent Chairman there were 13 representatives of the local authority associations and the Greater London Council, three representatives of the Employers Side of the N.J.C. and 13 representatives of trade unions— N.A.L.G.O. (4), N.U.P.E. (3), T.G.W.U. (3) and G.M.W.U. (3). The inclusion of representatives of the manual workers unions as well as N.A.L.G.O. reflected

8

the fact that the L.G.T.B. had full responsibility for the training of manual workers as well as officers.

STAFFING STRUCTURE

The Charter of 1946 dealt with (1) recruitment and training; (2) general conditions of service; (3) national salary scales; (4) official conduct; and (5) miscellaneous items (including an important provision for appeals). It came into effect on 1 April 1946.

At that time, the majority of the local government service was classified into five divisions: the General Division (£65 at 16 rising to £300 at 30) covering work 'in accordance with well defined instructions and regulations'; the Clerical Division for those doing clerical work which merited a higher classification (£315 to £360); the Higher Clerical Division for supervisors and those doing more responsible individual work (£380 to £425); the Miscellaneous Division, for males not normally recruited as juniors, whose duties were not wholly clerical but were of a specialized character (Grade I, £255 to £300 and Grade II, £315 to £360) and the Administrative, Professional and Technical Division which was sub-divided into eight grades (the lowest being £330 to £375, and the highest £625 to £700). Salaries are given here as a matter of historical interest but will not be hereafter.

The duties appropriate to the administrative division were said to be those concerned with the formation of policy, improvement of organization, general administration of instructions of the authority and the control of departments, higher work in the legal, technical, accounting and other departments. It also included subordinate officers engaged on professional or technical work of a minor character. The professional and technical group was separately defined to cover officers with qualifications awarded by professional bodies in amongst others the legal, medical, scientific, accountancy, secretarial, engineering, and surveying fields.

These five divisions were seen as covering the service by reference to the nature of duties performed but it is interesting to record, as suggestive of the thinking of the time, that Appendix 'B' to the Charter—a list of examinations appropriate to the local government service—was drawn up on a strictly departmental basis. The departments then listed were the Clerk's; Education; Engineer and Surveyor's; Estate, Land Agents and Small Holdings; Housing; Library; Parks; Public Assistance; Public Health; Rating and Valuation; Trading; Transport; Treasurer's; and Weights and Measures. Therefore, whilst for the purposes of national salary scales it was implied that work would be analysed by its nature and level of responsibility as in the Civil Service (although not with identical classification), organizationally the structure was seen as essentially departmental broadly following the lines of one department for each major service provided to the community, with a very few common service departments—principally the Clerk's (legal) and finance.

Although the Miscellaneous Division scales overlapped those of the General and Clerical Divisions none of the remaining four overlapped each other. It would therefore seem that, at the time, it was thought that levels of work within the Charter definitions for each division could be fairly strictly defined. However, as with other aspects of local government the practical operation of the scheme led to many local variations and consequential anomalies. Some councils made a conscientious effort to classify their officers by reference to duties performed, whilst others assumed that they could classify their staff by reference to the salaries they were paying them before 1 April 1946—slotting each one into the new salary grade nearest to the previous salary.

The self-contained nature of the local government divisions in terms of salary in 1946, however, was by no means intended to imply separate recruitment to them. There was a bar to promotion beyond the General Division on the basis of qualifications, which is dealt with more fully below, but movement between divisions was not only possible, it was expected.

One last point of note on the 1946 Charter—it provided salary scales for women at 80% of those agreed for men in all divisions except the Administrative, Professional and Technical where equal pay applied. Equal pay was agreed in principle in 1955 and implemented in all divisions over a seven-year period although doubts still exist on the question of equal opportunity.

In the next 20 years numerous changes were made in the Charter. Each edition was significantly larger than its predecessor, reflecting new problems which had presented themselves for national solution and the pressure from both staff and employers for greater uniformity and guidance on service conditions matters. The number of salary scales within the divisions was at times increased and at others reduced. Specified gradings were introduced for a number of occupational groups, including typists and machine operators, and the grades for which it was necessary to have full or part qualification were changed (usually upwards!).

In 1966, however, there was a significant reconstruction of the grades. The General Division scale was merged with the lowest of three Clerical Division scales and a routine work bar introduced to determine progression on the basis of the work performed, rather than qualifications held. The then Clerical Grades II and III were retained and an additional grade (IV) introduced to provide for officers doing more highly responsible clerical work or supervising large clerical units. A Trainee Grade was introduced to cater for staff appointed to train as administrative, or professional officers—the first example of planned national provision for direct recruitment to the AP divisions.

The most significant change introduced in 1966, however, was the reconstruction of the APT division. A separate Technicians and Technical Staffs Division was established to cover officers undertaking work of a technical nature which requires a special training or expertise but not such as to require a full professional qualification. The division had six grades the salaries for which overlapped the Clerical and most of the new AP grades. No qualifications were attached to the Technical grades because the object was to 'enable local authorities to make the fullest use of technicians . . . and thereby utilize fully their qualified professional officers on professional duties'. The higher grades, however, were intended to include those posts for which recognized technicians training schemes and/or qualifications existed.

Prior to the restructuring there were 13 APT grades. The five lowest were recast into a new 'AP division containing five grades. Above the AP grades provision was made for more senior administrative and professional staff by means of two new categories termed 'Senior Officers' and 'Principal Officers' respectively. They are descriptions of responsibility levels and not departmental titles. This reconstruction was a reflection of the need of the steadily enlarging local government units for a bigger upper structure of managerial staff and the difficulty of accommodating suitable salaries for them between the former ceiling of the AP divisions and that of chief officers and their deputies—particularly of the smaller authorities—which were separately negotiated by the J.N.C. using as a basis the population of the area governed by the local authority concerned.

At the time of re-organization in 1974 the salary structure—and the formal staffing structure—was similar to that agreed in 1966 but much more complex than in 1946. A simple table will help to make the point:

1946		1974			
General Division	Miscellaneous Divisions (2 grades)	Clerical Division (4 grades)	Typists and M.O.s (5 grades)	Miscellaneous Divisions (8 grades)	Technical Divisions (7 grades)
Clerical Division					
Higher Clerical Division					
A.P. Division (8 grades)		A.P. Division (5 grades)			
		Senior Officers (2 grades)			
		Principal Officers (2 ranges)			
Chief Officers		Chief Officers			

The table throws up some of the modernizing trends—a greater sophistication in the analysis of the nature and levels of responsibility of the work done, the emergence of a distinct technician group, and accommodation for a larger top management structure. However, it masks others. The list of examinations recognized for promotion purposes has long since ceased to be on a departmental basis—signalling at least a breach in rigid departmentalism. There has been a significant growth in the variety of occupational groups in response to the growth of services such as social work, consumer protection, and recreational, in compensation for those lost such as the hospitals and utility services in the 1940s. Greater acknowledgement of the importance of management or organizational functions has also added to the occupational groups in terms of O. & M. officers, personnel officers and work study assistants. These in turn have had their effect on patterns of work and even methods of payment. (It is not without significance that there is now an Appendix to the Charter on approved procedures for the introduction of management techniques.) Management considerations are also beginning to make a breach in the former invariable situation where, in contrast to the Civil Service, it was the professional and not the administrator who was on top. In 1946 a significant proportion of those in the higher ranges of the AP divisions and of the Chief Officers would not just have been 'professionals' but from the traditional professions of the law, medicine, accountancy and engineering. At the time of re-organization at least some of those in the senior officers grades and above were drawn from a wider field. These and other underlying trends will be further discussed later in this chapter.

RECRUITMENT

Before the Second World War local authorities recruited largely from 16-year-old boys who had left grammar school with a School Certificate. They thus took into their service many who would have profited from a period in the sixth form, possibly followed by a degree course at university, had those opportunities been more widely available. The National Joint Council in 1946 indicated that the Charter was intended 'to enable employing authorities to deal with their staffs on a basis intended to mark the Local Government Service as offering a career likely to attract entrants of the type required to meet the future needs of local government'. It envisaged a minimum age of entry of 16 years and provided that 'entrance shall be by examination . . . and shall consist of two stages (1) a qualifying stage and (2) a competitive stage (including interview)'. The standard of the qualifying examination was to be 'not less than that in force under the School Certificate examination'.

Clearly in 1946 it was expected that recruitment would go on much as before the war. Young people would come into the service at 16 and, if they had the will and ability, qualify themselves for promotion and work their way at least to the senior range of posts, if not to the top. This was in fact what happened in many cases. Not a few Clerks of local authorities had served articled pupilage in local government, qualified as solicitors and after a period in legal work had moved to administrative and managerial activities as deputy clerks. Financial Officers or Treasurers were largely the products of internal promotion having, during their service, passed the examinations of the Institute of Municipal Treasurers and Accountants. Most of the Chief Librarians, Parks Superintendents, Rating and Valuation Officers, and Chief Inspectors of Weights and Measures fell into the same category.

However, in thinking that recruitment at 16 would continue to produce enough senior officers, and that it would be possible—or necessary—to insist on all recruits having a School Certificate standard of education, the N.J.C. in 1946 was thinking too much in pre-war terms. Since 1945 there has been a steady increase in the number of children who stay on at secondary school, and the trend towards a longer school life and further period of full-time education has continued. By 1960 de *facto* had become *de jure* and it was accepted that school leavers could be recruited to the local government service without any educational qualifications. For those with a minimum of four G.C.E. passes, there were, however, higher starting salaries; and it is interesting to note that in that year 84% of those able to take advantage of the higher starting salary had more than the minimum number of G.C.E. passes required. The Entrance Examination of the L.G.E.B. held between 1951 and 1963 inclusive was accepted in place of the requisite G.C.E. passes. By 1964 the growing number of 18-year-old school leavers, and the value of the contribution they could make by qualifying for the APT division, was recognized by giving them a higher starting point within the General Division than their age warranted, provided they had a minimum of 5 'O' level passes.

The recruitment of university graduates was also specially mentioned in the 1946 Charter. The desirability of employing graduates was accepted, but 'To achieve this object' the Charter stated, 'facilities should be afforded by employing authorities for serving officers to obtain such qualifications, and also for a limited number of University graduates to be recruited direct'. It is known that in the late 1950s between 200 and 250 graduates a year were joining local government direct from university—most of them going to the large authorities. The majority had studied subjects relevant to the department they were entering. The two biggest graduate recruiting departments at that time were the Engineers and Libraries, with the Clerks (for those with law degrees), finance, children, and welfare accounting for most of the rest.

The Mallaby Committee on Staffing in Local Government reported in 1967 that in the years 1962–64 the annual average rate of graduate recruitment had risen to between 350 and 400. However, the Committee considered this to be inadequate. Because of full employment, the rate of increase in the total working population, the fall in the number of 18-year-olds, the raising of the school leaving age and increased opportunities for extending full-time education, the Committee concluded that local authorities could no longer rely on school leavers as their main source of recruitment. The point was well taken and in 1966, a trainee grade was introduced for direct entry to the AP divisions. This overlapped scales Clerical I and AP I and II. The starting point within the trainee grade was flexible, to be determined by the recruiting authority according to age and qualifications on entry. Progression was dependent on success at various stages of whatever approved qualification the trainee took. There were set minima for those passing the intermediate stage of their examinations and—near the top—for those passing their finals for whom no substantive post requiring the qualification concerned was immediately available. The minimum salary for those with an intermediate qualification also applied to graduates recruited to the trainee grade, as it was hoped the grade would prove attractive to them, as well as 18-year-old school-leavers. The Charter did not specifically state that the trainee's education and training would be paid for by the employer. As, however, the trainee was required to undertake and pursue it successfully in order to meet the requirements of the grade, appropriate finance and study leave was normally assumed, and normally granted.

By 1974, therefore, recruitment patterns in local government had become much more varied and flexible. The educationally qualified 16-year-old recruit to the lowest Division, who was the mainstay of the entry in 1946, is now in just one recruitment category. Recruitment is common at any age between 16 and 19 and after graduating. Depending upon educational qualifications, if any on entry, and upon career interest, recruits can be placed in the clerical, typing, technical or trainee grades. There are also more entrants direct to the lower AP grades. They are—at least nominally—fully trained outside the service. Social workers who are recruited straight from college are a significant group in this category. This greater variety and flexibility is not only a response to market forces, but the result of more attention being paid to job requirements—an underlying influence on the pattern of the local government service which will be returned to later.

PROMOTION POLICIES

At the beginning of the period under review, promotion prospects in the Civil Service existed mainly within, and not between, classes. During the period, however, promotion between classes became steadily more common. As we have seen in local government, the movement was, if anything, the other way. It was not until the mid-1960s that formal provision was made for direct recruitment to the middle (AP division) grades.

The concept that pay should reflect that local government was a 'qualified service' underlay the 1946 salaries agreement. The acceptance of the need to submit to independent rigorous and standard national tests of relevant knowledge was the 'quo' which the local government officer offered for his 'quid'. It was also local government's answer to strictures about favouritism in making appointments. In order to develop and maintain the qualified service, the 1946 Charter provided that 'a general division officer shall not be eligible for promotion to a higher grade unless he or she has passed successfully the promotion examination, or has secured the qualification of a recognized professional institute. The National Council has decided to establish a suitable promotion examination in the future, together with the necessary machinery.' The machinery was the Local Government Examinations Board.

In relation to promotion, the Local Government Examinations Board then had two functions:

(a) it had to advise on the examinations of 'professional institutes' which should be accepted for promotion purposes, and at what levels; and
(b) it had itself to provide the equivalent of a professional examination for administrative staff, who, as an occupational group had no organization of their own to conduct examinations for them. N.A.L.G.O. had given up its examining function to the L.G.E.B. and the two major Secretarial bodies were based mainly in industry and commerce.

With regard to the 'Promotion Examination' the National Joint Council, on the recommendation of the L.G.E.B., adopted a rather drastic policy. The examination was to qualify officers in the General Division for promotion 'throughout the Divisions' and was seen as a means of identifying a pool of suitably qualified candidates for even higher appointments. This scheme lasted only three years (1948–50) because it tried to meet two needs and in so doing met neither satisfactorily. The Promotion Examination was set at what would now be regarded as G.C.E. 'A' level and was of a similar academic nature. As such, it proved unrealistically difficult, and insufficiently job related, to serve as the hurdle every officer had to pass, in order to do work even one degree more responsible or specialized than that which obtained in the General Division. At the same time, it was supposed to select those from whom higher appointments could in due course be made; appointments which presumably would be at the same level as those held by professional officers such as lawyers, accountants, and engineers. Clearly an examination of the standard and nature of the Promotion Examination could not reasonably claim to do this. The result of a review of the situation was the creation of two new examinations. The first was a relatively straightforward 'Clerical Division Examination' set, in academic terms, just above G.C.E. 'O' level, intended primarily for those concerned only to qualify themselves for promotion into the Clerical Division. The second led to the award of the Board's 'Diploma in Municipal Administration'. This examination was structured on the general pattern of the major professional qualifications with Intermediate and Final stages. Its standards in academic terms related to those of the Intermediate and Final stages of an Ordinary (pass) degree. Success at the Intermediate stage qualified officers for promotion up to the (then) AP IV grade and at the Final for promotion beyond that grade.

It was indicated above that the Promotion Examination, like those which took its place, was mainly for the clerical and administrative staff. This was the case in practice, but it was not the original theory. In considering the examinations of 'professional institutes' which should be recognized for promotion purposes, the L.G.E.B. saw dangers in the tendency for the number of professional bodies to increase, either by duplicating work of existing bodies or by splintering the field of local government employment. In seeing this as a danger, the Board was not undervaluing the extent to which these bodies had steadily raised the standard of senior officers employed by the local authorities through the encouragement they had given to many kinds of education and training. The danger seen was undue specialization in the early stages of the young officer's career when it might be quite fortuitous which department of local government he entered, he might not know the extent of the opportunities available to him or be able to assess where his future interests lay. A broader training and education before specialization would be advantageous. It was therefore argued that the Promotion Examination should be accepted by professional bodies as their own intermediates with the addition perhaps of one or two specialist papers. To encourage this hoped-for development, and because the Promotion Examination itself gave eligibility for promotion throughout the grades, the National Joint Council decided to recognize as alternative to it only the final examination qualification of approved professional institutes.

Like the Promotion Examination itself, the provision whereby officers could only qualify for promotion from the General to the Clerical Division by passing a final professional qualification did not last long. With the replacement of the Promotion Examination by the D.M.A. the intermediates and finals of the major and professional bodies were given the same degree of recognition for promotion purposes as the Diploma, although those not regarded as of equivalent standard and status were equated only with the Intermediate D.M.A.

Although committed to the concept of a qualified service, the introduction of qualifications for promotion, in the rigid way in which it was done in 1946, left N.A.L.G.O. as the major union representing the staff with the problem of how to protect the interests of the many officers already in service. Many were of an age or seniority at which it would be unrealistic to expect them to qualify for further promotion when, at the time they joined the service, this was not a requirement. Negotiations within the National Joint Council defined and re-defined classes of officers exempted from the provisions for qualification for promotion on grounds of age and length of service. They also produced compensation in the form of accelerated increments for officers who qualified but failed to get early promotion. This, though, did not go far enough for some local authorities, which agreed with their staffs completely to ignore the requirements of the Charter relating to promotion. Others operated it strictly—so strictly that long serving officers normally in line for promotion were passed over because they were unqualified.

The most bitter arguments were in the 1950s when the number of staff who had never been required to qualify was at its greatest and education and training facilities, particularly the opportunity to study in working time, were far from fully developed. More recently, qualifications for promotion have been relaxed for quite different reasons—market forces and a more accurate assessment of work requirements. By 1966, therefore, when the grades were reconstructed,

8*

there was no longer a requirement to pass the Clerical Examination in order to move up through the Clerical Division, although local authorities were enjoined to give preference to those who did and they were given the right to accelerated increments. Similarly, qualifications were no longer necessary for the administrative and professional grades, although local authorities were advised 'to make every endeavour ... to ensure that officers appointed to these grades are appropriately qualified by examinations'. Qualifications were, however, required for the Senior Officers and Principal Officers grades. Comparing 1946 with 1974, therefore, we have moved from a situation in which it was, at least in theory, necessary to take quite an exacting examination merely to move from the lowest scale to the one immediately above it, to one in which no qualifications need be required below the Senior Officers scale—though, of course, in practice they often are, and certainly it is an advantage to have them.

Although formal qualifications for promotion had been introduced in local government, they could only provide the pool from which promotions were made. Experience and personal qualities other than intellectual must always count too. The assessment of personal qualities and performance standards has always been a sensitive area in local government. The 1946 Charter included a model form of annual report to be made on each member of staff. As from 1964, the model form was taken out and a more general reference made to reporting both at the end of the first year and, if the authority so desired, on further occasions. The removal of the form and the general terms of the paragraph tend to indicate that at national level the question of a formal system of reporting was being soft-pedalled. In recent years, however, with the development of the work of the Local Government Training Board as well as the growth of management training, questions of staff appraisal both in relation to responsibilities of line management and of the developing personnel function have again arisen. Appraisal systems, for good or bad, are being used in some authorities, particularly in connection with schemes of management by objectives and similar experiments, and so presently there may again be pressure for standardized forms and procedures. Where the personnel function is well developed and an appraisal system exists, clearly the resulting records will have some impact upon promotion prospects.

Seniority and breadth of experience have been quite common and acceptable criteria for promotion. This has meant not movement between departments as it might mean in the Civil Service, but movement between local authorities. There is much to be said for it, because different authorities have different problems and methods, and working in a new environment must always present a challenge, providing opportunities for the officer concerned. However, recently the cost of re-housing has made officers more resentful of the need to move to get promotion. If it results in officers remaining for a large part of their career with one authority—even a large one—it will deprive local govenment of some of the richness of experience which mobility encourages.

TRAINING

In its evidence to the Mallaby Committee (1964) N.A.L.G.O. listed many types of training which should be available in local government. They included induction, general education, on-the-job training in clerical skills and routines, training for supervision, preparation for administrative or professional qualifications, training in the principles of management, background, appreciation, refresher and integration courses for both administrative and professional staff, management development facilities for qualified officers, senior management courses for chief officers and re-training. The view was expressed that local authorities should pay in time and money for any training which was of use to them.

The 1946 Charter had envisaged that after entry to the service officers would continue study. Arrangements might include attendance at approved part-time classes for general education, for studies of the principles of local government and public administration and for any preliminary qualifications needed for acceptance as students by technical, professional or administrative examining bodies. Guidance and facilities were to be provided to enable officers to qualify, and officers were encouraged to undertake systematic study of local government and its problems, through courses of study, lectures, library facilities and facilities for research.

The nature and amount of training provided by individual local authorities varied greatly from one to another. Much depended upon the attitude of senior officers in each department. There were no training officers and there were many pressures arising from the post-war re-organization of services. Helping officers to qualify by examination was given the greatest emphasis, but again the level of help given varied greatly. In many cases officers were given grants for examination success, but initially had to pay course fees themselves. Although reference was made to guidance for young officers, it was quite often a matter of chance, influenced by the department to which he was appointed which led an officer to take one qualification rather than another. The emphasis placed in local government on preparation for professional qualifications has sometimes been adversely commented on. It was, however, evidence of a desire on the part of the employers to enforce high standards and of considerable effort, self discipline, and willingness to submit to independent tests of knowledge and understanding on the part of the staff. What was less widespread in local government was practical and skills training.

Looking to 1974 we see a rather different picture. The Charter recommendation is that students attending approved courses, whether for examination or non-examination purposes, should be fully financed by their employers and undertake training in their employers' time. One feature of note, which is more forward looking than in many other services, is that there is no age bar even for general education purposes—though obviously leave for study purposes is given more readily to the young. The variety of training available is much greater than in 1946. Induction training is now common. There has also been a great expansion in practical training both in relation to jobs as such and in association with theoretical preparation for formal qualification. Many officers now attend full-time courses on secondment although more could be made of 'post-professional' or 'second degree' courses for the development of experienced officers in the midst of their careers. Management training has blossomed. There have been crash programmes for senior officers: of ten weeks for the under 45s and three weeks for those over that age. Many others have attended shorter courses. Supervision training for officers on lower grades is, however, relatively less common.

How was the transformation achieved? Underlying influences such as the level of employment, changes in the public education system and public demand for improved personal services are dealt with in the last part of this chapter. Within local government, however, a number of organizations gave impetus to the change. Initially, a great deal of the push to improve education and training after the Second World War came from the officers themselves, principally through their union N.A.L.G.O. It had been long standing union policy that local government should be a fully qualified service. As early as 1912 the Association had—in default by the local authorities—started its own entrance and qualifying examinations for administrative staff, its own correspondence courses in 1920 and students' lending library in 1929. Also long before the 1939–45 War it tried to stimulate teaching in public administration and allied subjects by giving grants to assist the founding of university lectureships in the subject and by approaching local education authorities to provide classes. After the Second World War N.A.L.G.O. also expanded its own education services, regarding anything it could do to help its members climb the promotion latter as a legitimate union activity. In this respect the union regarded itself as an innovator— it held courses in management for local government officers long before they became fashionable—and a protector of the interests of the small specialist groups, the isolated student, and those not selected for training by their employers, by the provision of correspondence and residential courses for professional examinations and in a wide range of administration and management subjects. In so doing it gave the employers something to finance, to counter the plea, particularly in the 1950s and 1960s, that they were willing to send staff for training but suitable courses did not exist.

It was then, with the full support of the staff representatives as well as those of the local authorities, that the Local Government Examinations Board was set up in 1946 and to it N.A.L.G.O. willingly gave up its examining functions in the belief that the examinations were better conducted by an entirely independent body. The Board's advisory work on education and training was, however, greatly stimulated when in 1960 it set up its Education Committee. The Committee undertook a survey of recruitment and training methods and started to consider training methods and specific training needs. However, it was not until the establishment of the Local Government Training Board in 1968 that a substantial impetus was given to the analysis of training needs and the preparation of recommendations to meet them.

The L.G.T.B. was set up mainly at the instance of the local authority associations and did not emanate from the Industrial Training Act. In setting it up the associations were attempting both to deal with the problem of the small authority which had genuine difficulties in financing training, and to stimulate the less training conscious authorities to contribute to the total training effort instead of recruiting staff fully trained at the expense of other authorities. As the initial impetus was financial—to spread the load of the cost of training—each member authority paid according to the number of its staff and received back in grant sums calculated on the quantity and nature of the training provided. However, once the formerly less generous training authorities had been inveigled into a higher level of training activity the redistribution of finances became just that and a much less important part of the L.G.T.B.'s activities, as was the case with most of the industrial training boards.

As at 1974 the Training Board had drawn up 18 training recommendations covering such varied occupational groups as roadmen, personnel officers, swimming pool plant operatives, administrative staff, and on management development. On-the-job training was a field ripe for development in 1946. In most cases routine procedures were learned 'sitting next to Nellie' with consequential variations in standards of skill, thoroughness and awareness. The Local Government Training Board has given considerable impetus to effective on-the-job training, through the influence of its training recommendations, and by the appointment of training officers during the last five years.

In 1946, one of the purposes for which it was intended to use the Local Government Examinations Board was to give guidance towards suitable qualifications and help to cut down the proliferation which then existed. The position in 1974 is, if anything, more complicated. The number of examinations recognized for promotion purposes has grown—a reflection of the growing variety of specialized work and the attempt of specialized groups to achieve the same status, and indeed to submit themselves to the same sort of discipline, as those that were established at an earlier stage. The demand for education and training facilities from these professional and occupational groups is a feature of the development of education and training in local government and, whilst sometimes it has not been coherent, and outsiders always regard each group as being too narrow and self-centred, the gain in occupational 'know how' and the improvement of technical standards is to their credit.

The majority of the qualifications recognized for promotion purposes are awarded by professional bodies—in other words the scope and nature of the education, and to some extent the practical training involved are governed by the occupational group itself. There has, however, been a growth in the influence of statutory and other public qualifying bodies whose qualifications normally involve specified practical training. The main examples are the Central Council for Education and Training in Social Work, providing qualifications which include practical training for a range of social workers, the Youth Employment Examinations Board which does similarly for Careers Officers, and the Public Health Inspectors Examinations Board.

The development of training and qualifications for social workers is worthy of special mention, not only because social work has been one of the main growth areas in local government activity, but because it is an object lesson in opportunities forgone both from the point of view of local government retaining control of its own staff recruitment, training and development, and from that of an important occupational group failing to secure control of its standards. After the Second World War problems arose in caring effectively for children 'deprived of a normal home life', which led to the 1946 Curtis Committee investigation and report. As a result of that report wider responsibility for child care was placed squarely on the Home Office and there was set up in 1947 the Central Training Council in Child Care. The Council's activities in turn led to an extensive provision of special university courses. In 1955 the Younghusband Committee was appointed to inquire *inter alia* into the recruitment and training of social workers in local authority health and welfare departments. The Committee found that the services were limited by lack of appropriately trained staff and that a vacuum created when the Poor Law Examinations Board ceased to exist had not been filled. It concluded that a national qualification was needed, and agreed that this would call for provision of training on a national scale. The result was the statutory Council for Training in Social Work set up in 1962, and in 1971 its activities were joined with those of the Councils responsible for training in child care and probation work to form the Central Council for Education and Training in Social Work.

If social work can be regarded as a post-war profession one can see here that, for social-workers—as for administrators through the Local Government Examinations Board—a new pattern was emerging where those responsible for qualification and training were independent from those trained. It is a matter for debate as to where the responsibility for standards of professional competence of local government officers should lie as between local authorities, central departments, independent statutory bodies and the occupational groups themselves. In social work, however, it seems that government stepped in when there was an obvious need which neither local government nor the occupational group concerned had taken adequate steps to meet.

Now that the Local Government Training Board is well established and conducting examinations as agents for people who are not local government officers —e.g. Fire Brigade and the Police, it seems illogical that there should be other independent public examination boards for categories of officers who are wholly, or mainly, within local government, such as the careers officers and social workers. But, although the existence of these bodies with their sometimes overlapping functions, makes for confusion as well as variety, they have been significant developers and providers of education and training in the period under review.

Whilst the national bodies referred to above have all had significant parts to play in the development of education and training in local government there have also been contributions from organizations at regional and local levels. Most provincial councils set up education committees in the 1940s and early 1950s. Some of these committees drafted post-entry training schemes to give flesh to the bare bones of the Charter provisions on education and training and because they were jointly agreed they had force for the local authorities who were party to them.

The level of education and training activities did, of course, vary considerably between one provincial council and another. However, it is interesting to note how many features of national agreements or recommendations started out at regional or local level. The basis for the specific proposals on the nature and degree of financial assistance to be given to officers studying for recognized qualifications incorporated in the Charter in 1952 were formulated by N.A.L.G.O.'s Metropolitan District Council in 1949 and approved by the Metropolitan Education Joint Council (the provincial council for education matters in the Metropolitan area). Other examples from the Metropolitan area include the grouping of local authorities for training purposes, started in 1951 to develop induction courses, on which Appendix 'B' was added to the Charter in 1964. The first day release course for weights and measures inspectors (operated with N.A.L.G.O. on a combined oral/correspondence basis) was established by the M.E.J.C. and the block release version pioneered by the South-West Provincial Council is commended in the L.G.T.B. 1974 recommendations for the training of weights and measures inspectors. It was also the South-West Provincial Council which appointed the first full-time education and training officer (in 1961) and which now probably leads the field in the number of job related short residential courses which it provides for its area, although a number of others are fast catching up. Many also do excellent, if little publicized, work in providing courses for manual workers and in the stimulation that their full-time staff give to the development of education and training within the member authorities through advice and exhortation.

At the beginning of this chapter emphasis was placed upon variation as between authorities which comes (quite properly) from their autonomy. It therefore follows that whatever the recommendations from national and regional level, implementation is largely a matter for the individual local authority and in this respect the work of local joint committees has often been of considerable importance. It is significant that from the first edition of the national scheme of conditions of service it has been acknowledged that 'any scheme of post-entry training should come within the purview of such local joint committees. However, in the absence of such committees the authorities establishment committee should formulate schemes in consultation with staff representatives'. In some cases, local schemes added very little to the national provision, in other cases they improved upon it and set out in considerable detail the way in which the national scheme should be implemented to meet local circumstances. In any event they provided a forum or focus for staff demands for the development of education and training facilities where the initiative was not taken by the management.

In recent years training, like management, has become fashionable. This has eased the path for those who, for other and more legitimate reasons, have wanted to see it develop in local government. Now, however, the cost is being more meticulously counted. There is a growing insistence that the training provided—particularly off the job—shall be job related and effective which is good. On the other hand there is a tendency to be much more selective which, if in respect of the type of education and training which opens up career opportunities, is not only a danger to individual officers but in the long run to the quality of staffing in the middle and senior levels of local government. To tread sensibly and fairly between the two paths will be one of the many challenges to the development of the local government service of the future.

INFLUENCES AND TRENDS

The previous paragraphs have attempted to trace staffing developments in local government under the conventional headings of structure, recruitment, promotion policies, and training. Obviously they are inter-related and there are influences and trends which underlie them all. It is interesting to try to identify what these have been. However, these influences and trends are themselves inter-related and there is no significance in the order in which they are dealt with below.

The Second World War was a great impetus to technological change, which has continued to be a feature of the last 30 years. It is not only the fact of change, but the rate of change, that is important. Technological arguments have influenced the distribution of some services. The transfer of the utilities to *ad hoc* bodies came about mainly for this reason. Under this broad heading too, there have been major developments in the more mundane fields of mechanization. Local government has not been slow to introduce new methods and machines. The computer works not only for the finance department but in the drawing office. Engineers inspect their drains with miniature television sets and traffic wardens as well as policemen and ambulance drivers are directed by short-wave radio. These changes demand new skills and evoke new occupational categories.

If changes in communications, in terms of transport, have thrown up many of the major problems that local government has had to cope with in engineering and planning, changes in methods of communicating information and ideas have had their impact on local policy and local practices. New communication methods have on the one hand speeded up domestic administration and, on the other, influenced public attitudes. The growth of television and local broadcasting, for example, has reduced the time between decisions taken by local authorities and the announcement and critical examination of those decisions. More information given to the public and given more quickly has encouraged greater involvement in local issues. This has had its impact on the officer too. It tends to bring him nearer to the public at a time when the growth in the size of local authorities is making him more remote. Perhaps the net result will be to leave things much as they were—but without changes in communications remoteness would surely have won!

The movement in political thinking in the 1940s towards acceptance of the idea of a welfare state and a rising standard of living brought public demand for a wider range of local government services in general and more effective personal services in particular. This led to a considerable growth in some occupational groups, such as entertainment officers on the one hand and social workers on the other. The greater demand for staff coincided with a relatively high level of employment, making it more difficult to recruit. This in turn led to the changing patterns of recruitment, already referred to, and also to the search for more effective means of using the manpower resources available, adding impetus to the development of management techniques and their by-products, mentioned again below.

Amongst the growing public services education has had a significant place, and it is one of which local government is both a provider and a consumer. Several aspects of the education explosion have affected the local government service. The raising of the school leaving age, but still more and earlier the growing tendency to continue full-time education beyond school leaving age, both at school and in further and higher education, has affected recruitment patterns, as already indicated.

With the increasing variety of institutions providing further and higher education has come a greater variety of courses. Many of these are now providing a more sophisticated basis of study in subjects relevant to professional careers. In turn the professions are increasingly demanding attendance at full-time courses as part of their specified education and training patterns. These courses are often entered straight from school and, since the product of some of them is limited, this faces the employer with having to accept the college chosen recruit or itself seconding officers at very early stages in their careers on relatively long full-time courses before they have proved themselves on the job.

With the growth of full-time courses, the provision of part-time ones and particularly evening classes, formerly the mainstay of the man determined to help himself, has declined. This presents both the local authority and the local government officer with the problem of where to get tuition if full-time courses are not suitable or convenient for one or other party. Thus the trend towards exclusively full-time tuition has the tendency to stratify recruitment to local government, and to militate against upward mobility through the strata.

Full-time courses, however, have greatly improved the quality of professional education particularly in areas where, previously, establishments had not been adjusted to permit students and trainees a lighter load of productive work, and they had therefore in practice to cope with a full load in overtime in compensation for what was ostensibly study leave. However in hoping that full-time courses would improve their training and status, and as a result their comparative salary levels, some professional groups such as librarians and careers officers were chasing a mirage. Their position in the pecking order remains substantially the same, give or take a few small movements up and down from time to time. The lawyers, engineers and accountants remain in the lead. They have been joined recently by the top echelon of social workers—surely mainly as a result of public demand for improved personal services—and catching up the personnel officers impelled by local government's own managerial revolution.

There is also a rival trend which could rebound upon professional bodies wedded exclusively to full-time courses, in cases where the nature of the studies involved do not make these imperative—the development within the public education system of vocationally based qualifications which are, or could be by public demand, available on both a part-time and a full-time basis. This trend may be encouraged by greater contact with the European Community, and the degrees of the Open University are a pointer to what could develop in other fields.

The education explosion was paralleled in local government by an explosion in management thinking and practices. It was natural for people returning from their different war-time environments to look critically at the way in which their work was organized. Theories developed within the United States government, and the American business schools, crossed the Atlantic to vie with others which had developed and been experimented with here. Long before re-organization, the growth in the size of many local authorities, on the one hand justified greater specialization, and on the other, called for more planning, co-ordination and control within the units. The more numerous and larger capital projects undertaken, involving longer time-scales, also called for more sophisticated planning, progressing, and co-ordination. Thus the importance of the organizing, or managerial, function became more apparent and led to the examination of organizational patterns and procedures.

At the same time the economic pressures of labour shortage, and periodic measures to curb public expenditure, allied to the desire for good husbandry, encouraged the study of how to make the best use of human and capital resources. Indeed forward looking local authorities such as Coventry and the L.C.C. were in the van of the Organization and Methods (O. and M.) movement. The study of methods and procedures involved a careful analysis of job content. Thus it emerged, amongst other things, that some posts occupied by professional officers were mainly administrative in character, whilst others were more technical than professional and meat for the growing category of technicians referred to above. The effect of this job analysis on recruitment and promotion patterns has already been mentioned. Other by-products were the moves to measure work of a clerical and even technical and professional nature, that had previously been regarded as unmeasurable, and, albeit to a limited extent, to introduce productivity payments for some types of clerical work and machine operation.

In the early stages, however, most O. and M. practitioners found it tactful to concentrate on methods rather than organization, and their work rarely affected what would now be called top management. Gradually, however, work on the relationships between councils and their committees, and between councillors and their staff, developed to the point where the Local Authority Associations asked for a review of Management in Local Government, undertaken by a committee under the chairmanship of Lord Redcliffe-Maud, whose report was published in 1967, alongside that on Staffing in Local Government, which was the work of the Mallaby Committee. The report laid emphasis on the need for corporate management—the need to cut across traditional departmental thinking, and plan the use of the local authority's resources as a whole, determining priorities in the light of analysis of policies and objectives. This put a premium on machinery for policy planning, progressing, co-ordination and control, and led, on the Council's side to the concept of management boards and policy committees. In respect of internal administration it gave impetus to the grouping of related functions under one directorate, so that there were few enough top managers to form a viable management team. It also resulted in the growth or strengthening of common services departments dealing with personnel, management services, and the collection and analysis of information in support of the management team.

These developments were sanctified by the 1972 report of the Bains Working Group on *The New Local Authorities—Management and Structure*, and, at least in principle, have been accepted by most of the new authorities set up on re-organization. The impact on the staff has been to open up a panoply of new higher management posts, but to reduce people reaching the head of their own specialist unit from the unique position of Chief Officer to that of one of a number of chiefs under one directorate. It also calls in question one of the underlying assumptions of the major professions—that a professional man can only be subordinate, if at all, to one of his own kind.

The rigid departmentalism of earlier days had started to break down before Mallaby and Bains, which to some extent built on the experiments and practices of the more forward looking authorities. The common service departments with their co-ordinating influence grew in the 1950s and 1960s. Establishment services widened to include a range of management techniques, computer units serving all departments, and central purchasing were cases in point. The grouping of engineering, surveying, environmental planning, and architectural services, or some of them, into 'technical service departments' was taking place at the same time as children's and welfare departments were being compulsorily fused under the Social Services Act 1970. The latter was influenced by the Seebohm Report which argued that all those who might become involved in the care of a family should be under the control of one department.

Undoubtedly the old rigid departmentalism made little sense in terms of the problems of the 1970s. In terms of staffing, as mentioned above, it offered relatively narrow promotion prospects within any one authority, and led to the need to move between authorities to broaden experience. Will the new arrangements be better in this respect? Or are we to see the growth of a new style of departmentalism just as rigid in its turn as the old? Personnel departments, supplies departments, management services departments, are increasingly being staffed by specialists, separately recruited, and separately trained, sometimes outside the service. As these departments grow their staffs could find themselves doing just as narrow a job, and building just as defensive a hierarchy, as the public health or welfare departments of the past. At least when those departments fought selfishly for a bigger share of total resources they did so in aid of a service given directly to the public. When the new type of horizontal department comes to fight for its own, it will be doing just that, and not for something that the public can easily identify, judge, and vote upon.

So much for the structures, but what of the people who operate them? Growing awareness of the importance of the organizing function led to a steadily increasing demand for management training to which a variety of organizations responded—N.A.L.G.O., the R.I.P.A., the L.G.T.B., the growing Institute of Local Government Studies at Birmingham University, and many colleges within the public education system. It also gave a new twist to the fight of the administrator for parity of esteem with his colleagues in the traditional professions.

What was done by the officers themselves to establish administrative qualifications, and the provision of study facilities for them, has been mentioned above. When the L.G.E.B. took over responsibility for the administrative qualification in 1946 it also took from the Civil Service the assumption (with which the author does not quarrel) that in order to do his job well an administrator must be able to think, and to some purpose. He must have intelligence, judgement, and logic. These were the characteristics which, given suitable material, a university degree was supposed to develop. Hence the administrative qualification devised was of a very academic nature. Most of the papers were in relevant background and 'tool' subjects, demanding an approach similar to that required in comparable subjects in degrees in government or public administration. In 1967 the Mallaby Committee reported that the D.M.A. had not gained the hoped for degree of acceptance. The numbers who had obtained the Diploma, although growing steadily, did not average two per authority, and were in fact concentrated in the larger ones. Furthermore only a relatively small number of D.M.A. holders held posts above the then APT division.

Historically most of the professional and technical groups then entrenched in local government had taken as long, if not much longer, to establish themselves, but this was of little comfort to D.M.A. holders. Administrators had no professional body to back them. N.A.L.G.O. did what it could, mindful of the fact that it also represented the professional and technical staff. Perhaps the administrators expected too much too quickly given the domination of the large departments by senior officers from the traditional professions. Some of them, at least, tended to look upon anyone who had not followed their own discipline as mere 'pen pushers', and the posts of those involved were graded accordingly. Rationalizing their attitude some professional officers accused the D.M.A. of being of a low standard (untrue—academically it was assessed by perhaps the most distinguished university panel established by any examining body, with strict instructions as to the standards to be enforced), and/or that it was insufficiently job related, especially to the needs of staff in the early stages of their careers (true—but remediable had it been the only problem).

It is surprising that the Mallaby Committee, in recording the relative lack of progress of the D.M.A., did not link it more definitely with its own comments on the inadequate use made of the 'lay administrator'. The comparatively small number of D.M.A. holders in senior posts probably had much less to do with the suitability of their qualification than with the comparatively small number of posts for administrators at senior level at a time when the organizing function was just coming to be recognized. In the new situation, with more senior posts opening up for those undertaking organizing, co-ordinating and controlling functions, officers in the traditional professions have seen a threat to their access to managerial posts if the administrator strengthens his position. At the same time they have felt a real need to develop the skills necessary to work successfully in inter-disciplinary groups, to ensure that complex projects reach fruition, and to make corporate management a reality, so from them has come much of the demand for management training in recent years. It seems a pity that, just when the administrator could gain from the increasing recognition of the importance of the organizing function, changes in the D.M.A. regulations to bring them manifestly in line with recent changes in professional body requirements, impose such stringent demands in terms of full-time courses and practical training that even well-intentioned authorities will have difficulty in making the necessary facilities available, especially during the re-organization period.

The question of 'administrator—on top or on tap?' therefore remains unresolved. But it is interesting to note that the D.M.A. holders, despite their relatively small numbers, appear (from the first lists) to have obtained as many posts of chief executive with the new authorities as have finance staff, with the engineering group pretty well nowhere in the race, and the lawyers still holding their overwhelming position. The latter was only to be expected. Most of the Clerks and Chief Executives of the old authorities were lawyers, and it would have been quite unwarranted to fail to make full use of their experience and ability in setting up the new ones. Who will succeed them is an open question. Mallaby indicated that in future the officer who chose from the start to make his career on the administrative side, rather than train as a lawyer, or accountant *en route* to his final aim, should have equal access with the professionals to the post as chief executive. Paradoxically, the Report did not see administrators becoming heads, or even deputies, of executive departments. It is also interesting to note that at that time, when the whole trend of management thinking was in favour of generalists leading large units, and all government exhortation was towards using modern management principles and practices, Seebohm went the other way in insisting upon a professionally qualified head of the proposed new social services department. The government followed by specifying the qualifications and attributes it would find acceptable in the Head of such a department, at a time when it was proposed to reduce central control in respect of other local government appointments.

So where will the Chief Executive of the future come from? N.A.L.G.O. argued in its evidence to the Mallaby Committee that no one type of training or experience uniquely fitted an officer for the top managerial posts. Capacity, flair, and genuine interest in the wider policy considerations and resource allocation were needed in addition. One would expect administrators, orientated that way from the start, to make at least equal running with those of more specialist bent, who at the moment feel they must give up the exercise of their specialism, very often at a time when they could make their greatest contribution to it, in order to further their careers. For the historian it will be interesting to look back in, say, ten years' time and see what has occurred; for the administrator we can but hope that the weight of tradition will not make it another period of agonizing frustration.

The chief executives will have great influence on the success with which local government settles down on re-organization. But what of the several hundred thousand other local government officers? How does the character and temper of the local government service compare with that in 1946? No generalization made about half a million people and 400 independent units can be valid for all, but with that proviso it is fair to note some changes discernible to those who knew the service in the 1940s.

The ex-serviceman returning to his employment after the Second World War returned to a somewhat authoritarian environment. He generally regarded his employer as benevolent if autocratic, and the local government service as something safe, respectable, and socially useful. Since then local government officers have been affected by the same social, economic, and political developments as the rest of the community. Indeed, with their growing numbers, more varied recruitment, and greater variety of work, they mirror the community—or at least the white collar section of it, much more closely than hitherto. Many a local government office is a more colourful and cheerful place than one would have expected to find 30 years ago. The young local government officer tends to dress according to the vogue, in terms of clothes, hair and beard. He tends to put less of a premium on tidiness and quietness than did his predecessor. The advent of party politics in local government is accepted by most local government officers, and even regarded as a good thing for sound political science reasons. In the 1950s, at least in some parts of the country, it was still regarded as somewhat unseemly. Today it is not uncommon to see on an election address that the candidate 'works in local government'.

Today, too, most local government officers recognize that in joining N.A.L.G.O. they are joining a trade union, and one which they helped to take into the T.U.C. in 1964. In 1946 many of them would have regarded it as an association of gentlemen, and industrial action as something which, as the term implies, belonged to industry. Recently N.A.L.G.O. has had its official strikes, and has even been prepared to take industrial action against the results of government policy which could not really be blamed on the local authorities—an inevitable development with the growing government intervention into wage bargaining within the public sector.

At the grass roots there is some talk of 'worker-participation'—a more difficult concept to reconcile with an employer elected by, and responsible to, the public, than within the private sector context. But within council policy, the idea of corporate management, management by objectives, and team working all imply more positive participation by the officer, and with improved education and training he is more frequently asking 'why?' instead of accepting without comment what is handed down from on high. Certainly there is one group of local government officers, or rather a group within a group, which is even prepared to question who is the better custodian of the rights of the citizen, its members or the Council? For some social workers their first loyalty is to their client, as an individual, and they have been prepared to serve him, in whatever they think is the most effective way, irrespective of Council policy and perhaps the needs of the rest of the community. This, however, is the extreme attitude of a very small group. In general, as with the Civil Service, it can be said that councils can have confidence that their staff will carry out council policy to the best of their ability, whether as individuals they like it or not, and however much, if they are sufficiently senior, they may seek to influence it beforehand.

The local government service is certainly more colourful, varied and at one with the rest of the community than it was. It no longer attracts mainly because it is safe and superannuable, for other occupations are too. Some young people enter the service because they are philosophically opposed to the commercial rat-race and want to do what they regard as a socially useful job, but few would now want to take the triple traditional Civil Service vows of anonymity, poverty and silence.

Changes, then, there have been, but are they superficial or fundamental? As this chapter was being written another report on local government was published. It was the report on 'Conduct in Local Government', the latest in a great series prepared by committees and commissions under the chairmanship of Lord Redcliffe-Maud. It mentions the great size of local operations, represented in 1971/72 by an expenditure of £10,000 million (England, Wales and Scotland). It draws attention to the many and costly capital projects undertaken by local government which makes it so significant a purchaser of building and civil engineering services. The opportunity for patronage is great, the number who can influence it many, and the incentives laid before them prepared with insidious professional skill reflecting the activities of that new occupational growth area—public relations. And yet between 1964 and 1972 only 22 local government employees were convicted under the Prevention of Corruption Acts. Twenty-two too many perhaps, but given the number at risk they cannot be a very venal lot! The Report recommends a number of legal changes with regard to disclosure of interest, the use of information obtained on the job for private purposes, prohibition of all outside work analogous to that on which the officer is employed by the council, and something which would be new to local government, a register of the outside interests of senior local government officers, but for the information of councillors only. For councillors there is a longer list of recommendations, and, a recommended Code of Conduct. It is significant that for officers it is not necessary to recommend a code—they have had one since 1946. Its current version does not include all the details in the Report's proposals, but it does cover their spirit, and because it has been freely entered into by representatives of the staff, and is part of the conditions of service of every local government officer on appointment, it is worth quoting:

> 'The public is entitled to demand of a local government officer conduct of the highest standard and public confidence in his integrity would be shaken were there the least suspicion, however ill founded, to arise that he could in any way be influenced by improper motives.
>
> An officer's off-duty hours are his personal concern but he should not subordinate his duty to his private interests, or in any way weaken public confidence in the conduct of the authority's business . . .'

No mean undertaking, and one to which the vast majority of the local government service subscribes.

Northern Ireland

10

Professor R. J. Lawrence, B.Sc. (Econ.) Ph.D.

The primary purpose of this chapter is to give an account of reforms in Northern Ireland since the beginning of the civil rights movement in 1968. During this period, the scope and character of reform have had no parallel in the rest of the British Isles. Virtually every public institution in Ulster, whether legislative or executive, regional or local, has undergone change to a greater or lesser extent. And the reformers have not been concerned simply to make government more efficient, or to subject it to closer public control, or to devise policies for particular services, though they have tried to do all these things. They have been confronted by the infinitely more difficult problems of maintaining order without excessive coercion within a deeply divided community, and of creating a constitutional framework within which the Protestant majority and the Roman Catholic minority would be willing to settle disputes without recourse to violence.

These problems cannot be understood if they are set in the context of Northern Ireland alone, or if they are confined within the perspective of the recent past. For one thing, the Governments of the United Kingdom and of the Irish Republic are deeply involved in one way and another, and their power or influence profoundly affects affairs in Ulster. For another, the six counties of Northern Ireland have only existed as a distinct political entity since 1921, and the political attitudes of its people, like those in the rest of Ireland, are still moulded in large part by memories of strife that was endemic for centuries in Anglo-Irish relations. Before turning to the post-1968 reforms, it is therefore necessary to sketch the historical background.

THE BACKGROUND

In the history of Anglo-Irish relations, a dominant theme is the attempt by England to anglicize Ireland. A similar policy, by and large, was effective on the mainland of Great Britain. Wales was incorporated and united with England in 1536 by Henry VIII, himself of Welsh descent. It was effective, too, in Scotland, though the Union of 1707 was achieved by more diplomatic means and left the Scots with their distinctive legal system and form of church government. In Ireland it failed—except in part of the province of Ulster in the north-east. Military conquest, though at times energetic and barbarous, was never thorough

237

enough to be of lasting effect and left a legacy of hatred: the name of Cromwell still lives in Ireland as a symbol of English oppression. The Protestant Reformation, possibly the strongest unifying force in Britain, never took root in the greater part of Ireland, where most of the people clung tenaciously to the Roman Catholic faith. The ownership of land, and the relations between landlords and tenants, gave rise to bitter dissension because vast areas on which the mass of the population depended for a bare subsistence were sequestrated by the Crown and turned over to English and Scottish settlers. Bribery was used to secure the legislative Union of 1801, and the promise of Roman Catholic emancipation was not realized until 1829. During the first decades of the 19th century ill fortune took a hand. The population outstripped the means of subsistence, and British Governments were confronted by problems of famine and pestilence that defied the best economic thought of the day. It was not until the last quarter of the 19th century that Britain made really determined efforts to redress tangible grievances; but by that time Irish nationalism, deepened by a revival of Gaelic language and culture, was deeply rooted and found expression in demands for freedom from foreign domination.

British policy was more successful in parts of Ulster where the population was Protestant in religion and of English or Scottish descent. The English Revolution of 1688–89 and the Williamite campaigns in Ireland were more revered than in England itself as foundations of civil and religious liberty. The Orange Order, founded in 1795, was a powerful social and political force. Tenant farmers in Ulster were less subject to the rapacity of landlords, and in the 19th century the skill and enterprise of the people provided a basis for rapid expansion of manufacturing and commerce. Demands for self-government by Irish Catholics therefore encountered determined resistance by Ulster Protestants. The Protestant Churches, the landed gentry and small farmers, and the business, commercial and working classes found common cause in opposing Home Rule and in creating the Ulster Unionist Party in Belfast in 1905.

This conflict between South and North, Catholics and Protestants, Home Rulers and Unionists, presented W. E. Gladstone and other British politicians in the age of liberal democracy with intractable problems of statecraft. Attempts to give Home Rule to the whole of Ireland foundered. Irish Nationalists saw Home Rule as a step towards autonomy; Ulster Unionists, as a stage in the dismemberment of the United Kingdom. After 1910 it became clear that many Irish Catholics were prepared to fight and die to get freedom from Westminster rule, and that many Ulster Protestants were equally prepared to fight and die to be free from Dublin rule. The Government's final response in 1920 was to partition Ireland and to provide for two Parliaments and Governments, one in Dublin and one in Belfast, both with limited powers and both subordinate to Westminster.

Partition, like all crude operations, was not ideal. The boundary was a subject of bitter dispute, and there remained enclaves of Protestants in the South and enclaves of Catholics in the North. While, however, Southern Protestants accepted the new regime or packed their bags and left, many Northern Catholics were disaffected and expressed their views by staying in Northern Ireland and refusing to recognize the authority of the new Parliament at Stormont. From the outset, therefore, the community in Ulster was divided. And the division arose, not merely from differences of religion or culture or language that are common in many countries today but also from a cleavage of nationality and political allegiance.

On the other hand, partition was not indefensible. It was not 'unnatural' because all political boundaries are the outcome of will, not nature. It gave to a majority in the South and in the North what they wanted—and it also enabled them to unite if they wished. The Government of Ireland Act 1920, empowered the two Parliaments to end partition by mutual agreement and to set up a single Parliament and Government for the whole of Ireland. To this end, the Act provided for a Council of Ireland consisting of representatives of each Parliament to initiate proposals for united action. The Parliament of Northern Ireland appointed representatives to the Council in June, 1921, but Southern Ireland preferred to go its own way. In 1922 it seceded from the United Kingdom and gained dominion status with the title of the Irish Free State, and in 1949 it left the Commonwealth and became the Republic of Ireland.

Between 1921 and 1968 events were shaped in one way and another by three Governments—in London, Dublin and Belfast—and a brief indication must be given of the attitudes of each of these.

The general posture of successive British Governments may be summarized in a single phrase: let sleeping dogs lie. Having extricated herself from the Irish imbroglio, Britain by and large left political leaders in Northern Ireland to deal with the difficulties that remained after British rule. Two difficulties were of special importance. The first was to prevent and contain subversion. Although Westminster was responsible for the defence of the United Kingdom, the burden of repelling periodic raids from across the border, as well as the maintenance of internal order, fell on Stormont. For these purposes, Ministers established an armed police force (the Royal Ulster Constabulary), supported by a mainly part-time force (the Ulster Special Constabulary) and took draconian powers, including the power to intern without trial, by the Civil Authorities (Special Powers) Act (Northern Ireland) 1922 and later legislation colloquially known as the Special Powers Acts.

The second difficulty, which was confined to the period before the 1939–45 War, was to secure sufficient money to improve the low standard of services that Britain had left behind. Although taxes in Northern Ireland were for the most part levied by Westminster at the same rates as in Britain, Governments in Northern Ireland were unable to obtain enough money from the Treasury to remedy years of neglect. After the Second World War, however, the Labour Government under Mr C. R. Attlee (later Lord Attlee) made more generous arrangements. Thereafter, Governments at Stormont were able to make vast improvements, though only at the cost of making themselves increasingly dependent on British goodwill. The Attlee Government also confirmed Ulster's constitutional status as part of the United Kingdom in 1949 when Southern Ireland became a republic. In subsequent Labour Governments, backbenchers who disliked the Stormont regime or its policies occasionally tried to exert pressure on British Ministers to bring about reforms. However, Speakers of the House of Commons discouraged Questions and debates on matters that had been transferred to Stormont, and Ministers strictly observed the rules of the Constitution. By the Government of Ireland Act 1920 the Parliament of Northern Ireland was subordinate to Westminster, but Ministers at Stormont were not subordinate to those in Whitehall. Thus, on 8 August 1966 the Minister of State, Home Office, explained in the House of Commons:

'Section 75 [of the Government of Ireland Act] preserves the supreme authority of Parliament but not the Government of the United Kingdom over all persons, matters and things in Northern Ireland. I stress that the word used is "Parliament", not "Government". This means that in no event can there be any question of the United Kingdom Government interfering in transferred matters without legislation passed by virtue of that Section. It would need legislation by this Parliament . . . The Government them- selves acting as a Government or Cabinet could not pass legislation . . . We have authority as regards certain subjects but not those which have been reserved for the Northern Ireland Government unless this Parliament passes an Act on those transferred matters.'

The United Kingdom Government could, no doubt, have obtained a powers Act and placed upon themselves direct responsibility for affairs in Ulster, but they preferred not to do so. Administrative arrangements conformed to this pattern. When Mr James Callaghan became Home Secretary in December 1967 he found that Northern Ireland affairs occupied so little time and attention in the Home Office that they were grouped together with a variety of miscellaneous functions, including British summer time, London taxicabs, liquor licensing, protection of birds and animals, the Channel Islands, the Isle of Man and the Charity Commission.[1]

Governments in Dublin, by contrast, pursued courses that were irrational in the sense that they were calculated to frustrate, rather than to further, their objectives. Their professed objective was to secure the political unification of the whole island. Since this could not be attained by invasion, it would seem that the most sensible course would have been to assure Northern Protestants by word and deed that they had nothing to fear and something to gain from political union. The policies pursued by Southern Governments might have been expressly designed to antagonize Northern Protestants. Indeed, failure by Dublin to take effective action to curb sporadic armed raids across the border created a siege mentality in the North and helped Unionist politicians to win elections by emphasizing the dangers of republicanism.

Unionists also were less than rational. They failed to appreciate the need to retain Britain's sympathy and goodwill and to try and win the allegiance of the

Catholic minority. True, anti-partitionists constantly denied the legitimacy of the Stormont regime, while the Nationalist Party steadfastly refused to act as a responsible Opposition at Stormont, and these attitudes were so passionately and sincerely held and so deeply rooted in hatred of British rule that nobody can say whether magnanimity over a fairly short period of time would have changed them. What can be said, from the vantage point of today, is that Unionist Governments would have been wise to ensure that there was no vestige or even any appearance of political or religious discrimination. However, the greatest grievance of the minority, after partition itself, was probably that all the power and patronage of government rested with one political party representing only one section of the community. Unionists won solid majorities at Stormont at every election after 1920. This predominance was not attributable to gerrymandering or other malpractices. The effect of the abolition of proportional representation for Parliamentary elections in 1929 was (as one would expect) to reduce the strength of small parties, including Independent Unionists; and a proportional representation election in 1973 gave Loyalists and Unionists a clear majority of seats in the Northern Ireland Assembly. To expect Unionists themselves to take the initiative in inviting their bitter opponents to form coalition governments was unrealistic. The remedy lay with the United Kingdom Parliament, which had absolute authority to amend the constitution.

On the other hand, Ministers in Northern Ireland had much to their credit. For almost 50 years they governed without undue coercion. Political parties were free to compete for votes; the press was free from censorship; the judiciary was independent; the Supreme Court was a reserved service controlled by the British Government; and the Civil Service was efficient and free from any taint of nepotism or corruption. The Constitution, which Stormont had no power to amend, prohibited laws interfering with religious equality, and no such laws were passed. As Britain made more money available after 1945, immense improvements were made over the whole field of public services. Church schools in Ulster were treated more generously than in England. The Northern Ireland Housing Trust, established in 1945, built large numbers of houses and allocated them fairly. All the services of the Welfare State were available to the whole population. It was no doubt partly for these reasons that, despite a high level of unemployment and emigration, the population increased between the first census in 1926 and the 1961 census, whereas in the Republic of Ireland it fell. (See table overleaf.)

It may be argued that conflict between South and North was understandable, or even inevitable in the sense that no other courses were open to them, because their aims were irreconcilable. But mutual trust and confidence can transform the most obdurate problems and create conditions in which co-operation may grow. It seemed that events might develop in that direction when, in 1965, Captain O'Neill (later Lord O'Neill of the Maine), then Prime Minister of Northern Ireland, and Mr Sean Lemass, Taoiseach of the Irish Republic, met at Stormont to discuss common problems. In the same year the Nationalists accepted the role of official Opposition at Stormont for the first time since 1921. But within three years all was changed. In 1968 mobs took to the streets to demand civil rights. A massive programme of reforms enacted or prepared by Stormont was followed by different and more strident demands to merge Ulster in an all-Ireland republic. Violence and counter-violence spread until in March 1972 the Stormont Parliament and Government were replaced by direct rule from London.

TABLE 1   Population, 1926 and 1961

	Northern Ireland				Republic of Ireland			
	1926		1961		1926		1961	
	Persons 000s	%	Persons 000s	%	Persons 000s	%	Persons 000s	%
Roman Catholic	420	33·5	498	34·9	2751	92·6	2673	94·9
Others	836	66·5	927	65·1	221	7·4	145	5·1
Totals	1256	100·0	1425	100·0	2972	100·0	2818	100·0

THE CIVIL RIGHTS MOVEMENT AND ITS AFTERMATH

In 1966 the 50th anniversary of the Easter Rising in Dublin was celebrated in Belfast and other places in Northern Ireland. In the same year a committee met in Belfast to discuss the formation of a civil rights organization. The Northern Ireland Civil Rights Association, with a constitution modelled on that of the National Council of Civil Liberties, was established in 1967. These events symbolized the divergent aims and motives of many people in Northern Ireland, especially among the Catholic minority, and their sympathizers in Britain. One aim, inspired by the sentiment of Irish nationalism, was to end partition. The other, motivated by a desire for social justice, was to maintain civil liberties, abolish discrimination, and secure impartial government and administration. Though divergent, both movements expressed deeply-felt emotions of resentment and frustration which could easily give rise to violent protest and rebellion.

The Civil Rights Association was not the first body to be concerned with social justice in Northern Ireland, nor the last. In 1964 an organization known as the Campaign for Social Justice had been founded in protest against the allocation of houses by Unionist-controlled councils in Dungannon (County Tyrone); and after 1967 a variety of other bodies sprang up, including the People's Democracy, the Derry Citizens' Action Committee, and more than a score of other action committees and local civil rights committees throughout Northern Ireland. Collectively they may be said to constitute the civil rights movement.

At its inception the movement aimed to achieve its objectives by the tactics of peaceful marches and demonstrations in public places which had become popular and effective in the United States. The first march took place in August 1968 between Coalisland and Dungannon in County Tyrone. Its immediate occasion was the allocation by the local Unionist council of a house to a Protestant in preference to a Catholic whom the demonstrators considered to be in greater need. Bias in allocating houses was not confined to Unionist councils, but in the Dungannon area (where the Campaign for Social Justice originated) there had been resentment among Catholics for many years about housing. The march, which was re-routed by the police in order to avoid a counter-demonstration by Protestants, gave rise to some tension but passed off peacefully. The Cameron Commission (mentioned on p. 245 below) noted the hope among many of the participants that something new was taking place in Northern Ireland. People of different political antecedents and convictions had taken part in a non-violent demonstration and were united on a common platform of reform. But the Tyrone march proved to be the first breath of a storm during the next five years which, it seems safe to say, few of the original demonstrators had foreseen or intended. Demonstrations and marches in other places led to counter-demonstrations; and riot, disorder and lawlessness gradually became part of normal life. Thousands of people refused to pay rent, rates and taxes; squatting became commonplace; explosives, petrol bombs and incendiary devices were used against life and property; barricades were erected, first by one side, then by the other, and finally by the Army to keep them apart; town centres were sealed off; armed gangs and private armies emerged with the conflicting aims of destroying or maintaining Northern Ireland as a political unit; revolutionary movements of various kinds began to take a hand; and as the fabric of law and society crumbled, malicious and greedy men seized the opportunity to pay off old scores and enrich themselves by robbery and extortion. Episodes of this unfolding tragedy were magnified and distorted by some newspapers and by television, whose commentators' confidence in their ability to prescribe remedies was matched by their insolent treatment of those in authority.

As these events developed, British Governments were gradually impelled to concern themselves more closely with affairs which they had hitherto regarded as the constitutional responsibility of Northern Ireland. Thus on 25 October 1967 the Home Secretary told the House of Commons:

> 'Under the Northern Ireland constitution, certain powers and responsibilities are vested in the Parliament and Government of Northern Ireland. Successive Governments here have refused to take steps which would inevitably cut away not only the authority of the Northern Ireland Government but also the constitution of the province. Nevertheless, my right hon. Friend and I have not concealed from the Prime Minister of Northern Ireland, with whom we have had continuing discussions, the concern felt here . . . There is room for argument . . . about the pace which is practicable or desirable. But we must at least be satisfied about the

direction. Provided we can be so satisfied, there is a great deal to be said for not trying to settle the affairs of Northern Ireland too directly from London.'

Thereafter, Northern Ireland affairs were more frequently debated at Westminster, and British Ministers pressed insistently and publicly for reform. It was, no doubt, more convenient to proceed in this manner than to secure legislation to transfer contentious issues to Westminster; but after almost half a century the affairs of Northern Ireland, and the Irish question with which it was entangled, were beginning to reappear in British politics.

At the same time, Governments at Stormont formulated and put into effect a massive reform programme. There can be no doubt that this was in large part in response to British pressure, which was the more effective because of Ulster's financial dependence. Nevertheless, Prime Ministers of Northern Ireland had a choice. They could have pointed to the law of the Constitution and, if necessary, have offered their resignation to the Governor of Northern Ireland. Instead they undertook the task of persuading the Ulster Unionist Parliamentary Party, as well as the party outside Parliament, to accept reform. The difficulties were enormous. While some Unionists held that the best hope of stability lay in acceding to reasonable demands—though it was not always obvious what was reasonable—others feared that concessions would whet an appetite for Irish union in the foreseeable future. In February 1969 the Prime Minister, Captain O'Neill, went to the country in order to strengthen his position and gain wider acceptance of his policies of reform. The result showed that the power of dissolution can be two-edged. O'Neill split his party, carried his own constituency by only a minority vote, and was obliged to resign as Prime Minister in April. His successor, Major Chichester-Clark (later Lord Moyola) survived until March 1971 and was then replaced by Mr Brian Faulkner. Despite these internal dissensions, successive Unionist Governments carried through a host of reforms and instituted independent inquiries into the causes of the disorders. Indeed, Mr Faulkner's Government began to consider more far-reaching changes. In June 1971 they made firm proposals for functional committees of the Stormont House of Commons, with a membership reflecting the strength of parties in the House, to consider major policy and scrutinize administration. At least two committees were to be chaired by Opposition M.P.s. In October they suggested that the size of the Commons might be increased, declared that the single transferable vote system of proportional representation merited serious consideration, and said that it would be very desirable for members of both religious communities to take part in the executive Government, provided that they accepted Northern Ireland's status as part of the United Kingdom and were willing to preserve the processes of democratic government and to resist organizations which sought to advance their causes by violence and coercion.

In consequence of this activity, by 1971 virtually all the original claims for civil rights had been met and many more reforms had either been put into effect or were in prospect. By that time, however, protest was taking new directions.

The demands that were now put forward ranged from a complete reconstruction of the Northern Ireland Constitution in order to assure the Catholic minority of a share in government, to the ending of partition and the creation of an all-Ireland Republic. Protest had also become so violent that in August 1969 the British Government at the request of Major Chichester-Clark sent a contingent of the Army to the province. Constitutional responsibility for law and order, however, still rested with Stormont. This division between power and responsibility was clearly not satisfactory, and in March 1972 the British Government insisted on the transference of law and order to Westminster. Mr Faulkner and his colleagues then resigned and the British Government took powers to prorogue Stormont and to govern Northern Ireland by direct rule for a period of up to two years, i.e. until March 1974. Henceforth, Northern Ireland legislation took the form of Orders in Council, and executive functions vested in the Governor of Northern Ireland and Ministers were discharged by the Secretary of State. After March 1972 the British Government drove forward political and administrative reforms, including those already introduced at Stormont before direct rule. Now, however, the major task was to devise and put into effect before the end of March 1974 a new form of regional government which would be acceptable to both the majority and minority communities.

Thus, during the years 1968 to 1973 an extensive programme of political and administrative reform was enacted at Stormont and Westminster, and in the latter part of the period more fundamental attempts were made to secure a political settlement by means of constitutional reform. Even an outline of all these changes would fill a volume. It is necessary to select the most important. I therefore begin with the Cameron Commission, which diagnosed the causes of disorder as they appeared in 1969.

POLITICAL AND ADMINISTRATIVE REFORM

The Cameron Commission

In March 1969 the Governor of Northern Ireland appointed a Commission under the chairmanship of Lord Cameron to inquire into the violence and civil disturbances since October 1968. The Commission's Report, published in September 1969, first sketched the complex background. It pointed to the existence of one-party government since 1921 and the absence of any united Parliamentary opposition dedicated to support the Constitution. A party continuously in power tended to be complacent and insensitive to criticism or acceptance of any need for change or reform; an Opposition which could never become a Government tended to lose a sense of responsibility. The Report also noted the remarkable width of the powers given to the Royal Ulster Constabulary and the Ulster Special Constabulary under the Special Powers Act 1922, but pointed out that the Act was passed at a time of undoubted emergency caused by campaigns of mutual murder and reprisal in 1920 and 1921; that the

9

I.R.A. continued a campaign of violence between 1956 and 1962; and that its activities still continued and its objectives remained the same, even if temporarily its tactics varied. The Commission outlined the deep-seated political and religious divisions in Northern Ireland and the fears and suspicions they engendered, but declared that traditional patterns of antagonism had begun to erode and that this trend had coincided with 'a decline in preoccupation with the border as an immediate political issue among, and in the appeal of Nationalism to, the Catholic population'. The bulk of the Report examined the actual course of events in detail and the many complaints of injustice that were put forward. The Commission's summary of the general causes of the disorders was as follows:

(1) A rising sense of continuing injustice and grievance among large sections of the Catholic population in Northern Ireland, in particular in Londonderry and Dungannon, in respect of (i) inadequacy of housing provision by certain local authorities; (ii) unfair methods of allocation of houses built and let by such authorities, in particular, refusals and omissions to adopt a 'points' system in determining priorities and making allocations; (iii) misuse in certain cases of discretionary powers of allocation of houses in order to perpetuate Unionist control of the local authority.

(2) Complaints, now well documented in fact, of discrimination in the making of local government appointments, at all levels but especially in senior posts, to the prejudice of non-Unionists and especially Catholic members of the community, in some Unionist controlled authorities.

(3) Complaints, again well documented, in some cases of deliberate manipulation of local government electoral boundaries and in others a refusal to apply for their necessary extension, in order to achieve and maintain Unionist control of local authorities and so to deny to Catholics influence in local government proportionate to their numbers.

(4) A growing and powerful sense of resentment and frustration among the Catholic population at failure to achieve either acceptance on the part of the Government of any need to investigate these complaints or to provide and enforce a remedy for them.

(5) Resentment, particularly among Catholics, as to the existence of the Ulster Special Constabulary [the 'B' Specials] as a partisan and paramilitary force recruited exclusively from Protestants.

(6) Widespread resentment among Catholics in particular at the continuance in force of regulations made under the Special Powers Act, and of the continued presence in the statute book of the Act itself.

(7) Fears and apprehensions among Protestants of a threat to Unionist domination and control of Government by increase of Catholic population and powers, inflamed in particular by the activities of the Ulster Constitution Defence Committee and the Ulster Protestant Volunteers, provoked strong hostile reaction to civil rights claims as asserted by the Civil Rights Association and later by the People's Democracy which was readily translated into physical violence against Civil Rights demonstrators.

It will be seen that according to this diagnosis the general causes of the disorders lay mainly in four fields: local government, the absence of machinery to investigate and provide remedies for complaints, the Ulster Special Constabulary and the Special Powers Act.

Local Government

In 1967 local authorities in Northern Ireland comprised the elected councils of six counties (responsible chiefly for education, libraries, health and welfare services and roads in rural districts), two all-purpose county boroughs (Belfast and Londonderry), and 65 boroughs and urban and rural districts with housing, environmental and miscellaneous functions. There were in addition several *ad hoc* authorities. Belfast City and District Water Commissioners supplied water to Belfast and other places. The Northern Ireland Housing Trust built and managed houses. The Northern Ireland Hospitals Authority ran the hospitals. The Northern Ireland General Health Services Board provided general health services. In 1969, following the disorders in Londonderry, the powers of the corporation and the adjoining rural district council were transferred to the Londonderry Development Commission consisting of members appointed by the Minister from different sections of the community, with the aim of rapidly improving the economic and social life of the area.

The whole structure was transformed in October 1973, when the major functions of elected councils were transferred to the regional government. Local government survives in an attenuated form: 26 district councils, elected by proportional representation, have limited functions, chiefly minor environmental services. Appointed area boards are responsible for administering a number of former local government services, and their members include a minority nominated by the district councils.

The reasons for this transformation, which were partly political and partly administrative, are complex. It had been evident for years that a plethora of small local authorities was inefficient and a hindrance to economic development, and in 1966 the Government announced their intention to initiate talks on the re-shaping of local government. Two White Papers were published. One, a *Statement of Aims* in December 1967, set out the problem and examined various alternatives. The other, containing *Further Proposals* in July 1969, proposed the retention of one council in Belfast and the creation in the rest of the province of 16 authorities responsible for housing and other urban and rural functions in areas comprising both town and countryside. The Paper made no firm proposals for health, welfare, education and library services, which absorbed most local expenditure and required fairly large populations, but it was clear that none of the proposed new councils except Belfast would be suitable for their administration. Thus, it seemed necessary to transfer these functions to *ad hoc* bodies or to retain county councils.

Meanwhile, the Ministry of Health and Social Services was examining the health and personal social services in the light of proposed changes in Britain.

The structure of these services was tripartite, the Hospitals Authority being responsible for hospitals, the General Health Services Board for general health services, and county councils for personal health and social services. In a Green Paper published in July 1969 the Ministry discussed the merits of creating an integrated structure by dividing the province into three to five areas with a single board in each to provide the whole range of services. Two months later the Cameron Report was published. Its criticism of shortages of council houses and the manner of their allocation stimulated immediate action. In a joint communiqué in October the Westminster and Stormont Governments announced the intention to set up a single-purpose, efficient and streamlined central housing authority, and to make arrangements to ensure the provision of water, sewerage, roads, land, and social and recreational services.

The Ministry's local government proposals were therefore no longer realistic, and in December 1969 a Review Body under the chairmanship of Mr Patrick Macrory was appointed to make a new appraisal. Their Report in June 1970 pointed out that their terms of reference (unlike those of the Redcliffe-Maud and Wheatley Commissions in Britain) did not require them to take account of the need to sustain a viable system of local democracy. Macrory did, however, sketch the English and Scottish proposals for larger local government areas and he dwelt on the special circumstances of Northern Ireland—its small population (about $1\frac{1}{2}$ millions), its limited financial resources, and the fact that it already possessed a regional level of government. In the light of this, Macrory divided services into two groups, district and regional. For district services (environmental health, cleansing, recreation and other minor matters) he advocated 26 districts with elective councils to replace all existing local authorities. In the new districts there would be two sorts of local rate, a regional rate uniform throughout the province, and a district rate, but both would be collected together. Regional services, requiring larger areas for efficiency, included major environmental functions (planning, roads and traffic management, water and major sewerage) and personal services (education, libraries, personal health, welfare and child care). The report recommended that responsibility for these should be vested in Ministers accountable to the regional Parliament, with provision where necessary for administration by area boards, a minority of whose members could be nominated by the district councils. In view of the extra work that would fall on M.P.s, Macrory saw a need to enlarge the size of the Stormont House of Commons, while ministerial responsibility would be strengthened by the creation of more Parliamentary committees.

These ideas flowed naturally from the terms of reference, though it would not have been impossible to create a more democratic structure. But the proposals gained general acceptance. They offered a neat solution to the problems raised by the re-organization of housing and supporting services and the health and personal social services; and the removal from local authorities of most of their powers promised both the substance and the appearance of impartial administration. Legislation to establish the 26 district councils was passed in 1972, and elections by proportional representation using the single transferable vote followed on 30 May 1973. Candidates nominated by Unionist constituency associations won an overall majority in 12 of the 26 districts, and Loyalists gained a majority in one. In the other 13 districts no party gained control. Unionists formed the largest single group in nine, the Social Democratic and Labour Party in three, and no party was predominant in one. This degree of fragmentation, together with the fact that local authorities had lost their major powers, has apparently encouraged greater co-operation among rival groups and shifted the focus of discontent from local to regional government.

Re-organization of local government entailed extensive changes in other services. Public sector housing was formerly the responsibility of the Housing Trust and local authorities. Ulster's general housing record, within the limits of available resources, was impressive. About 45% of the total housing stock at the end of 1971 represented buildings completed since the Second World War, though a third of these were in the private sector (which received limited Exchequer subsidies), and a few councils were open to criticism for making unfair allocations. In 1969 the Ministry of Development prepared a model points scheme, and in 1971 the Northern Ireland Housing Executive was made responsible for the building, allocation and management of all publicly-owned houses. A minority of members of the Executive, and all the members of an advisory Housing Council, are drawn from district councils. Health and personal social services as well as education and libraries were transferred to Government departments, with management being devolved to four health and social services boards and five education and library boards on which district councils and various interests are represented. Roads, planning and conservation (including water and sewerage) were wholly centralized in one Ministry, though its officials stationed in the major towns are responsible for day-to-day administration and for liaison with district councils and with out-stations of other regional bodies.

Electoral Law

The Cameron Commission singled out as a cause of unrest the gerrymandering of local government boundaries. I outline below reforms in the general field of electoral law, including the franchise, since 'one man one vote' was a principal demand of the civil rights movement. At the outset it may be said that the franchise in Northern Ireland differed from that in Britain mainly because of changes made at Westminster after the last war which Stormont did not copy. The differences in Ulster thus reflected conservatism rather than religious discrimination and could be defended. If a regional legislature is given power to make law, whether on elections or other matters, it can hardly be accused of want of uniformity. The Northern Ireland Constitution Act 1973 reserved elections, including the franchise, to the United Kingdom Parliament, and this could have been done at any time before 1973 had that Parliament so wished.

So far as Parliamentary elections are concerned, the main differences in Northern Ireland were the absence of an independent boundary commission to review Stormont constituencies and the existence of plural voting, in the sense of voting more than once at the same election. (Multiple registration in respect of more than one address, which is permitted in Britain, was prohibited in Northern Ireland.) Legislation announced at Stormont at the end of 1966 came into effect in 1968. A permanent boundary commission was established. The occupation of business premises as a qualification to vote was abolished. It had never been important: the business electorate at the 1965 Stormont General Election was 12,510, or 1·4% of the total electorate. University graduates also lost the vote and the university constituency (which returned two Unionists, one Liberal and one Independent at the 1965 general election) was replaced by four new territorial constituencies, all of which were won by Unionists at the 1969 General Election. In 1972 an independent statutory officer, the Chief Electoral Officer for Northern Ireland, was made responsible for conducting all Northern Ireland elections. Finally, in July 1973 the Stormont Parliament was abolished and a new unicameral Assembly of 78 members was elected on 28 June by proportional representation.

Local government elections were criticized on three main grounds—gerrymandering, plural voting, and restriction of the franchise to ratepayers. Charges of gerrymandering, like charges of personation, are easy to make and hard to substantiate. They were probably well founded in respect of Londonderry county borough, and the Cameron Commission gave statistics for one county and five urban and rural districts which showed that electoral arrangements on a population basis were weighted against non-Unionists. Plural voting was in principle more obnoxious than at Parliamentary elections, since companies could cast up to six votes according to their rateable valuation. In 1967, of the total electorate of 694,483, there were 3322 company nominees, or 0·5%, and 990 of the 3322 were registered in Londonderry county borough. The local government franchise was assimilated to the Parliamentary franchise in 1969 and the voting age in both cases was reduced from 21 to 18. In 1971 the office of Local Government Boundaries Commissioner was established and boundaries of the 26 new districts were drawn before the 1973 election which, as noted above, was by proportional representation.

The Redress of Grievances

Until 1968 a citizen with a grievance could approach his elected representative, but in a divided community with one party always in power he could not be sure of a remedy. It was also possible to take action in the courts, since the Government of Ireland Act expressly prohibited legislation and the use of executive power which interfered with religious equality. This procedure could be slow, expensive and uncertain, though in view of the volume and gravity of complaints it may be thought remarkable that no actions were brought for a declaration or an injunction. In 1969 two Ombudsmen were appointed: the Northern Ireland Parliamentary Commissioner for Administration, and the Northern Ireland Commissioner for Complaints.[2]

The Parliamentary Commissioner investigates complaints of maladministration against Government departments and certain other bodies which are referred to him by members of the Northern Ireland Assembly (formerly by Stormont M.P.s). Since April 1970 he has been empowered to examine actions taken in respect of appointments, removals, discipline and other personnel matters in the Northern Ireland Civil Service. He also investigates complaints of any religious discrimination by contractors who undertake Government work. Table 2 has been compiled from the Commissioner's reports for 1970–72. It may be seen that relatively few complaints were received, that many were outside jurisdiction, and that the number found to be justified was negligible. In the three years the Commissioner received five complaints alleging discrimination and found discrimination in one case.

TABLE 2   Action on Complaints

	1970	1971	1972
References received	99	37	26
Uncompleted cases brought forward from previous year	—	8	4
Rejected as outside jurisdiction	58	20	13
Discontinued after partial investigation	—	—	1
Under investigation	8	4	7
Completed cases	33	21	9
of which:			
Complaint not justified	31	16	7
Justified and remedied	2	4	2
Justified and not remedied	—	1	—

The Commissioner for Complaints deals with grievances against local or public authorities which are addressed to him in writing by members of the public. Anybody whose complaint is upheld can if necessary seek redress in the courts, and the Commissioner himself can institute proceedings to stop continuing and persistent maladministration. Tables 3 and 4, taken from the Commissioner's reports for 1970–72, reveal more cases than Table 2. A large proportion were concerned with housing. Of the 1182 cases investigated during the three years, maladministration was found in 103.

In the three years 1970–72 the Commissioner received 127 complaints from people of various denominations alleging religious or political discrimination. In only one case (in the field of housing allocation) did he find that the action complained of had been motivated by discrimination of the form alleged. However, in his Report for 1972 the Commissioner pointed out that in this area more than any other it was dangerous to draw inferences from statistics, and he refrained from doing so. He continued:

'I merely record that a number of persons complained to me that they had suffered injustice as a result of discrimination, and that my investigation did not sustain this charge in any case. To say how far the figures reflect accurately the incidence of discrimination in the public sector is not my responsibility. It may be considered too that complainants are inhibited from bringing charges of discrimination, particularly in employment cases, by the fear, however illusory, of damaging prospects of future promotion or their relationship with fellow workers. Indeed these are factors which may be inherent in many complaints relating to employment, whether discrimination is alleged or not.'

TABLE 3   Complaints by Subject

	1970	1971	1972
Housing allocation	251	170	107
Housing repairs	163	83	59
Housing (other)	57	28	52
Employment	122	54	38
Planning	59	40	23
Vesting orders	31	13	1
Public utility services	90	17	10
Education	43	11	11
Roads	36	14	9
Miscellaneous	141	69	62
Totals	993	499	372

TABLE 4   Action on Complaints

	1970	1971	1972
Complaints received	1193	594	431
Ruled outside jurisdiction	344	176	102
Withdrawn	50	72	34
Discontinued	57	88	5
Investigated	285	594	303
of which:			
Settlement effected	125	202	88
Maladministration found	14	61	28
Number in action at the end of year	457	121	112

Until 1973 the Parliamentary Commissioner and the Commissioner for Complaints were precluded from investigating complaints if an aggrieved person had a remedy in a court of law. This restriction no longer applies in respect of complaints involving discrimination on the grounds of religious belief or political opinion. Nor (with some exceptions) does it apply if any person is required to take an oath or make an undertaking or declaration as a condition of membership of or employment by a public authority.

Police and the Administration of Justice

In August 1969 the Minister of Home Affairs appointed a committee under the chairmanship of Lord Hunt to examine the recruitment, organization, structure and composition of the Royal Ulster Constabulary and the Ulster Special Constabulary and their respective functions and to make recommendations. Hunt was pitched in a different key from Cameron. The Report deplored the effects of press and television coverage, which tended to enlarge and confuse rather than clarify complex issues in Northern Ireland. It stressed the peculiar difficulties confronting the police, referred to the distinguished history of the R.U.C., and declared that, despite adverse publicity, the best efforts of its members were directed towards ensuring fair treatment of all citizens under the law. It attributed the low level of Roman Catholic recruitment to the fact that they had not come forward in sufficient numbers, and heard no evidence of discrimination on religious grounds with regard to promotion. The report paid tribute to the gallant service by the U.S.C., particularly in times of emergency, but considered that the protection of the border and the State against armed attacks was not a role which should have to be undertaken by the police, whether regular or special. It noted that for a variety of reasons (which were not specified) no Roman Catholic was a member of the U.S.C. The Committee recommended that the R.U.C. should be relieved of all duties of a military nature, and that the U.S.C. should be replaced by a locally recruited part-time force under the control of the G.O.C., Northern Ireland, and by a volunteer reserve police force. Other recommendations included the establishment of a Police Authority with a membership reflecting the different groups in the community; vigorous efforts to increase Roman Catholic membership of the R.U.C.; and adoption of the Scottish system of independent public prosecutors. These and other reforms were put into effect. In 1969 two new forces, the Ulster Defence Regiment and the Royal Ulster Constabulary Reserve, were established. A Police Authority in 1970 was made responsible for maintaining an adequate and efficient police force. The office of Director of Public Prosecutions was created in 1972.

There remained the problem of dealing with terrorism. The provincial Government relied upon Regulations made under the Special Powers Act which (among other things) authorized the Minister of Home Affairs to detain and intern a person 'who is suspected of acting or having acted or being about to act in a manner prejudicial to the preservation of the peace and the maintenance of order'. The Act was temporary (i.e. renewable each year) until 1933, when it was made permanent, though it was only used in extreme emergency, as was also the case with similar powers in the Irish Republic. According to Barritt and Carter,[3] hardly anybody was interned in Northern Ireland in the period between the two wars, and the powers were only used on any scale during the Second World War and after 1956 when life and property were threatened by terrorist

9*

bombs and bullets. An advisory committee in Northern Ireland heard representations from internees. These powers were often attacked as being illiberal, and as often defended as being essential to protect innocent people.

The British Government in October 1972 sought advice from a Commission under the chairmanship of Lord Diplock. Speaking in the House of Lords on 10 July 1973, Lord Diplock said:

> 'Until I had been to Northern Ireland and seen what was happening, and talked to those concerned in the administration of justice, it was impossible to realize how terrorism could corrupt and ultimately destroy the administration of justice in courts of law. Witnesses risked their lives, families and properties if their identity could be guessed let alone their names known.'

The Northern Ireland (Emergency Provisions) Act 1973 repealed the Special Powers Acts, abolished the death penalty for murder, and prescribed new procedures. Part I of the Act deals with the trial and punishment of certain offences, including murder and manslaughter, arson and riot. Trials on indictment are held only in Belfast and by a judge without a jury. Written instead of direct oral evidence may be admissible, and in cases involving firearms or explosives found in a vehicle or on premises the onus of proof may rest in part on the person charged. The court is required to state reasons for conviction, and appeal lies to the Court of Criminal Appeal. If these provisions, and especially non-jury trial, had been enacted at Stormont they would probably have aroused a storm of protest in Britain. Part II of the Act gives carefully defined but very wide powers of arrest, detention and search to the police and the armed forces. For example, a constable may arrest without warrant any person whom he suspects of being a terrorist and enter any place for the purpose, and the arrested person may be detained for 72 hours. The period can be extended to 28 days by an interim custody order signed by the Secretary of State or a Minister of State or Under-Secretary of State, but cannot exceed 28 days unless the case is referred to a Commissioner. He may make a detention order if he is satisfied that: (a) the respondent has been concerned in any act of terrorism or the direction, organization or training of persons for the purposes of terrorism; and (b) his detention is necessary for the protection of the public. A detainee may within 21 days appeal to a Detention Appeal Tribunal which can dismiss the appeal or allow it and direct the discharge of the detainee. The Secretary of State is required to refer to a Commissioner the case of any person who has been detained for one year since the making of a detention order or for six months from the determination of the most recent review of the case. The Commissioner must direct his discharge unless he considers his continued detention is necessary for the protection of the public. Thus, internment gave place to detention, and safeguards against arbitrariness were strengthened.

Other Reforms

Other reforms included the establishment in 1972 of a Local Government Staff

Commission to exercise general oversight of personnel matters in local government. One of the Commission's functions is to establish fair procedures for the appointment and treatment of local government officers. Similar Commissions operate in other fields of public employment. In 1969 a Ministry of Community Relations and a Community Relations Commission were constituted. Measures to prevent religious and political discrimination were strengthened by the Northern Ireland Constitution Act 1973. The Act nullifies discriminatory legislation, whether passed by the old Northern Ireland Parliament or the new Assembly. The validity of such legislation can be determined by the Judicial Committee of the Privy Council on the recommendation of the Secretary of State. Discrimination by Ministers of the Crown, members of the Northern Ireland Executive, the Post Office and other public authorities is declared to be unlawful and actionable in the courts. The Act also set up a Standing Advisory Committee on Human Rights consisting of the chairman of the Community Relations Commission, the Commissioner for Complaints, the Parliamentary Commissioner and other persons appointed by the Secretary of State. Its purpose is two-fold: (a) to advise the Secretary of State on whether the law to prevent discrimination and to provide redress is adequate and effective; and (b) to keep him informed of the extent to which Ministers, the Northern Ireland Executive and other public authorities have prevented discrimination by other persons or bodies. The first chairman, Mr Victor Feather (later Lord Feather), former general secretary of the British T.U.C., was appointed in November 1973.

Constitutional Reform

As the causes of disorder diagnosed by the Cameron Commission were removed, violence increased and became more deadly and claims for civil rights were overtaken by a variety of new demands ranging from the formation of a coalition government to withdrawal of British troops and an end to partition. After direct rule in March 1972 Britain was therefore confronted with the problem of devising a new political settlement. The Conservative Government, with the general support of the Labour Opposition, stood firm on two points. One was the need for a settlement that would command the allegiance of both communities in Northern Ireland and evoke the co-operation of the government and people of the Irish Republic. The other was that there should be no change in the constitutional status of Northern Ireland without the consent of a majority of its people.

In 1949 the Labour Government incorporated in the Ireland Act 1949 the following declaration:

It is hereby declared that Northern Ireland remains part of His Majesty's dominions and of the United Kingdom and it is hereby affirmed that in no event will Northern Ireland or any part thereof cease to be part of His Majesty's dominions and of the United Kingdom without the consent of the Parliament of Northern Ireland.

Neither before nor after 1949 had any government asked the people of Northern Ireland what they wanted. Opinion polls gave various results; and it was argued that the Stormont Parliament did not accurately reflect the popular will, partly because it included an indirectly elected Senate and partly because of the electoral system. On 24 March 1972 the Prime Minister (Mr Edward Heath) told the House of Commons that successive governments had given solemn assurances that there would be no change in the constitutional status of Northern Ireland without the people's consent, and that a plebiscite would be held as soon as practicable, followed by further plebiscites at intervals of years.

The Border Poll, on 8 March 1973, proved to be contentious. However, 591,820 people (57·5% of the electorate) voted in favour of remaining within the United Kingdom, and 6463 (0·6%) voted to join the Republic of Ireland. While it is certain that, for one reason and another, many among the Catholic community did not vote, their number is anybody's guess.

The plebiscite was important, not only because it revealed for the first time the preferences of the electorate, but also because it showed that free elections could still be held despite constant disorder, terrorism and intimidation. The district council elections followed on 30 May and the Government, with the encouragement of the Opposition, brought forward to 28 June the date of a general election for a new Northern Ireland Assembly. Before discussing the outcome of the election, it will be convenient to sketch the relevant provisions of the Northern Ireland Constitution Act which was passed on 18 July, shortly after the election.

The Act was based on fundamental criteria which had been set out in a Discussion Paper in October 1972 and a White Paper in March 1973. Two of these criteria may be mentioned as being of special importance:

(1) Northern Ireland would remain part of the United Kingdom for as long as that was the wish of the majority of the people, but that status did not preclude taking into account what was described in the Discussion Paper as the 'Irish Dimension'.

The Constitution Act affirmed that Northern Ireland would not cease to be part of Her Majesty's dominions and of the United Kingdom without the consent of a majority of the people of Northern Ireland voting in a poll, which may be held not earlier than 9 March 1983, and thereafter at intervals of not less than ten years. At the same time, Northern Ireland was empowered to consult and enter into agreements with the Republic of Ireland, and to legislate for that purpose.

(2) New institutions in Northern Ireland must seek a wider consensus than hitherto and be capable of providing the concrete results of good government. The White Paper stated flatly that there was no future for devolved institutions unless the majority and the minority alike could be bound to their support.

The Act abolished the Parliament of Northern Ireland and the office of Governor and provided for an elected unicameral Assembly of 78 members with power to make laws (styled Measures), and for an Executive consisting of a chief Executive, the heads of Departments, and other persons, all of them appointed by the Secretary of State. The Act provided for participation by both the majority and the minority in two ways. First, the Assembly must establish consultative committees reflecting the balance of parties, which would advise and assist the heads of Departments in formulating policy. Secondly, an Executive was to be formed which, 'having regard to the support it commands in the Assembly and to the electorate on which that support is based, is likely to be widely accepted throughout the community'.

In framing this scheme the Government had, of course, to consider the situation that would arise if one party or another boycotted the election, or if the principal party leaders and their followers declined to co-operate after an election whose result could not be known. Co-operation cannot be forced, and threats to withdraw British troops and financial support could make a bad situation worse. Policy therefore provided for contingencies. In the first place, powers were withheld from the Assembly until it had made progress in the desired direction. The Constitution Act provided for the devolution of legislative and executive responsibility if it appeared to the Secretary of State: (a) that the Assembly had made satisfactory provision in its standing orders for consultative committees and certain other matters; (b) that an acceptable Executive could be formed; and (c) 'that having regard to those matters there is a reasonable basis for the establishment in Northern Ireland of government by consent'. Second, if powers were not devolved before 30 March 1974 (when direct rule was due to expire), the Assembly would be dissolved on that day. Third, the Assembly election on 28 June was held by proportional representation (the single transferable vote) in order to ensure that parties would gain representation in proportion to the votes cast for them.

The election revealed the strength of new political alignments. The Ulster Unionist Party had maintained its unity for more than 60 years, since its formation in 1905. At the 1969 General Election, as mentioned earlier, it split between pro- and anti-O'Neill supporters. In the storm and stress of the following years its divisions grew sharper and more numerous, and in 1973 it was fragmented into five main Loyalist and Unionist groups and a number of splinters. On the anti-partition side, by contrast, the Social Democratic and Labour Party had rapidly built up a sound organization since its foundation in 1970 and was displacing the traditional Nationalist Party. Two parties competed for the middle-of-the-road vote—the Northern Ireland Labour Party, and the Alliance Party founded in 1970.

All these divisions were reflected in the Assembly. Of the 78 seats, 19 went to the Social Democratic and Labour Party, eight to the Alliance Party and one to Northern Ireland Labour. The Loyalists and Unionists captured the other 50 seats, which represented a decisive majority (64%) of the Assembly.

The election, which was conducted by the Chief Electoral Officer and other officials of recognized impartiality, showed that Unionist strength was not based on gerrymandering or other malpractices. In that respect, nothing had changed.

What was new was the acute dissension within the Unionist movement. Of the 50 seats, the Vanguard Unionist Loyalist Coalition took seven, the Democratic Unionist Loyalist Coalition eight, other Loyalists three, Unionists eight, and Official Unionists 24. The Official Unionists, led by Mr Brian Faulkner, who was prepared to accept the new constitutional arrangements if satisfactory safeguards for the majority could be obtained, were themselves divided. The greater number pledged themselves during the election campaign to support their leader's policy, but others declined to do so. To add to the confusion, some of those who were pledged changed their minds after the election.

Nevertheless, at the invitation of the Secretary of State, Mr Faulkner and some of his colleagues, together with leaders of the Social Democratic and Labour Party and the Alliance Party, began negotiations to try to form a coalition Executive. They reached agreement on 21 November 1973, but during the negotiations various bargains were made which were not made public and which involved the Republic of Ireland.

Relations with the Irish Republic

As noted above, Irish Governments after 1922 pursued policies which could accurately be described as irrational. Instead of reassuring the majority in the North that they had nothing to fear from Irish union and might have something to gain from it, they antagonized them. Thus, the Irish Free State decided not to take part in a Council of Ireland in the 1920s. The Irish constitution of 1937 proclaimed that the national territory was the whole island of Ireland and claimed jurisdiction over it. The Irish Government remained neutral during the last war and seceded from the Commonwealth and became a Republic in 1949. Protestants in the North feared the influence of Catholicism in the South and were convinced that more could be done there to stop armed raids across the border and to bring fugitives to justice. There was, however, always a certain amount of co-operation in practical matters such as drainage, fisheries and electricity supply, and it appeared that relations might become more harmonious after Mr Lemass and Captain O'Neill met in 1965. The disorders that followed set back what seemed to be a promising development.

Nevertheless, it was always clear that North and South stood to gain by working together, especially after they entered the European Communities on 1 January 1973. More people on both sides of the border gradually inclined to the view that co-operation was preferable to conflict and possible civil war, and the British Government's Discussion Paper in October 1972 recognized that Northern Ireland's problems had an Irish dimension. A fortnight after the agreement to form an Executive, British and Irish Ministers together with leaders of political parties supporting the Executive met for four days at Sunningdale in England. They were able to agree on 9 December 1973 on a number of important matters, including some form of recognition by the Irish Government of the right of Northern Ireland to exist, and the formation of a Council of

Ireland. Of equal or greater importance was the fact that all the participants at Sunningdale were evidently determined to approach the problems of centuries in a spirit of conciliation. The Sunningdale agreement was debated by the Commons at Westminster on Thursday, 13 December and by the Dail in Dublin and the Assembly in Belfast on the following day. The Commons approved an Order to devolve powers to the Assembly with effect from 1 January 1974, and this marked the end of direct rule. The Dail decided by 59 votes to 54 to support the agreement. The Assembly, after nearly 18 hours' debate, welcomed the agreement by 43 votes to 27 on the morning of Saturday, 15 December.

Acknowledgement: I wish to acknowledge the help of Mrs S. Cox in preparing this chapter.

Editor's Note

At the General Election held on 31 January 1974, all the 'official' Unionist candidates in the Northern Ireland constituencies were defeated. The 12 seats were won by the following parties: Democratic Unionist one, United Ulster Unionist Council eight, Vanguard two, Social Democratic and Labour one. The last-mentioned was represented by Mr G. Fitt, the Deputy Chief Executive in the new administration. The other 11 members declined to follow their Unionist predecessors in earlier Parliaments in an alliance with the Conservatives. Instead, they formed the United Ulster Unionist Parliamentary Coalition with the *long-term* aim of overthrowing the Sunningdale Agreement and the Constitution Act, and the *short-term* aim of securing new elections to the Northern Ireland Assembly. In support of the latter, a body called the Ulster Workers' Council called for a general strike in the latter half of May, 1974, and secured enough support to bring the economic life of the province to a virtual halt. As a result, the Northern Ireland Executive resigned and the United Kingdom Government resumed direct rule, with the declared intention of restoring the Executive as early as possible.

NOTES AND REFERENCES

1 James Callaghan, *A House Divided* (Collins), London, 1973, p. 2.

2 Complaints involving maladministration by United Kingdom Government Departments in Northern Ireland fell within the jurisdiction of the United Kingdom Parliamentary Commissioner.

3 Denis P. Barritt and Charles F. Carter, *The Northern Ireland Problem*, (Oxford University Press), 1972, p. 129.

The Process of Decolonization

11

Sir Leslie Monson, K.C.M.G., C.B.

In 1950 there were some 36 territories for which the Colonial Secretary was responsible. To these should be added, first, the self-governing Colony of Southern Rhodesia and the South African High Commission Territories (Basutoland, the Bechuanaland Protectorate and Swaziland), where responsibility lay with the Secretary of State for Commonwealth Relations (responsibility for the High Commission Territories was transferred to the Colonial Office after South Africa left the Commonwealth) and secondly the Anglo-Egyptian Condominium of the Sudan where in the British Government the Foreign Secretary was the responsible Minister. By 1974, though there were still some 20 British dependent territories (other than Rhodesia), their total populations were about five million in all (four-fifths living in Hong Kong) as compared with the 70 millions or so who in 1950 were living in the territories for which the Colonial Secretary was then responsible. The Annex to this chapter tabulates the dates on which territories were 'decolonized' either by becoming independent sovereign states, by merger with other states, or by achieving 'Associated Statehood'.

Of the territories listed it is convenient to treat the Sudan as a special case. A condominium in form, its administration had been essentially British but largely controlled on the spot rather than from London. By 1950 it had achieved an advanced form of mixed British and Sudanese government and early in 1952 a locally appointed commission reported in favour of self-government. By mid-1952 draft legislation based on its recommendations was referred to the codomini. The British were ready to approve the draft legislation but the Egyptians, who had hitherto maintained that the condominium did not prejudice Egyptian sovereignty over the Sudan, now proposed radical amendments, providing in particular that after a term of three years the Sudanese could choose between union with Egypt or 'complete independence'; in the meantime to achieve 'a free and neutral atmosphere' international commissions would be appointed to supervise the Governor-General and 'sudanize' the Civil Service. These amendments were accepted by Sudanese politicians and embodied in an Anglo-Egyptian agreement of February 1953. In effect therefore the British lost from that date virtually all capacity to control the course of events leading up to independence. Sudanese independence on the other hand affected nationalist aspirations elsewhere in Africa.

As regards the other territories listed in the Annex, no such complications arose. Though British dependent territory Governments were separate entities from the Government of the United Kingdom, their constitutions were embodied in United Kingdom legislation (usually Orders-in-Council) over which local legislation could not prevail. Consequently the authority for constitutional change rested up to the date of independence with British Ministers and the British Parliament. But there was no attempt to regularize relations between Britain and her dependent territories on a generalized basis, as was done in this period by the French Government by the Loi-cadre of June 1956 or by the referendum of September 1958.

The policy was rather to seek agreement with the main political groupings in a territory as regards amendments to its constitution. The constitutional relationships of Britain and her dependencies were consequently tailored to a variety of local circumstances. Hence, in dealing with decolonization within the ambit of a single chapter, there is a risk of falling into the trap of an over-simplification, unwarranted by the essentially pragmatic approach which in fact successive British Governments attempted to follow. As an example of this danger, one may quote comments by Iain Macleod in the *Weekend Telegraph* of 12 March 1965. He there referred to the assumption then being made by students of British Colonial policy that, following the 1959 General Election (when he had become Colonial Secretary), some dramatic Cabinet decision had been taken to speed up the granting of independence in Africa and that Harold Macmillan's 'Wind of Change' speech in Cape Town on 3 February 1960 had been designed to announce this decision to the world, but went on, 'This is not true. What did happen was that the tempo accelerated as a result of a score of different deliberate decisions.' Nevertheless as will be clear from the sequel, by that stage, decisions taken in one area (not necessarily by the British Government or in British territories), were creating political circumstances in other British territories which led to analogous decisions there.

None of this was, however, clear by 1950. Though there was no central legislative framework within which Colonial government was carried on, there were statements of general policy to point the way. In 1948 Arthur Creech-Jones, then Colonial Secretary, had defined the central purpose of British Colonial policy as being 'to guide the colonial territories to responsible government within the Commonwealth in conditions that ensure to the people concerned both a fair standard of living and freedom of oppression from any quarter'. The Conservative Government after the 1951 General Election re-defined the fundamentals of policy as being to help Colonial territories to attain self-government within the British Commonwealth and to that end to seek to build up as rapidly as possible in each territory the institutions which its circumstances required; and as being to pursue the economic and social development of Colonial territories so that it kept pace with their political development. Oliver Lyttelton in making this statement in Parliament claimed that it showed there was no fundamental difference of policy between the two main political parties in Britain on this point and both on the text of his statement and on the record of the parties in office his claim can be justified.

In the light of hindsight, however, it could be said that the Conservatives' statement of policy did at least hint at a difficulty concealed in the earlier Labour statement. The latter involved really four aims—first, a political and constitutional evolution which would transfer control of the executive from the Governor, that is, from an official responsible to British Ministers, themselves responsible to the British Parliament, to a 'politician', constitutionally responsible to the local community: the second, the establishment of a stable local economy as a pre-requisite of a fair standard of living: the third, the protection of the territory as a whole from external aggression and, fourth, the protection of individuals or communities within the territory from arbitrary acts of oppression by the territory's government. If the policy is re-defined in these terms the problem becomes one of bringing each of the conditions to fruition in parallel, and Creech-Jones' use of the word 'guide' implies that Britain was to be the judge of when the criteria had been met. Lyttelton's statement could be read as implying that political evolution would be the pacesetter, though the policy of Conservative Governments in the 1950s still assumed that Britain had the power to control the pace of political evolution. Certainly not in the 1950s or later was there any readiness to return to the policy, reflected in the Anglo-Egyptian Agreement of 1953 on the Sudan, by which a target date for independence would be set well ahead of the actual date. British policy was rather as explained by Sir Andrew Cohen in discussion in 1957 in the United Nations Trusteeship Council, 'to proceed step by step, neither too quickly nor too slowly, judging each step in the light of the experience of the last one and consulting the representatives of the people on Legislative Council at each stage'. [This discussion was on the suggestion, frequently ventilated in U.N. debates that the Administering Authority (i.e. in this case Britain) should fix a target date for independence. Julius Nyerere in the same debate argued that an interval of 10–12 years should be ample to complete the process in Tanganyika (i.e. until 1967 or 1969). Tanganyika in fact became independent by agreement in December 1961.] That statement, though made in respect of Tanganyika, could be applied to the process of decolonization in all the territories covered by this chapter (including the Sudan, since Britain there took account of Sudanese politicians' views before signing the Anglo-Egyptian Agreement of 1953) with but two exceptions— Cyprus (where communal differences prevented the establishment of a legislative council to consult and the Governments of Greece and Turkey had to be involved in the formulation of the independence constitution) and South Arabia (where the Government, which was being 'guided' to independence, disintegrated in the face of armed rebellion).

The policy outlined in Sir Andrew Cohen's statement reflected the 'guidance' principle in the 1948 Creech-Jones' statement. But it was also shaped by the evolution over a long period of the system of Crown Colony Government which still applied in most Colonies. Since that system proved to be the vehicle by which the process of decolonization was carried out in the great majority of cases, some explanation of its working is necessary to the understanding of the events covered by this chapter.

In general the system comprised three elements—the Governor, the Executive Council and the Legislative Council. The Governor was generally responsible to the Colonial Secretary at Westminster for the good government of the territory: his position was constitutionally quite independent of any local institution. The Executive Council assisted him in the discharge of his day-to-day duties but in law its functions were, despite its title, not executive but advisory, and the Governor need not be bound by its advice: in its original form it was generally composed of his chief officials but there was usually an early resort to the practice of the Governor nominating to the Council a limited number of 'unofficials' of the 'elder statesman' variety, who could advise on public reaction to Government measures. The Executive Council could be regarded as the adaption to more 'primitive' conditions of the British Cabinet. The Legislative Council was a similar adaption of the British Parliament, more especially of the House of Commons. But again there were at the outset major differences. The earliest Legislative Councils were composed of members nominated by the Governor and the majority of these members were found from his officials (in the absence of a Ministerial system only an official could present Government legislation to the Council): in effect therefore the Governor could control the passage of legislation through the Council, but in addition to this he had the power to veto Bills passed by the Council (and the Crown through the Colonial Secretary could also disallow legislation to which he had assented). Moreover he had on the model, as finally evolved, the power also to enact legislation which the Council refused to pass if he considered this necessary 'in the interests of public order, public faith or good government'.

The Crown Colony system was adopted widely in the early and mid-19th century as a means of avoiding the dangers of a constitutional clash between Governors responsible to British Ministers and representative 'Assemblies' over which such Governors had at most a power of veto. (Such a clash had led to the American Revolution.) The system was also thought particularly suitable for territories where the population in general was regarded as incapable of working representative government or where only a minority of the inhabitants were thought to be so capable. In the latter case it was the role of the Governor and his officials to represent the interests of the supposedly inarticulate majority as well as those of the British Government.

The system has been described as autocracy, tempered by bureaucracy and slightly diluted by oligarchy, but the description is hardly fair. In the first place, the Governor was not a full autocrat since he was subject to the direction of the Secretary of State to whom any person in a Colony could submit a petitition of grievances and who was himself responsible to Parliament for anything that might happen in a Colony. Indeed it was primarily because of this responsibility that the Governor as the representative of H.M. Government was provided with such a seemingly formidable list of constitutional powers. Secondly and almost subconsciously the system, while being a substitute for responsible government, was regarded as a preparation for the introduction of such government. Colonial authorities were from the first ready to see a wider range of opinion represented in the Legislative Council than in the necessarily restricted Executive Council. They were ready at a comparatively early stage to let 'special interests' elect their representatives to Legislative Council. Such interests included in different territories Chambers of Commerce, the inhabitants of municipalities, racial communities (the European settlers in Kenya had asserted their 'natural-born right as Englishmen' to elect their own representatives as long ago as 1916), Councils of African chiefs and the like. Once in the Legislature unofficials were reluctant to appear as 'yes-men' to the Governor even if he had nominated them and the fact that the British Government, while expecting Colonies to pay for their own administration, still had atavistic fears of infringing the principle of 'no taxation without representation', gave the unofficial representatives in Legislative Council real power in the crucial field of supply. (In many Colonies it was the practice to remit questions of supply in the first place to a Finance Committee of Legislative Council, in which the unofficials were in a majority.)

For a century and a half before 1950 the system had worked by unwritten conventions on the part of the Governor and his metropolitan masters that their overriding powers would be used only on matters of major importance and then only as a weapon of last resort and on the part of the unofficials that they for their part would not force matters to this pass. On this basis the system had proved capable of almost indefinite modification. The trend had been generally in the direction of replacing the official majority in Legislative Council by an unofficial majority; of providing that the majority of that majority should be found by election rather than nomination; of then widening the method of election: and also, though at a slower rate, of increasing the numbers of unofficial members in Executive Council and reducing those of the official members. If this process were carried to the stage when the legislature was wholly elected and the Governor's Executive Council was composed of members of the legislature, responsible to that body, the Crown Colony system would have evolved naturally into a system of Cabinet Government. If, as was natural at such a stage, the Governor was also obliged by the constitution to accept the advice of his Cabinet, except on the subjects of special concern to the British Government such as defence and external affairs, the territory would have reached full internal self-government. This normally was to be rapidly followed by independence. Such a process was fully compatible with the concept of Britain 'guiding' the colonial territories to responsible government and the step-by-step approach advocated in the U.N. debates of 1957. It was also in fact the way in which most territories did proceed to independence. The question nevertheless remains for debate whether in pursuing it Britain did in fact go 'neither too quickly nor too slow'.

What is certain is that the British Governments of the 1950s followed in three important areas (the West Indies, Central Africa and East Africa) courses of political action which, in Central and East Africa at least, would have required much time to bring to fruition and which in all three areas never did in fact come to fruition. Nevertheless each of these courses of action can be directly related in its genesis to the achievement of the first of the criteria for responsible government which Creech-Jones had put forward, viz., the need to create conditions which would ensure a fair standard of living for the people in general. This line of thought was particularly evident in the recommendations which led to the creation of federations in the West Indies and in the Rhodesias and Nyasaland. [The other Federations created in this period (Nigeria and Malaysia) had different origins. The Nigerian Federation replaced a unitary constitution of British making and, like Malaysia, sprang from an initiative by local politicians taken because of local political considerations. This is not to deny that the inducement to the Northern Borneo territories to join Malaysia was economic but the initiative came from the Prime Minister of Malaya and not from anyone in Britain.] The Standing Closer Association Committee in the West Indies (a local body but one established on British initiative) reported in 1950 (Col. No. 255) that 'only states that paid their way could really be said to enjoy true independence and in a region like the West Indies where the economic balance was precarious and at the mercy of world prices, economic stability could not be attained while the region was made up of a large number of political units'. Similarly the Report of the Conference on Closer Association in Central Africa, published in 1951 (Cmnd. 8233) advocated the creation of a federation as offering the best means of stimulating the maximum economic development of the area as a whole and of facing with greater confidence the effects of any future economic recession. In putting forward such considerations, the authors of the latter report disclaimed any suggestion that they were influenced solely by material considerations: on the contrary they argued that the moral and social arguments for their proposal were equally strong. The greater prosperity, which they foresaw would come from associating the three territories in a federation, would lead to an expansion of Government revenues and to a consequent amelioration of Government social services. The chief beneficiary of this would be the African population, and its moral and social advancement would thus keep in step with the economic development of the federated territories.

But from these virtually identical points of departure, the political institutions of the two Federations followed a different course. Universal suffrage was the accepted rule in the West Indies. In Central Africa and in East Africa a much more limited franchise was still thought essential. Partly this was because Africans generally were still thought ready to exercise the responsibilities of the vote only at a very restricted local level but more generally the policy reflected the socio-economic argument that the bulk of the national income and therefore the capacity to raise standards to those set out in the Creech-Jones criteria, derived from the activities of the settlers and external investors in those countries. Too rapid a transfer of power to Africans as things stood was thought of as likely to have an inhibiting effect on such activities and therefore to be impossible in the interests of the Africans themselves. The thought is implicit in the quotations above from the report on Closer Association in Central Africa. It was even more bluntly put by the East Africa Royal Commission of 1953–55, viz. 'East Africa needs the skill and capital of the non-African more than the non-African needs East Africa'. It meant, however, that a much slower course of devolution had to be envisaged than that which developed in West Africa or in Malaya where it could be said that the non-European was making a much larger direct contribution to national wealth and consequently Government revenue. (In Malaya there was in any event the further consideration that success against the Communist insurrection had involved offering the people an alternative political future and associating their leaders with the Government in the struggle against the Communists: the 'Emergency' postponed the holding of elections but the confirmation in those elections of the political strength of the parties earlier associated with Government, made it inevitable that they would have independence as soon as they asked for it.)

In Central and East Africa therefore the British Government endeavoured to follow a policy of reassuring Africans as to the ultimate future and at the same time not going so fast in the direction of majority rule as to scare the other races or the outside investment which found its natural outlet in their business and farming activities. To reconcile Africans in the Federation to this situation they relied on undertakings in the preamble to the Constitution to the effect that the protectorate status of the northern territories (i.e. their link with the United Kingdom) would be preserved so long as the majority of the inhabitants desired it and that in the meantime those aspects of Government which affected the daily life of the African would remain with the territorial Governments and therefore ultimately under the control of the British Government and Parliament: similarly in Kenya there had been a statement of British policy as long ago as 1922 that the interests of the African should be paramount and that if and when those interests and those of the immigrants should conflict, the former should prevail. Taken on their face value, the British Government could have implemented these assurances by giving the Africans a formal veto on independence and rely on the hope that this would in itself bring about a politically acceptable modus vivendi between the races. But this seemed too passive a role for Government. Colonial administrators were only too aware that the practice of communal representation in the Legislature inhibited the expression of a 'national' point of view since a communally elected member naturally owed his first duty to those who had elected him to be their spokesman; moreover if members were simply the spokesmen of one community, it would be difficult to accelerate any increase in unofficial membership of the Executive Council without prejudice to the efficient working of that institution. There was therefore a conscious attempt made in the later 1940s and in the 1950s to foster in East and Central Africa political groupings that cut across race and so to create a national 'multi-racial' political system without at the same time swamping the influence of the immigrant communities by merging them in a common electoral roll. This attempt can be regarded as in line with the Lyttelton objective of building up in each territory the institutions which its circumstances required. The methods adopted, however, varied from territory to territory.

In Kenya it was thought best to concentrate on the members of Legislative Council rather than the electorate (there was in any event no African electorate until 1957). Between the end of the Second World War and 1957 the division of unofficial seats in Legislative Council was based on the principle of 'parity', interpreted in this instance as parity between Europeans on the one hand and the sum total of non-Europeans (Asians, Arabs and Africans) on the other. It was hoped that this would force local politicians to look to support from more than one race to ensure a majority in favour of their views, while the presence of a substantial number (though no longer a majority) of official members and of the Governor's reserve powers could serve, if need be, to keep the ship of state on course. To complete the picture, it may be added that at a later stage the idea of using the Legislative Council as a means of fostering multi-racial politics was carried further by forming the Council as a whole into an electoral college to fill a bloc of 12 seats allocated equally between Europeans, Asians and Africans.

In Tanganyika, thinking favoured the introduction of multi-racialism at the constituency level. The process was easier to introduce because communal elections had not been included earlier in the system, the Governor selecting members of Legislative Council from lists submitted by communal representative bodies. When direct elections were introduced, it was done on the basis of a common roll covering all races but with three seats per constituency, each seat being allocated by race so that the constituency would be represented by one European, one African and one Asian member. Each voter was given three votes each to be cast for a candidate of a different race and no vote would be valid unless all three were cast: candidates were also required to have a specified number of signatures by electors of their own race on their nomination papers.

In Central Africa, formal allocation of seats on a communal basis was eschewed (this would hardly be compatible with Rhodes' dictum of 'equal rights for all civilized men') and franchises were based on two electoral rolls with 'higher' and 'lower' qualifications, determined by income, education or experience of public affairs. In practice this meant that the Higher Roll would be predominantly European but it was hoped to encourage political parties which cut across race by a system of cross-voting between the Rolls.

The subsequent fate of these various experiments in multi-racial politics is discussed below but the point to be made here is that British Ministers of the day, while realizing that the slower rate of decolonization involved might well be emotionally distasteful to many Africans in East and Central Africa, felt justified in appealing to them to be patient in their own interests and those of their children.

The analysis so far has been concerned with territories which were considered capable at the appropriate stage, however long it took to reach that stage, of sustaining full independence. There was also considerable thought given in the 1950s in Whitehall and outside to the problem of finding a 'non-Colonial' status for territories which could not easily be combined with other territories but for whom full sovereign independence by the thinking of the time seemed impossible.

These territories fell into three main groups. Some were thought incapable of sustaining independence because of the threat from external powers. Hong Kong remains the classic example of such a territory and indeed its relationship with China has meant that the path of constitutional development followed elsewhere has been barred to Hong Kong.

Others were thought incapable of independence because of their financial position. The concept that independence normally involved the capacity to pay one's own way in the world had been deeply ingrained in British policy. (Gladstone for example in the 1860s had argued that since independence was the destiny of British colonies it would be wrong to provide them through the British taxpayer with services which they could not sustain after independence from their own resources.) Some Colonies of course could not make ends meet and in that event they had to be given budgetary grants-in-aid from the United Kingdom Exchequer but traditionally this had been at the cost of control of their budgets from London in a manner that seemed quite incompatible with political independence.

Finally there was a group of Colonies (Malta, Cyprus, and Singapore) where British defence considerations seemed in the circumstances of the 1950s to rule out a transfer of sovereignty. As regards Malta, for example, the British all-party representatives at the Round Table Conference of 1955 (Cmd. 9657) could not foresee a time when the territory could achieve complete independence. In the next year, British Government spokesmen, while not going so far as to say that the principle of self-determination could never be applicable to Cyprus, took the position that it was not at that time a practical proposition on account of the situation then existing in the Eastern Mediterranean. The farthest they could go was to work for a solution which would both satisfy the aspirations of the people of Cyprus and be consistent with the strategic interests of the United Kingdom.

No such solution was in fact ever found within the framework of British sovereignty over Cyprus (the solution was in fact to excise from the area of an independent Cyprus those small areas of land which were needed for a British base) but experiments to reconcile British defence requirements and the political aspirations of the inhabitants were made in Singapore in 1957 and Malta in 1962. Briefly the arrangements took the form of establishing a 'State' with internal self-government under its own elected Ministers, of separating the 'ceremonial' and executive functions of the Governor between a local 'head of State' and a United Kingdom Commissioner and of providing for a joint Council to oversee matters which impinged on the responsibilities of both the British and the local Government. These experiments were comparatively short-lived. Singapore passed in the early 1960s out of British sovereignty into membership of the new federation of Malaysia, becoming independent thereafter on its own in 1963. At the elections in Malta which followed the establishment of 'the State', both the main parties campaigned on a programme for independence and at a conference the following year the British Government accepted these claims, relying as in Singapore for the maintenance of its defence facilities on an agreement between two sovereign states rather than the retention of sovereignty for itself. There was, however, to be a further resort to the concept of statehood, as an alternative means of decolonization, after the disintegration of the West Indies Federation.

This is, however, to anticipate the course of events and in particular the greatly accelerated speed in the process of decolonization which took place from 1960 onwards. It had been said above that the vehicle for this process was the old Crown Colony system of Government itself which in the past had within the conventions, which governed its application, shown itself capable of almost indefinite modification. This system was, however, in the 1950s and 1960s exposed to new political forces which had grown up outside it and which in the event it could not contain for long.

These forces were those referred to in Harold Macmillan's Cape Town speech when he said that whether we liked it or not, the growth of national consciousness in Africa was a political fact and that national policies must take account of it. African nationalism was no new phenomenon, at least in West Africa. What was new was that it now grew up outside the existing constitutional framework and that it was much more widely spread in the community than earlier movements. Its origins were penetratingly analysed in the Gold Coast in the Coussey Commission Report of 1949 (Col. No. 248) but there were striking parallels elsewhere. It was distinguished by the emergence of new political elites, often educated in the secondary schools established in the inter-war period, who had kept in touch with each other after leaving school and many of whom had gone overseas for further education; and by the creation of a wider field of political activity in which they could operate through the presence in their communities of large numbers of men who had become politically conscious either through service in the forces overseas [c.f. 'Of the new forces at work the most important was the attitude of mind of the ex-servicemen . . . For the first time a relatively large proportion of the inhabitants of the country had travelled beyond its territorial limits . . . They returned with a knowledge of other nations, possessing no higher standards of cultural, social and intellectual development who nevertheless are now ordering their own affairs. Moreover having fought in the cause of freedom, they considered it their right that they should have some share in the government of their own land' (Colonial No. 248 p. 25)] or through being drawn into the money economy and into more urbanized living conditions, as a result of the war-time drive for greater production of raw materials. Political consciousness was heightened by post-war economic adjustments leading to employment difficulties and to higher prices for the consumer goods to which many more people had become accustomed. All this favoured the formation of 'mass' political parties, operating largely outside the Legislative Councils of the established system but going down to the grass-roots through a network of Party branches, ex-servicemen's associations, women's and youth groups. The instincts of party leaders and members more often than not were for action outside the constitution and this led to clashes with the law and imprisonment for many of their leaders, thus providing the movements with their martyrology. But their success in practical terms depended more on the use they made of widenings of the franchise to gain access to, and control of, Legislative Councils and access to membership of the Executive Councils. On this basis the crucial dates in decolonization in Africa are those on which Nkrumah, emerging from jail after his party had won an overwhelming electoral victory, accepted Sir Charles Arden-Clarke's invitation to enter the Government and that on which Nyerere persuaded his party, despite its dislike of the multi-racial electoral system in Tanganyika, to contest the elections there.

The history of the Gold Coast between Nkrumah's acceptance of office in 1951 and Ghana's independence in March 1957 had two features which were to be repeated elsewhere in the process of decolonization. First, for the period 1951–54 the Executive Council was composed of both official 'Ministers' (holding the 'portfolios' of Defence and External Affairs, Finance and Justice) responsible to the Governor and through him to the British Government and of unofficial Ministers basically responsible to the Legislative Council. This transitional stage, which by constitutional theory should have been impossible, in practice worked well, the officials bringing to it the fruits of experience and a tradition of 'government by consent' and the unofficials recognizing their good faith. Secondly when in 1956 the 'Cabinet', as it had by then become, asked for independence, the British Government in view of increasing political divisions in the country required the issue to be put to another General Election but agreed that if (as in fact happened) the legislature, resulting from the election, confirmed by 'a reasonable majority' the request for independence it would be granted. This was the first explicit mention on the British side of the principle of 'the People's wishes' which was to become increasingly the determining factor in 'decolonization'.

Nigeria and Sierra Leone in the 1950s followed the same course as the Gold Coast but the complications of federalism in Nigeria inevitably slowed the process there. These greater complications gave rise to two new practices which again were to form precedents for elsewhere. First, though it had been possible to negotiate the various stages of constitutional advance in the Gold Coast between the Governor and the elected Prime Minister, changes in Nigeria were made through conferences, comprising all the political parties in the legislature, under the chairmanship of British Ministers and secondly, though the first of these conferences was held in Nigeria, it later proved impracticable for a busy Secretary of State to be absent from Westminster for the time required to reach general agreement. It therefore became the almost invariable rule to hold such conferences in London, thus inscribing the names of the former aristocratic residences of Lancaster House and of Marlborough House in the history books of more than a score of successor states.

The electoral systems introduced in the early 1950s in West Africa had thus allowed the new nationalist parties there to gain admittance to and take over control of the central organs of government. In East and Central Africa 'nationalist' meant 'African nationalist' and, as has been explained above, the Colonial constitutions and franchises there had been tailored to foster multi-racial rather than African parties. Unlike their West African counterparts there-fore the African politicians in those territories had still to get to first base. (This generalization does not apply to Zanzibar and Uganda where the European stake in the economy was more akin to West Africa, but these territories had their own political and racial divisions of a different kind.) In Central Africa the issue was further complicated by the Federal set-up and, though the con-stitutional position in the Northern territories was the responsibility of the British Government, the latter had to have regard to the views of the Federal Government. Moreover the United Federal Party, which controlled the Federal Government, had its territorial parties in each of the constituent territories and these territorial parties were in a predominant position among the elected members of local legislatures.

In Kenya and Tanganyika nationalist politicians showed considerable adroit-ness in pursuing their immediate aims of overthrowing the existing multi-racial policies.

In Kenya they followed a policy of using the electoral provisions of the con-stitution to establish their bona fides as representatives of African political opinion but having established that, of refusing to participate in the institutions of government on the basis of political alliances across racial divisions—thus frustrating the strategy which had been thought of as providing the vehicle towards responsible government, most appropriate to the circumstances of Kenya. Their opportunity came with the introduction of a franchise for African voters in 1957. This, though qualitative and weighted, did admit some 60% of the adult African population to the franchise. They could then argue that so long as the number of African seats was limited by the requirement of parity between the numbers of European members and those of all the non-European members of Legislative Council, each African member's constituency would have so many electors that he could not possibly give them the service any member owed to his electors. On the basis of this argument they were allowed an increase in seats to give them parity with Europeans, who thereby became a minority as against non-European members as a whole. But the African elected members still refused to take up seats in the Council of Ministers and in 1959 walked out of Legislative Council. The British Government, while still main-taining that there was insufficient understanding of political institutions to warrant the introduction of responsible government, promised to hold a further constitutional conference.

Nyerere in Tanganyika had an easier course. He managed to secure sufficient numbers of European and Asian supporters to allow members of those races to be nominated on his Party ticket in each constituency. The deployment behind them of the African predominance on the common roll then ensured their return. The experiment in multi-racial politics in Tanganyika therefore resulted in a legislature, equally divided in membership between the races but overwhelmingly opposed to the whole multi-racial basis of the constitution.

In Central Africa the nationalists were still concentrating on extra-constitutional methods, which had led to the declaration of States of Emergency, and to the detention or imprisonment of their leaders.

This was the situation which awaited the Macmillan Government on its return after the 1959 General Election in Britain and which led to the 'different deliberate decisions' which were to accelerate the tempo in constitutional advance to independence in Africa. The first of these decisions was to accept the defeat of the parity concept in Tanganyika in the light of Nyerere's victory at the polls. A new constitution was agreed in 1960 which gave Africans predominance among members of the legislature and provided for a majority (up to 10 to 3) of elected over official Ministers in the executive. The constitutional conference promised to Kenya took place at Lancaster House in London in December 1960 and resulted in provision for a majority of African elected members in the legislature and for elections for non-African seats to be held on a common roll of electors—though with communal 'primary elections' to ensure that candidates for these seats had a minimum (25%) of support from their own community; and, on the unofficial side of the executive, Africans were given a majority of one over Europeans and Asians combined. In Uganda where the problem of racial representation had always been less acute than that of fissiparous movements among the Africans, the legislature also became almost entirely elected in composition and the Council of Ministers was composed substantially of members of the legislature. In Nyasaland the leader of the Nationalist Party was released from detention, participated with his Party in a subsequent constitutional conference and at the ensuing election won 22 out of the 28 seats in the legislature. Constitutional changes in Northern Rhodesia, put through despite a boycott of the constitutional conference by the local United Federal Party, brought African nationalists by 1962–63 into a coalition Government. This swing in political strength in the two northern territories in turn led to the dissolution of the Federation of Rhodesia and Nyasaland at the end of 1963.

The effect of these decisions by the British Government in the years following 1959 was the abandonment of the policy of setting up multi-racial governments in British Africa north of the Zambezi. It did not end the political influence of individual European politicians, many of whom continued to play an important part in the formulation of policy, but that influence was exercised within the framework of African-dominated parties, and where, as in Kenya and Uganda, African party divisions developed, the division was not about the timing of internal self-government or independence but about the constitutional forms appropriate to these conditions. At the same time, those African leaders who now had a direct share in the responsibilities of Government, worked, as in West Africa, harmoniously with their Governors and official colleagues in a manner that formed an agreeable contrast to the demagogy which often had characterized their performance in opposition.

It may indeed be asked why in view of the difficulties which were inevitably inherent in a political revolution of the kind that was taking place, African politicians were not content to hasten more slowly and why the British Government, in discharge of the responsibilities it still had towards the peoples of its dependencies, did not use the powers it still possessed to delay the process of decolonization until the foundations for independence had stood the test of further time.

The answer to the first of these questions lies in the nature of the new mass political movements which has been described above. (The importance of the role of the Party in the new African state can be judged from the fact that Nyerere found it necessary after independence to give up for the best part of a year his duties as Prime Minister and devote that time to re-organizing his Party at its grass-roots level.) Co-operation with the Colonial government put political leaders, however reasonable their conduct in office, in jeopardy of losing their political influence to more extreme influences in their parties who were not 'tainted' by association with Government. It has been said of the middle-of-the-road men who emerged as political leaders in Malaya that they were like a man riding a bicycle: they had to keep up the impetus in order to stay in control of the machine. If this was true in Malaya, it was even more true in Africa.

It would be unjust, however, to attribute the continued pressure for independence solely or even primarily to the exigencies of internal politics. Political convictions pointed the same way and were reinforced by honorable ideas of national pride, such as those already quoted from the Coussey Commission in the Gold Coast of 1950. The Monckton Commission on the Central African Federation in 1960 brought the record up to date by pointing out that the five countries in Africa, which were independent on the establishment of the Federation in 1953, had since then been joined by 20 others: that these included the Congo which was inhabited by people to whom the Africans in the Federation felt no sense of inferiority: and that in consequence it was 'natural and inevitable that the prospect of independence, seven years ago unthinkably remote, should now appear to many Africans a right from which they should no longer be debarred'.

The ever-increasing pressure for independence also brought the British Government face to face with a dilemma, which had indeed been implicit in British Colonial policy for a long time. Lord Cromer in Victorian days had pointed out that the British overseas in pursuing the ideals of good government and of self-government, were seeking ends which could be mutually destructive. The British Government now took precautions in the interests of good government, in case their change of policy went completely wrong. For example, even though the Kenya 1961 constitution provided for an African majority in the legislature, the Governor was still left with the power of nominating members of the legislature so that government could be carried on in face of an African boycott like that of 1959. (Indeed a boycott by the majority party after the 1961 elections was frustrated by the formation and successful functioning of a minority Government.) After the 1960 conference too the long-standing principle that Colonies should be responsible for the cost of their own defence was breached by taking the cost of the King's African Rifles on to U.K. votes so that the efficiency of this second line of defence against civil disorder need not be endangered by local legislatures refusing to vote the necessary supply. In any event the British Government still possessed the ultimate sanction of suspending the constitution, and had in fact used this sanction in two territories in the period under review. The constitutions of British Guiana and of Malta were suspended in 1953 and 1959 respectively as a result of refusals by the majority political party in each territory to co-operate in the spirit of the constitution with the official element in it. But the politics of both these countries had been marked by deep and roughly balancing divisions. (Even so the suspension in British Guiana was presented as a necessary period of 'marking time' before constitutional advance could be resumed, as it was in 1956 and 1957, and suspension in Malta was more or less immediately followed by the establishment of a Constitutional Commission to recommend in what form progress could best be resumed.) The situation where a 'colonial' government found itself at loggerheads with a nationalist movement commanding general popular support, carried a quite different kind of risk. Harold Macmillan quotes in his memoirs the counsel he received from one Colonial Governor. The latter accepted that his African Ministers would not be fully fitted to run their affairs for a dozen years or so but nevertheless advised that they should be given independence as soon as possible on the grounds that the alternative was for himself to spend the next dozen years suppressing political unrest and putting the leaders of African opinion behind bars; in such circumstances there could be no further training for independence and little hope of attracting the investment necessary to sustain a rising standard of life. In short, as things turned out, Lord Cromer's conflicting ideals were no longer in conflict, and the only chance of good government now seemed to lie in self-government despite all its imponderables.

This is to put the question in terms of colonial policy. The Home Government had also to consider the implications of resisting independence in terms of finance, defence and international relations. These considerations had in fact been on their minds when they decided after the 1959 election to seek to come to terms with African nationalism. They had if anything acquired greater force in the period of co-operation in government with African nationalist leaders. The British Government before that period had successfully fought 'colonial wars' in the 1950s against the Malayan communists and Mau Mau. Those movements had not commanded general support from the population in either Malaya or Kenya; nevertheless their defeat had called for considerable expenditure of British funds, and for the diversion of British forces from the country's first line

of defence in Western Europe. This was not a good augury for taking on movements which might have general support and there were those in Britain who had
noted the cost to France in money and political strife of the 'colonial' wars in
Indochina and Algeria. They noted also the revival of French influence abroad
that followed the granting of independence to French African territories in the
years 1958–60.

It was against such a background that British Ministers continued to hold to
the conclusion that manifest as were the risks of moving quickly towards independence, the dangers of being too slow were greater.

As has already been said, the first victim of the 'Wind of Change' in Africa
was the multi-racial policy which the British had tried to pursue in East and
Central Africa. There was now to be another victim in the shape of a British
policy of far longer history, viz. that independence must mean the ability to pay
one's own way in the world. It is true that the Gladstonian gloss on that philosophy that Colonies must be restricted to a level of services they could meet from
their own resources, had been modified in 1940 by the Colonial Development
and Welfare Act which had allowed the British Government to make grants to
Colonial governments for the purposes defined in the Act. This facility had been
a most important aid to carrying out the policy, formulated by the Conservative
Government of 1951, of pursuing the economic and social development of
Colonial territories so that it kept pace with the territories' political development.
But the assumption was that such help would cease on independence. Nevertheless the practice whereby the richer nations contributed by loans, gifts and technical assistance to the plans of independent underdeveloped countries was being
established in 1951 and was to spread widely during the rest of the decade. In
consequence, by February 1956 the Colonial Secretary of the day was able to
tell West Indian politicians that there would be nothing derogatory to the
dignity of an independent Federation of the West Indies in accepting help of
partners to improve its economic situation. Clearly, any idea that economic
independence had to be reached before political independence could be granted
was by now anachronistic.

But the speech just quoted also showed that as far as budgetary assistance was
concerned, the old doctrine was far from dead. In it the Colonial Secretary laid
down as still a pre-condition of independence that a country must be able to
finance its own administration. Over the next eight years this position was in
turn to be gradually eroded under the pressure of policies to the contrary pursued
by other powers with interests in Africa and by the result of the ending of the
Italian trusteeship over Somalia in 1960 and of British Somaliland joining the
new State. Britain and Italy found themselves having to contribute to the budget
of the new Republic since it was impossible for that State from its own resources
to balance it. Nor when French dependent territories became independent states
did the French Government have any regard to their budgetary position as a
factor to be taken into account in granting independence. The first purely British
territory to go independent without a balanced budget was Zanzibar but the

deficit was small and likely to be temporary. The conclusive break with past British doctrine came with Malawi which went into independence with a substantial deficit on its budget. But it would have been politically ludicrous and a false economy if, having given way to political pressure and allowed Nyasaland, though it could not balance its budget, to leave a federation in which it could only be held by force, Britain was then to contemplate keeping the country still dependent against its will. Political considerations pointed to the alternative policy of taking account of the need for budgetary aid within the total aid programme and tailoring capital assistance so as to remove the need for help to the budget.

Another consequence of the Gladstonian doctrine was that Britain had traditionally expected Colonies to pay for the cost of their civil service, including the salaries and pensions of expatriate officers, recruited for those services by the British Government. These expatriate officers had come to have special privileges in the shape of 'inducement' allowances over and above their basic pay which had generally been adjusted to that of locally recruited officers of identical rank; they also received special passage allowances and had the right to retire on compensation for loss of career following major constitutional changes. All of this fell on the funds of the Colonies where they were employed. In theory, under the doctrine that social progress should be assisted to keep pace with political development, colonial educational systems should have been turning out sufficient skilled manpower to replace expatriate civil servants by the time of independence. In India and Ceylon this had worked well enough to leave a comparatively small residual expatriate problem at the time of independence. In Africa, however, the speed at which power was transferred outstripped the ability of the educational services to produce sufficient trained local manpower. In these circumstances, the politicians taking over from the British were anxious to avoid a breakdown of administration and to that end wished to continue to employ experienced British officers in their territories and to recruit from Britain to meet vacancies which could not be filled locally. The expatriate officers in such territories, though ready for the most part to serve on there, were apprehensive lest, if they did so, their terms of service might be altered to their detriment. The first British attempt to meet these difficulties came in 1954. The British Government then declared its readiness, at the time it lost effective control over the terms and conditions of service of a territory's civil service (i.e. at internal self-government), to make agreements with the territorial government by which the latter would undertake that the terms of service of officers who had been recruited by the British Government, would be preserved. This undertaking did not entirely assuage the apprehensions of expatriate officers since, even though employing governments might enter into such an agreement, this did not remove the risk that their legislatures might refuse to vote the funds necessary to implement it. (The special privileges in expatriate terms of service were an obvious target for more extreme politicians.) After some limited amendments within the framework of the 1954 arrangements, the British Government took an entirely

10

new approach to the problem in 1960 and for the first time itself assumed a financial responsibility in respect of those it recruited to serve in overseas territories. This took the form of the Overseas Service Aid Scheme (O.S.A.S.). This was open to participation by all territories, dependent or independent, where officers recruited by the British Government were serving. Under it that government undertook to pay the cost of inducement and educational allowances for the officials it had recruited, to make a contribution towards their passage costs and to meet half the cost of any compensation for which they might become eligible. It also proved ready to help governments with loans to meet their half of these compensation costs. In the first year the scheme, which was widely adopted by overseas governments, cost the British taxpayer over £13m. But it did seem to allow the transition to independence to be bridged without the collapse of administration that had once been feared. Its principles were also applied to officers recruited on contract by the British Government for service with overseas governments and in this way it also bridged the gap between the pre-independence Colonial Service and post-independence schemes of technical assistance. In the later 1960s, however, the Tanzanian Government professed itself incapable of meeting the cost of expatriate pensions which arose from service before the time of self-government, without undue damage to its expenditure on social and economic matters. In 1970 the British Government declared its willingness, if a government so asked, to consider assuming responsibility for pensions arising in respect of service before the date of self-government.

The decision not to regard the need for budgetary assistance as an impediment to decolonization opened the way to the independence of the former South African High Commission Territories. This had a bearing in the fears, felt earlier, in London, that countries incapable of their own protection could not become independent. In an historical sense the South African High Commission Territories were the perfect example of such a category since they had come under British rule and had remained under it because their peoples had wanted protection from South Africa. When, however, they were now asking for independence, their representatives made it clear that they had accepted as a necessary condition of that independence that they could no longer look to Britain for help in maintaining a state of co-existence with South Africa. From now on Britain made it clear to territories seeking independence that they must rely on their own efforts for defence against external aggression or on international or regional security organizations. This decision was to keep British Honduras poised on the brink of independence for many years after 1964. The British Government also made it clear from this time that a country seeking independence must be prepared to deal with any internal security threats without British assistance. The only departure from this rule was in the special circumstances of Mauritius where the price of maintaining after independence British defence facilities in the Island was an undertaking to consult with the Mauritius Government in the case of internal security difficulties.

The acceleration towards independence in Africa had also brought to a head the problem of Southern Rhodesia. The white population there, who had controlled the government of the Colony since 1923 with the minimum of intervention from Britain, felt no less than their African neighbours to the north that the spread of independence elsewhere in Africa confirmed their own claims to independence. But the course of events to the North made them no less determined to resist the advent of African majority rule in their own country. They therefore pressed for independence on the basis of their existing constitution. The British Government's powers of intervention on the spot were practically non-existent: local Ministers controlled the security forces and the civil service, both of which were recruited locally. The assertion of British control by armed intervention was geographically very difficult even if it had been politically practicable in the United Kingdom. British Governments were reluctant, however, to accept responsibility for Rhodesian independence except on conditions, the chief of which were that the independence constitution should provide for unimpeded progress to majority rule and should be acceptable to the people of Rhodesia as a whole.

Their main weapon was that their consent was properly a prerequisite of international recognition of an independent Rhodesia. Discussions with the Conservative Government in 1963–64 and with their Labour successors ended in deadlock and in November 1965 the Rhodesian Government purported to make a declaration of independence. The British Government carried the problem into the international sphere by securing a United Nations mandate for the imposition of economic sanctions on Rhodesia. Sanctions worked slowly and two attempts by the Labour Government to negotiate a settlement ended in failure. The newly-independent African states had found the policy of negotiation with white 'rebels' offensive to their sense of African nationality and the transfer of the issue to the international arena gave them scope to voice their resentment. The incident therefore soured any hopes the British Government on the precedent of France might have had of securing a wide measure of goodwill in the underdeveloped world by their record of decolonization, and the vehemence of African criticism also soured large parts of British public opinion towards the new states. The Conservative Government in 1970–71 did reach agreement with the regime, which by that time in the absence of international recognition was running short of development capital but the settlement failed the test of acceptability which was carried out by an independent commission, appointed by the British Government. Stalemate therefore continued with the British Government making it clear that it looked to Africans and Europeans to reach agreement direct on the solution of their difficulties.

Elsewhere in Africa the main problem remaining for the British Government had been to leave behind safeguards for the rights of minorities (tribal and racial) in independence constitutions. Radical solutions like separate independence for Ashanti and the Northern Territories in Ghana or for Buganda in Uganda had been firmly resisted in the past on the grounds that they would mean a fall back on the standards of life of the general population. But the independence constitutions of Uganda and Kenya now established 'regional' bodies, deriving their existence from 'entrenched' sections of the constitution, which would share in day-to-day government and so impose some restraint on the central executive. Provision was also made, as had been done in Ceylon in 1948, for the appointment of independent Judicial, Public Service and Police Commissions with a view to offering guarantees to minorities that appointments and promotions in these services would not be determined on communal, political or tribal lines. Following a Nigerian precedent provision was also made for the recognition of fundamental rights, based on the International Convention of 1953 on Human Rights and Fundamental Freedom (Cmd. 8969) and the constitutions provided individuals with the right of appeal to an independent High Court for protection or enforcement of any of these provisions.

In some of these respects, as in other matters, independence constitutions tried to reflect the unwritten practices of the Westminster Constitution. There were those at the time who were doubtful whether these principles, built up over so many years and reflecting the peculiar course of British history, could be transplanted successfully to new countries overseas. The post-independence fate of many constitutions in Africa has added to the number of such critics. But it is difficult to see what other course the British Governments of the time could have taken. They were fully aware that no constitutional provision they could devise and however they might entrench it by special amendment procedures, would be proof against a *coup d'etat* and, though they may not fully have appreciated what effect the transfer of local armed forces from expatriate command to a new élite officer class with ideas of its own on government and the power to enforce them, might have, any greater degree of foresight would not have been likely to have altered the basic decision that the balance of advantage lay in going faster rather than slower. Moreover they had no alternative form of constitution which they could put forward with confidence as better fitted to the circumstances of new states. But the conclusive factor was that the politicians of the emerging states demanded the Westminster Constitution. They had been conditioned towards it by membership of Legislative Councils whose procedures reflected Westminster and nurtured in its ways by attendance at meetings and seminars of the Commonwealth Parliamentary Association. The argument that it could not be transplanted seemed to them basically a reflexion on the abilities of their own race. This, as nationalists, they resented; they also claimed that there was no fundamental difference between the Westminster model and the African tradition of reaching decisions at the tribal level by a process of full discussion and not by diktat.

There was, however, a difference that became clear after independence. The African tribal tradition was concerned with reaching a consensus behind which all would then fall in line. It left no room for the continuing legitimacy of organized political opposition. (Nor could an opposition in an African state be relied on, as in the Westminster model, to exercise restraint sufficient to secure that defeat of the Government of the day would not mean destruction of the

State itself.) In these circumstances effective political debate tended after independence to be confined to party caucuses and Parliamentary proceedings to become as short a ritual as was necessary to give the force of law to the party consensus: this led naturally to the establishment *de facto* or *de jure* of one-party states, so distasteful to the Westminster tradition. Even more distasteful to Western political thought was the adulation of the Head of Government which so often accompanied the creation of one-party states. Again African politicians saw this as part of African tradition on which the British themselves had been only too happy to rely in order to buttress their policy of indirect rule through traditional authorities. By this African tradition, leadership and the enforcement of the law, even though the law was made by a group, is the responsibility of a person with authority, who should be answerable for his actions to the group but not hampered by them in effecting them—a concept far removed from the Westminster ideal of Parliament as a continuing check on the Executive but one into which 'adulation' fits as strengthening the day-to-day authority of the head of the Executive. But pre-independence there was in the Colonial Governor an authority with the means to remove a traditional authority who had lost the confidence of his group. After independence control of such means had passed to the Head of Government himself and so long as he retained that control, the analogy with the tribal past was imperfect. Hence one-party states in Africa have remained vulnerable to unconstitutional *coups d'état* and their proponents have still to work out the reconciliation of their ancestral traditions with the necessity in a modern state of ensuring peaceful methods of political change. (The Tanzanian experiment in allowing constituencies a choice of candidates of the same Party may contain the seeds of a solution.)

The Westminster model was more successfully transplanted to the West Indies but plans for decolonization there foundered with the break-up of the West Indies Federation. This had occurred at the stage when inter-Governmental agreement had actually been reached on an independence settlement to come into effect in 1962. But Jamaican opposition to West Indian customs union led to a 54% majority for secession in a referendum there. The British Government accepted this as a final indication of the wishes of Jamaica which then proceeded independently to independence. Trinidad soon followed as did Barbados after a four-year interval. The Government of Montserrat declared that because of its small size and economic vulnerability the island should remain a dependency but the legislatures of the other smaller territories of the former Federation accepted a form of statehood in association with Britain. The genesis of this particular form of statehood was a Declaration of Principles by the General Assembly of the United Nations in December 1960. [General Assembly Resolution No. 1541 (XV).] This declaration had recognized that, as an alternative to emergence as a sovereign independent state, a non-self-governing territory could, within the terms of the Charter, reach 'a full measure of self-government through free association (or integration) with an independent state'. The criteria for free association were that the choice should be made freely and voluntarily by the people of the territory concerned, expressed through informed and democratic processes: that they should retain the freedom to modify their status through the same processes and have the right to determine their internal constitution, without outside interference, by their own constitutional processes. In the view of the British and Associated States' Governments, the first criterion was met by approval of the island legislatures, the members of which were elected on the basis of universal suffrage: provision for the remainder was made in British legislation and in formal agreements with the respective state governments. Each Associated State was given complete control of its internal affairs, including the power to amend or replace its constitution without resort to British Orders-in-Council: Britain remained responsible for external relations and defence, retaining legislative and executive authority as necessary for this but undertaking to discharge this responsibility in close consultation with the state government concerned. Limited delegations of authority on external affairs have been made to state governments. Association was to be terminable by either party to it and Britain has agreed to give six months' notice of any intention to terminate and to hold a conference on its implications. Special procedures (approval by two-thirds of the elected members of the legislature and, except where association with another Commonwealth Caribbean country was envisaged, two-thirds of the votes cast in a referendum) were laid down for the exercise of the option by an Associated State. [When however the Grenada Government sought in 1973 to proceed to sovereign independence, it requested the British Government to arrange for this by acting on its power to terminate Association. The British Government, after holding a conference with representatives of the Government and the Opposition in Grenada, agreed to proceed in this way, thus obviating the need to resort to the special procedures described in this sentence.] The United Nations in fact did not accept the arrangements as meeting their criteria for 'free association' on the grounds that there had been no United Nations presence associated with the choice of the status by the West Indian legislatures involved, but this did not greatly worry either Britain or the Associated States.

Britain, however, met difficulties of another kind arising from the new association. The 6000 inhabitants of Anguilla professed to prefer a direct relationship with Britain to inclusion in the State of St Kitts–Nevis–Anguilla and carried their objections to the extent of bundling the State officials and police out of the Island. While this was primarily an internal affair, the State lacked the means of re-establishing its authority across 70 miles of sea. A vacuum was created which might be filled by undesirable foreign influences and therefore affect Britain's responsibilities for external affairs. In discharge of these responsibilities British security forces and a British Commissioner were despatched to the island, an operation which attracted considerable publicity at home and abroad. The British Government made it clear that it was no part of their policy to force the Anguillans to live under a government of which they disapproved but efforts at reconciliation, despite assistance from a Caribbean commission of enquiry, were fruitless. The vacuum in government continued and in particular courts of law under the State constitution could not be held in the island. This again could clearly affect the British Government's international responsibilities for the State since they would be held responsible by other governments whose nationals might be denied justice by the situation. Accordingly the British Government, without formally excising Anguilla from the Associated State, took powers temporarily to place the British Commissioner in control of the whole internal government of the island. These events disenchanted British Ministers with the experiment of Associated Statehood and no encouragement was given to any idea that the British Parliament would be prepared to give legislative authority to repeating the experiment in any of the remaining dependent territories.

A definitive statement of policy as regards these was made at the Bahamas Constitutional conference in 1968. It was to the effect that it was no part of British policy to force independence on a people who did not want it or to deny it to a people who wanted it—it was for the people to decide. There is no mention here, as there had been in 1948 and 1952, of any political, social or economic criteria for independence or any implication that Britain was the final arbiter as to whether those criteria had been met. On the contrary any territory could choose independence. Statements in other contexts however made it clear that if it did so, it had to accept as a corollary that it must rely for defence against external aggression on its own forces and on international or regional machinery: nor could its government count on British assistance in the event of civil disorder. It was not debarred from continuing British financial aid but that would be considered within the framework of British policy to independent countries. If it opted for continued dependence on Britain its reasonable needs, as assessed by Britain, would have the first call on British aid funds, Britain would fulfil its obligation to protect it against external aggression and generally observe an obligation to promote to the utmost the well-being of the territory's inhabitants, including in particular the maintenance of law and order. In this connexion, the context in which the statement was made at the Bahamas conference is important. At that conference there had been no demand for immediate independence. The representatives of the majority Party sought, however, to have internal security entrusted to local Ministers and as a corollary that the latter should have full control over the police force. The British Government were unwilling to give up ultimate responsibility in this sphere which in any dependent territory was one on which British Ministers were likely to find Parliament sensitive. In addition responsibility for internal security involved responsibility for determining, in the event of disorder, the right moment for calling in British armed forces in support of the civil power. The statement was therefore to be read as implying that if the people of any dependency wished for their own reasons to retain their link with Britain, they had, as a corollary, to accept that this could only be done in terms of a constitution agreeable to the British Government. But the choice still remained with the subject and not with the ruler. If therefore it did not complete the process of decolonization, it at least firmly established the principle of self-determination.

The progress of decolonization increased the size and geographical spread of the Commonwealth. It has also been credited with altering the concept of the Commonwealth. To a large extent this is true but there had been a major change in the working of the Commonwealth even before the new members joined it in such large numbers. Before the Second World War, only Canada of the 'Old Dominions' had had a Foreign Service of any size. The rest had depended for the protection of their interests abroad on British Ambassadors and in matters of foreign policy they naturally in these circumstances tended to look first for guidance to Britain. After the war, they had become deeply involved in political and military relationships in their own part of the world and had greatly extended their own Diplomatic Services. The arrival of the new members, who followed the same policies, greatly accentuated this trend.

On the other hand the expansion of the Commonwealth had occurred at a time when the more developed countries of the world had come to accept that they had both an interest and a duty to help underdeveloped countries raise their economic standards. The Commonwealth, embracing as it did, on a basis of equality, a wide range of countries in both categories, was particularly well placed to take part in and foster developments of this type. Heads of Government meetings began to be supplemented by more specialized Commonwealth Conferences meeting regularly—as for example on Finance, Trade and Economics and Education and some of these had resulted in schemes of Commonwealth co-operation as for the provision or training of teachers or the exchange of Fellowships in the educational field. Nevertheless such arrangements had tended to be made *ad hoc* until the establishment in 1965 of a Commonwealth Secretariat, staffed from and financed by Commonwealth countries. This provided an organization specifically charged with promoting closer and more informed understanding between Commonwealth governments and one which could and did take a lead in fostering on a more general basis intra-Commonwealth contacts and arrangements for mutual help.

The Secretariat was responsible to the meetings of Heads of Government and serviced these meetings. The increase in the number of governments represented at the meetings did, however, carry with it the risk that proceedings would take the form of a series of set speeches prepared beforehand. Some of these seemed to be aimed more at audiences back home rather than to bring about closer meetings of minds round the table. A deliberate and generally successful attempt was therefore made at the Ottawa conference of 1973 by procedural methods to foster a return to the informality and intimacy of discussion which had marked earlier Commonwealth conferences and had been recognized as a distinctive and particularly fruitful mark of the Commonwealth connexion.

In parallel with the changes in the working of the Commonwealth came questions about Britain's own government machinery for dealing with its overseas responsibilities and interests. When technical assistance and financial aid had become a major factor in the international field, did it make sense for responsibility for this work in Whitehall to be divided between the three Departments of the Foreign, Commonwealth Relations and Colonial Offices, to say nothing of the Treasury? When Commonwealth Governments were basing their own external policy on regional arrangements and at the U.N. were taking positions in all sorts of international questions, did it really make sense for Britain to have one department (the Commonwealth Relations Office) responsible for relations with Commonwealth countries and one (the Foreign Office) responsible for relations with foreign countries and for work at the United Nations? Did the existence of two Departments with separate services and communications tend to hamper the formulation of coherent British policies in regions of the world where they were both represented? Questions such as these led to a restructuring in the 1960s of British Government machinery over the whole overseas field though, as with decolonization, this was reached through a succession of different decisions.

In 1960 the Select Committee on the Estimates recommended that the Commonwealth Relations Office and the Colonial Office should be merged in a new Commonwealth Office on the grounds that the two Departments had marked similarities of function and in light of the changes then taking place in Africa. The Conservative Government of the day, however, while recognizing that this might be the ultimate solution thought it premature at that particular time. They did undertake a measure of co-ordination in the overseas field in 1961 when they set up the Department of Technical Co-operation to take over responsibility for the provision of technical assistance and staff to Commonwealth, foreign and colonial governments and for British participation in internationally organized technical assistance. In the next year they made some changes in responsibility for Commonwealth and Colonial relations. In the first place as a temporary measure pending the settlement of the future of the Federation of Rhodesia and Nyasaland, they established a Central African Office with its own Ministerial head. But they placed the Colonial and Commonwealth Relations Office under the direction of a single Secretary of State though the two Departments themselves still remained distinct. In the field of external relations they also in 1962 appointed a Committee under Lord Plowden to examine the services responsible for representing British interests in foreign and Commonwealth countries. The Committee reported by the end of 1963. Their report included a statement that the logic of events pointed to the amalgamation of the Commonwealth Relations Office with the Foreign Office but the Committee hesitated to recommend this at that juncture as it would be liable to be misinterpreted as a sign of loss of interest in the Commonwealth partnership. They did, however, recommend the creation of a unified Diplomatic Service covering posts in both Commonwealth and foreign countries. This recommendation was accepted by the Government who also expressed the hope that when it had been put into effect, they could proceed to the merger of the Colonial and

10*

Commonwealth Relations Office. They expected to be able to do this in the latter half of 1965.

By that time, however, the Conservative Government had fallen and the new Labour Government had reverted to the system of having separate Secretaries of State for Commonwealth Relations and for the Colonies. They, however, set up a new Ministry of Overseas Development to deal with the British economic aid programme as a whole. As a result of this decision it was possible to draw up a coherent and centrally directed British aid programme in place of the previous position where that programme tended to be an unco-ordinated series of separate projects each considered, by the Department responsible for it, on its own merits and in the light of that Department's policies. A problem did, however, arise over aid to dependent territories. Control of this, both budgetary and development aid, was an important instrument in the hands of the Colonial Secretary for the discharge of his general responsibility for the administration of the remaining dependent territories. If he transferred any part of this responsibility to another Minister, could he realistically still discharge those responsibilities? In the end a judgment of Solomon awarded development aid to the Ministry of Overseas Development and left budgetary aid with the Colonial Office, both Departments being urged to work closely together and the principle was laid down that the reasonable needs of the remaining dependent territories should have the first claim on the British aid programme ('reasonable' still remained a somewhat subjective term of judgment).

In 1966 the Labour Government did effect the merger of the Colonial and Commonwealth Relations Office into a single Commonwealth Office as the Select Committee on the Estimates had recommended six years before. In 1968 the Commonwealth Office was itself merged with the Foreign Office to form a new Foreign and Commonwealth Office. It was recognized that the administration of the remaining dependent territories was a specialized form of work and a division for those duties was preserved in the new office. Responsibility for relations with Commonwealth countries and for the external relations of dependent territories was, however, arranged on a geographical basis, departments dealing with relations with such countries and with foreign countries in the same geographical regions. A Commonwealth Co-ordination Department was, however, maintained to preserve the special traditions of the Commonwealth relationship and to ensure that these were not overlooked in the work of the rest of the Office.

The Conservative Government in 1970 decided that overseas aid should also be the responsibility of the Foreign and Commonwealth Secretary. The intention behind this was to unify Ministerial responsibility for overseas policy but, at the same time, it was recognized that it would be important to maintain a coherent direction of the aid programme and not to dissipate the store of expertise in this field that had been built up in the Ministry of Overseas Development. These objects were achieved by the transformation of the Ministry (now called the Overseas Development Administration) into a functional 'wing' of the Foreign and Commonwealth Office. This 'wing' in turn was placed in the charge of a Minister with direct access to the Foreign and Commonwealth Secretary. A minor but consequential adjustment was to set up a joint division, serving Ministers in both 'wings', to deal with business concerning the remaining dependent territories, thereby obviating any duplication of effort arising from the division of responsibility in this field which had resulted from the creation of the Ministry of Overseas Development.

The Labour Government, on assuming office in 1974, however, re-established the Ministry of Overseas Development as an independent department. This was in accordance with the terms of their election programme. In that programme the principles which should determine policies for overseas development were enumerated. The conclusion was reached that if Third World countries were to be assisted by a British Government to achieve their aim of economic independence and viability, policy could not be just a matter of aid but must include other considerations such as trade, monetary reform, and international co-operation in this field. It was recognized that these policy objectives would require a greater degree of integration between the several Government Departments involved than had been the case under Labour in 1964–70 or under the succeeding Conservative administration. The election programme, besides announcing the proposal to re-create the separate Ministry of Overseas Development, declared the intention to create machinery in Whitehall to give expression to the objective of assisting the Third World in trade and monetary matters and to implement overseas development policies as a co-ordinated programme of action. Though a separate Ministry of Overseas Development had been established, the joint division, dealing with the dependent territories, was preserved with the responsibility of serving Ministers concerned with those territories in both the Foreign and Commonwealth Office and the re-created Ministry.

ANNEX
Dates of 'decolonization'

1956 Sudan

1957 Ghana* : Malaya

1960 Nigeria : Cyprus
British Somaliland (as part of the Republic of Somalia)

1961 Sierra Leone : Tanganyika
Southern Cameroons (as part of the Federal Republic of Cameroons)

1962 Jamaica, Trinidad and Tobago and Uganda

1963 Kenya : Zanzibar, Sabah, Sarawak and Singapore (as part of the Federation of Malaysia)

1964 Malawi, Malta and Zambia

1965 The Gambia (Singapore seceded from Malaysia and became independent)

1966 Guyana, Botswana, Lesotho and Barbados

1967 South Arabian Federation
Antigua, St. Kitts–Nevis–Anguilla, Dominica, Grenada and St. Lucia as States in association with Britain

1968 Swaziland : Mauritius

1969 St. Vincent as State in association with Britain

1970 Tonga : Fiji

1973 The Bahamas

* States underlined become members of the Commonwealth.

Britain and Europe

12

Professor S. C. Holt, M.A. Ph.D.

Perhaps the very first thing which should be mentioned in a chapter of this kind is that a book about British Government now has to include a consideration of 'the European dimension'. Traditionally, Britain's relations with Europe and with the Common Market in particular have been thought of primarily as issues of foreign affairs. Only when the prospects of British membership of E.E.C. became really imminent did the ordinary citizen, outside the political class, seem to appreciate its likely impact on his everyday life and on the way he might be governed. But if the European Community ultimately achieves the objectives of its founders it will have the most far-reaching implications both at home and abroad. It is probably fair to say that *in terms of the balance of power*, it may turn out to be the most important thing that has happened in Europe since the French Revolution. But will the Community achieve the objectives of its founders and, more important, perhaps, at present for Britain, will all the Member States continue to feel that the benefits of the enterprise make it all worthwhile?

In most areas of policy for which it is responsible the Community is behind schedule, but in the original six founder states the organization continues to command the support of a majority of the political class, of industry, the trade-union movement and, most important, of public opinion. While many of these supporters are disappointed with the speed of progress, there is no sizeable movement in any of these countries which favours abandoning the whole enterprise and taking off in another direction. With the enlargement of the Community the speed of progress is likely to slow down further for a combination of two reasons—the method of taking decisions and the different conflict of interests that the three new member states have added.

Britain, of course, as a Member State faces all these difficulties too but has quite a few extra ones of her own. These arise partly because she joined the organization late when some inconvenient rules had been made and partly because she is a different kind of country, in economic, political and psychological terms. The latter is extremely important. During the police hunt for Frederick Sewell in 1971, the B.B.C. reported the fears of the authorities that in spite of their careful watch on the ports he might have 'escaped to Europe'. It will probably take a long time before the British start thinking of Europe as being here rather than somewhere else. By using the word 'European' in this way, the British, of course, really mean 'continental'. For a number of straight-forward historical reasons Britain is not 'continental' and President De Gaulle used regularly to remind us of this fact. He would either make this point directly or occasionally incorporate it in a backhanded compliment like referring to us as 'that great island people'.[1]

Whether one takes the view that this historical legacy has been an advantage or a disadvantage we cannot alter it. On the other hand, if the people of Britain are to make the psychological readjustments necessary to make a success of membership of the Community, they will need a lengthy period of good news from Brussels. While the supporters of the Community in the founder states are 'content but not satisfied', their counterparts in Britain are not yet in that happy position. As a majority of public opinion continues to be hostile, the pro-marketeers in Britain have found themselves still on the defensive, even after the country has actually joined the Community. This is because in Britain, unlike in any other Member State there *is* a sizable section of the political class that wishes to abandon the enterprise and move in a different direction. A further complication is that those who feel this way are not agreed about what this direction should be, indeed the issue would be much simpler if they were. But whatever comfort the pro-marketeers may take from this latter situation is matched by the prospect of the issue being kept alive for some time yet. Even if it were to happen that the new Labour Government took Britain out of the E.E.C. this could only be done on the basis of a whole new economic and political strategy which might conceivably bring about even greater changes in our lives and the way we are governed.

While Britain has had a very eventful political history, she has been lucky in being able to face some of the great convulsions with a high degree of national unity, as in the two World Wars. In other crises such as the inter-war depression, the divisions have usually been along coherent ideological lines. Indeed, the clarity and consistency of political decision in Britain both for politicians and for the voters has been the vital key to our stability. Many other countries in Europe have not been so lucky; their stability has been frequently upset by deep and bitter divisions in their societies. These divisions, moreover, have sometimes been so complex that it has been impossible to predict just when a crisis would come. Italy, France, Finland, Spain, Greece, Germany (under the Weimar Republic) have all known this kind of situation. Such stability as they have had has often been bought at an appalling price. Happily for the British, only occasionally does a great issue arise which shatters the regular political align-ments. Home Rule for Ireland was one, the Munich crisis of 1938 was another, and in the 1960s and 1970s the Common Market has done the same. There are not many exposed nerves in the British body politic, but when they are hit the patient goes into a convulsion. The traumatic experience of coming to terms with the Common Market has been highly significant for what it has taught us about ourselves, the nature of our institutions and our methods of taking decisions. The rest of the chapter will accordingly be devoted to a survey and analysis of the way the British political system has responded to the European challenge. It will *not* be a reiteration of the economic arguments for and against the decision to join. Because the issue was so hotly contested, however (both for economic and political reasons), all kinds of quite fundamental questions were asked, which would not have been otherwise, concerning such matters as holding a referendum, the processes of constitutional change etc. Nothing can be quite the same again.

Neither those who have been for nor those against British membership of E.E.C. can look back with much satisfaction on the 'Raikes progress' of Britain's European policy since the Second World War. While she would undoubtedly have liked to pursue an independent policy while retaining the dignity and respect which she had enjoyed in recent history, this proved not to be possible. Once it had been decided to change direction and go into the Common Market it turned out to be very difficult to make a success of this policy either. Not only did a long series of indignities have to be endured at the hands of Britain's historic rivals, the French, but when an agreement was eventually reached the terms of entry were such as not to arouse great enthusiasm.

Any young student looking back over the last 25 years could be forgiven for wondering how the previous generation managed to get the worst of both worlds. The explanation is not easy because the whole story is highly complex, involving a subtle interplay of factors and forces, some well outside our shores with others inside our own political system.

Having made these few introductory remarks, we must now look at the main events as they happened and consider their significance.

The full story from 1945–73 has been told in detail in a number of standard works whose high quality is unlikely to be surpassed.[2] There is clearly not space here to go over all this ground again but an attempt will be made to look at the main turning points and to try and explain why the British reacted the way they did. All this, of course, can only be one writer's judgement and it may well be revised as greater distance in time brings a clearer perspective.

The first thing to be said is that while successive British Governments since the Second World War have produced their plans for what should happen in the field of European Co-operation, they have never been pioneers. What has some-times looked like a British initiative has actually been a counter-initiative to the pioneering work of other countries whose proposals the British Government did not like. To understand the reason for this one has to appreciate the psychology of the British people at the end of the war. While the victory over Germany was a joint victory of the Allies, the British felt themselves, together with the Com-monwealth, to be the principal *moral* victors of that struggle. All the other allies had skeletons in the cupboard somewhere. The Americans had come in late, the Soviet Union had to explain the Hitler-Stalin Pact, some of the French had given in, the Dutch and Belgians had been defeated and so on. While Britain too had made a pact with Hitler at Munich in 1938, the country was being run during and after the war by people who had repudiated it at the time.

The British did not feel the need nor did they have the desire to become integrated, or, as they felt, 'entangled' with a group of discredited countries. It is only much more recently that the true extent of Britain's financial loss in the Second World War has been acknowledged. In the immediate post-war years, national self-confidence was very much intact.

Now, of course, it was considered desirable, to prevent another European war, that the countries of Europe should unite. Winston Churchill, whose international popularity was unrivalled at this time, referred to the need for European unity in a number of speeches but it is clear, particularly from his Zurich speech in 1946, that he did *not* intend Britain to take a leading part in this process.[3] It has to be remembered that the British Empire, at the height of its prestige, was still within the memory of living people. Even as it slowly changed into a Commonwealth of 'free and equal partners', most people in Britain believed that the word 'equal' was included in that phrase only for the sake of politeness. The British Prime Minister always took the Chair at Commonwealth Prime Ministers' conferences and they took place in London. Both these practices have now been changed. The last two conferences have taken place in Singapore and Ottawa and in neither case was Mr Heath in the Chair. The fact that these moves have been generally accepted, indicates not so much a change in Britain's relative position in the Commonwealth, but an increase of realism on the part of public opinion. The Commonwealth as an organization has acted as a kind of parachute for Britain, letting her down gently from her status as a great world power. The rules of membership of the Commonwealth have been so flexible as to be difficult to define and have been modified in important respects to prevent member states from leaving. The British Monarch used to be Head of State in all Commonwealth countries but this was modified to accommodate India in 1947 when she wanted to become a republic. When Malaya obtained independence in 1957 she remained a Monarchy but wanted her own king. This too was allowed. Following the Rhodesian U.D.I., two Commonwealth states—Ghana and Tanzania—actually broke off diplomatic relations with Britain but remained in the Commonwealth. Until the last few years, British Governments have attached the greatest importance to keeping the organization together. When South Africa was forced to discontinue her membership in 1961, the British Prime Minister went to great lengths to prevent it happening. It was pressure from other member states that finally forced the break.[4]

Unlike most other organizations, the Commonwealth is so flexible and places such minimal demands on its members that everyone involved can hold a different view about what it is for and how far they acknowledge British leadership. In the view of some, this gave British prestige a much needed lease of life; in the view of others, it simply perpetuated illusions that distracted the country from other opportunities.

The point of saying all this is to suggest that whichever party had been in office in the 1945–51 period, it would have been difficult, if not unthinkable, for a British Government to have taken a lead in the European integration movement. The country's historic ties with other continents were seen as being *competitive* and not complementary with ties in Europe. To the extent that, of course, a Customs Union, such as the E.E.C. was to become, legally conflicted with the existing system of Commonwealth (tariff) Preference, this was true. Britain's system of feeding her own people was also not 'continental'; it was, generally speaking, based on the principle of support (i.e. direct subsidy) of farmers rather than protection.

These kinds of differences were early warning signs to British Ministers about how the country's freedom of action might be limited if too close ties with the continent were formed. But the main obstacle in the early post-war years was still a psychological one, based on beliefs to which we have already referred about Britain's relative position in the post-war world. Winston Churchill stimulated these beliefs at the Conservative Party Conference of 1948 when he spoke of Britain being situated in the overlapping area of three rings—the Commonwealth, Europe and the U.S.A. The clear implication of this statement was that it would be difficult and undesirable for one of these three relationships to be given permanent precedence over the others.

This was the thinking behind the European policy of both Labour and Conservative Governments in the 1940s and 1950s. They were prepared to join European organizations as long as they were of an orthodox *inter-governmental* character. In other words, the organizations they joined had not to contain any major element of 'supra-nationality'. The word supra-national is a little difficult to define, but broadly speaking, it is used to describe an organization in which the member states commit themselves in advance to be bound by the decisions of the majority. There can, of course, be degrees of 'supra-nationality' and there can be different kinds of majority decision from one country one vote to the 'weighted' majority voting provided for in the European Community Treaties.[5]

In a traditional inter-governmental organization, however, decisions are taken by the agreement of the participating Governments. By withholding its agreement, therefore, a country can retain control of its own destiny. If life becomes intolerable it is also possible to leave, even if a period of notice has to be given. This, at any rate, is the *de jure* position; in practice, of course, it is now difficult for a country to isolate itself from the effects of the decisions of other countries, even if it leaves the organization in which these decisions are taken. Accordingly, therefore, British Governments of the 1940s and 1950s joined a number of inter-governmental organizations whose membership was entirely or mainly European.

The most important of these were the Brussels Treaty Organization (1948) and N.A.T.O. (1949)—both military/political organizations, the Organization for European Economic Co-operation (1948) which was formed to administer Marshal Aid and the Council of Europe (1949).[6] In the case of the Council of Europe the British distaste for supra-nationality was brought clearly into the open. The idea of the Council emerged from the 'Congress of Europe' held at The Hague in May 1948 and attended by over 600 delegates from 16 countries.

It adopted a series of ambitious resolutions calling for an economic and political union among the nations of Europe and one of these resolutions expressly stated that these nations 'must agree to merge certain of their sovereign rights'; another called for the setting up of a Consultative Assembly.[7] Although Winston Churchill was President of Honour of the Congress and Britain sent the second largest delegation (140), it was clear soon afterwards that the British had not been carried along in the general federalist euphoria. When concrete negotiations to set up a Council of Europe began after The Hague Congress, the British began by opposing the idea of a Consultative Assembly. Although the strength of opinion in favour of it finally induced the Government to accept the idea, it did so with great reluctance.[8] It soon became clear that if there was to be a Council of Europe which included Britain, it would have to be based on a treaty with limited commitments other than the obligation to co-operate.

Britain, however, was not the only country with reservations. It was clear that unless some clause was put into the Statute excluding matters relating to National Defence, a number of countries would not be able to join. This applied to countries with traditional or potential neutrality policies—Switzerland, Sweden, Ireland and Austria. A clause to this effect was duly inserted.[9] But the most significant change between the Hague Congress and the Statute setting up the Council of Europe was the replacement of the word 'union' by the word 'unity'. As A. H. Robertson has pointed out 'union' implies integration or constitutional links of a federal character; 'unity' means nothing of the sort.[10] Since its inception, the Council of Europe has proceeded to 'discuss questions of common concern' and 'reach agreements on common action' as its Statute enjoined it to do, in economic, social, cultural, scientific, legal and administrative matters and in the field of human rights.

The Council of Europe fulfilled one other important general function which was to allow a start to be made among countries who agreed to differ on the ultimate objectives. These differences of opinion tended to settle into two principal camps that became known as the 'functionalists' and the 'federalists'. The federalists, who were more numerous on the Continent of Europe, believed, as their name implies, in the formation of a new region-state on federal lines in which existing nation states would be willing in the last analysis to take a subordinate part. The functionalists, on the other hand, took a decidedly agnostic view about whether this could be achieved, at least in the foreseeable future. However, as their disagreement was about the form of integration at its later stages, it was possible to agree on how to proceed in the early stages. The reservations of many of the functionalists concerned not so much their own views but their opinions about what other people would be likely to accept. If a start could be made in the economic sector where tangible, measurable results could be achieved, who knows, so the argument ran, the necessary consent for something more ambitious in the sphere of political integration might be created.

While the federalists were prepared 'to settle for half a loaf', they pointed out that there were definite risks in proceeding with economic integration unless political integration followed fairly rapidly afterwards. Such historical evidence as there is seems to be on their side. The Zollverein did *not* lead to the peaceful unification of Germany, whereas Italy was able to construct an economic union on the Italian peninsula after the political unification had first taken place. The latter process, of course, was itself achieved by force, so producing this kind of historical evidence is just as capable of alienating support from those who advocate the limiting of national sovereignty.

In the late 1940s, however, there was one kind of historical argument which obtained a ready response, namely the tendency for national rivalries in Europe, particularly between France and Germany to cause wars. Indeed, the so-called 'hereditary enmity' between France and Germany even has a special name in German, the '*Erbfeindschaft*'. While, therefore, there was disagreement, as we have noted, about the 'theology' of integration, there was a universal desire so to arrange Europe's affairs that France and Germany should not be able to fight again. The political climate was accordingly favourable when Robert Schuman announced his plan in May 1950 to pool the resources of the principal war industries of France and Germany—coal and steel. Negotiations began for the setting up of a European Coal and Steel Community, and other countries besides France and Germany were invited to join. In the event, only Italy, Belgium, the Netherlands and Luxembourg actually did so. The British Labour Government of the time showed no serious interest; having recently nationalized the coal and steel industries, there was no enthusiasm for placing them under any degree of foreign control. Considering the expectations the Labour Party then had for their nationalized industries, their attitude is understandable. The powers given to the High Authority which was to do the day-to-day running of E.C.S.C. were considerably more 'supra-national' than were those given to the Commissions of the E.E.C. and Euratom in the Rome Treaties of 1957. Nor were the Labour Party alone in wishing to stand aside from the E.C.S.C. Very few British politicians advocated that the British Government should become seriously involved in the negotiations. Among these few, however, was one new Conservative backbencher making his maiden speech—his name was Edward Heath.

The E.C.S.C. Treaty was signed by the Six in April 1951 and began work in August 1952. The President of the High Authority was Jean Monnet, a former French civil servant, who had actually drafted the original text of the Schuman Plan in 1950. If there is one name, more than any other, which is associated with the post-war drive for European integration it is that of Jean Monnet. He gave up the Presidency of the High Authority in 1954 so as to devote all his energies to the campaign for a united Europe.

While the British aloofness from the E.C.S.C. did not prevent its birth, the same cannot be said of the next major development in integration we must consider—the European Defence Community. The idea of a European Army was first proposed by Churchill at the Council of Europe in August 1950. The outbreak of the Korean War two months previously meant that the Americans had to reduce their troop levels in Europe and the most obvious way of doing it was to rearm Germany. Even looking back from this distance in time, it is easy to appreciate that the countries who five years before had been occupied by the Germans found this thought unbearable. The blow might be softened if German troops were incorporated in a 'European' army along the lines that Churchill suggested. Even this, however, was unpalatable to many people at the time and it was only after the Americans called for German rearmament in September 1950 that the French Government formally proposed the setting up of a European Defence Community. In this organization, German battalions could be distributed amongst European Brigades. It was also to be linked to a European Political Community which would bring about the indispensable harmonization of the foreign policies of the member states. Both Communities, however, were stillborn and are important mainly as an object lesson in the dangers of Governments trying to force the pace of political union before the grass roots have been adequately prepared. It was not to be the last mistake of this kind in the story of European integration. While the E.D.C. Treaty was signed by France, Germany, Italy and the Benelux countries in 1952, its ratification in the French National Assembly was defeated by 319 votes to 264. Successive French Governments had delayed presenting the Treaty for ratification fearing that it would be defeated by one of those 'unholy' voting alliances of the Fourth Republic when Left and Right combined. Eventually in 1954 the Government of Mr Mendès-France presented the Treaty to the National Assembly but did *not* make its approval a question of confidence.

It was a combination of right wing chauvinism and left wing fear of Germany that caused the E.D.C. to be voted down. But there was another theory, widely held then and since, which is relevant to our consideration in this essay of Britain's relations with Europe. It is possible that had Britain been willing to join this Defence Community, the French National Assembly would have ratified. However, just as the Labour Government of Mr Attlee had stood aside from the E.C.S.C. and the E.D.C. when they were proposed in 1950, so when the crunch came on the E.D.C., the Conservative Government of Winston Churchill (with Eden as Foreign Secretary) made it clear that their help would be from *outside.*

As far as the attitude of Britain is concerned, it should *not* be assumed that because they wished to remain outside they also wished the E.D.C. to fail; the contrary is the case as Anthony Eden made clear in his memoirs.[11] The British Government's objections stemmed from the fact that the organization had unrealistic 'federal' implications for the future. The following passage from Eden's memoirs sums up very clearly the policy and the temperamental objections to this kind of integration, not just from the Government's point of view, but from that of most of the British also:

> 'I had no quarrel with the conception of a European Defence Community. On the contrary, I liked the idea, for I have never thought that my country need have any apprehension on account of a closer union between the nations of continental Europe. We have suffered too much from the lack

of it, and the trend these days should be towards larger units. My reservation arose from other causes. I feared that the plan, imaginative as it was, might fail for just that reason. It seemed to attempt too much, to ask more of the nations concerned than they could freely give and then the outcome might be disillusion, leaving Europe in disarray. On the other hand, I was prepared to admit that I could be wrong in this judgement, which might be the result of our English preference for taking our changes in doses rather than at a gulp. This was the temper in which I approached E.D.C.'[12]

On this occasion, the British Government were right in that the E.D.C. did 'attempt too much' and it failed. It is probably also true to say that at this stage Britain did not have 'any apprehension on account of a closer union between the nations of continental Europe'. But when the British had to face the next round of integration on the continent—the formation of the Common Market—this kind of reaction was to lead them into a blind alley. They again thought the Six would not succeed in agreeing on a Treaty, and when this happened, it was not too long before they found there was serious cause for apprehension about the effects on themselves.

The defeat of the E.D.C. caused a profound depression amongst the supporters of European integration. It also resulted in the initiative passing from the adherents of the 'federalist' approach to the 'functionalists'. Nothing happened immediately except that the defence situation in Western Europe could not be left as it was. Britain entered into a looser defence organization with the Six called the Western European Union[13] in 1955. Britain, in this Treaty undertook not to reduce its armed forces below certain minimum levels without the agreement of a majority of member states except in the event of an acute overseas emergency. Those who had campaigned against the E.D.C. failed to prevent re-armament of West Germany which joined N.A.T.O. in 1955. The only morsel of comfort for those who remained opposed was that she was not to have her own High Command—this was to be fully integrated into the Command structure of N.A.T.O.

It was not long after the setback of the defeat of E.D.C. that the promoters of European integration recovered their morale and support grew for an attempt to 'relaunch' the European idea. Accordingly, in June 1955 a conference was held at Messina in Sicily of the Foreign Ministers of France, West Germany, Italy and the Benelux countries. They considered what further steps could be taken towards full integration in Europe. To many people's surprise they decided that there was a realistic basis not just for the integration of further separate sectors of their economies like Coal and Steel, but of all of them at the same time. Although the resolution with which the Messina Conference ended was a cautious one in which any commitment to supra-nationality seemed to have been abandoned, the 'Europeans' were encouraged. There were prospects of half a loaf in the near future and who could say that there would not be a whole one eventually?

The Messina Conference did not just produce a declaration of intent but a commitment to formal negotiations in the form of an Intergovernmental Committee presided over by the Belgian Foreign Minister Paul-Henri Spaak. These negotiations began a month after the Messina Conference in July 1955 and, awkward though it was for the British Government, they found themselves once again having to adopt a policy position on a development in which they were in no way making the running. While on the one hand Britain was not formally involved, the countries who were wanted her to become so; indeed, after Messina, they had sent the Dutch Foreign Minister as an emissary to London to discuss the terms on which the British might become associated with the work.[14] In the event, when the negotiations started at the Chateau Val-Duchesse outside Brussels, the British did send a representative from the then Board of Trade who was more of an observer than a participant. It soon became clear, however, that the paths that Britain and the Six intended to take were fundamentally divergent and he was withdrawn after only five months in November 1955. Miriam Camps has described the withdrawal of the British representatives from the Spaak Committee as 'a critical turning-point in the development of relations between the Six and the United Kingdom and the beginning of a long period of tension between the two'.[15]

It is now clear that the British Government's posture at this time was based on a serious misjudgement both of the nature of the enterprise which the Six wished to undertake and the strength of their determination to pursue it. Whereas the Six placed the main responsibility with their Ministries of Foreign Affairs (both at Messina and subsequently), it is significant that the British treated it all mainly as a Board of Trade matter and kept saying that they would prefer this kind of work to be kept under the auspices of the Organization of European Economic Co-operation rather than creating new institutions. The British attitude passed from cool indifference to a period of outright opposition to the plans of the Six in the last weeks of 1955. It was probably the clear support the Six were getting from the United States that induced the British to change their attitude of opposition into one of accommodation at the beginning of 1956. By then it was clear that there was a good chance that the Six would succeed in their efforts to form a Common Market and that it was potentially a rather serious matter if they did.

The need for this reappraisal of British foreign policy coincided with the arrival at the Exchequer of Harold Macmillan. He had been Foreign Secretary, and represented the United Kingdom, when M. Spaak reported to a meeting of the Council of Ministers of the Western European Union at the very end of 1955. According to Miriam Camps . . .

'This seems to have been the first time that the essentially political nature of the Common Market question was really brought home to the United Kingdom. And it is perhaps not without significance that it was Mr Macmillan who represented the United Kingdom at this meeting and bore the brunt of M. Spaak's indignation at the British policy with respect to the Six.'[16]

But the official conversion of Mr Macmillan to the necessity of membership of E.E.C. for Britain was to be delayed another five and a half years. It was to be a very costly delay and both Conservative and Labour Governments had cause to regret it. Macmillan has since honestly expressed his regret about the missed opportunities in the middle 1950s in the Prologue to his Memoirs: 'I shall never cease to blame myself that I did not, even from my comparatively junior position in the Cabinet, raise as a matter of high principle the question of Britain joining actively at least in the preliminary talks which ultimately led to the Treaty of Rome'.[17] But over the next five and a half years Britain was to be taken up with two distractions—the still-born 'big' European Free Trade Area and the European Free Trade Association.

In the autumn of 1956 the British Cabinet decided to try and negotiate a Free Trade Area between the Six, the United Kingdom and any other countries of O.E.E.C. who wished to participate. This was accepted by Parliament in November of that year without a vote. The advantage of this proposal was that it did not prevent the Six from proceeding with their own customs union, in other words, they could join the Free Trade area as one unit, simply extending free trade concessions to the other countries who joined this larger grouping. Had this proposal succeeded, the United Kingdom would have had the best of both worlds and avoided a prolonged struggle with France and a bitter dispute at home. In a customs union, member states are *not* free unilaterally to fix their own external tariffs, this has to be done by agreement between all the members. The complicated series of tariff preferences which Britain gave to Common-wealth countries (and sometimes received in return) made a customs union too restrictive for her trade policy. Speaking in the House of Commons on 26 November 1956, Mr Macmillan undoubtedly spoke for the overwhelming majority of the House when he said:

'I do not believe that this House would ever agree to our entering arrangements which, as a matter of principle, would prevent our treating the great range of imports from the Commonwealth at least as favourable as those from the European countries. So this objection, even if there were no other, would be quite fatal to any proposal that the United Kingdom should seek to take part in a European Common Market by joining a Customs union.'[18]

There was, however, another serious obstacle which made it difficult for Britain to join the Common Market at this stage and that was her cheap food policy. By importing half her own food at the (then) low world prices, Britain could keep down the cost of living while giving direct subsidies to the very small number of farmers. The Six Community countries by contrast were in a quite different situation. They were nearer to being self-sufficient in basic foodstuffs and had so many farmers that a system of direct subsidies would have been impractical. Besides being numerous, the farmers of the Six were politically powerful and it would not have been realistic for the Governments of the Six to leave agriculture out of their arrangements. As things have turned out in the

Common Market, agriculture has not only been the most important sector of co-operation, but by far the most costly.

It is easy, therefore, to see that a big Free Trade Area with the Common Market joining as one unit would have been highly advantageous to Britain. It is equally easy to see, however, why, after two years of both multilateral and bilateral negotiations, the British got nowhere. There were serious French objections both before and after De Gaulle came to power in mid-1958. There was strong (and vocal) opposition to the proposal from the Patronat and from other influential industrial groups in France.[19] To understand this opposition and the anxieties elsewhere in the Six, one has to remember that the Common Market was intended to be much more than a customs union. The Treaty of Rome provided for transition eventually to a full economic union involving a process of harmonization in a vast number of policy sectors. The costs of undertaking such an elaborate programme were clearly going to be considerable, and for the Six to have exposed themselves to the full force of competition from surrounding states not faced with these costs would have been extremely risky.

However, to cut a long story short, by the time the Free Trade Area negotiations ran into the sand, the Common Market Treaty had been signed and had come into effect (on 1 January 1958). Signed at the same time between the same Member States was the Euratom Treaty providing for the pooling of resources connected with the peaceful uses of nuclear energy. Britain stood aside from this second Treaty also, although in February 1955 she had ratified a Treaty of Association with the European Coal and Steel Community. There was no doubt that it was now with the Six that the initiative lay and their Common Market got off to a very promising start. Their surprising success, even in establishing the organization, was something to which the British could not now remain indifferent. Whether they liked it or not, there was growing on their doorstep a potential world power. This would have been serious enough if the enterprise had been confined to the economic sphere alone, but there were prospects that the Six might follow their economic endeavour with a political union as well. Such a development of course had serious implications for the balance of power and for Britain's relative position in the world.

The E.E.C. Treaty does not, in fact, use the words 'political union' or 'political community' at all, there is simply a commitment in the preamble 'to lay the foundations of an ever-closer union among the peoples of Europe'. There was no doubt, however, that this omission was occasioned by lack of agreement on what could meaningfully be said at that stage. There was no doubt concerning the opinions of many of the 'activists' who had promoted the various stages in European integration. Jean Monnet, for example, who had drafted the Schuman Plan from which the E.C.S.C. emerged published a book in 1955 called 'Les Etats-Unis d'Europe ont Commencé'.[20] But it was not necessary to share the beliefs of the professional 'Europologists' to realize that some kind of political community was likely to follow the establishment of an economic union. Some of the nation states of Western Europe like Britain have had only indifferent success in running their national economies even when they have had strong central Governments. It would seem to be contrary to common sense to suppose that any greater success could be made of running an economy of continental size, unless there were strong central institutions with real powers. Once these central institutions are established, however, they can be effective in *external* relations as well as in domestic affairs.

For these and other reasons, therefore, the United Kingdom had to make some response to the establishment of the Common Market and the failure of the big Free Trade Area proposal. Accordingly, a new proposal was produced to set up the European Free Trade Association of Britain, Norway, Denmark, Sweden, Switzerland, Austria and Portugal. Negotiations were rapidly concluded and the E.F.T.A. came into force in May 1960. The main thing these countries had in common was that they were unable, or did not wish, to join the Common Market. From Britain's point of view the E.F.T.A. was never viewed as an end in itself. The British Government expected to be able to perform some 'bridge-building' with the Six, in the hope of persuading them or forcing them to agree to the substance of what they had refused in the context of the big Free Trade Area. The attempt at 'bridgebuilding' failed and Britain was left in the situation that she had been instrumental in founding an organization which was simply too small as a base for the expansion of her trade. The total population of the E.F.T.A. countries was nearly 90 million of which Britain accounted for over half—nearly 53 million. Since Britain already had access to her own market, she was gaining much less than were the other E.F.T.A. states in the way of new markets and it is not altogether surprising that once 'bridgebuilding' had failed there had to be a change of policy.

All this is easier to understand with the benefit of hindsight, but when the Conservative Government announced in the middle of 1961 that it was requesting negotiations aimed at full membership of the Common Market, it opened a Pandora's box of trouble. Apart from some hurried consultation of Commonwealth Governments beforehand, there had been no preparation for the move. There was consternation among the E.F.T.A. countries who woke up to find that Britain, after being instrumental in arranging the marriage was already seeking other partners. In response to this wholly reasonable reaction, the British Government rashly made a pledge that it would only join the Common Market if special arrangements acceptable to the rest of E.F.T.A. could be negotiated to protect their interests. This might well have been a very difficult pledge to redeem in the end, if the negotiations had not been terminated by the French veto. Two other E.F.T.A. countries—Denmark and Norway—applied to join E.E.C. along with Britain; so also did the Irish Republic whose trade was so bound up with Britain's that she had virtually no choice.

But the reaction from the rest of E.F.T.A. was the least of the Government's problems. There were the Commonwealth Governments, the British farmers and sections of the Conservative and Labour parties.[21] In voicing their objections these groups were doing no more than indicating that they believed what the

British Government had so recently been telling them. For Britain to join a customs union would constitute a serious barrier to Commonwealth trade. The British system of agricultural support so favourable for producers and consumers would have to be changed for a system of protection with its attendant greater risks for the farmer and higher prices for the consumer. Those in the Conservative and Labour parties who feared, for different reasons, that the British Parliament would lose the right unilaterally to make and alter its own laws, had only to read the Treaty of Rome. Industry on the whole supported entry and began to give financial support to the European Movement.

The Conservative Government nevertheless were on very difficult ground; the recent statements of its own Ministers could so easily be quoted. There was really only one way out in these circumstances and that was to give reassurances that the implications of membership were not what they seemed. The pledge to E.F.T.A. has already been mentioned. Commonwealth Governments were assured that Britain was confident of being able to negotiate long lists of exceptions to the Community rules. Farmers were assured that their interest would be safeguarded. Indeed, August 1961 marks the appearance of a form of resolution which was to appear in similar guises many times at party conferences and in Parliament over the next decade. The Government's motion, approved by the House of Commons read as follows:

> 'That this House supports the decision of Her Majesty's Government to make formal application under Article 237 of the Treaty of Rome in order to initiate negotiations to see if satisfactory arrangements can be made to meet the special interests of the United Kingdom, of the Commonwealth and of the European Free Trade Association; and further accepts the undertaking of Her Majesty's Government that no agreement affecting these special interests or involving British sovereignty will be entered into until it has been approved by this House after full consultation with other Commonwealth countries, by whatever procedure they may generally agree.'[22]

There is not much there to object to; while the Labour Party tabled its own amendment, it did not oppose the Government's substantive motion. No-one was committed to anything other than to explore possibilities and the motion allowed everyone voting for it to hold a different view of precisely what the 'special interests' of the United Kingdom were and thereafter what arrangements to meet these interests would be 'satisfactory'. Naturally the Government hoped that it could prove easier to get agreement on concrete issues as the negotiations proceeded than to try and do so in the abstract and in advance. To have been more precise might also have given away their negotiating hand. But while there is much to be said for this argument, the wording of the Government's motion had one intrinsic weakness which would not have mattered if so many later motions and resolutions of both parties had not taken their cue from it. The weakness lay in the motion's commitment simply to talk. It did not require anyone voting for it to take a positive or negative position towards the essentials of the enterprise on which the Six had embarked. Members claiming to be anxious about the 'terms' were not required to answer the basic question as put by Roderick Bowen in the House of Commons in a subsequent debate, 'Do they regard the creation of the Community as it now exists as a backward or a forward step in international affairs?'[23] It soon became clear that there were wide differences of view inside Britain about what 'terms' would be necessary before the country could join. Some of the reservations expressed hit at the whole basis of the Common Market's future programme as set out in the Treaty—the customs union, the free movement of capital, the harmonization of taxation systems etc. Had the original Six conceded these points they would have had to abandon their key objectives and become another kind of organization altogether. Those who held the more extreme reservations and yet continued to vote for resolutions aimed at entry were only stoking up trouble for later. If one draws up a resolution favouring marriage in such a way that supporters of free love can vote for it, one should not be surprised if later on, those involved in the exercise feel disappointed and let down.

The British two-party system only works properly if the two main parties maintain an image before the public of reasonable unity. On the Common Market issue this unity did not exist, so the only way out was for a large number of M.P.s on both sides of the House to lapse into a kind of neutral position, saying that they were not for or against entry into E.E.C., they were 'waiting for the terms'. To some this seemed an appalling abdication of leadership on one of the greatest issues of the 20th century. As Jo Grimond, the Liberal leader, said:

> 'Is one of the great political decisions in history to be reduced to a question of 5% more or less on the tariff on canned peaches? It is as if at the Reformation someone had said they were unable to make up their mind until they knew what price the monasteries were likely to fetch.'[24]

As far as the Government was concerned, it was difficult for its members to conduct a positive campaign for entry while conducting the negotiations.

It is only fair to remember also that at this stage no one expected the first set of negotiations to drag on so long; still less did anyone contemplate that Britain would have to wait ten years before being accepted as a full member of the Community. The negotiations, however, did drag on. The Government had drawn up an over-ambitious list of the 'special arrangements' it said it needed. Furthermore, the longer the negotiations continued the more there was time for the pressure groups in the Commonwealth countries who would be affected by the outcome to work on their Governments. At the Commonwealth Prime Ministers' Conference of September 1962 Mr Macmillan had quite a rough time. Public opinion which had been showing a majority in favour of the idea of joining E.E.C. seemed to be turning against. On 12 December 1962, the *Daily Telegraph* gave the results of a Gallup Poll showing that since October 1962 the percentage of those in favour of joining 'on the facts as you know them at present' had declined from 41 to 29 and the percentage against joining had risen from 28 to 37.[25]

However, as is now well known, the veto on the continuation of the negotiations was pronounced by President De Gaulle at a press conference in January, 1963, and Britain's first attempt at joining the Community came to an end.

The failure of this first attempt not only prevented a major row in the Commonwealth but prevented one also in the Labour Party. Had they remained in opposition this might not have been important, but we need to consider their situation for two reasons. First, it was to be a Labour Government that was to make the next attempt to re-open negotiations and secondly, it was to be a Labour Government in 1974 that was to attempt the task of 'renegotiating' the terms agreed by the Conservatives, with the possibility that Britain might leave the Community. The Labour Party's initial difficulty was a psychological one. To use the current jargon, joining E.E.C. was not originally their 'thing'. The British two-party system institutionalizes automatic conflict and for many Labour supporters, the fact that entry was proposed by a Conservative Prime Minister meant that it never had a chance of getting their support. Mr Macmillan's move, moreover, came at a time when the Government were losing support at by-elections and there was some suspicion that a great issue like Europe might make it possible for the Conservatives to inflict on Labour their fourth successive defeat.

However, the thing that 'immobilized' the Labour Party more than anything else was that it was split in its basic attitude then as it has been ever since. The moderate, 'social democratic', wing of the party led by Roy Jenkins welcomed the Government's move in their individual speeches and adopted a similar attitude towards the E.E.C. to their counterparts on the continent. The left wing, however, were hostile to the basically capitalist principles of the Common Market. They were and have been undoubtedly right when saying that the kind of socialism they wished to see adopted in Britain would conflict with the Treaty of Rome. Mr Gaitskell as party leader was in a very difficult position. While he belonged to the 'social democratic' wing of the party he wanted to try and restore party unity so recently shattered by disputes over defence and nationalization. At the Party Conference of 1961, Mr Gaitskell made a speech that was hostile in tone but did not close the door to British membership. The cordial reception it received from his old enemies on the left indicated that it was the least divisive stand he could take. On the other hand it dismayed many of his friends.

However, as we have seen, a serious split was avoided because de Gaulle's veto postponed the whole issue for several years and (with some relief) the parties returned to their more customary battles.[26] The Common Market issue played no part in the General Election of 1964 and only a small part in that of 1966. Both parties were now formally committed to opening negotiations again with the Six 'if the opportunity should arise'. Like the various resolutions to which we have referred the Labour manifesto tells us very little about the party's real position; it said:

'Labour believes that Britain, in consultation with her E.F.T.A. partners, should be ready to enter the European Economic Community, provided essential British and Commonwealth interests are safeguarded.'

There was no sign that an early opportunity of reopening negotiations would be forthcoming so there was not much incentive for either party to stir up the whole divisive controversy again. Several Ministers, however, made speeches referring to the Common Market which indicated that a Labour Government's bargaining position might be prohibitively high. Barbara Castle, for example, in a speech at Hartlepool could not be restrained from an attack on the free movement of labour and capital that a merger with the Six would involve.[27]

The election resulted in a Labour majority of 96 and to the great surprise of many observers Mr Wilson entered into what has come to be called his 'romantic' phase in his relations with Europe. He seems to have undergone a conversion in his basic attitude to the Community. Like Hugh Gaitskell he had always claimed not to be against entry into E.E.C. on principle, but his most important speeches on this issue during the 1961–62 period were highly sceptical and hostile in tone.[28] However, in November 1966 he announced that he and the Foreign Secretary, George Brown, would tour the capitals of the Six between January and March of the following year to see if favourable conditions existed for a further attempt to reopen negotiations. Four days after this announcement Mr Wilson spoke at the Lord Mayor's banquet at the Guildhall and called upon Britain to take a lead in promoting technological co-operation in Europe. He said 'I believe the tide is right, the time is right, the winds are right to make the effort'.[29]

When Mr Wilson and Mr Brown had concluded their series of visits to Community capitals, the Cabinet was advised that it was worth proceeding and the Government put in a formal application for membership on May Day, 1967. It seemed unlikely that the Government would risk a public rebuff unless it had reason to believe that negotiations would be allowed to proceed. The Brussels Commission made a study of the problems involved and concluded by recommending that negotiations should be opened.[30] There was, however, no clear encouragement from Paris and all Europe had to wait until November 1967 for de Gaulle to make some kind of clear pronouncement at his press conference. He again objected to British entry and the negotiations never began. Given that the political veto still existed, it was probably wise from the point of view of the French for negotiations not to be allowed to start. Mr Wilson and the Foreign Office spokesmen were showing such determination in their European enterprise that they might not have given the French any plausible excuse to break the negotiations off once they had begun. The British application of 1 May had been a short, simple request without any formal strings attached. The only guide we have, which is publicly available, to what the Labour Government's negotiating position was in 1967, is contained in a speech delivered by George Brown to the W.E.U. on 4 July 1967.[31] This speech concentrated on only three main conditions—special arrangements for New Zealand, for Commonwealth sugar, and a fair bargain over Britain's contribution to the Community's budget. But while the Ministers responsible for relations with Europe were bending over backwards to ensure that the negotiations would be straightforward, Mr Wilson was doing his best to maintain the momentum of the British application. Speaking at the Annual Dinner of the C.B.I. on 17 May, he said: 'At the beginning of this year I said we should not take no for an answer and that remains our position'.[32] It would be wrong, however, to presume that all the members of the Cabinet shared this determination. The official policy both of the Government and the party allowed them to maintain their separate and different reservations until a concrete decision had to be made on a precise set of terms agreed with the Six.

As far as the mass of activists in the Labour Party were concerned there undoubtedly were many who were persuaded to look more favourably on a Labour sponsored application to the E.E.C. than they had on the earlier Conservative one and all they were asked to do was to vote for the same kind of innocuous resolutions which allowed those voting the same way to have in mind quite different things.[33] This writer has questioned a number of journalists and delegates who have attended every Labour Party Conference since 1961 and none could remember any atmosphere of real enthusiasm for the Common Market in the various debates. There was rather a feeling of relief on the part of the platform each time the E.E.C. debate was over that greater differences of opinion had not been exposed. In 1967 the Foreign Office Ministers did display enthusiasm for entry as did other pro-Market Ministers in the Cabinet, but there are contradictory views about how far the Labour Cabinet was committed 'in intention and in principle' to the desirability of entry in E.E.C. George Brown has asserted that it was,[34] Mr Richard Crossman has asserted equally strongly that it was not. He has declared that at no time did the Cabinet make a collective decision to approve entry and added that 'it was clearly appreciated that the application had been made on the understanding that while entry into the Common Market was an objective of policy, if the terms proved reasonable, it was just as much of an objective to stay out if they proved too high'.[35] For two former members of the same Cabinet to disagree in this way would seem to indicate that there was no clear collective view. Clearly, some Ministers very much wanted negotiations with the Six to succeed, others only did so on conditions which at that time made the whole exercise a waste of time.

It was on this basis that the Labour Government and Party drifted towards the third attempt to enter the E.E.C. following the replacement of President de Gaulle by Georges Pompidou in 1969. But it was a short-sighted policy for the pro-Market Ministers at the Foreign Office to work away on their own without their enthusiasm being shared by the whole Cabinet. Their statements were taken by many people at home and abroad at their face value and it exposed the party to later charges of bad faith.

The Labour Government having presided over the preparation for the third and successful negotiations, it fell to the Conservatives to conduct them following their victory at the election of 1970. When the Conservatives finally produced a set of 'terms' in 1971, the Labour Party officially turned them down. It did so for the same mixture of reasons that immobilized it ten years earlier. But the measure of unity it found in saying no, concealed a wide range of different policy positions. Some rejected the terms because they fell short of what they genuinely expected, others rejected them because they would only have accepted terms that were never remotely negotiable in Brussels. This became increasingly clear from the nature of the attacks on the 'Tory terms'. It was very difficult for observers at home and abroad to reconcile the apparent determination to join the E.E.C. of the Labour Government's spokesmen of 1967, with the open contempt in which so many leading supporters of the party seemed to hold the Community after 1971. There is not space to set out here the details of the terms of entry secured by Mr Rippon in 1971. These were set out in a White Paper[36] and replied to by the so-called 'anti-white paper' published by the *New Statesman*.[37] The debate on the E.E.C. at the Labour Party Conference of 1971[38] as well as the earlier special one-day conference[39] gave a fair picture of the basis of the opposition of members of the party outside Parliament. As far as Labour Members of Parliament were concerned, the differences of opinion were more clearly recorded when the vote, on the principle of entry into E.E.C. on the terms negotiated, took place on 19 October 1971; 89 Labour M.P.s voted in favour or abstained. The Conservative Government got their motion passed by a majority of 112.[40] They had had considerable trouble with their own anti-Market wing and on this vote 41 Conservative M.P.s voted against or abstained. The most prominent of these was Enoch Powell who felt so strongly about this and other issues that he left Parliament at the dissolution of 1974 and even decided to vote for a Labour candidate. The balance of opinion within the Labour Party as a whole thereafter swung more and more strongly against the 'Tory terms' and the Labour M.P.s who had supported the Government became progressively more isolated. They were eventually forced into the absurd position of having voted in favour of entry but of having to vote *against* all the implementing legislation. Accordingly, parts of this were only passed by wafer thin majorities. The party remained officially unreconciled to the idea of joining the E.E.C. even after Britain officially became a member on 1 January 1973. No British Labour delegation went to the European Parliament at Strasbourg and the Party pledged itself to a 'fundamental renegotiation' of the terms of entry (followed by a referendum or an election) with complete withdrawal remaining a possibility. Mr Peter Shore, Opposition spokesman on E.E.C. affairs in the last Parliament set out his own views in a Fabian pamphlet about how this renegotiation should be conducted.[41] Referring to the 'far-reaching nature' of the changes required, he says

'It is no good pretending that they can easily be secured—and we have from the start to envisage that the prospects of failure are greater than those of success.'

However, after Labour took office in March 1974, Mr Shore was not put in principal charge of the renegotiation. This duty fell to Mr Callaghan as Foreign Secretary and it was clear from the outset that a more moderate and conciliatory approach was to be adopted. The Government, for example, did not carry out Mr Shore's proposal immediately to suspend the Treaty of Accession during the period of renegotiation.

Just how long this renegotiation will take is not clear, but eventually, a new set of 'terms' on which Britain's continued membership of E.E.C. is possible will emerge. When that happens, the Party will again have to face its own internal contradictions but this time in a more acute form than ever before. Because even if the final decision is left to the voters in a referendum, it is surely inconceivable that the incumbent Government could decline to give them its clear advice? The other Member States of the Community, of course, have serious problems of their own; it is just possible that they may choose to abandon the main objectives of their enterprise and turn themselves into a quite different kind of organization. But assuming this does *not* happen, assuming the other states wish broadly to continue with their planned programme, the final question which has to be asked is this. 'Does there exist a set of terms, which are at all likely to be granted by the Community, on the basis of which the Labour Party can agree that Britain should either leave the organization or stay in?' Looking back over the past, the strong implication is that there does not. The decision to be taken (either way) is fraught with the most far-reaching consequences and the responsibility involved is of a totally different order than that which the Party has ever faced on this issue before.

While supporters of the European Community evinced dismay at the prospect of a Labour Government pursuing a renegotiation, there is actually an excellent case for saying that these same people should welcome it. This argument stems from the persistent problem of the unreconciled state of public opinion.[42] It is difficult to see how Britain can make any real success of her E.E.C. membership unless positive support is built up for the idea at the grass roots. This is unlikely to be done while the normal opinion leaders of half the country are continuing to attack the Community and encouraging people to feel that the problems connected with membership are somehow unnecessary. It may be, therefore, that even the pro-marketeers have something to gain by the Labour Party having to face the issue squarely from the position of office. It may abandon its opposition to membership, either because it negotiates new terms so good that most of its members can accept them and recommend them to the electorate; alternatively, it may negotiate new terms which it is not very happy with, but which nevertheless prove acceptable to the British public in a referendum. If neither of these two things happen, it may well be the pro-marketeers who find themselves reconsidering their position.

The long-term changes which membership of E.E.C. will bring are hard to determine at this early stage. During the negotiations and since entry, Common Market affairs have been co-ordinated under the aegis of the Prime Minister's office.[43] This is likely to accelerate the development of this office, already begun, into a full Department of State. As far as Westminster is concerned there is an urgent need for the earliest possible scrutiny of proposals for European Instruments. Select Committees of the House of Lords and the House of Commons both recommended in 1973 that a Special Committee should be set up to deal with these as a matter of urgency.[44]

Finally, the Common Market may be the occasion on which the device of referendum is introduced into the British system of government. It is too early to tell whether the Labour Government will conduct its electoral consultation on E.E.C. by referendum, by an election, or by asking the electorate to vote in both ways on the same day. The longer term consequences that membership may lead to, such as direct elections to the European Parliament and majority voting in the Council of Ministers, seem too far ahead to see. The most promising area for a new step forward seems to lie in the progressive alignment of foreign policies arising out of the regular meetings of the Foreign Ministers of the Nine. If this trend continues, it will represent a major change of direction for Britain. Oddly enough, it will not have happened as part of a programme of integration but as a response to the international economic crisis which would have come upon the Western world even if the Common Market had never been born.

NOTES AND REFERENCES

1 See anthology of De Gaulle's key pronouncements on Britain in the *Sunday Times*, 13 November 1966.

2 For the early post-war period see *The Recovery of Europe* by Richard Mayne (Weidenfeld & Nicolson) London, 1970. For Britain's relations with the Common Market see *Britain and the European Community 1955–63* by Miriam Camps (O.U.P.), *The Second Try* by Uwe Kitzinger (Pergamon Press) Oxford, 1968, *Diplomacy and Persuasion: how Britain joined the Common Market* by Uwe Kitzinger (Thames & Hudson) London, 1973. The latter volume concentrates on the period 1970–72.

3 See the extract from this speech in *The European Common Market and Community* by Uwe Kitzinger (Routledge & Kegan Paul) London, 1967, p. 37.

4 *At the End of the Day 1961–1963* by Harold Macmillan (Macmillan) London, 1973, p. 312.

5 See articles 148–50 of E.E.C. Treaty, article 28 of E.C.S.C. Treaty and articles 118–20 of Euratom Treaty.

6 For a detailed description of these and other post-war organizations see *European Institutions—Co-operation; Integration; Unification* by A. H. Robertson (Stevens/Matthew Bender, 3rd edn), 1973.

7 *Ibid.*, p. 11.

8 *Ibid.*, p. 13.

II

9 Article 1, para. (d).

10 *Ibid.*, p. 37.

11 See *Full Circle* (Cassell) London, 1960, pp. 29–52.

12 *Ibid.*, p. 32.

13 The Western European Union was an expanded and renamed version of the Brussels Treaty Organization of 1948. The latter was a collective self-defence agreement between the U.K., France and the Benelux Countries. Italy and the Federal Republic of Germany were invited to join thus forming the W.E.U. in 1955.

14 For the best detailed account of this stage see *Britain and the European Community 1955–63* by Miriam Camps (O.U.P.) London, 1964, pp. 29–53.

15 *Ibid.*, p. 45.

16 *Ibid.*, p. 48.

17 *Winds of Change 1914–39* by Harold Macmillan (Macmillan) London, 1966, p. 23.

18 Quoted in *Britain and the European Community* by Miriam Camps, p. 106.

19 *Ibid.*, p. 131.

20 Published by R. Laffont: Paris, 1955.

21 The Liberals as a party were in favour of Britain's application to become full members of E.E.C. They had formally divided the House on the subject in 1960. A small number of individuals in the party, some of them prominent, have remained opposed to entry.

22 Hansard, 2 August 1961, col. 1480.

23 Hansard, 8 November 1962, col. 1221.

24 Press release of speech to Liberal Assembly, 22 September 1962 (Liberal Party Press Office).

25 *Britain and the European Community 1955–63* by Miriam Camps, p. 464n.

26 For details of the situation at the breakdown see *Report to the European Parliament on the State of the Negotiations with the United Kingdom*— Commission of the European Communities (Brussels, February 1963).

27 *The British General Election of 1966* by D. E. Butler and Anthony King (Macmillan) London, 1966, p. 112.

28 See in particular Section IV of Mr Wilson's own selection of his speeches *Purpose in Politics* (Weidenfeld & Nicolson) London, 1964.

29 *The Times*, 15 November 1966.

30 *Opinion on the Applications for Membership received from the United Kingdom, Ireland, Denmark and Norway*—Commission of the European Communities (Brussels, 29 September 1967).

31 Cmnd. 3345, reprinted in full in *The Second Try* by Uwe Kitzinger, pp. 189–203.

32 *The Times*, 18 May 1967.

33 See in particular the resolutions passed at the Labour Party Conferences of 1967 and 1969 (the latter was reaffirmed in 1970).

34 *The Times*, 16 February 1971, quoted in article by Michael Wheaton, 'The Labour Party and Europe 1950–71' in *The New Politics of European Integration* (ed. Ghita Ionescu) (Macmillan) London, 1972, p. 96.

35 'The Price of Europe'—R. H. S. Crossman, *New Statesman*, 12 February 1971. Quoted in *ibid*.

36 *The United Kingdom and the European Communities* (Cmnd. 4715) H.M.S.O., July 1971. See also *The Enlarged Community: outcome of the negotiations with the applicant states*—Commission of the European Communities (Brussels, 1972).

37 *The Case against Entry: the United Kingdom and the European Communities: the answer to the White Paper*—the *New Statesman* (London, 1971).

38 See report of the Seventieth Annual Conference of the Labour Party— Brighton, 1971.

39 *Labour and the Common Market—Report of a Special Conference of the Labour Party Central Hall Westminster 17th July 1971*.

40 For the best detailed account of Britain's third and successful attempt to join E.E.C. see *Diplomacy and Persuasion: How Britain joined the Common Market* by Uwe Kitzinger (Thames & Hudson), London, 1973.

41 *Europe: the way back* by Peter Shore (Fabian Tract 425) (Fabian Society: London, 1973).

42 For the trends in British public opinion on the Common Market see surveys undertaken by Social Surveys (Gallup Poll) Ltd., London, W.1. For the 1970–72 period an excellent selection of a variety of poll figures has been put together by Dov. S. Zakheim in the *Journal of Common Market Studies*, vol. XI, No. 3, March 1973.

43 See 'The Impact of Community Membership on the British Machinery of Government'—Helen and William Wallace, *Journal of Common Market Studies*, vol. XI, No. 4, June 1973.

44 See Second Report by the Select Committee on Procedures for Scrutiny of Proposals for European Instruments—The House of Lords (25 July 1973), and Second Report from the Select Committee on European Community Secondary Legislation—the House of Commons (25 October 1973). Both the Special Committees were set up in May 1974.

Index